Meet the only team to _____ _____ despite posting the low___ _____ average in its league.

Meet Babe Ruth's first pennant-winning team.

Discover the all-star teams for each of baseball's seven eras.

Chart the course of each team, from its roots to its present location.

Be surprised by what team has been most dominant in the American League during the current era.

Learn who were each team's top rookies and most important contributors.

Decide for yourself which was the greatest team of all time.

Every fan of every baseball team has his or her own questions about the glory of baseball's past. And now every fan has a book that can be read from cover to cover, dipped into again and again, and enjoyed as thoroughly as the crack of the bat and the roar of the crowd.

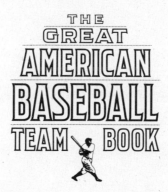

THE
GREAT
AMERICAN
BASEBALL
TEAM BOOK

DAVID NEMEC, a noted baseball historian, has authored such popular triumphs as *Great Baseball Feats, Facts & Firsts* and *The Baseball Challenge Quiz Book*, both in Signet editions. He lives in San Francisco.

THE GREAT AMERICAN BASEBALL TEAM BOOK

DAVID NEMEC

A PLUME BOOK

DEDICATION
To all the members of my first organized team, the Minnie Minosos, the scourge of the Lakewood "D" League in 1951.

PLUME
Published by the Penguin Group
Penguin Books USA Inc., 375 Hudson Street,
New York, New York 10014, U.S.A.
Penguin Books Ltd, 27 Wrights Lane,
London W8 5TZ, England
Penguin Books Australia Ltd, Ringwood,
Victoria, Australia
Penguin Books Canada Ltd., 10 Alcorn Avenue,
Toronto, Ontario, Canada M4V 3B2
Penguin Books (N.Z.) Ltd, 182-190 Wairau Road,
Auckland 10, New Zealand

Penguin Books Ltd, Registered Offices:
Harmondsworth, Middlesex, England

First published by Plume, an imprint of New American Library, a division of
Penguin Books USA Inc.

First Printing, April, 1992
10 9 8 7 6 5 4 3 2 1
Copyright © David Nemec, 1992
All rights reserved

 REGISTERED TRADEMARK—MARCA REGISTRADA

Library of Congress Cataloging-in-Publication Data

Nemec, David.
  The great American baseball team book / David Nemec.
    p. cm.
ISBN 0-452-26781-1
1. Baseball—United States—Clubs—Miscellanea. 2. Baseball—United States—
Miscellanea. 3. Baseball—United States—History.
I. Title.
GV875.A1N46   1992
796.357'64'0973—dc20   91-35163
                                                                            CIP

Printed in the United States of America
Set in Aster
Designed by Leonard Telesca

BOOKS ARE AVAILABLE AT QUANTITY DISCOUNTS WHEN USED TO PROMOTE PRODUCTS OR
SERVICES. FOR INFORMATION PLEASE WRITE TO PREMIUM MARKETING DIVISION, PENGUIN
BOOKS USA INC., 375 HUDSON STREET, NEW YORK, NEW YORK 10014.

ACKNOWLEDGMENTS

As always in a book like this one, there have been many helping hands. Among those who have been of special assistance are James Murphy and John Fox, two fine baseball writers who gladly shared their information with me on the 1914 Providence Grays and the 1918 Binghampton Bingos; Kevin Mulroy, my editor; and Fran Collin, who once again shepherded one of my romanesque projects from inception to publication.

CONTENTS

• •

INTRODUCTION

If you ask ten baseball historians what team was the greatest ever, you're liable to get ten different answers, ranging from the 1869 Cincinnati Red Stockings to the 1989 Oakland A's. Reshape your query so that you're now seeking opinions on the greatest team over the entire course of baseball history, and it's unanimous—the New York Yankees. Yet not even the Yankees have always been a great team. During the early part of the century they were never more than an occasional contender, and as late as the spring of 1921 were still in search of their first pennant. Since then, of course, the Yankees have won more than twice as many pennants and World Championships as any other team. The Chicago White Sox, in contrast, have claimed just one league title since the close of the deadball era, and the Boston Red Sox have to stretch all the way back to 1918 to boast of their last World Championship. As you will discover in this book, these two teams were the best in the American League prior to 1920, when each did something foolish that forever altered its course. Eight members of the White Sox sold out the 1919 World Series, thereupon gutting the team of several of its greatest players, and the Red Sox sold quite possibly the greatest player of all time, Babe Ruth, to the Yankees at the finish of the 1919 campaign.

When the deadball era ended, the Chicago Cubs had won more pennants than any other major league team. They continued to be strong for another twenty years before going into a decline from which they have never really righted themselves. The Cubs' reversal of fortune can't be traced to any single event or front-office move, but is more the result of a general lack of where-withal. But notwithstanding their current all-time record for the longest span of time without winning a pennant, the Cubs have had two teams that will always rate among the greatest ever. The 1880 outfit had a .798 winning percentage, still a National League record, and the 1906 Cubs won an all-time major league record 116 games and became one of the elite few nines to garner a team Triple Crown (lead its league in batting average, fielding average and earned run average).

Oddly, the American League also had a team Triple Crown winner in 1906. It would have marked the lone time that two Triple Crown winners met in a World Series but for one small problem. The American League club was the only Triple Crown winner since 1885 that failed to capture a pennant. As you might suspect if you know how certain teams have traditionally seemed to squander their resources and opportunities, it was Cleveland. Not only didn't Cleveland triumph, it couldn't even manage to finish in second place that year. Were the 1906 Cleveland Naps a great team? No, but they were certainly the weirdest American League club during the deadball era, if only because their failure is contrary to everything we know about what makes for a winner in baseball. The Naps not only won the team Triple Crown in 1906; in addition, they paced the American League in runs, on-base percentage, slugging average and double plays.

In some respects every team has a treasure to offer us, even the most mediocre. The 1932 Phillies, for one, won just two more games than they lost and finished an uneventful fourth in the National League race. A season like that would have been shameful to Yankees followers of that time, but in Philadelphia it was a rare occasion to rejoice. It was in fact about the only year that an entire generation of Phillies fans could celebrate. That fourth place in 1932 was their team's lone first-division finish between 1918 and 1949.

If you root for the Indians or the Astros these days, you know what those folks in Philly suffered. Even if your allegiance lies with the Dodgers or the A's, you understand that life has not always automatically included a contending team. History tells us that every major league organization of any duration has at some point suffered at least one dreadful lapse. Likewise, each club has had some proud moments. Yet there has never been anything even remotely approaching an even ebb and flow. With all the efforts to equalize talent and promote a competitive balance, some teams have hugged the floor of the ocean for years on end while others hardly ever seem to slip below the surface.

This book is intended to provide you with a kind of ship's log, a handy device that can be useful in plotting the historical course of all the current major league teams and most of their ancestors. As you're sailing along, you can expect to be hauled off on a side junket now and then to a part of the sea where the hulk of some famous or interesting major or minor league team lies at bottom. But first a look at your cruise itinerary.

Leg One—1876, the year the National League (generally recognized to have been the first major league) began, through 1892, the last season in which pitchers plied their trade from inside a rectangular box located only 50 feet from home plate.

Leg Two—1893, the season when the pitcher's mound was first established at its present 60'6" distance from home plate, through 1900, the last year there was only one major league.

Leg Three—1901, the American League's inaugural season as a major league, through 1919, the final year of what is considered to have been the deadball era.

Leg Four—1920, the beginning of the lively ball era, when hitting and scoring were at an all-time zenith, through 1941, the last season in which the game was still relatively unaffected by World War II.

Leg Five—1942–60, the era in which most historians believe the game reached its peak both in popularity and the quality of play, particularly at the major league level.

Leg Six—1961–76, the era in which both major leagues expanded, first to ten and then to 12 teams apiece, causing the minor leagues to dwindle accordingly and the game to suffer through a long period of readjustment before experiencing a renewed surge of popularity.

Leg Seven—1977 to the present, the era of free agency, astronomical increases in players' salaries and further expansion, resulting in longer careers, violent fluctuations in both team and individual performances, and the shattering of many season and career records that only a generation ago had seemed unassailable.

By this time you no doubt have a hunch that the purpose of this journey is pure pleasure rather than a somber exploration of all the statistical gadgets that have been invented in recent years to measure and predict a team's performance. It's true. I have to confess to seeing most of baseball as sheer entertainment. Yet I've been known to have my serious side at times, enough that I'll be surprised if you aren't given some things to think about while you're having fun. And if what you find here whisks you off from time to time to plunge into your favorite baseball record book or encyclopedia for further edification, well and good. That, I might also confess, is one of my objectives. I like to jog the eye, beam my light into the brain at odd angles. *Bon voyage.*

LEG ONE

1876–1892

INTRODUCTION
TO TEAM NOTES AND
RECORD HOLDERS

• •

The team notes in each section of this book are meant to serve several purposes. In addition to tracking a team's progress or lack of it during a particular era, key highlights and lowlights have been provided to help in understanding why a team performed as well or as poorly as it did. The following is an explanation of each item found in the notes:

Pennants—A list of the years a team finished in first place. Years followed by a "(D)" indicate that a team won only its division that season.

Manager—The manager who served the longest at the team's helm during the era under consideration.

Park—Where the team played its home games. When more than one park was used, the years are given for each along with significant opening and closing dates and games.

Best Year—The season in which the team compiled its best won-lost record. In some cases the team might have had a higher finish in the standings in another season during the era or even won a pennant with a poorer record.

Worst Year—The season in which the team compiled its poorest won-lost record.

Top Rookie—The player who had the best rookie season for the team. In most cases the player's impact on the team's performance is also taken into account. A 20-game winner on a pennant winner that finished fourth the previous year generally gets higher marks than a .340 hitter on a cellar dweller.

Biggest Disappointment—The player whose unexpectedly poor performance caused the team the greatest grief. For some players, particularly highly touted young ones, the disappointment sometimes extended over several seasons.

Best Deal—In general the team's best trade, but occasionally a waiver deal, a free agent signing or even a bold front-office move. The year cited is the one in which the deal first impacted on the team. For pre-1901 clubs this item has been labeled "Best Move" because deals were rather rare in the game's early days.

Worst Deal—Usually the team's worst trade, but again it could be some other act of stupidity by the club.

Other—A chronology of the team's high points and low points during the era. The sampling is necessarily representative, otherwise we would have to do a whole book for each team. For not only did every team do, or fail to do, something worthy of mention every year, it was usually involved in enough events of interest to merit a whole page of notes.

As for the charts of team hitting and pitching record holders during each era, they too can do duty in a number of different ways. Along with the Ruths, Hornsbys, Aarons, Musials, Carltons, Mathewsons and Koufaxes who dominate the charts of every team for which they played, as you would naturally expect, there are many interesting and illuminating surprises. Quite a few players whose names are largely unremembered today, even in the cities where they achieved their greatest success, emerge as having been important team catalysts. One such in the game's second phase is Bert Cunningham. No more than an average pitcher for most of his career, in 1898 Cunningham had a year that was so outstanding it not only set many club records but had a large hand in lifting his team, the Louisville Colonels, out of the depths for the first time and making its assets suddenly valuable enough to Barney Dreyfuss, who owned a piece of the club, that he held on to his interests rather than selling out as he had been previously inclined. After the 1899 season, when the Louisville franchise was dumped by the National League, Dreyfuss was allowed to cart its best players off to Pittsburgh, which he also owned. Imagine if Honus Wagner and Fred Clarke had played for a team other than Louisville at the tag end of the nineteenth century. The odds are substantial that they would have been in the upstart American League by 1901 and not in Pittsburgh, one of the few National League clubs willing to pay its players enough to keep them from jumping to the ambitious new circuit. And if the two of them had been lost, Wagner especially, it seems a fair possibility that the National League, already beginning to crumble, might have come apart at the seams. So Bert Cunningham, if only tangentially, is owed a bit of belated recognition for having helped to hold the fabric of the game together.

Bill Sweeney of the Boston Braves is another intriguing figure. He too had only one great season, that in 1912, but without it there would probably have been no miracle in Boston two years later. For Sweeney was not only the first player to provide the Braves with any offensive spark since the early 1900s, when American League raiders had looted the team of most of its top players, but he was also the bait Boston used to land Johnny Evers from the Cubs. Without Evers it is almost inconceivable that the Braves would have been a contender in 1914, let alone won the pennant.

But invitations to historical speculation are only one use to which these charts of team record holders can be put. They also reveal the most productive players during each era and suggest which elements of the game were emphasized and why certain teams floundered while others excelled. More than that, they offer some insights into which players truly have been the game's greatest and most enduring superstars. Many players appear as record holders for more than one team during an era, but few have managed to bridge the gap between changing styles of play and continue to be record setters in a later era as well. Part of the fun in a book like this, of course, is finding out at your own pace who they are, and you can rest easy. No one here is about to spoil it for you.

TEAM NOTES AND RECORD HOLDERS: 1876–92

At first glance the game's inaugural era appears to have been so tumultuous that even to attempt a meaningful examination of the many teams that existed during the period is a waste of effort. There were four major leagues, two of which—the Union Association and the Players League—survived only a single season, and both of the other two circuits fielded a different cast of teams nearly every year. To further complicate the task, teams frequently switched leagues or combined with other franchises, or cannibalized the rosters of rival clubs.

Yet upon closer inspection some threads of sanity emerge from those first seventeen years of major league history. Both the National League and the American Association had a certain underlying stability, enough that six teams from each circuit can be offered for the kind of capsule study that will mark every future era. In the National League only two of the six teams were on board from the loop's inception in 1876 right on through the 1892 season. The Association, though short lived, was in a sense luckier. Two teams survived the entire decade the loop lasted, and two other cities—Baltimore and Philadelphia—were also represented in each of the ten Association seasons, though not always by the same franchise.

In any event, here for your enjoyment is one historian's assessment of the teams that highlighted the game's initial era. The composite standings of the two leagues reflect each club's comparative strength for however long it survived in its respective league or leagues.

NATIONAL LEAGUE	AMERICAN ASSOCIATION
1. Chicago	1. St. Louis
2. Boston	2. Cincinnati
3. New York	3. Philadelphia
4. Providence	4. Brooklyn
5. Philadelphia	5. Louisville
6. Pittsburgh	6. Baltimore

NATIONAL LEAGUE

CHICAGO WHITE STOCKINGS (1876–92)

Pennants: 1876, 1880, 1881, 1882, 1885, 1886
Manager: Cap Anson, 1879–92
Park: State Street Grounds, 1876–77
  Lakefront Park, 1878–84
  Westside Park, 1885–92
Best Year: 1880 (67–17, .798)
Worst Year: 1877 (26–33, .441)
Top Rookie: Larry Corcoran, 1880 (43–14 and a 1.95 ERA)
Biggest Disappointment: George Bradley, 1877
Best Move: Acquiring John Clarkson in 1884
Worst Move: Selling King Kelly to Boston, 1887
Other:
  1876—.337 team BA sets era record; club outscores opponents 624–257 and cops first NL flag
  1877—Ross Barnes done in by fair-foul rule change; Al Spalding done in by inability to throw curveball or hit one
  1880—Corcoran and Fred Goldsmith divide pitching chores; club becomes the first to have two 20-game winners
  1884—142 homers as a team, 103 more than runner-up Buffalo; first team to make 100 or more double plays (107) in a season
  1885—White Stockings post .777 winning percentage, third highest in NL history; franchise also has the record for the highest (1880) and the second highest (1876)
  1886—Rookie pitcher Jocko Flynn is 24–6 with top .800 winning percentage; never pitches another game in the majors
  1888—John Clarkson sold to Boston; this, coupled with the Kelly sale, helps end the team's dominance
  1892—Bill Hutchinson collects 123 wins in a three-year period, 1890–92 (in 1891 he was the last 40-game winner in major league history)

HITTING		PITCHING	
Batting Ave.	.429, Ross Barnes, 1876	Wins	53, John Clarkson, 1885
Slugging Ave.	.590, Ross Barnes, 1876	Losses	36, Bill Hutchinson, 1892
Home Runs	27, Ned Williamson, 1884	Innings	627, Bill Hutchinson, 1892
RBIs	147, Cap Anson, 1886	Games Started	71, Bill Hutchinson, 1892
Total Bases	287, Jimmy Ryan, 1889	Complete Games	68, John Clarkson, 1885
Hits	187, Cap Anson, 1886	Strikeouts	316, Bill Hutchinson, 1892
Runs	155, King Kelly, 1886	Bases on Balls	199, Bill Hutchinson, 1890
Doubles	49, Ned Williamson, 1883	Winning Pct.	.875, Fred Goldsmith, 1880
Triples	15, Jimmy Ryan, 1891	ERA	1.75, Al Spalding, 1876
Bases on Balls	113, Cap Anson, 1890	Shutouts	10, John Clarkson, 1885
Stolen Bases	60, Jimmy Ryan, 1888		

With the exception of the three-year period between 1877 and 1879, the White Stockings never lacked for an outstanding pitcher during the game's first era. In 1880 they were fortunate enough to have two, Larry Corcoran and Fred Goldsmith. Goldsmith's .825 winning percentage was the highest in the nineteenth century by a 20-game winner. One of his losses came on July 10 to Cleveland, when he was beaten 2–0 on a two-run ninth-inning home run by Fred Dunlap. Dunlap's blow ended the White Stockings' nineteenth-century-record 21-game winning streak, which helped the club to register a .798 winning percentage, still an NL record.

BOSTON RED STOCKINGS (1876–92)

Pennants: 1877, 1878, 1883, 1891, 1892
Manager: John Morrill, 1882–88
Park: South End Grounds
Best Year: 1877 (42–18, .700)
Worst Year: 1885 (46–66, .411)
Top Rookie: Kid Nichols, 1890
Biggest Disappointment: Hoss Radbourn, 1886–89
Best Move: Snaring Dan Brouthers, Hardy Richardson and Charlie Bennett for the 1889 season from Detroit after the Detroit franchise folded
Worst Move: Blackballing slugger Charley Jones during the 1880 season
Other:
    1877—Lead NL in every major team department except FA
    1878—Tommy Bond wins 40 of the club's 41 victories
    1880—Club's first sub-.500 finish
    1881—Score fewest runs in league, 43 less than the next most punchless team, Cleveland
    1883—Career year by second baseman Jack Burdock is instrumental in club's only pennant during the 1880s
    1889—Lose pennant on the last day of the season when ace John Clarkson is beaten unexpectedly
    1890—Frank Selee named manager, brings Kid Nichols to the club
    1892—Hugh Duffy, Tommy McCarthy and Jack Stivetts acquired from former American Association teams as part of peace settlement between the two leagues

HITTING		PITCHING	
Batting Ave.	.387, Deacon White, 1877	Wins	49, John Clarkson, 1889
Slugging Ave.	.545, Deacon White, 1877	Losses	33, Jim Whitney, 1881
Home Runs	12, Dick Johnston, 1888	Innings	620, John Clarkson, 1889
RBIs	118, Dan Brouthers, 1889	Games Started	72, John Clarkson, 1889
Total Bases	276, Dick Johnston, 1888	Complete Games	68, John Clarkson 1889
Hits	184, Hugh Duffy, 1892	Strikeouts	417, Charlie Buffinton. 1884
Runs	129, Herman Long, 1891	Bases on Balls	203, John Clarkson, 1889
Doubles	41, King Kelly, 1889	Winning Pct.	.750, Charlie Buffinton, 1884
Triples	20, Dick Johnston, 1887	ERA	1.96, Tommy Bond, 1879
	20, Harry Stovey, 1891		
Bases on Balls	93, Tommy McCarthy, 1892	Shutouts	12, Tommy Bond, 1879
Stolen Bases	84, King Kelly, 1887		

Buffinton's remarkable 48–16 season in 1884 was obscured by Hoss Radbourn's 60 wins and 441 strikeouts. White's 1877 season was his last with Boston; he skipped to Cincinnati the following year to join his brother Will in forming the first all-sibling battery. Johnston is the one name on the chart that even many students of the last century may not recognize. He played only three full seasons with the Red Stockings. In 1889, his last, he hit .228, and one might imagine that the team was not overly distressed when he jumped to the Players League the following year.

NEW YORK GIANTS (1883–92)

Pennants: 1888, 1889
Manager: Jim Mutrie, 1885–91
Park: Polo Grounds, 110th St., 1883–88
  Polo Grounds, 155th St., 1889–90
  Polo Grounds, 157th St., 1891–92
Best Year: 1885 (85–27, .759)
Worst Year: 1892 (71–80, .470)
Top Rookie: Mike Tiernan, 1887
Biggest Disappointment: Joe Gerhardt, 1885, hit .155 as club's regular second baseman to contribute heavily to its losing the pennant by a narrow two-game margin
Best Move: Obtaining Amos Rusie from the defunct Indianapolis franchise in 1890
Worst Move: Not retaining Fred Pfeffer when the franchise moved from Troy to New York in 1883; Pfeffer went to Chicago and became the NL's top second baseman in the late 1880s
Other:
  1883—Buck Ewing is the first catcher to be a league home run leader
  1885—In a weird season finish 2nd, two games out of 1st but 28 games ahead of 3rd-place Philadelphia; become only pre-1900 club to lose a pennant despite winning a team Triple Crown
  1886—Tim Keefe and Mickey Welch win 75 games between them, all but one of the team's 76 victories; team draws record crowd of 20,709 on Memorial Day and later in the year has nearly 30,000 at a game
  1888—First flag won by an NL team in New York
  1889—Win pennant on the closing day of the season, the first time in NL history this happened
  1892—Poor fielding—565 errors in 153 games—helps doom team to its lowest winning percentage (.470) since joining the NL in 1883

HITTING		PITCHING	
Batting Ave.	.371, Roger Connor, 1885	Wins	44, Mickey Welch, 1885
Slugging Ave.	.541, Roger Connor, 1887	Losses	34, Amos Rusie, 1890
Home Runs	17, Roger Connor, 1887	Innings	557, Mickey Welch, 1884
RBIs	130, Roger Connor, 1889	Games Started	65, Mickey Welch, 1885
Total Bases	274, Mike Tiernan, 1890	Complete Games	62, Mickey Welch, 1884
			62, Tim Keefe, 1886
Hits	184, Monte Ward, 1887	Strikeouts	345, Mickey Welch, 1884
Runs	147, Mike Tiernan, 1889	Bases on Balls	289, Amos Rusie, 1890
Doubles	36, Jim O'Rourke, 1889	Winning Pct.	.800, Mickey Welch, 1885
Triples	22, Roger Connor, 1887	ERA	1.58, Tim Keefe, 1885
Bases on Balls	96, Mike Tiernan, 1889	Shutouts	8, Tim Keefe, 1888
Stolen Bases	111, Monte Ward, 1887		

Ward had to wait a long time to get into the Hall of Fame because he alienated a lot of magnates with his attempts to unionize players and generally create havoc, but there is no good explanation for why it took Connor and Welch so long to be enshrined. Connor's case is especially baffling. As the chart suggests, he had many outstanding seasons. Rusie's 1890 walk total is an all-time record. He's the only hurler in the Hall of Fame who averaged over four bases on balls for every nine innings he pitched.

PROVIDENCE GRAYS (1878–85)

Pennants: 1879, 1884
Manager: Harry Wright, 1882–83; Frank Bancroft, 1884–85
Park: Messer Street Park
Best Year: 1884 (84–28, .750)
Worst Year: 1885 (53–57, .482)
Top Rookie: Monte Ward, 1878
Biggest Disappointment: Lee Richmond, 1883
Best Move: Pilfering Paul Hines from Chicago in 1878
Worst Move: Releasing Charlie Sweeney in 1884
Other:

1879—Feature the first protective wire screen behind home plate in its park and also the first turnstile; lead NL in BA

1882—Barney Gilligan arrives to give the club a solid catcher; George Wright hits .162 at shortstop

1883—Art Irwin replaces Wright at shortstop; club's BA improves by 22 points

1884—Hoss Radbourn wins a record 60 games and three more in post-season play to give the Grays a sweep of the first World Series ever played to a conclusion

1885—Team's chances killed by horrible hitting, a .220 BA in particular, which is last in the NL; poor attendance causes Providence to exit from the major league scene, never to return

HITTING		**PITCHING**	
Batting Ave.	.358, Paul Hines, 1878	Wins	60, Hoss Radbourn, 1884*
Slugging Ave.	.486, Paul Hines, 1878	Losses	26, Dupee Shaw, 1885
Home Runs	9, Jerry Denny, 1882, 1884	Innings	679, Hoss Radbourn, 1884
RBIs	53, Monte Ward, 1881	Games Started	73, Hoss Radbourn, 1884
Total Bases	213, Paul Hines, 1884	Complete Games	73, Hoss Radbourn, 1884
Hits	148, Paul Hines, 1884	Strikeouts	441, Hoss Radbourn, 1884
Runs	94, Paul Hines, 1883, 1884	Bases on Balls	99, Dupee Shaw, 1885
Doubles	36, Paul Hines, 1884	Winning Pct.	.833, Hoss Radbourn, 1884*
Triples	10, Paul Hines, 1879, 1882, 1884 10, Joe Start, 1882	ERA	1.38, Hoss Radbourn, 1884
Bases on Balls	44, Paul Hines, 1884	Shutouts	11, Hoss Radbourn, 1884
Stolen Bases	Not available		

*One of Radbourn's wins in 1884 is still disputed; as a result some current reference books credit him with only 59 wins and an .831 winning percentage.

Paul Hines died in 1935 unaware that he was the first player in major league history to win a Triple Crown. RBIs were not regarded as a particularly important stat in 1878, the year he won, so nobody got too excited when he knocked home a loop-leading 50 runs. No one cared much either about his four home runs. But what really stung Hines was that the bat title was awarded that year to Abner Dalrymple. Not until much later did it emerge that Hines actually had a higher BA. So just how good was he, really? The best player that Providence ever had, at the very minimum. And that includes its several Hall of Famers.

PHILADELPHIA PHILLIES (1883–92)

Pennants: None
Manager: Harry Wright, 1884–92
Park: Recreation Park, 1883–86
  Philadelphia Baseball Grounds, 1887–94, also known as Palace Park
Best Year: 1886 (71–43, .623)
Worst Year: 1883 (17–81, .173)
Top Rookie: Ed Daily, 1885
Biggest Disappointment: Charlie Reilly, 1892, hit .196 at third base after the club got rid of Bill Shindle, a much better player
Best Move: Getting Sam Thompson from the defunct Detroit franchise in 1889
Worst Move: Letting John Coleman go to the rival Philadelphia AA club in 1884—a bust with the Phillies, he later became quite a good outfielder for several years
Other:
  1883—5.33 staff ERA and 887 runs allowed in 99 games; club also known as the Quakers during the 1880s
  1885—Break .500 for the first time and finish 3rd
  1888—Star pitcher Charlie Ferguson dies
  1889—Fall below .500 for the first time since 1884
  1890—Top NL in team batting for the first of what will be many ti nes
  1891—Star outfielder Jim Fogarty dies in May, eliminating the question of whether he'd have been able to hold his job with Sam Thompson, Ed Delahanty and Billy Hamilton all on the club by now
  1892—Lead NL in BA, homers and SA; Hamilton, Delahanty and Thompson all hit .306 or better (a remarkable showing in that apart from the trio of Phils outfielders the NL only had seven .300 hitters in 1892)

HITTING		**PITCHING**	
Batting Ave.	.340, Billy Hamilton, 1891	Wins	38, Kid Gleason, 1890
Slugging Ave.	.495, Ed Delahanty, 1892	Losses	48, John Coleman, 1883
Home Runs	20, Sam Thompson, 1889	Innings	538, John Coleman, 1883
RBIs	111, Sam Thompson, 1889	Games Started	61, John Coleman, 1883
Total Bases	263, Sam Thompson, 1892	Complete Games	59, John Coleman, 1883
Hits	186, Sam Thompson, 1892	Strikeouts	222, Kid Gleason, 1890
Runs	141, Billy Hamilton, 1891	Bases on Balls	168, Gus Weyhing, 1892
Doubles	41, Sam Thompson, 1890	Winning Pct.	.769, Charlie Ferguson, 1886
Triples	21, Ed Delahanty, 1892	ERA	1.90, Ben Sanders, 1888
Bases on Balls	116, Roger Connor, 1892	Shutouts	8, Ben Sanders, 1888
Stolen Bases	111, Billy Hamilton, 1891		

Coleman later became an outfielder, Gleason later became a second baseman, Ferguson later died while still at his peak, and Sanders later defected to the Players League. August "Gus" Weyhing later opened a bar and restaurant. When it failed he put a sign in the front window that said: "Attention, patrons. The first of July will be the last of August." The 1883 season was nearly the last of the Phillies. The club was so bad that it finished 23 games behind seventh-place Detroit, this despite playing only a 98-game schedule.

PITTSBURGH PIRATES (1882–92)

Pennants: None
Manager: Horace Phillips, 1884–89
Park: Exposition Park, 1882–86, 1891–92
  Recreation Park, 1887–90
Best Year: 1886 (80–57, .584)
Worst Year: 1890 (23–113, .169)
Top Rookie: Ed Swartwood, 1882
Biggest Disappointment: Jim McCormick and Abner Dalrymple, 1887
Best Move: Getting Ed Morris and Tom Brown from Columbus when the Ohio franchise went belly-up after the 1884 season
Worst Move: Replacing Ned Hanlon as manager and letting him move on to Baltimore in 1892
Other:
  1882—Team known as the Alleghenies and later was called the Innocents; became the Pirates in 1891, when the club bagged second baseman Lou Bierbauer, who was left unprotected through an oversight by the Philadelphia Association club
  1883—Ed Swartwood wins the Association batting crown, the only Pittsburgh winner prior to Honus Wagner
  1884—In an expansion year, with four new teams added to the Association, the Alleghenies hit .211 and finish 10th
  1886—Ed Morris and Pud Galvin win 70 games between them as the club finishes 2nd in its final Association season
  1887—Franchise shifts to the National League after an argument over the rights to St. Louis Browns pitcher Jumbo McGinnis; first baseman Alex McKinnon dies after playing 48 games and hitting .340
  1890—Franchise record 113 losses, including three in one of the last tripleheaders played
  1891—Club is last when great pitching—a strong second in team ERA—is overridden by weak attack; Pirates are last in BA and also have lowest SA and OBP
  1892—First above-.500 finish since joining the NL

HITTING		PITCHING	
Batting Ave.	.356, Ed Swartwood, 1883	Wins	41, Ed Morris, 1886
Slugging Ave.	.499, Fred Carroll, 1887	Losses	35, Fleury Sullivan, 1884
Home Runs	10, Jake Beckley, 1892	Innings	581, Ed Morris, 1885
RBIs	97, Jake Beckley, 1889	Games Started	63, Ed Morris, 1885, 1886
Total Bases	234, Jake Beckley, 1892	Complete Games	63, Ed Morris, 1885, 1886
Hits	162, Jake Beckley, 1891	Strikeouts	326, Ed Morris, 1886
Runs	106, Tom Brown, 1886	Bases on Balls	118, Ed Morris, 1886
Doubles	32, Sam Barkley, 1886	Winning Pct.	.672, Ed Morris, 1886
Triples	19, Jake Beckley, 1891, 1892	ERA	2.31, Ed Morris, 1888*
Bases on Balls	82, Elmer Smith, 1892	Shutouts	12, Ed Morris, 1886
Stolen Bases	71, Billy Sunday, 1888		

*Denny Driscoll had a 1.21 ERA in 201 innings in 1882, enough to qualify for an ERA crown in any era, but still . . . 201 innings in the 1880s was nothing; for many pitchers it was about a couple of weeks work.

Beckley could hit, no question, but he was a huge liability in the field. His arm was so bad that he would sometimes run the ball across the diamond rather than throw it in an effort to catch a runner trying to advance an extra base. Morris's arm, in contrast, was so good that he was the first really great lefthander, and his 12 shutouts in 1886 still stand as an all-time southpaw record. It was even good enough to make Hall of Famer Pud Galvin no better than the club's second-string pitcher during most of the seasons both were with Pittsburgh. Look up Sullivan, if you don't already know him, and wonder, as does everyone, who he was, with which arm he threw, and on and on.

AMERICAN ASSOCIATION

ST. LOUIS BROWNS (1882–92)

Pennants: 1885, 1886, 1887, 1888
Manager: Charlie Comiskey, 1883, 1885–89, 1891
Park: Sportsman's Park
Best Year: 1885 (79–33, .705)
Worst Year: 1882 (37–43, .463)
Top Rookie: Silver King, 1887
Biggest Disappointment: Bill White, 1888
Best Move: Purchasing Bob Caruthers in 1884
Wort Move: Selling Caruthers and Dave Foutz to Brooklyn in 1888 rather than give them a pay hike
Other:
  1882—5th in a six-team league; only sub-.500 finish while in Association; feature Bill and Jack Gleason, first brothers to play side by side in the same infield
  1884—Team short of pitching after Tony Mullane jumped to Union Association and subsequently wound up with rival Toledo AA club
  1885—Set AA records for the highest winning percentage (.705) and the greatest margin of victory (16 games) by a pennant winner
  1887—Club showcases Tip O'Neill, who set an AA record for the highest batting average and won the Triple Crown
  1888—Win team Triple Crown and become first team ever to grab four straight pennants
  1891—Finish 2nd in AA in loop's final season, then loses most of its top players to already existing NL teams as part of the peace settlement between the two leagues and tumbles all the way to 11th place in 1892 as the reformed Browns in the NL

HITTING		PITCHING	
Batting Ave.	.435, Tip O'Neill, 1887	Wins	45, Silver King, 1888
Slugging Ave.	.691, Tip O'Neill, 1887	Losses	22, Jack Stivetts, 1891
Home Runs	14, Tip O'Neill, 1887	Innings	586, Silver King, 1888
RBIs	110, Tip O'Neill, 1889*	Games Started	65, Silver King, 1888
Total Bases	357, Tip O'Neill, 1887	Complete Games	64, Silver King, 1888
Hits	225, Tip O'Neill, 1887	Strikeouts	289, Jack Stivetts, 1890
Runs	167, Tip O'Neill, 1887	Bases on Balls	232, Jack Stivetts, 1891
Doubles	52, Tip O'Neill, 1887	Winning Pct.	.763, Bob Caruthers, 1887
Triples	19, Tip O'Neill, 1887	ERA	1.64, Silver King, 1888
Bases on Balls	119, Dummy Hoy, 1891	Shutouts	11, Dave Foutz, 1886
Stolen Bases	129, Arlie Latham, 1887		

*RBI totals for the 1887 AA season are still unavailable, but O'Neill almost certainly had more than 110 that year; several books credit him unofficially with 123.

O'Neill's great season in 1887 happened to coincide with a rule change that year that counted bases on balls as hits. Hence he was credited at the time with a .492 BA that has since been reduced to a figure that is still the second highest in history. Yet to be done is a careful examination of his performance in 1887. For those of you out there looking to make your mark as a baseball researcher, you just received my hint for the day. King's early career is also well worth exploring. Actually, this whole Browns dynasty has never gotten anywhere near the attention it deserves. For four years there they dominated their loop to a degree that no other team ever has, with the sole exception of the 1936–39 Yankees.

CINCINNATI RED STOCKINGS (1882–92)

Pennants: 1882
Manager: Gus Schmelz, 1887–89
Park: Bank Street Grounds, 1882–83
  American League Park, 1884–92
Best Year: 1882 (55–25, .688)
Worst Year: 1891 (56–81, .409)
Top Rookie: Tie between Bug Holliday and Jesse Duryea, 1889
Biggest Disappointment: Tom Mansell, a flop in 1884 after he was picked up from St. Louis to play center field
Best Move: Acquiring Frank Fennelly in late 1884 from the folding Washington AA club to fill a glaring hole at shortstop
Worst Move: Cutting Joe Knight, the club's top hitter in 1890 and the fifth best batter in the league
Other:
  1883—Lose a chance to win the pennant when the team wins just four of 14 games against the New York Mets
  1885—Club secretary O. P. Caylor becomes manager
  1887—Win 80 games and post .600 winning percentage but finish 14 games behind powerful Browns
  1889—Hick Carpenter, probably the greatest lefty infielder ever, plays his final season as the club's regular third baseman
  1890—Franchise switches to NL along with Brooklyn after its owners lose a power struggle with Browns mogul Chris Von der Ahe
  1892—Club shows 24½ game improvement over 1891 after four decimated AA franchises join the NL and bring up the loop's rear

HITTING		PITCHING	
Batting Ave.	.342, Hick Carpenter, 1882	Wins	43, Will White, 1883
Slugging Ave.	.551, Long John Reilly, 1884	Losses	27, Tony Mullane, 1886
Home Runs	19, Bug Holliday, 1889	Innings	577, Will White, 1883
RBIs	104, Bug Holliday, 1889	Games Started	64, Will White, 1883
Total Bases	280, Bug Holliday, 1889	Complete Games	64, Will White, 1883
Hits	181, Bug Holliday, 1889	Strikeouts	250, Tony Mullane, 1886
Runs	139, Bid McPhee, 1886	Bases on Balls	166, Tony Mullane, 1886
Doubles	35, Long John Reilly, 1887	Winning Pct.	.769, Will White, 1882
Triples	26, Long John Reilly, 1890	ERA	1.54, Will White, 1882
Bases on Balls	86, Hugh Nicol, 1887	Shutouts	8, Will White, 1882
Stolen Bases	138, Hugh Nicol, 1887		

The Red Stockings' record totals in almost every instance are significantly less than those of the other good teams during the era. Cincinnati's biggest weapon was its fielding. In Bid McPhee the club had the best middle infielder during the 1880s, and many historians of the period consider Pop Corkhill to have been among the finest outfielders. Holliday, on the other hand, was reportedly not much of a fielder. Some sources still credit him with 193 hits and a .343 BA in 1889, but most now feel that there were discrepancies in his totals that year and that the stats on the chart here are the true ones.

PHILADELPHIA ATHLETICS (1882–90)

Pennants: 1883

Manager: Bill Sharsig, served all or part of every season but 1882 and 1883

Park: Oakdale Park, 1882

Jefferson Street Grounds, 1883–90

Best Year: 1883 (66–32, .673)

Worst Year: 1890 (54–78, .409)

Top Rookie: Denny Lyons, 1887, hit .367 and cemented his status as the club's number one third baseman after looking bad in a late-season trial the previous year

Biggest Disappointment: Bill Conroy, 1890, a .171 hitter as the club's regular shortstop

Best Move: Garnering Harry Stovey in 1883 after the Worcester franchise in the NL folded and was moved to Philadelphia to become the Phillies

Worst Move: Failing to put Lou Bierbauer and Harry Stovey on the club's reserve list when they jumped to the Players League in 1890; as a result both joined NL teams after the rebel loop collapsed

Other:

1883—Become first team in ML history to need to win its final game of the season in order to clinch a pennant

1884—Finish 6th with the best-hitting team in the AA owing to weak pitching and poor defense

1885—First sub-.500 finish

1887—Much-traveled Frank Bancroft takes a turn as the club's manager and is a flop

1889—Club as usual has fine hitting but can finish only a distant 3rd as its trio of pitchers is not on a par with those of St. Louis and Brooklyn

1890—Despite execrable pitching, the A's lead the AA in July, only to come apart in the stretch and finish 7th; ousted from AA after season for financial reasons and replaced in 1891 by Philadelphia Players League club which retains Athletics nickname

HITTING		PITCHING	
Batting Ave.	.367, Denny Lyons, 1887	Wins	35, Ed Seward, 1888
Slugging Ave.	.545, Harry Stovey, 1884	Losses	28, Gus Weyhing, 1887
Home Runs	19, Harry Stovey, 1889	Innings	519, Ed Seward, 1888
RBIs	119, Harry Stovey, 1889	Games Started	57, Ed Seward, 1888
Total Bases	298, Denny Lyons, 1887	Complete Games	57, Ed Seward, 1888
Hits	209, Denny Lyons, 1887	Strikeouts	286, Bobby Mathews, 1884, 1885
Runs	152, Harry Stovey, 1889	Bases on Balls	212, Gus Weyhing, 1889
Doubles	39, Curt Welch, 1889	Winning Pct.	.698, Bobby Mathews, 1883
Triples	23, Harry Stovey, 1884	ERA	2.01, Ed Seward, 1888
Bases on Balls	79, Denny Lyons, 1889	Shutouts	6, Ed Seward, 1888
Stolen Bases	95, Curt Welch, 1888		

Some books still credit Stovey with a .404 BA in 1884 and the AA hitting crown, but most now reduce his figure to .326 and give the honor to Dave Orr of the New York Mets, who hit .354. In any case, Stovey remains the top all-around slugger of the 1880s and the first player to collect over 100 career home runs. Seward was a small, chunky righthander who won 81 games in his first three seasons with the A's before his arm went on the blink. Despite his short career, he rates as the club's best pitcher. Unlike the other well-run AA clubs, the Athletics lacked continuity. As an illustration, Jack O'Brien was the only member of the A's inaugural team in 1882 who was still on its roster when it began its fourth season in 1885.

BROOKLYN BRIDEGROOMS (1884–92)

Pennants: 1889 (AA), 1890 (NL)
Manager: Bill McGunnigle, 1888–90
Park: Washington Park, 1884–90
  Eastern Park, 1891–92
Best Year: 1889 (93–44, .679)
Worst Year: 1884 (40–64, .385)
Top Rookie: Mickey Hughes, 1888
Biggest Disappointment: Jackie Hayes, 1885; expected to be the club's regular catcher, he saw his career nosedive when he could not hit overhand pitching, allowed in the AA for the first time in 1885
Best Move: Keeping the team intact during the 1890 Players League threat
Worst Move: Allowing Bill McGunnigle to exit Brooklyn and become Pittsburgh's manager in 1891
Other:
  Known as the Grays when they originally join the AA; become the Bridegrooms in the late 1880s when they have a number of newlyweds on the team
  1884—Jack Remsen, the last bearded player in the majors until the 1970s, occupies center field in team's initial season in AA
  1885—Owner Charlie Byrne takes a try at managing the club
  1888—Bob Caruthers and Dave Foutz purchased from St. Louis
  1889—Set 19th century attendance record by drawing an estimated 353,000 fans
  1890—Become only team in major league history to win flags in consecutive seasons in two different leagues when they cop NL bunting after deserting the AA following the 1889 season
  1891—Monte Ward replaces McGunnigle as manager; team topples from 1st to 6th
  1892—Hub Collins dies of typhoid fever; team tops NL in runs, BA, and FA but has only seventh-best ERA and finishes 3rd

HITTING		**PITCHING**	
Batting Ave.	.335, Dan Brouthers, 1892	Wins	40, Bob Caruthers, 1889
Slugging Ave.	.480, Dan Brouthers, 1892	Losses	35, Adonis Terry, 1884
Home Runs	13, Oyster Burns, 1890	Innings	476, Adonis Terry, 1884
RBIs	128, Oyster Burns, 1890	Games Started	55, Adonis Terry, 1884
Total Bases	282, Dan Brouthers, 1892	Complete Games	54, Adonis Terry, 1884
Hits	197, Dan Brouthers, 1892	Strikeouts	230, Adonis Terry, 1884
Runs	148, Hub Collins, 1890	Bases on Balls	163, George Haddock, 1892
Doubles	36, Mike Griffin, 1891	Winning Pct.	.784, Bob Caruthers, 1889
Triples	20, Dan Brouthers, 1892	ERA	2.13, Mickey Hughes, 1888
Bases on Balls	85, Hub Collins, 1890	Shutouts	7, Bob Caruthers, 1889
Stolen Bases	91, Darby O'Brien, 1889		

O'Brien died in 1893, approximately a year after Collins; both were swift base runners and good fielders who were sorely missed. Brouthers also holds many period batting records for Buffalo and Detroit, two NL teams that did not last quite long enough to be considered here. Perhaps Brooklyn's best player throughout the period was one who does not appear on the chart, George Pinkney, a fine all-around third baseman who once played 577 consecutive games, still thought by many historians to be the pre-1893 record.

LOUISVILLE COLONELS (1882–91)

Pennants: 1890
Manager: Jack Chapman, 1889–92
Park: Eclipse Park
Best Year: 1890 (88–44, .667)
Worst Year: 1889 (27–111, .196)
Top Rookie: Pete Browning, 1882
Biggest Disappointment: Juice Latham, 1884, hit .169 as the club's regular first baseman and team captain
Best Move: Obtaining Bill White from Washington of the Eastern League in 1886 to plug a hole at shortstop
Worst Move: Letting Sam Weaver jump to the Union Association in 1884 and leave the team without a reliable backup pitcher, a flaw that probably cost the club the 1884 flag
Other:
  1882—On the team are the Reccius brothers, Phil and John, the first twins to play in the majors; club known as the Eclipse, a name that is gradually discarded in mid-1880s.
  1884—Lead AA race in mid-July before lack of pitching depth makes itself felt
  1887—Last season a Louisville team in the majors finishes above .500 with the exception of the 1890 club
  1889—Record 26 consecutive losses; team is dissension-ridden
  1890—Win flag largely because most of its holdovers from 1889 team are too weak to be coveted by Players League raiders; team also known by now as the Cyclones
  1891—Franchise absorbed by the NL when AA folds; top finish in the NL comes in 1892 when club wins 63 games and posts .414 winning percentage

HITTING		PITCHING	
Batting Ave.	.402, Pete Browning, 1887	Wins	52, Guy Hecker, 1884
Slugging Ave.	.547, Pete Browning, 1887	Losses	29, Red Ehret, 1889
Home Runs	9, Pete Browning, 1885	Innings	671, Guy Hecker, 1884
RBIs	82, Chicken Wolf, 1891	Games Started	73, Guy Hecker, 1884
Total Bases	299, Pete Browning, 1887	Complete Games	72, Guy Hecker, 1884
Hits	220, Pete Browning, 1887	Strikeouts	499, Toad Ramsey, 1886
Runs	137, Pete Browning, 1887	Bases on Balls	207, Toad Ramsey, 1886
Doubles	35, Pete Browning, 1887	Winning Pct.	.722, Guy Hecker, 1884
Triples	19, John Kerins, 1887	ERA	1.80, Guy Hecker, 1884
Bases on Balls	83, Reddy Mack, 1887	Shutouts	6, Guy Hecker, 1884
Stolen Bases	103, Pete Browning, 1887		

RBI totals for many AA teams during the 1880s are incomplete. Since Louisville is one of them, no one knows how many runs Browning knocked home in 1887, but almost certainly he had enough to wipe Wolf's name off the chart. No one will ever know either how great a pitcher Hecker might have been if Louisville had had another decent hurler in 1884. Unable to spell Hecker, the club used him to the hilt. He was never again so good a pitcher but was so good an all-around player that he could not be kept out of the lineup. The Billy Goodman of his day, Hecker won a batting crown in 1886 without a regular position and also contrived to collect 27 victories.

BALTIMORE ORIOLES (1882–89)

Pennants: None
Manager: Billy Barnie, 1883–89
Park: Union Park
Best Year: 1887 (77–58, .570)
Worst Year: 1882 (19–54, .206)
Top Rookie: Matt Kilroy, 1886
Biggest Disappointment: Milt Scott, 1886
Best Move: Retaining Oyster Burns; a flop in 1885, he became a star upon his return in 1887
Worst Move: Letting Dennis Casey, the team's best hitter in 1885, drift away following a salary dispute
Other:
  1883—Second straight last-place finish
  1884—Hit just .233 as a team but play .594 ball in an expansion year
  1886—Record low .204 team BA and .258 SA; only pre-1900 ML team to average as many as six pitcher K's per game (exactly 6.00)
  1887—Team undergoes 27-game improvement over 1886 finish, largely thanks to standout rookie Mike Griffin in center field
  1889—Tommy Tucker wins AA batting crown with the highest BA in history by a switch hitter; franchise folds at the season's end owing to the Players League threat; another franchise plays part of the 1890 season in Baltimore and the original Orioles are then revived in 1891 with an entirely different cast of players

HITTING		PITCHING	
Batting Ave.	.372, Tommy Tucker, 1889	Wins	46, Matt Kilroy, 1887
Slugging Ave.	.519, Oyster Burns, 1887	Losses	34, Matt Kilroy, 1886
Home Runs	9, Oyster Burns, 1887	Innings	589, Matt Kilroy, 1887
RBIs	99, Tommy Tucker, 1889	Games Started	69, Matt Kilroy, 1887
Total Bases	286, Oyster Burns, 1887	Complete Games	66, Matt Kilroy, 1886, 1887
Hits	196, Tommy Tucker, 1889	Strikeouts	513, Matt Kilroy, 1886
Runs	152, Mike Griffin, 1889	Bases on Balls	182, Matt Kilroy, 1886
Doubles	33, Oyster Burns, 1887	Winning Pct.	.708, Matt Kilroy, 1887
Triples	19, Oyster Burns, 1887	ERA	2.75, Bob Emslie, 1884
Bases on Balls	91, Mike Griffin, 1889	Shutouts	6, Matt Kilroy, 1887
Stolen Bases	94, Mike Griffin, 1887		

The chart creates a powerful impression that Kilroy was the only pitcher of consequence this club had. That's almost the case. The Orioles were typical of all the weak teams in this era. When they happened to stumble on a strong young pitcher while they were at a low ebb, they did not hesitate to abuse him. Kilroy hurled 1172 innings and 132 complete games in his first two seasons. Both figures represent about half of his career totals. In 1886, Kilroy's rookie season, the team gave him so little support that he could not win even half his games despite notching an all-time record number of strikeouts. The club's best hitting regular that year was rightfielder Jack Manning, who hit all of .223.

THE BEST, THE WORST AND THE WEIRDEST TEAMS BETWEEN 1876 AND 1892

• •

NATIONAL LEAGUE

THE BEST

1880 CHICAGO WHITE STOCKINGS
W-67 L-17
Manager: Cap Anson

Regular Lineup—1B, Cap Anson; 2B, Joe Quest; 3B, Ned Williamson; SS, Tommy Burns; RF, King Kelly; CF, George Gore; LF, Abner Dalrymple; C, Silver Flint; P, Larry Corcoran; P, Fred Goldsmith

Playing an 84-game schedule, the White Stockings romped to the flag by a 15-game margin. Anson not only had Corcoran, one of the era's top pitchers, but in Goldsmith the first change boxman to notch 20 or more victories. Moreover, the club had four of the loop's top five hitters, including Burns, probably the best all-around shortstop in the game at the time. Early in the season the White Stockings reeled off 21 straight wins, marred only by a 1–1 tie with Providence. During their record skein they won six games from Providence, their closest rival, six each from Troy and Worcester and three from Boston, omitting only Buffalo and Cincinnati, the two weakest clubs in the league that year, and Cleveland, the third-place finisher, which ended the streak on July 10. The White Stockings triumphed again in 1881 with the same lineup, adding only Hugh Nicol as a utility out-fielder, and took their third successive pennant a year later with Kelly moving to the infield to replace Quest and Nicol at Kelly's old post. The club then underwent some reshuffling after both Corcoran and Goldsmith had arm problems and Nicol jumped to the American Association, but rebounded to win again in 1885 with a team some consider to have been as good as the 1880 crew. Although the White Stockings finished that year just two games ahead of the New York Giants, who were studded with several of the star players from the 1884 AA champion New York Metropolitans, they came in 30 games in front of third-place Philadelphia.

THE WORST

1890 PITTSBURGH INNOCENTS
W-23 L-113
Manager: Guy Hecker

Regular Lineup—1B, Guy Hecker; 2B, Sam LaRoque; 3B, Doggie Miller; SS, Ed Sales; RF, Billy Sunday; CF, Tun Berger; LF, John Kelty; C, Harry Decker; P, Kirtley Baker; P, Guy Hecker; P, Dave Anderson; P, Bill Sowders

A decent team in 1889, Pittsburgh suffered more than any other NL club from defections the following year to the Players League. Sunday, one of the two regulars not to jump ship, was sent to Philadelphia late in the 1890 campaign when the situation became hopeless, leaving Miller the club's lone holdover from 1889 to finish the 1890 season with Pittsburgh. Hecker, nearing the end as a player, would have preferred to be a bench manager but soon found he did not have that luxury. The Innocents were woefully short of both hitting and pitching, posting the lowest BA and by far the highest ERA in the NL, but it was as fielders that they really distinguished themselves. Hecker's crew made 607 errors and had the last sub.-900 FA in major league history. Baker, the staff ace, had just three wins, and Miller was the only major contributor who was retained by the club when the Players League deserters returned in 1891. The team billed itself as the Troubadours but became the Innocents when it began the season with inexperienced players at almost every position. Among the club's untested hopefuls were the Gil-bert brothers, who formed the first sibling keystone combination on a major league level (albeit a very short-lived one), and Harry Decker, acquired from Philadelphia to be the club's interim catcher. Decker led the team in hitting with a .274 BA but is better known as the inventor of a catcher's mitt that was remarkably similar to those in use today.

THE WEIRDEST

1878 CINCINNATI RED STOCKINGS
W-37 L-23
Manager: Cal McVey

Regular Lineup—1B, Chub Sullivan; 2B, Joe Gerhardt; 3B, Cal McVey; SS, Billy Geer; RF, King Kelly; CF, Lip Pike; LF, Charley Jones; C, Deacon White; P, Will White

After finishing a very distant last in 1877, the Red Stockings shocked the baseball world by beginning the 1878 season with six straight wins at home and then took to the road, where they continued to play well before faltering late in the summer and giving way to Boston. This club had something for everyone, numbering twenty-year-old rookie Kelly, destined to become the most notorious rules violator of his time, Pike, who was blacklisted during the 1878 season and replaced by Buttercup Dickerson, himself later blacklisted, and Jones, one of the game's first great sluggers, who was blacklisted by Boston during the 1880 season and played outlaw ball for two years in Portsmouth, Ohio, before joining the American Association. It also had the Whites, the first brother battery and the last pair of major leaguers who were not at all shy about arguing their conviction that the world was flat, and the first "Pony Battery" in diminutive change pointsmen, catcher George Miller and pitcher Bobby Mitchell, who was furthermore the first southpaw in major league history. The franchise was owned by Wayne Neff, an ice-refrigerating mogul, who had prevented it from going belly up the previous year by cavalierly making good a slew of debts left behind by the previous owner, Josiah Keck, the operator of a fertilizer company that was called Si Keck's Stink Factory to distinguish it from his ball club, known as Si Keck's Stinker Nine. What it must have been like to play for this team has never been adequately documented, but one still prays that McVey, perhaps its lone reliable spokesman, left behind a diary of his last days in Cincinnati that will someday be found.

AMERICAN ASSOCIATION

THE BEST

1887 ST. LOUIS BROWNS
W-95 L-40
Manager: Charlie Comiskey

Regular Lineup—1B, Charlie Comiskey; 2B, Yank Robinson; 3B, Arlie Latham; SS, Bill Gleason; RF, Bob Caruthers/Dave Foutz; CF, Curt Welch; LF, Tip O'Neill; C, Jack Boyle; P, Silver King; P, Bob Caruthers; P, Dave Foutz

Until recently pitching stats for the 1887 season indicated that the Browns actually won 97 games and lost only 38, but King has since been credited with two less victories and an additional loss. In any event, the team finished at least 14 games ahead of second-place Cincinnati and paced the AA in every important hitting and fielding department except triples and double plays. O'Neill had the most awesome pre-1900 season of any hitter with the possible exception of Fred Dunlap with the 1884 St. Louis Maroons, and the three main hurlers all won 25 or more games and worked between 339 and 390 innings to give the Browns the game's first "Big Three." Considered by many historians to have been the strongest club in either major league before owner Chris Von der Ahe, rankled by salary demands, broke up his juggernaut by shipping Caruthers and Foutz to Brooklyn and Gleason and Welch to Philadelphia (Welch was replaced in 1888 by Harry Lyons, who hit .194), the Browns disappointed their followers in just one respect: they lost the 1887 World Series to Detroit after many of their players, with Latham the most vociferous, had confidently pledged victory.

THE WORST

1886 BALTIMORE ORIOLES
W-48 L-83
Manager: Billy Barnie

Regular Lineup—1B, Milt Scott; 2B, Mike Muldoon; 3B, Jumbo Davis; SS, Jimmy Macullar; RF, Jack Manning; CF, Buster Hoover; LF, Joe Sommer; C, Chris Fulmer; P, Matt Kilroy; P, Jumbo McGinnis

During the AA's decade as a major league other clubs had poorer records than the 1886 Orioles, but none achieved so little with what seemed like so much. Barnie, normally a players' manager, curiously did not intervene the previous season when outfielder Dennis Casey had a falling-out with the club's owners, and so lost his main offensive weapon. Had Casey teamed with record-shattering rookie pitching star Kilroy, the Orioles might have been competitive in 1886. Lacking Casey, they had a .204 team BA and just one player, Fulmer (.244), who hit above .223. Macullar, one of the last lefty shortstops, was the lone infielder to top .200, and to add to Barnie's misery, McGinnis proved to be pitched out after the Orioles went through a protracted legal battle with Pittsburgh over which club should have the right to acquire him from St. Louis. The following season, bolstered by several rookies at key positions, the team rocketed to third place, its highest finish during Barnie's lengthy and for the most part frustrating tenure at its helm.

THE WEIRDEST

1890 LOUISVILLE COLONELS
W-88 L-44
Manager: Jack Chapman

Regular Lineup—1B, Harry Taylor; 2B, Tim Shinnick; 3B, Harry Raymond; SS, Phil Tomney; RF, Chicken Wolf; CF, Farmer Weaver; LF, Charlie Hamburg; C, John Ryan; P, Red Ehret; P, Scott Stratton; P, George Meakim; P, Herb Goodall

Beyond all doubt the largest collection of unknowns ever to win a major league pennant (I've yet to meet anyone who could name even one member of the club's infield), the Colonels, prior to 1991, were also the only team in history to snare a flag after finishing last the previous season.* Not only did they win, they breezed, cruising home ten games ahead of the Columbus Senators—and with a patched-together lineup that had been rated

*Let's settle something right here. In 1991 the Atlanta Braves matched Louisville's previously unparalleled achievement by going from worst to first, but Minnesota did not. While the Braves had the poorest record in the NL in 1990, the Twins tied Milwaukee for the 12th-worst record in the 14-team AL—not a true worst to first leapfrog. For those who might disagree, ask yourself this: How do you stand if the Angels, the AL's 11th best team in 1991 but last in the West, win in 1992 following an even .500 finish?

among the AA's weakest in the preseason forecast. The team was so lowly regarded that the Players League raiders virtually ignored it, pilfering just three players of note, Pete Browning, Dan Shannon and John Ewing. Wolf, the best of the lot who remained with Louisville and the only player to participate in all ten of the AA's seasons as a major league, won the batting crown. After managing the 1877 Louisville club that was decimated by scandal, Chapman spent the next 12 years skippering some of the worst clubs of the period before returning to the Falls City late in the dreary dissension-ridden 1889 season and was fired in 1892 when the club was once again mired deep in the second division. But in 1890 he and Wolf and a supporting cast that contained no players who would have any significant impact after the two major leagues merged two years later were magical. Louisville fans, for years convinced their nine was among the best in the game and certain to triumph one day, expected nothing but further heartbreak in 1890 and got nearly everything when the Colonels culminated their stunning season by tying the heavily favored Brooklyn Bridegrooms in the last NL versus AA World Series after being down 3 games to 1 as Ehret saved the team's second victory for Stratton and then went the route the following day to knot the affair. A deciding game to settle the issue and make up for an earlier contest that ended in a 7–7 deadlock was never played because the weather by then was so cold—it was nearly November—that fan interest was nil.

SPECIAL FEATURE TEAM

• •

1884 ST. LOUIS MAROONS
W-94 L-19
Managers: Ted Sullivan/Henry Lucas

Regular Lineup—1B, Joe Quinn; 2B, Fred Dunlap; 3B, Jack Gleason; SS, Milt Whitehead; RF, Orator Shaffer; CF, Dave Rowe; LF, Buttercup Dickerson; C, George Baker; P, Charlie Sweeney; P, Bollicky Billy Taylor; P, Henry Boyle; P, Perry Werden; P, Charlie Hodnett

Sullivan resigned as manager in mid-June when he found himself powerless to enforce disciplinary rules he instituted largely to curb notorious lushers like Taylor and Dickerson. At that point Lucas became an owner-manager, but Dunlap really ran the club on the field. In any case, Lucas was the prime mover and shaker behind the Union Association, which afforded professional baseball the sternest challenge to its reserve clause prior to the 1970s. Lucas believed the reserve clause was nothing more than a fancier form of slavery and organized his league around the premise that a player was bound to a particular team for only the length of his current contract.

What sank Lucas's experiment after a single season was that he was too good a recruiter. While the other seven UA teams began the 1884 season with ragtag lineups comprised of raw rookies and minor league castoffs, the Maroons featured Dunlap, Shaffer, Dickerson and several other standout performers who had been plundered from National League teams. The all-veteran cast enabled St. Louis to begin the season with a record 20 consecutive victories and swiftly end all pretense of a pennant race. Interestingly, though, the Maroons were not necessarily the UA's strongest team at the season's close. The Cincinnati Outlaw Reds won 24 of their last 26 games after snatching Jack Glasscock, Jim McCormick and Fatty Briody from Cleveland of the National League in August, whereas St. Louis was only 20–7 down the home stretch. McCormick, Glasscock, Dunlap and Charlie Sweeney were the class of the UA. Dunlap hit .412 and scored 160 runs in a mere 101 games, Glasscock batted .419 during the few weeks he spent in Union livery, and both McCormick and Sweeney were nearly unbeatable, losing just ten games between them while combining for 45 wins. All four returned to the National League in 1885 when Lucas's circuit collapsed, but only Glasscock was still a productive player by the end of the decade. In fact, the lone Union Association graduate who went on to have a career judged worthy of Hall of Fame selection was Tommy McCarthy, a rookie flop in 1884 with the Boston Unions, who were owned by George Wright, the star shortstop of the legendary 1869–70 Cincinnati Red Stockings.

Baseball historians have yet to unearth solutions to several mysteries that surround the Maroons. One is the fate of Charlie Hodnett, the club's Opening Day pitcher who beat Chicago 7–2 in a rain-abbreviated six-inning contest and had a 12–2 record when his career was ended by an ulcerated foot. Despite diligent efforts to track Hodnett's path after he left baseball, nothing is known about his later life. Then there is the curious case of Roche (first name unknown), the Maroons shortstop when the club played the first game in its history on April 6, 1884, against its own reserve team. Although reportedly an excellent fielder, Roche for reasons as yet undiscovered was no longer with St. Louis two weeks later when the Union Association campaign opened, and indeed never played a single game for any major league team that season or any other. What is especially strange about Roche's disappearance is that his ultimate replacement at shortstop, Whitehead, was a disaster. In 99 games Whitehead made 87 errors, fielded .803 and hit just .211.

THE FIRST MINOR
LEAGUE CHAMPION

• •

1877 TECUMSEH STARS
W-14 L-4
Manager: Jake Knowdell

Regular Lineup—1B, Foghorn Bradley; 2B, M.H. Dinnin; 3B, Herm Doscher; SS, Ed Somerville; RF, None; CF, Jake Knowdell; LF, Joe Hornung; C, Grandma Powers; P, Fred Goldsmith

The Tecumseh club represented London, Canada, in the six-team International Association, now recognized by most historians to have been the first minor league, although the IA did not regard itself as "minor" in any sense of the word but rather as the first of many attempts to challenge the National League's monopoly on urban markets and the best players available. Another loop, the League Alliance, also tested the waters in 1877 but failed to last out the season. Although Tecumseh played only 18 "championship" games, the team actually had a fairly busy schedule, playing numerous nonchampionship contests against rival clubs in its own circuit as well as exhibitions with teams in the year-old National League. In addition, Tecumseh played several games against the Live Oak nine from Lynn, Massachusetts, which were considered exhibitions despite having been originally designated as championship contests. For reasons that are now impossible to unearth, the International Association viewed Live Oak as a league member in good standing at the beginning of the season but subsequently decided to bar the Massachusetts club from participating in championship play.

The IA's fledgling campaign was full of many such vagaries. The Rochester team played four championship games against Tecumseh and none against fourth-place Manchester. Tecumseh won the pennant with a .191 team batting average and had only one regular, Powers, who hit over .250. Manager Knowdell batted a minuscule .112 but held his job because Hornung was the team's lone first-rate outfielder—six different men served in right field during the course of the season. Second-place Allegheny was even more inept at the plate, averaging a meager .175. The circuit had just two .300 hitters, in fact: Rochester second baseman Steve Brady, the leader with a .375 mark, and Chub Sullivan, who hit .333 at first base for the Buckeye club. Unsurprisingly, outstanding pitching accounted for the spate of low batting averages. Goldsmith later put in four good seasons with the Chicago White Stockings before his arm blew out; the Buckeyes had Bobby Mathews, who had been cut earlier in the summer by Cincinnati; and Live Oak, the loop's outlaw team, showcased Candy Cummings, allegedly the first pitcher to discover how to throw a curveball. But the IA's top boxman was Pud Galvin of Allegheny. Galvin, who played two seasons in the IA before debuting in the National League in 1879 with 37 wins for Buffalo, was handled by Bill Holbert, a fine defensive catcher who had been squeezed out of the majors after the 1876 season when the National League dropped New York and Philadelphia and pared its ranks from eight teams to just six. Also on the Allegheny nine were Ned Williamson and the IA's top keystone combination in shortstop Jack Nelson and second baseman Chick Fulmer. Going by future performance on the major league level, Allegheny would seem to have had a much stronger lineup than Tecumseh, and that was borne out in head-to-head competition. The Alleghenys won three of the four championship contests played between the two teams. Against the other four clubs, however, Allegheny had only an 8–4 record while Tecumseh was 13–1. Below are the final standings for the 1877 season.

TEAM	W–L	PCT.	RECORD VS. CONTENDERS
Tecumseh (London, Can.)	14–4	.778	3 losses to Allegheny, 1 to Rochester
Allegheny (Allegheny, Pa.)	11–5	.688	2 losses to Rochester, 1 to Tecumseh
Rochester (Rochester, N.Y.)	7–7	.500	3 losses to Tecumseh, 2 to Allegheny
Manchester (Manchester, N.H.)	6–10	.375	4 losses to Tecumseh, 3 to Allegheny
Buckeye (Columbus, Oh.)	4–8	.333	2 losses to Tecumseh
Maple Leaf (Guelph, Can.)	4–12	.250	4 losses to Tecumseh

ERA ALL-STAR TEAMS

NATIONAL LEAGUE (1876–92)		AMERICAN ASSOCIATION (1882–91)	
1B	Dan Brouthers	1B	Dave Orr
2B	Fred Dunlap	2B	Bid McPhee
3B	Deacon White	3B	Arlie Latham
SS	Jack Glasscock	SS	Germany Smith
OF	Sam Thompson	OF	Pete Browning
OF	Jim O'Rourke	OF	Tip O'Neill
OF	George Gore	OF	Harry Stovey
C	Buck Ewing	C	Jocko Milligan
P	John Clarkson	P	Bob Caruthers
P	Tim Keefe	P	Ed Morris
UTIL	King Kelly	UTIL	Guy Hecker
MGR	Cap Anson	MGR	Charlie Comiskey
*	Roger Connor	*	Charley Jones

* Best player who failed to make the team

LEG TWO

1893–1900

NATIONAL LEAGUE TEAM NOTES AND RECORD HOLDERS: 1893–1900

∙∙∙∙∙∙∙∙∙∙∙∙∙∙∙∙∙∙∙∙∙∙∙∙∙∙∙∙∙∙∙

Number of Years Finishing in Each Position

Team	1	2	3	4	5	6	7	8	9	10	11	12	Aggregate
Boston	3	1	1	2	1	0	0	0	0	0	0	0	1
Baltimore	3	1	0	1	1	0	0	1	0	0	0	0	2
Cleveland	0	2	1	0	2	1	0	0	0	0	0	1	3
Philadelphia	0	0	3	2	0	1	0	1	0	1	0	0	4
Brooklyn	2	0	0	0	2	2	0	0	1	1	0	0	5
Pittsburgh	0	2	0	0	0	1	3	2	0	0	0	0	6
Cincinnati	0	0	2	1	0	1	2	1	0	1	0	0	7
New York	0	1	1	0	1	0	2	1	1	1	0	0	8
Chicago	0	0	0	2	2	0	0	2	2	0	0	0	9
St. Louis	0	0	0	0	1	1	0	0	1	1	2	2	10
Washington	0	0	0	0	0	1	0	0	1	1	3	1	11
Louisville	0	0	0	0	0	0	0	0	2	0	2	3	12

The NL was a twelve-club circuit until 1900, when Cleveland, Washington, Louisville and Baltimore were jettisoned. The aggregate standings therefore include one season—1900—in which there were only eight clubs. Since New York finished last that year, its lone eighth-place finish during the period is thus a bottom and worth zero points in the calculations here. All other eighth-place finishes merited four points in determining the aggregate standings. A first-place finish correspondingly earned seven points in 1900 and 11 points in every other season during the period.

It should be noted also that the rule for what constituted a stolen base was tightened considerably in 1898, which explains why every team's record was set prior to that season. Once again the "Save" department has been omitted from the charts because relief pitchers were still employed too seldom for it to be meaningful—in 1898, for example, five teams registered no saves at all.

BOSTON BEANEATERS

Pennants: 1893, 1897, 1898
Manager: Frank Selee, 1893–1900
Park: South End Grounds
Best Year: 1897 (93–39, .705)
Worst Year: 1900 (66–72, .478)
Top Rookie: Tie between Chick Stahl, 1897 (.358) and Vic Willis, 1898 (25–13)
Biggest Disappointment: Cliff Carroll, 1893
Best Move: Obtaining Billy Hamilton from Philadelphia for Billy Nash in 1896
Worst Move: No egregious errors during the period; the club was either incredibly astute or very lucky; with Selee at the reins, suspect the former was the case
Other:
1893—Win pennant easily but lead NL in no major team departments
1894—Score record 1222 runs; Jack Stivetts and Kid Nichols have composite 58–27 record while the rest of the staff is 25–24
1896—Nichols and Stivetts have 51–28 record between them; other pitchers are 23–29
1898—Win franchise record 102 games
1899—Top FA of .952 and allow the fewest runs in the league
1900—Catcher Marty Bergen slays his family and then commits suicide
1890s—At some point during the decade, the club becomes more commonly called the Beaneaters than the Red Stockings

HITTING		PITCHING	
Batting Ave.	.440, Hugh Duffy, 1894	Wins	34, Kid Nichols, 1893
Slugging Ave.	.694, Hugh Duffy, 1894	Losses	19, Kid Nichols, 1899
Home Runs	18, Hugh Duffy, 1894	Innings	425, Kid Nichols, 1893
RBIs	145, Hugh Duffy, 1894	Games Started	46, Kid Nichols, 1894
Total Bases	374, Hugh Duffy, 1894	Complete Games	43, Kid Nichols, 1893
Hits	237, Hugh Duffy, 1894	Strikeouts	160, Vic Willis, 1898
Runs	160, Hugh Duffy, 1894	Bases on Balls	148, Vic Willis, 1899
Doubles	51, Hugh Duffy, 1894	Winning Pct.	.738, Kid Nichols, 1897
Triples	19, Chick Stahl, 1899	ERA	2.13, Kid Nichols, 1898
Bases on Balls	110, Billy Hamilton, 1896	Shutouts	5, Kid Nichols, 1898
Stolen Bases	83, Billy Hamilton, 1896		5, Vic Willis, 1899

About half the record totals on this chart have been changed just in the past ten years after box scores of the period were subjected to vigorous scrutiny by researchers. As a result, Duffy's 1894 season has been made to appear even greater as well as all the more inexplicable. It tends to hide the fact that Nichols's name is nearly as dominant on the pitching chart. Without question the era's top pitcher, Nichols is seldom recognized as such because he didn't achieve Cy Young's mammoth career stats or Amos Rusie's strikeout totals. All he did was win—300 games before he turned 31—and for a team that man for man was not the period's best but was made such largely by his unremitting excellence.

BALTIMORE ORIOLES

Pennants: 1894, 1895, 1896
Manager: Ned Hanlon, 1893–1898
Park: Union Park
Best Year: 1896 (90–39, .698)
Worst Year: 1893 (60–70, .462)
Top Rookie: Bill Hoffer, 1895 (31–6)
Biggest Disappointment: Tony Mullane, 1893
Best Move: Looting Willie Keeler from Brooklyn for George Treadway
Worst Move: The transfer by syndicate ownership of Dan McGann, Willie Keeler, Joe Kelley, Jim Hughes, Hugh Jennings, Doc McJames and more from Baltimore to Brooklyn in 1899
Other:

1893—Last sub-.500 finish

1894—First Baltimore flag in any major league; .944 FA is by far the NL's best; first team to play 100 games and make less than 300 errors

1895—First baseman Scoops Carey is the only regular (400 or more at bats) to hit below .300 in either 1894 or 1895

1897—Joe Corbett, brother of Jim, the heavyweight champ, wins 24 games and then quits majors to pitch on the Pacific coast

1898—.644 winning percentage is team's lowest since 1893

1899—Rookie skipper John McGraw brings a decimated team home 4th; steal post-1898 record 364 bases led by McGraw, Jimmy Sheckard and Ducky Holmes; after the season the franchise is dropped from the NL

HITTING		**PITCHING**	
Batting Ave.	.424, Willie Keeler, 1897	Wins	31, Bill Hoffer, 1895
Slugging Ave.	.602, Joe Kelley, 1894	Losses	18, Sadie McMahon, 1893
Home Runs	10, Joe Kelley, 1895	Innings	374, Doc McJames, 1898
RBIs	134, Joe Kelley, 1895	Games Started	42, Doc McJames, 1898
Total Bases	307, Willie Keeler, 1897	Complete Games	40, Doc McJames, 1898
Hits	239, Willie Keeler, 1897	Strikeouts	178, Doc McJames, 1898
Runs	165, Joe Kelley, 1894	Bases on Balls	156, Sadie McMahon, 1893
Doubles	48, Joe Kelley, 1894	Winning Pct.	.838, Bill Hoffer, 1895
Triples	31, Heinie Reitz, 1894	ERA	2.10, Al Maul, 1898
Bases on Balls	124, John McGraw, 1899	Shutouts	5, Jim Hughes, 1898
Stolen Bases	87, Joe Kelley, 1896		

One look at the pitching half of the chart and you'd bet plenty, wouldn't you, that the Orioles won the pennant in 1898. They didn't. They finished second, six games back of Boston, despite outscoring and outhitting the Beaneaters and having a lower staff ERA. There's no way now that I can prove it, of course, but I'm morally certain the main difference was Kid Nichols. Contrary to legend, the Orioles had good pitchers all during the 1890s. But they seldom had more than one at a time or any who excelled for longer than a season or two. Hoffer was the leading example, breaking in with three fine seasons and then being traded when he started slowly in 1898. It so embittered him that he never returned to Baltimore after his playing days were over, although he lived to be 88.

CLEVELAND SPIDERS

Pennants: None
Manager: Patsy Tebeau, 1893–98
Park: League Park
Best Year: 1895 (84–46, .646)
Worst Year: 1899 (20–134, .130)
Top Rookie: Jack Powell, 1897, with Lou Sockalexis, who hit .338 in 66 games that same year, a close second
Biggest Disappointment: Harry Colliflower, 1899, was 1–11 as a pitcher with an 8.17 ERA but was a good enough hitter to hit .303 and bat leadoff on occasion while playing center field, albeit not very well
Best Move: Plucking Zeke Wilson from Boston in 1895
Worst Move: The transfer of almost the entire team to St. Louis in 1899 by the Robison brothers, who also owned the Mound City club
Other:
  1893—Cy Young, 34–16; rest of pitching staff, 39–39
  1895—Young and Nig Cuppy, 61–24; rest of pitching staff, 23–22
  1896—Jesse Burkett hits .410; the other two regular outfielders bat .288 and .240
  1897—Outscore opponents by a margin of 93 runs but finish only seven games above .500
  1898—A bad last in attendance, causing Robison brothers to despair
  1899—6.37 ERA, the period's worst; the team is outscored, 1252–529; Knepper and Hughey, the two top pitchers, are a composite 8–52; club plays almost all its games on the road after mid-season owing to abysmal attendance

HITTING		**PITCHING**	
Batting Ave.	.410, Jesse Burkett, 1896	Wins	35, Cy Young, 1895
Slugging Ave.	.541, Jesse Burkett, 1896	Losses	30, Jim Hughey, 1899
Home Runs	9, Ed McKean, 1898	Innings	423, Cy Young, 1893
RBIs	133, Ed McKean, 1893	Game Started	47, Cy Young, 1894
Total Bases	317, Jesse Burkett, 1896	Complete Games	44, Cy Young, 1894
Hits	240, Jesse Burkett, 1896	Strikeouts	140, Cy Young, 1896
Runs	160, Jesse Burkett, 1896	Bases on Balls	112, Jack Powell, 1898
Doubles	33, Bobby Wallace, 1897	Winning Pct.	.778, Cy Young, 1895
Triples	21, Bobby Wallace, 1897	ERA	2.53, Cy Young, 1898
Bases on Balls	120, Cupid Childs, 1893	Shutouts	6, Jack Powell, 1898
Stolen Bases	47, Buck Ewing, 1893		

The scrappiest and also the most uneven team of the period, the Spiders constantly were a player or two short of being the best nine in the game. While the Phillies had an all-.400 hitting outfield in 1894, Burkett was the only Spiders gardener who topped .300. But the horrible excuse for a team in 1899 notwithstanding, Cleveland still finished a strong third in the aggregate standings. Young and Burkett were the principal reasons, naturally, but Childs and McKean were also among the top players of the 1890s. That the Spiders were the only team during the period without a player who stole at least 50 bases in a season suggests that their reputation for being intimidatingly aggressive on the basepaths may be exaggerated.

PHILADELPHIA PHILLIES

Pennants: None
Manager: Bill Shettsline, 1898–1900
Park: Philadelphia Baseball Grounds, 1892–94
  Baker Bowl, 1895–1937 (known as Huntington Street Grounds, 1895–1913)
Best Year: 1899 (94–58, .618)
Worst Year: 1897 (55–77, .417)
Top Rookie: Wiley Piatt, 1898 (24–14 and led NL in strikeouts and shutouts)
Biggest Disappointment: Phil Geier, 1896–97; one of the first great hitters in the high minors who was unable to produce anywhere near the same numbers on the major league level
Best Move: Got Monte Cross from St. Louis in 1898, filling a weakness at shortstop that had existed ever since Bob Allen's beaning in 1894
Worst Move: Handing over Billy Hamilton to Boston in 1896 for Billy Nash
Other:
  1894—Record .349 team BA and 1143 runs in 138 games
  1895—Jack Clements, the last lefty to be a regular catcher in the majors, hits .394, a record for backstoppers
  1896—Billy Hulen is at shortstop most of the season, the last lefty to be a regular player at any infield position besides first base; opponents hit NL-high .315 against team's pitchers
  1899—Club has .618 winning percentage, franchise record that stands until 1976
  1900—Despite allowing 791 runs, the most of any NL team, club finishes a solid 3rd

HITTING		PITCHING	
Batting Ave.	.410, Ed Delahanty, 1899*	Wins	26, Jack Taylor, 1895
Slugging Ave.	.686, Sam Thompson, 1894	Losses	21, Jack Taylor, 1896
Home Runs	19, Ed Delahanty, 1893	Innings	359, Jack Taylor 1896
RBIs	165, Sam Thompson, 1895	Games Started	41, Jack Taylor, 1896
Total Bases	352, Sam Thompson, 1895	Complete Games	35, Jack Taylor, 1896, 1897
Hits	238, Ed Delahanty, 1899	Strikeouts	121, Wiley Piatt, 1898
Runs	192, Billy Hamilton, 1894	Bases on Balls	145, Gus Weyhing, 1893
Doubles	55, Ed Delahanty, 1899	Winning Pct.	.724, Red Donahue, 1899
Triples	27, Sam Thompson, 1894	ERA	3.02, Al Orth, 1898**
Bases on Balls	126, Billy Hamilton, 1894	Shutouts	6, Wiley Piatt, 1898
Stolen Bases	98, Billy Hamilton, 1894		

*Tuck Turner hit .416 in 1894 but had only 339 at bats.
**Orth had a 2.49 ERA in 1899 while working only 145 innings.

Nap Lajoie and Elmer Flick are just two of the many great Phillies players during this period who couldn't crack the hitting chart. Delahanty, Thompson and Hamilton were the most potent outfield unit ever assembled. Uninspired pitching handicapped the team throughout the 1890s, but what hurt it equally as much was the beaning shortstop Bob Allen suffered early in the 1894 season. As a result of it, he was out of action until 1897, and without him the Phillies infield crumbled. The 1899 team was strong enough to have won the pennant if many of Baltimore's best players hadn't been shifted to Brooklyn prior to the season or if Orth had been healthy all year.

BROOKLYN SUPERBAS

Pennants: 1899
Manager: Dave Foutz, 1893–96
Park: Eastern Park, 1893–97
  Washington Park, 1897–1900
Best Year: 1899 (101–47, .682)
Worst Year: 1898 (54–91, .372)
Top Rookie: Fielder Jones, 1896
Biggest Disappointment: Tommy McCarthy, hit .249 in 1896 after he was acquired from Boston
Best Move: Being stocked with most of Baltimore's best players prior to the 1899 season by owners who had a piece of both clubs
Worst Move: Trading Willie Keeler to Baltimore for George Treadway prior to the 1894 season
Other:
  1893—Brickyard Kennedy leads the club in starts and innings pitched for the first of six straight season
  1895—Finish above .500 for the last time until 1899
  1897—Dave Foutz dies; Billy Barnie named manager of sagging team
  1898—Owner Charlie Ebbets manages the team when Mike Griffin gives up the reins after only four games; Griffin retires after the season while still at his peak and thus misses being part of the 1899–1900 championship squad
  1899—Fielder Jones is the lone holdover regular from the 1898 club; team becomes known as the Superbas because Ned Hanlon is now the manager and there is a famous vaudeville outfit called "Hanlon's Superbas" in the late 1890s
  1900—Pace NL in both runs and BA for the last time until 1941

HITTING		PITCHING	
Batting Ave.	.379, Willie Keeler, 1899	Wins	28, Joe McGinnity, 1900
			28, Jim Hughes, 1899
Slugging Ave.	.518, George Treadway, 1894	Losses	22, Brickyard Kennedy, 1898
Home Runs	9, John Anderson, 1895	Innings	383, Brickyard Kennedy, 1893
RBIs	108, Candy LaChance, 1895	Games Started	44, Brickyard Kennedy, 1893
Total Bases	257, Willie Keeler, 1899	Complete Games	40, Brickyard Kennedy, 1893
Hits	216, Willie Keeler, 1899	Strikeouts	107, Brickyard Kennedy, 1893, 1894
Runs	140, Mike Griffin, 1895	Bases on Balls	171, Ed Stein, 1894
	140, Willie Keeler, 1899		
Doubles	38, Mike Griffin, 1895	Winning Pct.	.824, Jim Hughes, 1899
Triples	26, George Treadway, 1894	ERA	2.68, Jim Hughes, 1899
Bases on Balls	93, Mike Griffin, 1895	Shutouts	3, Jim Hughes, 1899
Stolen Bases	51, Tom Daly, 1894		

A strong club early in the decade, Brooklyn plunged into the second division after a series of bad trades and the inability of its top pitcher, George Haddock, to adapt to the increased mound distance in 1893. The team vaulted back to the top in 1899 when syndicate ownership delivered several of the Orioles stars such as Keeler, Hughes and McGinnity to Brooklyn along with manager Ned Hanlon. Griffin, a fine centerfielder, was the club's best player through the period but unfortunately opted to retire before the resurgence occurred when he was not named the Brooklyn manager, the job instead going to Ned Hanlon.

PITTSBURGH PIRATES

Pennants: None
Manager: Connie Mack, 1894–96
Park: Exposition Park
Best Year: 1893 (81–48, .628)
Worst Year: 1897 (60–71, .458)
Top Rookie: Jimmy Williams, 1899, .355 and 116 RBIs; that same
   year the club had another rookie, Ginger Beaumont, who also
   hit over .350, to make it the only team in history to debut two
   players who topped the .350 mark
Biggest Disappointment: Bill Grey, 1898, hit .229 and fielded
   .879 at third base
Best Move: Obtaining Honus Wagner, Fred Clarke and all of
   Louisville's other rising young stars after the Kentucky club
   folded following the 1899 season
Worst Move: Shipping George Van Haltren to New York in 1894
Other:
   1893—Frank Killen, 36–14, is NL's top hurler
   1894—Pirates' 2nd-place finish in 1893 sparks club mogul Wil-
      liam Temple to start the Temple Cup series, pitting the 1st-
      place team against the 2nd-place team after each season; it
      comes a year too late as the Pirates plummet to 7th place
   1896—Connie Mack dumped as manager after 6th-place finish;
      Frank Killen is the last NL southpaw to win 30 games
   1897—First sub-.500 team of the period
   1898—Last time team finishes below .500 two years in a row
      until 1914–15
   1900—Finish a strong 2nd after the Louisville contingent joins
      the team

HITTING		PITCHING	
Batting Ave.	.381, Honus Wagner, 1900	Wins	36, Frank Killen, 1893
Slugging Ave.	.580, Jake Stenzel, 1894	Losses	23, Frank Killen, 1897
			23, Sam Leever, 1899
Home Runs	13, Jake Stenzel, 1894	Innings	444, Pink Hawley, 1895
RBIs	121, Jake Stenzel, 1894	Games Started	50, Pink Hawley, 1895
			50, Frank Killen, 1896
Total Bases	328, Jimmy Williams, 1899	Complete Games	44, Pink Hawley, 1895
			44, Frank Killen, 1896
Hits	219, Jimmy Williams, 1899	Strikeouts	142, Pink Hawley, 1895
Runs	148, Jake Stenzel, 1894	Bases on Balls	157, Pink Hawley, 1896
Doubles	45, Honus Wagner, 1900	Winning Pct.	.769, Jesse Tannehill, 1900
Triples	27, Jimmy Williams, 1899	ERA	2.37, Rube Waddell, 1900
Bases on Balls	77, Elmer Smith, 1893	Shutouts	5, Frank Killen, 1896
			5, Jesse Tannehill, 1898
Stolen Bases	61, Jake Stenzel, 1894		

Hawley and Killen each had some great seasons but could never seem to produce them in the same year. Williams, in 1899, had one of the greatest rookie years ever. Stenzel was the Chuck Klein of his day. His early fade causes most historians not to include him on their lists of great players, but during his peak years there were few better. Wagner played mostly right field in 1900, his first year with the team after the deal that Dreyfuss worked out with the league brought it all of Louisville's best players.

CINCINNATI REDS

Pennants: None
Manager: Buck Ewing, 1895–99
Park: League Park, 1893–1900 (known as American League Park until team joined the National League in 1890)
Best Year: 1898 (92–60, .605)
Worst Year: 1894 (55–75, .423)
Top Rookie: Noodles Hahn, 1899
Biggest Disappointment: Charlie Comiskey, 1892–94, saddled the club with the weakest-hitting first baseman in the league and was a failure as a manager after an initial flurry of success in 1892
Best Move: Picking up Jake Beckley in 1897 after he was released by the Giants
Worst Move: Released Jesse Tannehill after a five-game trial in 1894; he later became an outstanding pitcher
Other:
  1890s—Early in the decade the team becomes known almost universally as the Reds rather than the Red Stockings
  1893—Second team in history (1889 Chicago White Stockings were the first) to play a full schedule and finish above .500 without a 20-game winner
  1896—Team has carefully assembled a solid lineup but is still a cut below Baltimore and Cleveland
  1898—Strong 3rd-place finish is the best performance by a Cincinnati NL team prior to 1919
  1899—Perfect 14–0 record versus hapless Cleveland
  1900—Pitcher Jack Taylor dies of Bright's Disease; team falls to 7th, only 1½ games out of the basement

HITTING

Batting Ave.	.372, Bug Holliday, 1894		
Slugging Ave.	.523, Bug Holliday, 1894		
Home Runs	13, Bug Holliday, 1894 13, Jimmy Canavan, 1894		
RBIs	119, Bug Holliday, 1894		
Total Bases	267, Bug Holliday, 1894		
Hits	190, Bug Holliday, 1894		
Runs	129, Arlie Latham, 1894		
Doubles	38, Dusty Miller, 1896		
Triples	16, Dusty Miller, 1895		
Bases on Balls	94, Bid McPhee, 1893		
Stolen Bases	76, Dusty Miller, 1896		

PITCHING

Wins	27, Pink Hawley, 1898
Losses	22, Frank Dwyer, 1894
Innings	348, Frank Dwyer, 1894
Games Started	40, Frank Dwyer, 1894
Complete Games	34, Frank Dwyer, 1894
Strikeouts	145, Noodles Hahn, 1899
Bases on Balls	126, Tom Parrott, 1894
Winning Pct.	.742, Noodles Hahn, 1899
ERA	2.45, Billy Rhines, 1896
Shutouts	4, Noodles Hahn, 1899, 1900

A deceptively good team, the Reds also had Jake Beckley, Elmer Smith, Dummy Hoy, Buck Ewing and Ted Breitenstein at various junctures during the period and ended it with Harry Steinfeldt at third base. Moreover, Tommy Corcoran teamed with McPhee to give the club the era's top keystone combination. Yet the Reds never quite succeeded in breaking through and, in fact, began the twentieth century by finishing in the cellar. Appendicitis felled Holliday in 1895 at 28, and he never played regularly again. Rhines was the only hurler to lead the NL in ERA both before and after the mound was moved to its present distance from the plate, although he did it in 1896 while pitching in only 143 innings.

NEW YORK GIANTS

Pennants: None

Manager: Monte Ward, 1893–94; Owner Andrew Freedman was so hard to work for—and play for—that no other manager was able to survive for two full seasons during the period

Park: Polo Grounds

Best Year: 1894 (88–44, .667)

Worst Year: 1899 (60–90, .400)

Top Rookie: Bill Carrick, 1899

Biggest Disappointment: Les German, 24–27 in 1893–95 while serving as the team's number-three pitcher behind Amos Rusie and Jouett Meekin

Best Move: Bagging Jouett Meekin from Washington in 1894

Worst Move: Passing Willie Keeler on to Brooklyn after a seven-game test in 1893; Keeler had also looked good in a late-season trial with the club in 1892

Other:

1894—Unable to endure Freedman any longer, Monte Ward quits the game

1895—Finish 9th with a .504 winning percentage, the lowest finish ever by a team able to win more than half its games

1896—Amos Rusie holds out for the entire year; the team drops below .500

1897—George Davis moves from third base to shortstop to shore up a chronic weak spot; team ascends to 3rd place after Rusie returns to the fold

1899—Have a 13–1 record versus Cleveland but only 47–89 against the other ten teams

1900—First New York major league team to finish in the cellar, albeit with a .435 winning percentage, the highest ever to that point by a last-place club

HITTING		PITCHING	
Batting Ave.	.369, Mike Tiernan, 1896	Wins	36, Amos Rusie, 1894
Slugging Ave.	.554, George Davis, 1893	Losses	27, Bill Carrick, 1899
Home Runs	14, Mike Tiernan, 1893	Innings	482, Amos Rusie, 1893
RBIs	136, George Davis, 1897	Games Started	52, Amos Rusie, 1893
Total Bases	304, George Davis, 1893	Complete Games	50, Amos Rusie, 1893
Hits	204, George Van Haltren, 1898	Strikeouts	239, Cy Seymour, 1898
Runs	136, George Van Haltren, 1896	Bases on Balls	218, Amos Rusie, 1893
Doubles	36, George Davis, 1895	Winning Pct.	.786, Jouett Meekin, 1894
Triples	27, George Davis, 1893	ERA	2.54, Amos Rusie, 1897
Bases on Balls	88, Bill Joyce, 1898	Shutouts	4, Amos Rusie, 1893, 1895, 1898 4, Cy Seymour, 1898
Stolen Bases	65, George Davis, 1897		

Easily the best of the rest, but nevertheless not much of a team after the mid-1890s. Davis may be the only player to miss the Hall of Fame because he spent his prime years with a New York club. It's hard to imagine that the team strikeout leader could be someone other than Rusie, but Seymour, from reports, had terrific stuff when his arm was sound. Tiernan and Van Haltren, with a better club, also might have received serious Hall of Fame consideration. The past tense is used here because there's absolutely no chance, what with the way the Veterans Committee operates, that any of these players will ever be selected.

CHICAGO WHITE STOCKINGS

Pennants: None
Manager: Cap Anson, 1893–97
Park: West Side Grounds
Best Year: 1898 (85–65, .567)
Worst Year: 1894 (57–75, .432)
Top Rookie: Bill Everett, 1895, .358 and 129 runs
Biggest Disappointment: Bill Hutchinson, 1893; the increased mound distance from home plate that year pretty well finished him as a top-flight pitcher
Best Move: Picking up Adonis Terry in 1894 when Pittsburgh cut him; he turned out to have two decent years left
Worst Move: Packing off Bill Dahlen to Brooklyn in 1899
Other:
 1893—First sub.-500 team since 1877
 1894—Second-worst FA and ERA in the league
 1895—Clark Griffith and Adonis Terry are a composite 47–28; the rest of the hill staff is 25–30
 1898—The club's first year in history without Anson, and it has its best season in over a decade
 1900—Outscored by more runs (116) than any other club in the league but nevertheless manages to finish tied for 5th; club is now more commonly known as the Colts or the Orphans

HITTING		PITCHING	
Batting Ave.	.389, Bill Lange, 1895*	Wins	26, Clark Griffith, 1895
Slugging Ave.	.575, Bill Lange, 1895	Losses	24, Bill Hutchinson, 1893
Home Runs	15, Bill Dahlen, 1894	Innings	353, Clark Griffith, 1895
RBIs	130, Walt Wilmot, 1894	Games Started	41, Clark Griffith, 1895
Total Bases	284, Bill Dahlen, 1894	Complete Games	39, Clark Griffith, 1895
Hits	197, Walt Wilmot, 1894 197, Bill Everett, 1895	Strikeouts	107, Ned Garvin, 1900
Runs	149, Bill Dahlen, 1894	Bases on Balls	181, Willie McGill, 1893
Doubles	45, Walt Wilmot, 1894	Winning Pct.	.706, Clark Griffith, 1898
Triples	19, Bill Dahlen, 1896	ERA	1.88, Clark Griffith, 1898
Bases on Balls	76, Bill Dahlen, 1894	Shutouts	4, Clark Griffith, 1898, 1900
Stolen Bases	84, Bill Lange, 1896		

*Cap Anson hit .395 in 1894 but in only 347 at bats.

Griffith would have been a star pitcher regardless of what team's uniform he wore. For the White Stockings he was nothing less than the franchise savior. Nixey Callahan was the team's second-best pitcher during the era, and he didn't arrive until the late 1890s. Lange had some great seasons, as did Wilmot and Dahlen, but Jimmy Ryan, who appears nowhere on the chart, was probably the club's best all-around player. Cap Anson, although he could still hit some, didn't help matters by holding down the first base job long past the time he stopped serving as anything more than a stationary target.

ST. LOUIS CARDINALS

Pennants: None

Manager: Patsy Tebeau, 1899–1900

Park: Robison Field (renamed after the Robison brothers, who picked up the club on the cheap after it bankrupted Chris Von der Ahe)

Best Year: 1899 (84–67, .556)

Worst Year: 1897 (29–102, .221)

Top Rookie: Dick Harley, 1897

Biggest Disappointment: Jake Stenzel, 1898

Best Move: Putting its uniforms on almost the entire 1898 Cleveland Spiders team in 1899

Worst Move: Allowing Steve Brodie to escape to Baltimore in 1893

Other:

1893—57–75 mark is club's best until 1899

1895—5.76 team ERA

1896—5.33 ERA, worst in NL; Billy Hart, Red Donahue and Ted Breitenstein lose 79 games among them

1897—Donahue and Hart have composite 19–62 record; rest of staff is 10–40; finish 23½ games behind 11th-place Louisville with 6.21 team ERA

1899—Known first as the Browns and then as the Maroons or Perfectos, the team from here on is called the Cardinals

1900—.291 BA is second in NL but team finishes a bad 5th

HITTING		**PITCHING**	
Batting Ave.	.396, Jesse Burkett, 1899	Wins	27, Ted Breitenstein, 1894
Slugging Ave.	.508, Roger Connor, 1895	Losses	35, Red Donahue, 1897
Home Runs	12, Bones Ely, 1894 12, Bobby Wallace, 1899	Innings	447, Ted Breitenstein, 1894
RBIs	108, Bobby Wallace, 1899	Games Started	50, Ted Breitenstein, 1894, 1895
Total Bases	279, Jesse Burkett, 1899	Complete Games	46, Ted Breitenstein, 1894, 1895
Hits	221, Jesse Burkett, 1899	Strikeouts	140, Ted Breitenstein, 1894
Runs	116, Jesse Burkett, 1899	Bases on Balls	191, Ted Breitenstein, 1894
Doubles	29, Roger Connor, 1895	Winning Pct.	.619, Cy Young, 1899
Triples	29, Perry Werden, 1893	ERA	2.58, Cy Young, 1899
Bases on Balls	121, John Crooks, 1893	Shutouts	4, Cy Young, 1899, 1900
Stolen Bases	59, Tommy Dowd, 1893		

This team had so many holes that neither a change in its nickname nor the mass transfusion of Cleveland talent could lift it into contention in 1899. Some will find it fun to determine who the club's offensive record holders were prior to the Cleveland contingent's arrival. Those with an attachment to the Brownie powerhouses in the 1880s will probably just find it depressing. We'll never know now whether Breitenstein was one of the game's greatest pitchers in the 1890s or merely the unluckiest. Red Donahue was another good one who narrowly survived. By the time he escaped the club in 1898 he was carrying a 17–60 career won-lost record. For his nine remaining seasons Donahue was 148–115.

WASHINGTON SENATORS

Pennants: None

Manager: Gus Schmelz, 1894–97; his red beard was about the only bit of flair the club had during his sojourn at its helm

Park: National Park

Best Year: 1897 (61–71, .462)

Worst Year: 1893 (40–89, .310)

Top Rookie: Bad as this team was, it kept coming up with outstanding rookies: Bill Hassamaer and Win Mercer, 1894; Gene DeMontreville, 1896; Buck Freeman, 1899—take your choice

Biggest Disappointment: Les German, 2–20 in 1896 after he was dispatched to DC by the Giants

Best Move: Getting Bill Joyce from Brooklyn for Danny Richardson in 1893; Joyce promptly held out the whole year but later gave the club a very potent bat

Worst Move: Sending Kip Selbach to Cincinnati in 1899

Other:

    1893—Piloted by Orator Jim O'Rourke in his final major league season

    1894—Opponents hit pre-1930 major league record high .331 against team's pitchers; club sets post-1893 record when its hurlers fan only 190 hitters in 132 games

    1896—Win Mercer (25–18) gives the club its first 20-game winner since 1892

    1897—Schmelz fired after dismal 9–25 start; club catches fire under leadership of centerfielder Tom Brown and plays over .500 ball for the rest of the season

    1898—Brown fired after 3–13 start

    1899—Saved only by Cleveland from being last in the team's final NL season; franchise left out in the cold when the loop cut back to eight teams in 1900

HITTING		PITCHING	
Batting Ave.	.343, Gene DeMontreville, 1896*	Wins	25, Win Mercer, 1896
Slugging Ave.	.563, Buck Freeman, 1899*	Losses	28, Duke Esper, 1893
Home Runs	25, Buck Freeman, 1899	Innings	366, Win Mercer, 1896
RBIs	122, Buck Freeman, 1899	Games Started	45, Win Mercer, 1896
Total Bases	331, Buck Freeman, 1899	Complete Games	39, Gus Weyhing, 1898
Hits	193, Gene DeMontreville, 1897	Strikeouts	156, Doc McJames, 1897
Runs	110, Bill Joyce, 1895	Bases on Balls	156, Duke Esper, 1893
Doubles	35, Ed Cartwright, 1894	Winning Pct.	.581, Win Mercer, 1896
Triples	25, Buck Freeman, 1899	ERA	3.25, Win Mercer, 1897**
Bases on Balls	105, Paul Radford, 1893	Shutouts	3, Doc McJames, 1897
Stolen Bases	50, Ed Cartwright, 1895		3, Win Mercer, 1897

* In 1894 Bill Joyce had a .355 BA and a .648 SA in 355 at bats.
** In 1895 Al Maul had a 2.45 ERA in 136 innings and was awarded the ERA crown; many would thus consider him the true record-holder.

The team was also known at times as the Statesmen, but without any improvement in its performance. A seventh-place finish in 1897 instilled a spark of hope, only to be followed by a franchise-record 101 losses in 1898. Deacon McGuire, the club's best player, lucked out when he was traded to Brooklyn in 1899 and got to play on two pennant winners after a decade and a half of catching for basement dwellers. Mercer, his favorite batterymate, was not as lucky. After the franchise folded, he went to the last-place Giants in 1900 and then jumped to the American League, where he pitched for two more poor teams before committing suicide prior to the 1903 season.

LOUISVILLE COLONELS

Pennants: None

Manager: Fred Clarke, 1897–99

Park: Eclipse Park, located across the street from the original Eclipse Park (used by the Louisville AA team), which was destroyed by fire in 1892

Best Year: 1899 (75–77, .493)

Worst Year: 1895 (35–96, .267)

Top Rookie: Deacon Phillippe, 20–17 in 1899

Biggest Disappointment: Luke Lutenberg, .192 in 1894 with no power as a replacement at first base for Willard Brown, who hit .304 in 1893

Best Move: Obtaining Jimmy Collins on loan from Boston in 1895; this kind of transaction was fairly common in that era, as contending teams were so much stronger than weaker clubs that they saw no threat in loaning their impoverished cousins talented players who were still in need of a little on-the-job training

Worst Move: Letting Hugh Jennings get off to Baltimore in 1893

Other:

1893—5.90 ERA as pitchers don't have a clue in the first year the mound is stationed at its current distance from the plate

1894—First of three straight cellar finishes

1897—Player-manager Jim Rogers hits .147 but keeps penciling himself into the lineup at second base until he's replaced after 43 games by Fred Clarke

1898—Team for the second year in a row has no regular second baseman

1899—Team outscores opponents 827–775, but still finishes below .500; is dropped by NL after the season and is the only one of the four jettisoned franchises that is not subsequently offered a spot in the newly reorganized American League

HITTING		PITCHING	
Batting Ave.	.390, Fred Clarke, 1897	Wins	28, Bert Cunningham, 1898
Slugging Ave.	.533, Fred Clarke, 1897	Losses	28, Still Bill Hill, 1896
Home Runs	10, Honus Wagner, 1898	Innings	362, Bert Cunningham, 1898
RBIs	113, Honus Wagner, 1899	Games Started	42, Bert Cunningham, 1898
Total Bases	282, Honus Wagner, 1899	Complete Games	41, Bert Cunningham, 1898
Hits	202, Fred Clarke, 1897	Strikeouts	104, Still Bill Hill, 1896
Runs	122, Fred Clarke, 1899	Bases on Balls	176, George Hemming, 1893
Doubles	43, Honus Wagner, 1899	Winning Pct.	.651, Bert Cunningham, 1898
Triples	18, Fred Clarke, 1896	ERA	3.11, Pete Dowling, 1899
Bases on Balls	61, Dummy Hoy, 1899	Shutouts	3, Bill Magee, 1898
Stolen Bases	66, Tom Brown, 1893, 1894		

It's ironic that the era's worst team would discover Wagner, a player whom many rate the best ever, and then be made to fold its tent just when he was starting to emerge. There are other, smaller ironies here: For one, the Pirates, along with inheriting Louisville's players, also seemed to inherit the Colonels' inability to find one who was any good at drawing bases on balls. Witness the Pirates' 1901–1919 chart for evidence of this. The Colonels' two ninth-place finishes, for the benefit of any who haven't already surmised as much, came in 1898 and 1899. In the latter season only an unwillingness to beat up on Cleveland cost them a higher finish. Louisville was 10–4 against Cleveland, while eighth-place Chicago won 13 of 14; the three-game difference left the Colonels two games behind Chicago.

THE BEST, THE WORST AND THE WEIRDEST NATIONAL LEAGUE TEAMS BETWEEN 1893 AND 1900

THE BEST

1898 BOSTON BEANEATERS
W-102 L-47
Manager: Frank Selee

Regular Lineup—1B, Fred Tenney; 2B, Bobby Lowe; 3B, Jimmy Collins; SS, Herman Long; RF, Chick Stahl; CF, Billy Hamilton; LF, Hugh Duffy; C, Marty Bergen; P, Kid Nichols; P, Ted Lewis; P, Vic Willis; P, Fred Klobedanz

Selee's 1897 club had a slightly higher winning percentage, perhaps because it was chased harder by Baltimore, but it lacked one key ingredient the 1898 crew had: Willis. With the addition of Willis, Selee now had both the strongest regular lineup of the era and the soundest pitching staff in the league. Until very recently individual mound stats for the 1898 season credited Beaneaters hurlers with only 99 wins, three short of the club's total. When the discrepancy was ironed out, Nichols was assigned two more victories and Willis one. Had an extra win gone instead to Klobedanz, it would have given him an even 20 for the season and resulted in the Beaneaters being recognized, long after the fact, as the first team in history with four 20-game winners. There is still a possibility that this recognition may one day be forthcoming, but the club scarcely needs it. With Bergen having by far his best season at the plate and a careful blending of aging stars like Duffy and Long with the budding talents of

Willis and Stahl, Selee had a team without a weakness. In all likelihood, if syndicate ownership had not stocked Brooklyn with several of Baltimore's best players, the Beaneaters would have won a third straight pennant in 1899 before age and owner Arthur Soden's mode of operation caught up with the club. Soden was so aloof from his players that he did not even know the names of most of his subs, and so tightfisted that the majority of his regulars deserted the club for the American League the moment they were given the opportunity.

THE WORST

1897 ST. LOUIS MAROONS
W-29 L-102
Managers: Tommy Dowd, Hugh Nicol, Bill Hallman and Chris Von der Ahe

Regular Lineup—1B, Mike Grady; 2B, Bill Hallman; 3B, Fred Hartman; SS, Monte Cross; RF, Tuck Turner; CF, Dick Harley; LF, Bill Lally; C, Klondike Douglas; P, Jack Taylor; P, Red Donahue; P, Bill Hart; P, Kid Carsey; P, Wee Willie Sudhoff

The 1899 Cleveland Spiders and the 1890 Pittsburgh Innocents had poorer records than Von der Ahe's Maroons (nee the once-proud Browns), but the Spiders were ravaged by mercenary syndicate owners and the Innocents by Players League raiders, whereas Von der Ahe had only himself to fault for a pitching staff that gave up 1.57 earned runs per game more than the next worst team's. As evidence of how far Von der Ahe's gears had slipped, he briefly employed Con Lucid, Mike McDermott, and Bill Kissinger, three of the era's weakest hurlers, all of whom had previously flopped egregiously with other clubs, plus Bill Hutchinson and Duke Esper, outstanding pitchers early in the decade who had already amply demonstrated a total inability to adapt to the increased mound distance. Donahue, the team's ace, dropped a record 35 games and Hart lost 27, giving the Maroons a post-1893 record for the most losses (62) by a pitching duo. Taken individually, the everyday lineup wasn't bad, no worse certainly than that fielded by the other second division teams in 1897, but as a unit it failed to produce, scoring the fewest runs in the league by a wide margin despite putting more men on base than several teams that finished a comfortable distance ahead of it. The combination of execrable pitching and a penchant for leaving hordes of runners stranded thrust the team deep into the cellar, 23½ games behind the 11th-place Louisville Colonels.

THE WEIRDEST

1893 PITTSBURGH PIRATES
W-81 L-48
Manager: Al Buckenberger

Regular Lineup—1B, Jake Beckley; 2B, Lou Bierbauer; 3B, Denny Lyons; SS, Jack Glasscock; RF, Patsy Donovan; CF, George Van Haltren; LF, Elmer Smith: C, Doggie Miller/Connie Mack; P, Frank Killen; P, Red Ehret; P, Adonis Terry; P, Ad Gumbert

The club started the season with Frank Shugart at shortstop and did not really begin to gel until Glasscock was picked up from St. Louis. Once the best shortstop in the game, Glasscock was still the surest fielder at the position and proved also to be the club's steadiest run producer during the closing weeks of the season. Another midsummer acquisition, rookie outfielder Jake Stenzel, led the club in hitting with a .362 BA, albeit in only 224 at bats, and a third latecomer, pitcher Hank Gastright, paced the NL in winning percentage. The prospect of having this trio for a full season in 1894 to join with Killen, the NL leader in wins with 36, and the stingiest defense in the loop made dreams of a first-ever pennant in Pittsburgh seem realistic. Instead the Pirates dipped to seventh place when both the pitching and the defense caved in under the pressure of having to cope with teams like Philadelphia and Baltimore, which hit .349 and .343 respectively. Bewildered by the sharp reversal of fortune, team officials took the expected measure to remedy the situation, firing Buckenberger late in the 1894 season and replacing him with Connie Mack, but the change brought only another seventh-place finish in 1895. In retrospect, a wiser move might have been to retain backup catcher Billy Earle. A student of mesmerism and reputed to possess an evil eye, Earle was never an easy man to be around on the bench or in the clubhouse and consequently changed teams so often he was nicknamed "The Little Globe-trotter." One can suppose that he was unhappy to leave Pittsburgh, a contender, to play in 1894 for Louisville, the cellar dweller that year, and in addition to hitting .348 in his backup role with the Colonels might have found some other ways to gain revenge.

SPECIAL FEATURE
TEAM

• •

1894 BALTIMORE ORIOLES
W-89 L-39
Manager: Ned Hanlon

Regular Lineup—1B, Dan Brouthers; 2B, Heinie Reitz; 3B, John McGraw; SS, Hugh Jennings; RF, Willie Keeler; CF, Steve Brodie; LF, Joe Kelley; C, Wilbert Robinson; P, Sadie McMahon; P, Bill Hawke; P, Kid Gleason; P, Bert Inks; P, Tony Mullane; P, Duke Esper

For all that has been written about the rough and resourceful brand of ball the Orioles played in the mid-1890s, comparatively little attention has been devoted to the manner in which the team was assembled. McGraw, Robinson and McMahon were the only regulars who came with the club just two years earlier when it joined the National League after the American Association folded. Most of the others were acquired by Hanlon from other NL clubs via a series of deft trades. Keeler and Brouthers both came from Brooklyn prior to the 1894 season; Jennings was stolen from Louisville; Kelley was obtained from Pittsburgh during the 1892 season; and Gleason, Hawke, and Brodie were all garnered from St. Louis at little or no expense. Reitz, a twenty-six-year-old rookie in 1893, was purchased on Hanlon's recommendation from a minor league team in California, and Mullane was picked up from Cincinnati and Esper from Washington. The club needed so many pitchers—Hanlon used ten all told in 1894—because all of them except McMahon were either over the hill, having difficulty adjusting to the new 60′6″ mound distance from home plate, or never destined to be more than secondary contributors. In contrast, Baltimore used only ten position players all season—the eight regulars, plus Frank Bonner, who filled in everywhere but at catcher and first base, and Boileryard Clarke, the backup catcher and first sacker.

An eighth-place team in 1893, the Orioles caught the rest of the NL by surprise when the 1894 campaign opened and held a four-game lead on June 25 after winning 24 of their first 34 games. Predictions that the team had been playing over its head then seemed to be proven correct as a collective hitting slump sent the Orioles into a downward spiral that left them five games in back of Boston at the end of July. Hanlon countered by moving McGraw into the cleanup slot in the batting order, an odd maneuver that seemed to make no sense, since McGraw had little power and ended the season with the fewest RBIs of any of the team's regulars. Whatever Hanlon's logic was, though, that it got results cannot be denied. With McGraw at the heart of the order, the Orioles regained first place on August 30 and held it the rest of the way by reeling off 18 straight victories and winning 28 of their last 31 games.

At the close of the regular season the Orioles were made to face the New York Giants, who had passed Boston in the last weeks of the campaign and captured second, in a newly devised postseason series called the Temple Cup. The proposed division of the players' purse from the gate receipts was 65% to the winning team and 35% to the loser, but the Orioles vetoed that arrangement. Their salaries had ended when the season finished, and they felt that the chance of winding up with the losers' share made the series not worth playing. Hence the two teams agreed to a 50–50 split, but when league officials learned this they demanded a return to the 65–35 formula. Many of the players on each team made secret 50–50 deals, however, and the series was a travesty. The Giants won four straight one-sided games as their twin aces, Amos Rusie and Jouett Meekin, bagged two victories apiece. Hanlon meanwhile held out McMahon, his top winner, who was not up to par physically, and Baltimore's other pitchers surrendered 33 runs and 57 hits to the Giants in the sweep.

The resounding Temple Cup defeat blunted the Orioles, but it was only temporary. The club came back to win pennants again in 1895 and 1896, although with a slightly altered cast. Brouthers, who was 36 in 1894 and playing his last full season, was replaced by Scoops Carey, and Gleason, nearly finished as a pitcher, began the conversion to second base, filling in there after Reitz was shelved by an injury for much of the 1895 campaign. The team seemed only to be improved by the changes. In fact, beginning in 1894, the Orioles had a winning percentage of .679 over a five-year period, still an all-time record for a span of that length.

THE HITTING HOOSIERS: THE GREATEST MINOR LEAGUE TEAM BETWEEN 1893 AND 1900

. . . .

1895 INDIANAPOLIS HOOSIERS
W-78 L-43
Manager: Bill Watkins

Regular Lineup—1B, Frank Motz; 2B, Jimmy Canavan; 3B, Fred Roat; SS, John Newell; RF, George Hogriever; CF, Marty Hogan; LF, Jack McCarthy; C, Ed McFarland; P, Chauncey Fisher; P, Lem Cross; P, Whoa Bill Phillips; P, George Blackburn; Util., Tom Gettinger

In 1895 the Western League, the forerunner of the American League, was the strongest minor league, and Indianapolis became its reigning champion by beating out St. Paul and Kansas City in a hard-fought tussle. The Hoosiers led the circuit in fielding and in Fisher had one of the only two hurlers in the loop with an ERA under 3.00, but offense was the club's real forte. As has happened throughout history, trends in the majors during the mid-1890s were paralleled in the minors. In 1894, owing to the increased distance of the pitcher's mound from home plate, the National League as a whole hit .309. The following season, taking its cue, the Western League saw all eight of its teams top the .300 mark, with Indianapolis leading the way. The Hoosiers blasted .354 in 1895 and at that only narrowly paced the circuit as Minneapolis clocked an even .350. Indianapolis furthermore averaged nearly ten runs a game, plating 1201 tallies in 121 contests, while the Minnesota club did even better, scoring 1282 runs in 123 games.

Minneapolis was led by first baseman Perry Werden, who topped the WL in batting with a .438 mark and clubbed 45 home runs, a single-season professional record that stood until 1920 when Babe Ruth hit 54 dingers for the Yankees. Also on the Minneapolis team was Bud Lally, a .400 hitter in 1895 with 36 homers and a league-best 205 runs scored, and Minneapolis's sister city, St. Paul, had Bill George, who rapped .403 and amassed 63 doubles. But Minneapolis lacked pitching and St. Paul had little more than Tony Mullane, then 36 years old and approaching the end after a long career in the majors. The Hoosiers, in contrast, possessed Fisher and Cross, the league's best mound duo, as well as McFarland, its most durable and top all-around catcher.

Watkins had previously managed in the majors—he piloted the champion 1887 Detroit Wolverines, among other teams—and would work up top again before the decade was out. Most of his players, likewise, were former major leaguers who were trying to earn another chance. Many, however, did not receive it, including Hogan, Roat, Motz, and Newell, and of the few who did only McCarthy, Phillips, and McFarland made a significant mark. Phillips pitched for poor Cincinnati teams around the turn of the century, McCarthy made over 1200 career hits despite not reaching the majors to stay until he was nearly 30, and McFarland developed into one of the best-hitting catchers of his time, retained as a pinch hitter long after his defensive skills had eroded.

The Western League in 1895 played a 126-game schedule, teams meeting each of their seven rivals 18 times. Indianapolis split its 16 games with Minneapolis (two were postponed) and had a winning record against all of the other clubs. Watkins's men did especially well in games with the three tailenders, Milwaukee, Toledo and Grand Rapids, winning 40 of 52 contests. McCarthy and Motz shared the club lead in batting with identical .420 figures, and every Hoosiers regular hit at least .315. Indeed, virtually every club in the league had an all .300-hitting lineup, as only one player who participated in 100 or more of his team's games, shortstop Bobby Wheelock of Grand Rapids, hit below .290. The complete standings for the 1895 Western League season follow:

TEAM	W	L	Pct.	Manager
1. Indianapolis	78	43	.645	Bill Watkins
2. St. Paul	74	50	.597	Charlie Comiskey
3. Kansas City	73	52	.584	Jimmy Manning
4. Minneapolis	64	59	.520	J. S. Barnes
5. Detroit	59	66	.472	J. C. Strothers
6. Milwaukee	57	67	.460	Larry Twitchell
7. Toledo	52	72	.419	Bill Schneider
8. Grand Rapids	38	86	.306	G. E. Ellis

ERA ALL-STAR TEAMS

. . . .

	MAJOR LEAGUE			MINOR LEAGUE**
1B	Jake Beckley		1B	Bill Krieg
2B	Bobby Lowe		2B	Bad Bill Eagan
3B	Jimmy Collins		3B	Jud Smith
SS	Hugh Jennings		SS	Billy Hulen
OF	Ed Delahanty		OF	Joe Knight
OF	Willie Keeler		OF	Bud Lally
OF	Jesse Burkett		OF	Bill George
C	Wilbert Robinson		C	Art Twineham
P	Kid Nichols		P	Willard Mains
P	Cy Young		P	Ernie Beam
UTIL	George Davis		UTIL	Rasty Wright
MGR	Frank Selee		MGR	Billy Murray
*	Billy Hamilton		*	Irv Waldron

*Best player who failed to make the team

**Herewith are the ground rules used in the minor league selection process. Note first that no minor league all-star squads were chosen for the game's first era because of insufficient data or for the two postexpansion eras due to the greatly reduced number of minor leagues and the corresponding absence of players who were still able—or willing—to fashion outstanding careers below the major league level.
1. At some point in his career a player must have played the position for which he's been selected.
2. Minor league All-Stars in the 1893–1900 era cannot have played more than 200 games or pitched more than 300 innings in the majors.
3. Minor league All-Stars in every subsequent era cannot have played more than 620 games or pitched more than 1200 innings in the majors.

LEG THREE

1901–1919

TEAM NOTES AND RECORD HOLDERS: 1901–19

●●●●●●●●●●●●●●●●●●●●●●●●●●●●●●

AMERICAN LEAGUE

Number of Years Finishing in Each Position

Team	1	2	3	4	5	6	7	8	Aggregate*
Boston	6	3	2	3	2	1	1	1	1
Chicago	4	2	4	4	1	3	1	0	2
Philadelphia	6	3	1	2	1	1	0	5	3
Detroit	3	2	4	3	1	3	3	0	4
Cleveland	0	3	5	2	4	2	2	1	5
Baltimore–New York	0	3	2	3	3	4	1	3	6
Washington	0	2	2	1	1	2	7	4	7
Milwaukee–St. Louis	0	1	0	1	5	4	3	5	8

*To establish the order of finish, seven points were awarded for each pennant a club won, six points for each second-place finish, etc., on down to no points being credited for cellar finishes. Under this system, the clubs ranked in the following order:

Team	Points
Boston	91
Chicago	86
Philadelphia	78
Detroit	77
Cleveland	69
New York	58
Washington	40
St. Louis	36

The separation between the good teams and the poor ones was probably greater during this period than at any other time in major league history as only four AL clubs won pennants during the nineteen-year span. The period between 1942 and 1960 was similar—in the AL at any rate—but with one very important difference: Over that span the separation was between one team, the Yankees, and the rest of the league.

BOSTON RED SOX

Pennants: 1903, 1904, 1912, 1915, 1916, 1918
Manager: Jimmy Collins, 1901–06
Park: Huntington Avenue Grounds, 1901–11
Fenway Park, 1912–present (opened on April 20, 1912)
Best Year: 1912 (105–47, .691)
Worst Year: 1906 (49–105, .318)
Top Rookie: Patsy Dougherty, 1902
Biggest Disappointment: Harry Lord, 1910
Best Deal: Acquiring Herb Pennock on waivers from the A's in 1915
Worst Deal: George Stone for Jesse Burkett, 1905 trade with the Browns
Other:
1901—Known originally as the Puritans or Pilgrims and later the Somersets; become the Red Sox when John Taylor takes over the ownership of the club
1904—Six regulars play 155 or more of the team's 157 games; pitchers set post-1893 record for fewest walks allowed per game (1.49)
1905—Use AL–record low 18 players all year
1907—Player-manager Chick Stahl commits suicide in spring training
1910—First year that Tris Speaker, Harry Hooper, and Duffy Lewis play together as an outfield unit
1911—Only AL team with an ERA under 3.00 after a livelier ball is introduced that season
1914—Go 51–24 from July 11 to the end of the season but lose ground to the A's, who go 55–22 during the same period and pull away; unveil 19-year-old rookie pitcher Babe Ruth
1916—Tight defense covers up for spotty offense; team is sixth in AL in runs but wins second straight flag when it makes only 183 errors, the fewest in the majors
1918—Pitching staff totals 105 complete games and only two saves
1919—Finish 6th in Ruth's last year with the club; Ruth hits 29 of the team's 33 home runs

HITTING		PITCHING	
Batting Ave.	.383, Tris Speaker, 1912	Wins	34, Joe Wood, 1912
Slugging Ave.	.657, Babe Ruth, 1919	Losses	21, Bill Dinneen, 1902 21, Cy Young, 1906 21, Joe Harris, 1906
Home Runs	29, Babe Ruth, 1919	Innings	385, Cy Young, 1902
RBIs	121, Buck Freeman, 1902	Games Started	43, Cy Young, 1902
Total Bases	329, Tris Speaker, 1912	Complete Games	41, Cy Young, 1902
Hits	222, Tris Speaker, 1912	Strikeouts	258, Joe Wood, 1912
Runs	136, Tris Speaker, 1912	Bases on Balls	118, Babe Ruth, 1916
Doubles	53, Tris Speaker, 1912	Winning Pct.	.872, Joe Wood, 1912
Triples	22, Tris Speaker, 1913*	ERA	0.96, Dutch Leonard, 1914
Bases on Balls	101, Babe Ruth, 1919	Saves	8, Frank Arellanes, 1909
Stolen Bases	52, Tris Speaker, 1912	Shutouts	10, Cy Young, 1904 10, Joe Wood, 1912

*Some sources still credit Chick Stahl with 22 triples in 1904.

Babe Ruth, unsurprisingly, is the only player in any era to appear on both his team's hitting and pitching charts. Moreover, he might have appeared several more times if Wood hadn't had such a great year in 1912. From first place in 1904 the Red Sox skidded to the cellar two years later but then managed to right themselves just as quickly. By 1908 they were once again a decent team and a year later they had Speaker.

CHICAGO WHITE SOX

Pennants: 1901, 1906, 1917, 1919
Manager: Fielder Jones, 1904–08
Park: South End Grounds, 1901
   South Side Park, 1901–10
   Comiskey Park, 1910–90 (opened July 1, 1910, with a typical
   game for the Sox of that time; they were held scoreless by the
   Browns, losing 2–0)
Best Year: 1917 (100–54, .649)
Worst Year: 1903 (60–77, .438)
Top Rookie: Reb Russell, 1913
Biggest Disappointment: Ping Bodie, 1914, with Jack Fournier,
   1916, a very close second
Best Deal: Fleecing Cleveland of Joe Jackson, 1915
Worst Deal: Letting Nixey Callahan quit the club after the 1904
   season to run a local semipro team
Other:
   1901—Originally called the Invaders but quickly become
      known as the White Stockings, usurping the Chicago NL
      team's old nickname; win AL pennant in loop's first season
      as a major league with many of the same cast that won pen-
      nant in 1900 while AL was still a minor league; club's skip-
      per Clark Griffith becomes the lone pitcher in the 20th
      century to win a flag as a player-manager
   1905—Finish second, two games behind pennant-winning A's
      but with the same number of victories as both clubs fail to
      make up postponed games that could have given the White
      Sox the flag
   1906—Win AL-record 19 straight games
   1908—Finish 3rd just 1½ games out despite .224 team BA
   1909—.221 team BA and .275 SA
   1910—Set AL records with .211 team BA and .261 SA
   1913—Give up the fewest runs in the majors and have the ma-
      jors' best ERA (2.33) but finish 5th as team also tops the
      majors in fewest runs scored and lowest BA
   1918—Sag to 6th after losing Joe Jackson and several other
      key players to military service in last year of World War I
   1919—Eight team members conspire to throw the World Se-
      ries to the Reds

HITTING		PITCHING	
Batting Ave.	.351, Joe Jackson, 1919	Wins	40, Ed Walsh, 1908
Slugging Ave.	.506, Joe Jackson, 1919	Losses	25, Patsy Flaherty, 1903
Home Runs	8, Ping Bodie, 1913	Innings	464, Ed Walsh, 1908
RBIs	102, Happy Felsch, 1917	Games Started	49, Ed Walsh, 1908
Total Bases	293, Joe Jackson, 1916	Complete Games	42, Ed Walsh, 1908
Hits	202, Joe Jackson, 1916	Strikeouts	269, Ed Walsh, 1908
Runs	120, Fielder Jones, 1901	Bases on Balls	111, Frank Smith, 1907
Doubles	40, Joe Jackson, 1916	Winning Pct.	.806, Eddie Cicotte, 1919
Triples	21, Joe Jackson, 1916	ERA	1.27, Ed Walsh, 1910
Bases on Balls	119, Eddie Collins, 1915	Saves	10, Ed Walsh, 1912
Stolen Bases	53, Eddie Collins, 1917	Shutouts	11, Ed Walsh, 1908

The White Sox weren't a great team until the very end of the era, but they rank second because they were never really bad either. Walsh obviously set many all-time club records in 1908. Until Jackson, Collins and Felsch came along, however, several other fine White Sox pitchers who might also have achieved some outstanding stats burned out prematurely from a combination of overwork and a lack of offensive support. Walsh, for that matter, did too. Bodie had a .397 slugging average and knocked home only 48 runs the year he set the club's period home run mark; low as those totals were, he led the Sox that year in SA and was second in RBIs, only four behind leader Buck Weaver. And 1913 was one of the Sox' better offensive seasons.

PHILADELPHIA ATHLETICS

Pennants: 1902, 1905, 1910, 1911, 1913, 1914
Manager: Connie Mack, 1901–19
Park: Columbia Park, 1901–08
  Shibe Park, 1909–54 (opened April 12, 1909)
Best Year: 1910 (102–48, .680)
Worst Year: 1916 (36–117, .235)
Top Rookie: Scott Perry, 1918
Biggest Disappointment: Scott Perry, 1919
Best Deal: Luring Rube Waddell east from the Los Angeles team
  early in the 1902 season
Worst Deal: Allowing Mack to dismantle the 1914 powerhouse
  rather than pay his stars what they felt they were worth
Other:
  1902—Win first flag; tie for most runs in the majors with 775
  1907—Lose flag to Detroit by 1½ games when four postponed
    contests that might have enabled team to catch the Tigers
    are not made up
  1908—Finish 6th and win just 68 games but 23 are by shutouts
  1910—AL record 1.78 ERA
  1911—$100,000 infield unit of Home Run Baker, Jack Barry,
    Eddie Collins, and Stuffy McInnis plays its first full season
    together
  1914—First team to win a pennant without a 20-game-winning
    pitcher
  1915—Record 56-game drop from 1914 finish; use ML-record
    56 players
  1916—AL-record worst winning percentage (.235), worst
    performance on the road (13–64) and record 19 straight
    losses on the road; last ML team to commit over 300 errors
    in a season (314)
  1919—First of many times that both Philadelphia ML teams
    finish in last place

HITTING		**PITCHING**	
Batting Ave.	.426, Nap Lajoie, 1901	Wins	31, Jack Coombs, 1910
Slugging Ave.	.643, Nap Lajoie, 1901	Loses	23, Elmer Myers, 1916
Home Runs	16, Socks Seybold, 1902	Innings	383, Rube Waddell, 1904
RBIs	133, Home Run Baker, 1912	Games Started	46, Rube Waddell, 1904
Total Bases	350, Nap Lajoie, 1901	Complete Games	39, Rube Waddell, 1904
Hits	232, Nap Lajoie, 1901	Strikeouts	349, Rube Waddell, 1904
Runs	145, Nap Lajoie, 1901	Bases on Balls	168, Elmer Myers, 1916
Doubles	48, Nap Lajoie, 1901	Winning Pct.	.850, Chief Bender, 1914
Triples	21, Home Run Baker, 1912	ERA	1.30, Jack Coombs, 1910
Bases on Balls	121, Topsy Hartsel, 1905	Saves	13, Chief Bender, 1913
Stolen Bases	81, Eddie Collins, 1910	Shutouts	13, Jack Coombs, 1910

Eddie Plank was the club's top pitcher during the period if only for his consistent excellence over a long span of time. Waddell was by far the best, however, while at his peak. Choosing the A's top player is more difficult than it may appear. Collins would seem the logical candidate, with Baker the runner-up, but Harry Davis also must merit much more than passing support. Lajoie's 1901 season is dismissed by many analysts, who feel the AL was little more than a minor league that year, but even if he is excluded from consideration many of the figures on both the hitting and the pitching charts here are deadball era records.

DETROIT TIGERS

Pennants: 1907, 1908, 1909
Manager: Hugh Jennings, 1907–19
Park: Bennett Park, 1901–11 (named after Charlie Bennett, star catcher with the old Detroit Wolverines NL team, who lost both legs in a railway accident)
Navin Field, 1912–present (now called Tiger Stadium; opened on April 20, 1912, the same day as Fenway Park, putting the two in a flat tie for the honor of the oldest facility now in use)
Best Year: 1915 (100–54, .649); the 1915 Tigers were the first club in AL history to win 100 games without claiming a pennant
Worst Year: 1902 (52–83, .385)
Top Rookie: Roscoe Miller, 1901
Biggest Disappointment: Roscoe Miller, 1902
Best Deal: Obtaining Claude Rossman from Cleveland in 1907 to plug a huge first base leak
Worst Deal: Letting Wally Pipp go to New York on waivers in 1915
Other:
1901—Finish 3rd in inaugural season; top majors in errors with 410 but also turn most double plays (127)
1903—Pitcher Win Mercer, recently named the team's player-manager, commits suicide prior to the season
1908—Win flag by ½ game, the smallest margin of victory in AL or NL history
1909—First AL team to win three straight pennants
1912—Team goes on strike for one game after Ty Cobb is suspended, never regains stride and plummets to 6th after finishing 2nd in 1911
1915—First team ever to have the top three men in its league in RBIs
1916—Top ML with a .264 team BA
1918—Come in 7th, lowest finish since 1904

HITTING		PITCHING	
Batting Ave.	.420, Ty Cobb, 1911	Wins	29, George Mullin, 1909
Slugging Ave.	.621, Ty Cobb, 1911	Losses	23, George Mullin, 1904
Home Runs	9, Ty Cobb, 1909 9, Sam Crawford, 1913	Innings	382, George Mullin, 1904
RBIs	127, Ty Cobb, 1911	Games Started	44, George Mullin, 1904
Total Bases	367, Ty Cobb, 1911	Complete Games	42, George Mullin, 1904
Hits	248, Ty Cobb, 1911	Strikeouts	187, Bill Donovan, 1903
Runs	147, Ty Cobb, 1911	Bases on Balls	138, George Mullin, 1905
Doubles	47, Ty Cobb, 1911	Winning Pct.	.862, Bill Donovan, 1907
Triples	26, Sam Crawford, 1914	ERA	1.64, Ed Summers, 1908
Bases on Balls	118, Donie Bush, 1915 118, Ty Cobb, 1915	Saves	6, Bernie Boland, 1917
Stolen Bases	96, Ty Cobb, 1915	Shutouts	8, Ed Killian, 1905

It's something of a puzzle how the Tigers could have won only three pennants in this era with Cobb, by far its most dominant player—until you examine some of the players they had at other positions. There were always a couple of glaring weaknesses, and once Donovan and Mullin were gone, the pitching got pretty skimpy. Have you ever wondered what would have happened if Cobb had played for the White Sox during this period rather than Detroit?

CLEVELAND INDIANS

Pennants: None
Manager: Nap Lajoie, 1905–09
Park: League Park, 1901–09
New League Park, 1910–46 (opened on April 21, 1910)
Best Year: 1919 (84–55, .604)
Worst Year: 1914 (51–102, .333)
Top Rookie: Joe Jackson, 1911, hit .408; Vean Gregg, who also debuted in 1911, won 20 or more games in each of his first three seasons
Biggest Disappointment: Willie Mitchell, 1911
Best Deal: Tie between getting Jackson from the A's in 1910 and Tris Speaker from the Red Sox in 1916
Worst Deal: Failing to take the Tigers up on their offer of Ty Cobb for Elmer Flick during spring training in 1907
Other:
  1901—Known originally as the Blues; become the Naps in 1905 when Lajoie takes over as manager of the club and then later the Mollie McGuires; in 1915 adopt the present nickname of Indians
  1902—.289 team BA leads majors but team can finish only 5th as it surrenders the third most runs in the AL
  1904—Only AL team to score more than four runs a game
  1906—Lone twentieth-century club to fail to win pennant despite bagging the team Triple Crown
  1908—Lose flag by ½-game margin to the Tigers when Detroit doesn't make up a postponed game
  1911—Addie Joss dies of meningitis
  1914—Only cellar finish prior to 1969
  1918—Score most runs in AL (804) and have highest team BA (.260); finish a close 2nd, just 1½ games behind Red Sox; team feels cheated because war-abbreviated schedule requires it to play most of its games on the road while Boston plays majority at home
  1919—Tenth first division finish during the era but still no pennants

HITTING		PITCHING	
Batting Ave.	.408, Joe Jackson, 1911	Wins	27, Addie Joss, 1907
Slugging Ave.	.590, Joe Jackson, 1911	Losses	22, Pete Dowling, 1901*
Home Runs	12, Piano Legs Hickman, 1903	Innings	339, Addie Joss, 1907
RBIs	102, Nap Lajoie, 1904	Games Started	38, Addie Joss, 1907
Total Bases	337, Joe Jackson, 1911	Complete Games	35, Bill Bernhard, 1904
Hits	233, Joe Jackson, 1911	Strikeouts	184, Vean Gregg, 1912
Runs	126, Joe Jackson, 1911	Bases on Balls	136, Gene Krapp, 1911
Doubles	49, Nap Lajoie, 1904	Winning Pct.	.773, Bill Bernhard, 1902**
Triples	26, Joe Jackson, 1912	ERA	1.16, Addie Joss, 1908
Bases on Balls	105, Jack Graney, 1919	Saves	7, Jim Bagby, 1917
Stolen Bases	52, Ray Chapman, 1917	Shutouts	9, Addie Joss, 1906, 1908
			9, Stan Coveleski, 1917

*Includes only Dowling's losses with Cleveland—he also had five with Milwaukee and led the AL with twenty-seven.
**Includes only Bernard's record with Cleveland.

Good strong arguments can be made that the Indians ought to have won the pennant in 1906, 1908 and 1918—surely one of those years anyway. Unfortunately there were 16 other seasons during the period, and the Tribe wound up pretty far out of the hunt at the end of most of them. Joss's record-setting stats point up one of the problems. They're good but hardly awesome—whereas most of the other teams had somebody like Young or Chesbro or Johnson or Walsh or Waddell to serve as a mound fulcrum.

NEW YORK YANKEES

Pennants: None
Manager: Clark Griffith, 1903–08
Park: Oriole Park (Baltimore), 1901–02
  Hilltop Park, 1903–12
  Polo Grounds, 1913–19
Best Year: 1904 (92–59, .609)
Worst Year: 1912 (50–102, .329)
Top Rookie: Russ Ford, 1910
Biggest Disappointment: Fritz Maisel, 1917
Best Deal: Obtaining Roger Peckinpaugh from Cleveland, 1913
Worst Deal: Shipping Hal Chase to the White Sox in 1913 for a
  bunion and an onion
Other:
  1901–02—Franchise based in Baltimore, known as the Orioles;
    moved to New York in 1903 and first called the Highlanders;
    nickname changed to Yankees soon thereafter, though not
    officially until the early teens
  1901—Top the AL in batting under manager John McGraw but
    finish only 5th, largely because the club is the worst fielding
    unit in the majors
  1902—Team decimated by NL raiders, dependent on handouts
    from the other AL teams in the form of players and cash in
    order to finish the season; come in last despite scoring third
    most runs in the majors
  1904—Lose the pennant on the last day of the season on Jack
    Chesbro's famous wild pitch
  1908—Only team in the majors with an ERA above 3.00 (3.16)
    and give up 146 more runs than the next most generous
    team, the Cardinals
  1914—Club finishes 7th for the second consecutive season un-
    der Frank Chance; shortstop Roger Peckinpaugh replaces
    Chance with 17 games left in the season and becomes the
    youngest manager in history at twenty-three; last ML team
    to post slugging average below .300 (.287) as Doc Cook leads
    club with .326 SA
  1915—Yankees first wear pinstriped uniforms
  1919—3rd-place finish is club's best since 1910; hit most home
    runs in majors (45) despite not yet having Babe Ruth

HITTING		PITCHING	
Batting Ave.	.348, Birdie Cree, 1911	Wins	41, Jack Chesbro, 1904
Slugging Ave.	.513, Birdie Cree, 1911	Losses	22, Joe Lake, 1908
Home Runs	12, Wally Pipp, 1916	Innings	455, Jack Chesbro, 1904
RBIs	96, Jimmy Williams, 1901	Games Started	51, Jack Chesbro, 1904
Total Bases	264, Birdie Cree, 1911	Complete Games	48, Jack Chesbro, 1904
Hits	193, Hal Chase, 1906	Strikeouts	239, Jack Chesbro, 1904
Runs	113, Jimmy Williams, 1901	Bases on Balls	116, Slim Love, 1918
Doubles	31, Jimmy Williams, 1904	Winning Pct.	.813, Russ Ford, 1910
Triples	22, Birdie Cree, 1911	ERA	1.65, Russ Ford, 1910
Bases on Balls	80, Harry Wolter, 1913	Saves	8, Bob Shawkey, 1916
Stolen Bases	74, Fritz Maisel, 1914	Shutouts	8, Russ Ford, 1910

The franchise moved from Baltimore to New York at the beginning of the 1903 season. There are some members of the current Yankees family who've pretended for so long that the team wasn't born until 1920 that they now believe it themselves. You can't really blame them. Some of the club hitting records are ludicrously low, even for the deadball era, and if Chesbro's 1904 season is taken away, the pitching chart wouldn't look so hot either. Cree had only one great season, but he almost certainly would have had others like it if he hadn't wrecked his leg.

WASHINGTON SENATORS

Pennants: None
Manager: Clark Griffith, 1912–19
Park: American League Park, 1901–02
  National Park, 1903–10
  Griffith Stadium, 1911–60 (opened on April 12, 1911)
Best Year: 1912 (91–61, .599)
Worst Year: 1904 (38–113, .251)
Top Rookie: Joe Boehling, 1913
Biggest Disappointment: Patsy Donovan, 1904
Best Deal: With the help of the other seven AL teams, kept Walter Johnson from jumping to the rebel Federal League in 1914
Worst Deal: Sending Al Orth to New York, 1904
Other:
  1901—New Washington AL franchise is also known as the Nationals or Nats; team's .455 winning percentage remains club record until 1912
  1902—Team has most homers in the majors and generally good hitting, but execrable pitching dooms it to 6th place
  1903—Defending batting titlist Ed Delahanty dies in a fall from a railway trestle over Niagara Falls
  1906—Shortstop Joe Cassidy dies
  1909—Score AL-record low 382 runs, finish 20 games behind 7th-place St. Louis
  1913—Walter Johnson and Joe Boehling post a combined 53–14 record; the rest of the pitching staff is a combined 37–50
  1916—Finish 7th despite being just one game under .500 (76–77); .497 winning percentage is all-time highest for a team so low in the standings
  1917—Hit only four home runs all year
  1919—Walter Johnson and Jim Shaw have a combined 36–33 record; other pitchers are 20–51

HITTING		**PITCHING**	
Batting Ave.	.376, Ed Delahanty, 1902	Wins	36, Walter Johnson, 1913
Slugging Ave.	.590, Ed Delahanty, 1902	Losses	26, Jack Townsend, 1904
			26, Bob Groom, 1909
Home Runs	10, Ed Delahanty, 1902	Innings	374, Walter Johnson, 1910
RBIs	93, Ed Delahanty, 1902	Games Started	42, Walter Johnson, 1910
Total Bases	279, Ed Delahanty, 1902	Complete Games	38, Walter Johnson, 1910
Hits	194, Clyde Milan, 1911	Strikeouts	313, Walter Johnson, 1910
Runs	109, Clyde Milan, 1911	Bases on Balls	137, Jim Shaw, 1914
Doubles	43, Ed Delahanty, 1902	Winning Pct.	.837, Walter Johnson, 1913
Triples	19, Joe Cassidy, 1904	ERA	1.14, Walter Johnson, 1913
Bases on Balls	81, Joe Judge, 1919	Saves	6, Long Tom Hughes, 1913
Stolen Bases	88, Clyde Milan, 1912	Shutouts	11, Walter Johnson, 1913

I toyed with the idea of running a second chart for this team that excluded Johnson and Delahanty. But it would only be kicking a dead horse—everyone with any knowledge of the franchise already knows how little it had going for it in the early part of the century—and besides, you'd be deprived of all the rainy-day excitement of doing it on your own. You might find it interesting, though, that some writers in Washington were disappointed by Delahanty's performance in 1902. They expected more after all the hoopla his theft from the Phillies aroused in DC. Goes to show that you just never know when you have it so good.

ST. LOUIS BROWNS

Pennants: None
Manager: Jimmy McAleer, 1902–09
Park: Lloyd Street Grounds (Milwaukee), 1901
  Sportsman's Park, 1902–53
Best Year: 1902 (78–58, .574)
Worst Year: 1911 (45–107, .296)
Top Rookie: George Stone, 1905
Biggest Disappointment: Willie Sudhoff, 1904
Best Deal: George Stone from Boston, 1905
Worst Deal: Trading Jack Powell to New York in 1904 for Harry
  Howell and Jack O'Connor
Other:
  1901—Franchise begins as the Milwaukee Brewers, finishes
    last in inaugural AL season
  1902—Team moves to St. Louis, the first franchise shift of the
    new century
  1906—Barney Pelty is second in AL in ERA, one of only two
    Browns pitchers to do that well in team's fifty-two-year his-
    tory (the other was Ned Garver in 1950)
  1908—Last time until 1920 that team finishes in first division
  1912—Third straight year 100 or more losses
  1914—Rise to 5th place under rookie pilot Branch Rickey
  1915—Only time between 1909 and 1921 that team finishes
    above .500
  1917—George Sisler hits .353, 108 points above the team BA
  1918—Team hits only five home runs and generates so little
    offense that Sisler can collect only 41 RBIs on a .341 BA

HITTING		PITCHING	
Batting Ave.	.358, George Stone, 1906	Wins	22, Red Donahue, 1902
			22, Jack Powell, 1902
Slugging Ave.	.530, George Sisler, 1919	Losses	25, Fred Glade, 1905
Home Runs	10, George Sisler, 1919	Innings	328, Jack Powell, 1902
RBIs	103, Del Pratt, 1916	Games Started	39, Jack Powell, 1902
Total Bases	291, George Stone, 1906	Complete Games	36, Jack Powell, 1902
Hits	208, George Stone, 1906	Strikeouts	232, Rube Waddell, 1908
Runs	105, Burt Shotton, 1913	Bases on Balls	133, Grover Lowdermilk, 1915
Doubles	46, John Anderson, 1901	Winning Pct.	.667, Red Donahue, 1902
Triples	20, George Stone, 1906	ERA	1.59, Barney Pelty, 1906
Bases on Balls	118, Burt Shotton, 1915	Saves	4, done by many different pitchers
Stolen Bases	46, Armando Marsans, 1916	Shutouts	6, Fred Glade, 1904
			6, Harry Howell, 1906

Powell was the AL equivalent of Vic Willis. At the end of the 1904 season, his eighth in the majors, he looked almost certain to win 300 games. But he had only one more winning season after that and instead departed in 1912 with the most career losses (254) of any pitcher in history who failed to win 300 games. Anderson's doubles mark came while the club was still in Milwaukee; the most any Brownie could achieve during the period was 37, by Frank LaPorte in 1911.

NATIONAL LEAGUE: 1901—19

Number of Years Finishing in Each Position

Team	1	2	3	4	5	6	7	8	Aggregate*
New York	5	3	5	2	3	1	0	0	1
Chicago	6	7	1	2	0	0	1	2	2
Pittsburgh	4	4	3	4	1	1	1	1	3
Philadelphia	1	4	1	5	2	2	2	2	4
Cincinnati	1	1	2	0	6	4	4	1	5
Brooklyn	1	0	2	5	3	3	3	2	6
Boston	1	1	2	0	2	4	4	5	7
St. Louis	0	0	2	1	2	4	5	5	8

*See the American League standings for the period on p. 83 or an explanation of how points were awarded to determine the aggregate order of finish.

Team	Points
New York	97
Chicago	98
Pittsburgh	89
Philadelphia	68
Cincinnati	55
Brooklyn	53
Boston	41
St. Louis	33

The separation between the haves and the have-nots in the NL during this period is even more apparent than what you saw in the AL. Although seven of the eight NL teams won pennants at one point or another, only three managed to stay in contention throughout most of the era.

NEW YORK GIANTS

Pennants: 1904, 1905, 1911, 1912, 1913, 1917
Manager: John McGraw, 1902–19
Park: Polo Grounds, 1901–57; when a fire devastated the park in 1911, the club shared Hilltop Park with the Yankees while its home was being rebuilt
Best Year: 1904 (106–47, .693)
Worst Year: 1902 (48–88, .353)
Top Rookie: Christy Mathewson, 1901
Biggest Disappointment: Dan McGann, 1906
Best Deal: Obtaining Christy Mathewson from the Reds for Amos Rusie, 1901; Matty had previously belonged to the Giants before being drafted by the Reds; the method by which the Giants got him back would be considered illegal now
Worst Deal: Throwing in Edd Roush in a 1916 trade with the Reds; since Mathewson was also part of the deal, in a sense the Reds got a measure of justice for the reaming they took fifteen years earlier
Other:
1902—Second last-place finish in three years
1904—Win team Triple Crown
1906—Club sets all-time record for most games finished behind pennant winner by a team playing .600 ball or better when it trails the Cubs by 20 games despite posting a .632 winning percentage (96–56)
1908—Lose pennant to Cubs by one-game margin when Chicago wins makeup game made necessary by Fred Merkle's boner
1911—Set twentieth-century ML record with 347 stolen bases
1913—Fourth 100+ wins season in ten years
1915—Best last-place team ever; finish just 14 games below .500 and only 21 games behind pennant-winning Phillies
1916—Win ML-record 26 games in a row without a loss and ML record 17 straight games on the road; for all that, the club can finish no better than 4th
1919—Lead NL in runs, BA, and SA but finish a distant 2nd, nine games back of Cincinnati

HITTING		PITCHING	
Batting Ave.	.356, Mike Donlin, 1905*	Wins	37, Christy Mathewson, 1908
Slugging Ave.	.527, Larry Doyle, 1911	Losses	27, Dummy Taylor, 1901
Home Runs	13, Larry Doyle, 1911	Innings	434, Joe McGinnity, 1903
RBIs	108, Sam Mertes, 1905	Games Started	48, Joe McGinnity, 1903
Total Bases	300, Mike Donlin, 1905	Complete Games	44, Joe McGinnity, 1903
Hits	216, Mike Donlin, 1905	Strikeouts	267, Christy Mathewson, 1903
Runs	124, Mike Donlin, 1905	Bases on Balls	128, Jeff Tesreau, 1914
Doubles	40, Larry Doyle, 1915	Winning Pct.	.814, Joe McGinnity, 1904
Triples	25, Larry Doyle, 1911	ERA	1.14, Christy Mathewson, 1909
Bases on Balls	89, George Burns, 1914	Saves	7, George Ferguson, 1906
Stolen Bases	62, George Burns, 1914	Shutouts	11, Christy Mathewson, 1908

*Chief Meyers hit .358 in 1912 but in only 371 at bats.

Awesome pitching coupled with decent, if never exceptional, offensive production kept this club in the hunt all during the deadball era. After both of their cellar finishes—in 1902 and 1915—the Giants rebounded to win a pennant just two years later. Between them, Mathewson and McGinnity accounted for 68% of the club's 139 decisions in 1903, by far the most of any pitching tandem in this century. Apart from Burns and Doyle, two vastly underrated players, and Donlin, a potentially great player who pretty much threw his career away, the Giants' most consistently productive performer in the early part of the century was probably Fred Merkle.

CHICAGO CUBS

Pennants: 1906, 1907, 1908, 1910, 1918
Manager: Frank Chance, 1905–12
Park: West Side Grounds, 1901–15
 Wrigley Field, 1916–present (originally known as Weegham Park and used by the Chicago Whales of the Federal League; first used by the Cubs on April 20, 1916)
Best Year: 1906 (116–36, .763, setting an all-time ML record for wins by a team and a twentieth-century team record for the highest winning percentage)
Worst Year: 1901 (53–86, .381)
Top Rookie: Tie between King Cole, 1910, and Charlie Hollocher, 1918
Biggest Disappointment: Wildfire Schulte, 1912
Best Deal: Snaring Three Finger Brown from the Cardinals, 1904
Worst Deal: Sending Heinie Zimmerman to New York, 1916
Other:
 1902—Become known as the Cubs when Chicago sportswriters begin calling the team that after AL raiders force it to use lots of young unproven players
 1906—Outscore opponents, 704–381; win team Triple Crown with ease
 1907—ML record low 1.73 staff ERA
 1908—Win pennant by one game by beating Giants in makeup contest made necessary by famous "Merkle boner"; beat Detroit in the World Series to give the club its second and last World Championship
 1909—Set twentieth-century ML record for the highest winning percentage (.680) by an also-ran
 1912—Jim Doyle dies; club is forced to move Heinie Zimmerman to third base to take Doyle's place and Zimmerman wins Triple Crown
 1915—First sub-.500 season since 1902
 1918—2.14 staff ERA is best in NL by .34 runs
 1919—2.21 staff ERA tops majors

HITTING

Batting Ave.	.372, Heinie Zimmerman, 1912
Slugging Ave.	.571, Heinie Zimmerman, 1912
Home Runs	21, Wildfire Schulte, 1911
RBIs	107, Wildfire Schulte, 1911
Total Bases	318, Heinie Zimmerman, 1912
Hits	207, Heinie Zimmerman, 1912
Runs	121, Jimmy Sheckard, 1911
Doubles	41, Heinie Zimmerman, 1912
Triples	21, Wildfire Schulte, 1911
	21, Vic Saier, 1913
Bases on Balls	147, Jimmy Sheckard, 1911
Stolen Bases	67, Frank Chance, 1903

PITCHING

Wins	29, Three Finger Brown, 1908
Losses	23, Long Tom Hughes, 1901
Innings	343, Three Finger Brown, 1909
Games Started	40, Larry Cheney, 1914
Complete Games	33, Jack Taylor, 1903
Strikeouts	205, Orval Overall, 1909
Bases on Balls	140, Larry Cheney, 1914
Winning Pct.	.833, Ed Reulbach, 1906
	.833, King Cole, 1910
ERA	1.04, Three Finger Brown, 1906
Saves	13, Three Finger Brown, 1911
Shutouts	9, Three Finger Brown, 1906, 1908
	9, Orval Overall, 1909
	9, Pete Alexander, 1919

The Cubs dominated the NL throughout the deadball era in most pitching departments, but had few hitting leaders. Schulte's slugging in 1911 and Zimmerman's Triple Crown season the following year were virtually the club's only offensive bright spots during the period. The 1907 club, as an example, won the pennant without a single .300 hitter and was led in RBIs by Harry Steinfeldt with just 70.

PITTSBURGH PIRATES

Pennants: 1901, 1902, 1903, 1909
Manager: Fred Clarke, 1901–15
Park: Exposition Park, 1901–09
Forbes Field, 1909–70 (opened June 30, 1909; first all steel and concrete park in the majors)
Best Year: 1902 (103–36, .741)
Worst Year: 1917 (51–103, .331)
Top Rookie: Jim Nealon, 1906
Biggest Disappointment: Jim Nealon, 1907
Best Deal: Getting Vic Willis from the Braves, 1906
Worst Deal: Giving Kitty Bransfield to the Phillies in 1905 and opening a hole at first base that would haunt the club for the next decade
Other:
1902—Win flag by ML-record 27½ games; set NL record with 56–15 mark at home
1903—First ML team in this century to win three straight flags; share with Red Sox the honor of playing in the first modern World Series
1907—Only NL team to score over four runs a game, but poor defense scotches club's chances
1908—Lose pennant on the final day of the season when beaten by the Cubs (had the Pirates won the game they would have taken the flag and rendered the Merkle boner essentially meaningless)
1909—Franchise record 110 wins and second-highest winning percentage in history (.724) on a 154-game schedule
1912—.972 FA tops majors by a huge margin as team makes just 169 errors, 72 less than any other club in the majors and 94 less than Philadelphia, the AL's best fielding team
1914—First sub-.500 finish of the century
1917—Football coach Hugo Bezdek hired as manager; club finishes last for the first time since 1891 as Wilbur Cooper goes 17–11 and the rest of the pitchers are 34–92

HITTING

Batting Ave.	.357, Ginger Beaumont, 1902
Slugging Ave.	.542, Honus Wagner, 1908
Home Runs	12, Owen Wilson, 1911
RBIs	126, Honus Wagner, 1901
Total Bases	308, Honus Wagner, 1908
Hits	209, Ginger Beaumont, 1903
Runs	137, Ginger Beaumont, 1903
Doubles	44, Honus Wagner, 1904
Triples	36, Owen Wilson, 1912
Bases on Balls	80, Fred Clarke, 1909 80, Goat Anderson, 1907
Stolen Bases	63, Max Carey, 1916

PITCHING

Wins	28, Jack Chesbro, 1902
Losses	19, Elmer Jacobs, 1917 19, Frank Miller, 1917
Innings	322, Vic Willis, 1906
Games Started	38, Vic Willis, 1908
Complete Games	32, Vic Willis, 1906
Strikeouts	176, Claude Hendrix, 1912
Bases on Balls	151, Marty O'Toole, 1912
Winning Pct.	.824, Jack Chesbro, 1902
ERA	1.56, Howie Camnitz, 1908
Saves	4, Deacon Phillippe, 1910 4, George McQuillan, 1914 4, Wilbur Cooper, 1915
Shutouts	8, Jack Chesbro, 1902 8, Lefty Leifield, 1906 8, Al Mamaux, 1915

The NL's best-balanced team by far—at least until the mid-teens. Wagner almost every season found himself sandwiched in the batting order between two fairly potent hitters, and during the team's lengthy stretch as a contender three or four hurlers customarily took turns leading the club in wins. To drive home the mound depth the Pirates had Sam Leever, who was arguably the team's most effective pitcher for nearly a decade, doesn't even appear on the chart. Eight different pitchers were 20-game winners at various times for the club between 1901 and 1909, including Nick Maddox, who gives Jim Nealon stiff competition for being the Pirates' biggest disappointment in this era.

PHILADELPHIA PHILLIES

Pennants: 1915
Manager: Red Dooin, 1910–14
Park: Baker Bowl
Best Year: 1916 (91–62, .595)
Worst Year: 1904 (52–100, .342)
Top Rookie: Pete Alexander, 1911
Biggest Disappointment: Fred Osborn, 1909, hit .185 and was history after seeming in 1908 as if he would be the club's centerfielder for years to come
Best Deal: Getting Fred Luderus from the Cubs for Bill Foxen, 1910
Worst Deal: Making the Cubs a gift of Pete Alexander and Bill Killefer, 1918
Other:
- 1902—Fall from 2nd to 7th after losing the core of one of the NL's strongest teams to AL raiders over the past two years
- 1903—Cut Bill Keister after he hits .320 and leads the club in homers and RBIs
- 1904—Last team to make 400 or more errors in a season
- 1907—Rise to 3rd place under rookie manager Billy Murray
- 1911—Lead majors with 60 homers two years after having fewest four-baggers in NL
- 1913—2nd place, club's best finish since 1901; play pre-1961 ML-record 1453 innings
- 1915—First pennant in franchise history
- 1917—Finish above .500 for the last time until 1932
- 1919—No pitchers on the club work more than 185 innings; player–manager Gavvy Cravath leads the NL in homers for the final time despite collecting just 214 at bats

HITTING		**PITCHING**	
Batting Ave.	.354, Ed Delahanty, 1901	Wins	33, Pete Alexander, 1916
Slugging Ave.	.568, Gavvy Cravath, 1913	Losses	24, Chick Fraser, 1904
Home Runs	24, Gavvy Cravath, 1915	Innings	389, Pete Alexander, 1916
RBIs	128, Gavvy Cravath, 1913	Games Started	45, Pete Alexander, 1916
Total Bases	298, Gavvy Cravath, 1913	Complete Games	38, Pete Alexander, 1916
Hits	192, Ed Delahanty, 1901	Strikeouts	241, Pete Alexander, 1915
Runs	118, Roy Thomas, 1905	Bases on Balls	164, Earl Moore, 1911
Doubles	42, Bert Niehoff, 1916	Winning Pct.	.756, Pete Alexander, 1915
Triples	17, Elmer Flick, 1901 17, Sherry Magee, 1905, 1910	ERA	1.22, Pete Alexander, 1915
Bases on Balls	107, Roy Thomas, 1902, 1903, 1906	Saves	4, Dut Chalmers, 1911
Stolen Bases	55, Sherry Magee, 1906	Shutouts	16, Pete Alexander, 1916

Whereas the pitching records for most teams in this era were established in the early part of the century, the bulk of the Phillies' mound records came in the teens. It was not that they had no outstanding pitchers prior to Alexander, it was that he was so extraordinary. Magee, a fine hitter, had to shoulder the team's offensive load himself for most of his career. His best years were behind him by the time Cravath came on the scene. Flick, Thomas and Delahanty, the trio of outfielders with which the Phillies began the century, were probably the best outfield combination during the period but played together for only three years before being broken up by AL raids.

CINCINNATI REDS

Pennants: 1919
Manager: Joe Kelley, 1902–05; the club ran through eleven different managers during the period, with Clark Griffith the only one besides Kelley to last at least three seasons
Park: League Park, 1901
  Palace of the Fans, 1902–11
  Redland Field, 1912–69 (opened on April 11, 1912; later known as Crosley Field)
Best Year: 1919 (96–44, .686)
Worst Year: 1901 (52–87, .374)
Top Rookie: Mike Mitchell, 1907
Biggest Disappointment: Mike Mitchell, 1908; he later rebounded to become an excellent player
Best Deal: Obtaining Heinie Groh from the Giants, 1913
Worst Deal: Sending Mike Donlin to the Giants for Moose McCormick, 1904
Other:
  1903—Have top NL team BA for the first time in club history as outfielders Mike Donlin and Cy Seymour both finish among loop's top five hitters
  1904—Finish a solid 3rd with 88–65 record but trail the powerful pennant-winning Giants by 18 games
  1905—Fred Odwell is the club's last NL home run leader until 1954
  1909—Art Fromme and Harry Gaspar have a combined 37–24 record; club's other pitchers are 40–52
  1912—Team's batters lead the NL in fewest strikeouts but also hit the fewest home runs in the league
  1914—Set new franchise record with 94 losses
  1917—First season above .500 since 1909
  1919—First NL pennant in franchise history is accompanied by the club's first of many FA crowns in this century

HITTING		PITCHING	
Batting Ave.	.377, Cy Seymour, 1905	Wins	24, Fred Toney, 1917
Slugging Ave.	.559, Cy Seymour, 1905	Losses	23, Red Ames, 1914
Home Runs	16, Sam Crawford, 1901	Innings	375, Noodles Hahn, 1901
RBIs	121, Cy Seymour, 1905	Games Started	42, Noodles Hahn, 1901 42, Fred Toney, 1917
Total Bases	325, Cy Seymour, 1905	Complete Games	41, Noodles Hahn, 1901
Hits	219, Cy Seymour, 1905	Strikeouts	239, Noodles Hahn, 1901
Runs	120, Bob Bescher, 1912	Bases on Balls	147, Orval Overall, 1905
Doubles	40, Cy Seymour, 1905	Winning Pct.	.760, Dutch Ruether, 1919
Triples	22, Sam Crawford, 1902	ERA	1.73, Bob Ewing, 1907
Bases on Balls	103, Miller Huggins, 1905 103, Johnny Bates, 1911	Saves	7, Harry Gaspar, 1910
Stolen Bases	81, Bob Bescher, 1911	Shutouts	7, Fred Toney, 1917 7, Hod Eller, 1919

You'll be interested in discovering how long Crawford's club home run record lasted and who broke it. Seymour's dominance here makes it seem as if the Reds had no other hitters of consequence during this period, and that was almost the case. At the same time his 1905 season was the best one overall by any NL hitter during the deadball era. Seymour had only one other near it, however, and as a result Bescher, Mike Mitchell and Edd Roush, whose best years were still ahead of them, rate as the club's top offensive performers during the period.

BROOKLYN DODGERS

Pennants: 1916
Manager: Wilbert Robinson, 1914–19
Park: National League Park, 1901–12
  Ebbets Field, 1913–57 (opened on April 9, 1913)
Best Year: 1916 (94–60, .610)
Worst Year: 1905 (48–104, .316); the only time the franchise finished in last place
Top Rookie: Henry Schmidt, 1903, won 22 games and never pitched again in the majors; in the early 1900s the club was notorious for allowing talented pitchers to drift away
Biggest Disappointment: Tie between Jake Daubert and Mike Mowrey, 1917; poor years by them and several other members of the 1916 team sent the Dodgers tumbling all the way down to 7th place after winning the pennant
Best Deal: Obtaining Burleigh Grimes from Pittsburgh, 1918
Worst Deal: Letting Henry Schmidt get away after his marvelous rookie year
Other:
  1901—Club still known as the Superbas; begin to be called the Trolley Dodgers during the century's first decade and soon become just the Dodgers
  1901—Top NL in BA for the second year in a row
  1905—3.76 ERA and .937 FA are both the worst in the majors by a huge margin; team gives up 807 runs, 73 more than the next most generous club; Doc Scanlan is 14–12, rest of pitchers are 34–92
  1908—NL-record low .213 BA and 1358 total bases
  1909—Top NL in complete games with 103, a total that would have been last in the league just three years earlier
  1911—Score fewest runs in majors (539) and have lowest team BA (.237)
  1915—First above-.500 finish since 1903
  1918—Set NL record by losing nine straight games to open the season; score just 360 runs, by far the fewest in the majors

HITTING		PITCHING	
Batting Ave.	.354, Jimmy Sheckard, 1901	Wins	25, Bill Donovan, 1901
			25, Jeff Pfeffer, 1916
Slugging Ave.	.534, Jimmy Sheckard, 1901	Losses	27, George Bell, 1910
Home Runs	12, Tim Jordan, 1906, 1908	Innings	377, Oscar Jones, 1904
RBIs	104, Jimmy Sheckard, 1901	Games Started	41, Oscar Jones, 1904
Total Bases	296, Jimmy Sheckard, 1901	Complete Games	38, Oscar Jones, 1904
Hits	202, Willie Keeler, 1901	Strikeouts	226, Bill Donovan, 1901
Runs	123, Willie Keeler, 1901	Bases on Balls	152, Bill Donovan, 1901
Doubles	40, Red Smith, 1913	Winning Pct.	.694, Jeff Pfeffer, 1916
Triples	19, Jimmy Sheckard, 1901	ERA	1.58, Rube Marquard, 1916
Bases on Balls	82, Bill Dahlen, 1903	Saves	5, Elmer Stricklett, 1906
			5, Rube Marquard, 1916
Stolen Bases	67, Jimmy Sheckard, 1903	Shutouts	7, Burleigh Grimes, 1918

Between 1901 and Jake Daubert's emergence in the mid-teens as one of the NL's top batters, the Dodgers were the most punchless club in the majors. In 1908, for example, Jordan led the team with a .247 BA, and save for Jack Doyle, who had 91 RBIs in 1903, no other Brooklyn player between 1902 and 1922 had more than 90 in a season. As late as 1918, when a war-abbreviated schedule was played, the Dodgers scored just 360 runs in 126 games—an average of 2.86 runs per contest. In contrast, the team consistently had fine pitching, though the winning percentages of most of its hurlers during the era don't reflect that. Nap Rucker, an outstanding lefthander, was the principal victim.

BOSTON BRAVES

Pennants: 1914
Manager: George Stallings, 1913–19
Park: South End Grounds, 1901–15
   Braves Field, 1915–52 (opening game on August 18, 1915)
Best Year: 1914 (94–59, .614)
Worst Year: 1911 (44–107, .291)
Top Rookie: Irv Young, 1905
Biggest Disappointment: Bill James, 1915
Best Deal: Snagging Johnny Evers from the Cubs for Bill Swee-
   ney, 1914
Worst Deal: Sending Jesse Barnes and Larry Doyle to the Giants
   in 1918 for Buck Herzog
Other:
   1901—Only team in the majors to hit below .250; club still
      known as the Beaneaters
   1906—Top majors in complete games while posting no saves,
      the last time a pitching staff does this during a season in
      which a full schedule is played
   1907—Arthur Soden sells the club to the Dovey brothers and
      team briefly becomes known as the Doves; 3.33 staff ERA is
      the poorest in the ML, .63 higher than the next worst team,
      the Cardinals
   1909—NL record low .274 slugging average
   1911—Lose NL-record 14 straight games at home and also set
      NL season mark for the worst home performance, 19–54;
      staff ERA of 5.08 is worst in majors by 1.26 runs
   1912—Team becomes known as the Braves because new owner
      Jim Gaffney is a Tammany Hall chieftain
   1914—Win pennant after occupying last place as late as mid-
      July; put on torrid stretch drive while playing most of their
      home games at Fenway Park, the Red Sox's new domicile
   1915—Only 2nd-place finish in this century for the franchise
      while it is based in Boston
   1918—Top NL in complete games and become last team in ML
      history to achieve no saves
   1919—Pitcher Dick Rudolph has typical year for him while
      with the Braves, finishing high among the NL leaders in
      starts, innings, complete games and ERA but nevertheless
      compiling a losing record (13–18)

HITTING		PITCHING	
Batting Ave.	.344, Bill Sweeney, 1912	Wins	27, Togie Pittinger, 1902
			27, Vic Willis, 1902
			27, Dick Rudolph, 1914
Slugging Ave.	.494, Joe Connolly, 1914*	Losses	29, Vic Willis, 1905
Home Runs	10, Dave Brain, 1907	Innings	410, Vic Willis, 1902
	10, Fred Beck, 1910		
RBIs	100, Bill Sweeney, 1912	Games Started	46, Vic Willis, 1902
Total Bases	264, Bill Sweeney, 1912	Complete Games	45, Vic Willis, 1902
Hits	204, Bill Sweeney, 1912	Strikeouts	225, Vic Willis, 1902
Runs	102, Vin Campbell, 1912	Bases on Balls	149, Chick Fraser, 1905
Doubles	36, Doc Miller, 1911	Winning Pct.	.842, Tom Hughes, 1916
Triples	14, Ginger Beaumont, 1907	ERA	1.90, Bill James, 1914
Bases on Balls	87, Johnny Evers, 1914	Saves	9, Tom Hughes, 1915
Stolen Bases	57, Hap Myers, 1913	Shutouts	7, Togie Pittinger, 1902

*Connolly had only 399 at bats in 1914 but is regarded as the record holder because even if he'd gone hitless in another at bat, which would have given him 400, he'd still have the top SA.

Apart from Sweeney's sensational 1912 season and the freak pennant in 1914, only Willis and Rudolph saved this team from being the drabbest in the majors. As an example of the franchise's lack of wherewithal, Campbell was dumped after being the first Braves player in years to score over 100 runs in a season. A real odd note: Hughes in 1915 set a club save record that stood until the franchise moved from Boston.

ST. LOUIS CARDINALS

Pennants: None
Manager: Miller Huggins, 1913–17
Park: Robison Field, the last all-wooden park in the majors, it was abandoned by the Cardinals during the 1920 season
Best Year: 1901 (76–64, .543)
Worst Year: 1903 (43–94, .314)
Top Rookie: Tie between Jack Harper, 1901, and Rogers Hornsby, 1916
Biggest Disappointment: Mike O'Neill, 1903
Best Deal: Looting the Reds of Miller Huggins and more, 1910
Worst Deal: Sending Lee Meadows and Gene Paulette to the Phillies, 1919
Other:

1901—Lead NL in runs but finish only 4th

1903—Sink to last place when no pitcher wins more than nine games

1908—Average twentieth-century ML record low 2.41 runs per game and are blanked in a record 33 games

1911—Helen Britton (Lady B) becomes the first woman to be the controlling owner of a major league team

1914—Finish 3rd, first time in the first division since 1901

1916—Branch Rickey leaves the Browns to run the team's front office

1917—Team finishes 12 games over .500 despite giving up 36 more runs than it scores

1918—Last cellar finish in franchise history

1919—Third baseman Rogers Hornsby narrowly misses becoming first Cardinal to win an NL batting crown and also finishes high among the leaders in RBIs, total bases and SA, but team still languishes in 7th place

HITTING		PITCHING	
Batting Ave.	.378, Jesse Burkett, 1901	Wins	23, Jack Harper, 1901
			23, Bob Harmon, 1911
Slugging Ave.	.509, Jesse Burkett, 1901	Losses	25, Stoney McGlynn, 1907
			25, Bugs Raymond, 1908
Home Runs	10, Jesse Burkett, 1901	Innings	352, Stoney McGlynn, 1907
RBIs	91, Bobby Wallace, 1901	Games Started	41, Bob Harmon, 1911
Total Bases	306, Jesse Burkett, 1901	Complete Games	39, Jack Taylor, 1904
Hits	226, Jesse Burkett, 1901	Strikeouts	145, Bugs Raymond, 1908
Runs	142, Jesse Burkett, 1901	Bases on Balls	181, Bob Harmon, 1911
Doubles	38, Ed Konetchy, 1911	Winning Pct.	.760, Bill Doak, 1914
Triples	25, Tommy Long, 1915	ERA	1.72, Bill Doak, 1914
Bases on Balls	116, Miller Huggins, 1910	Saves	8, Red Ames, 1916
Stolen Bases	48, Red Murray, 1908	Shutouts	7, Bill Doak, 1914

Burkett and Wallace jumped to the AL Browns after the 1901 season along with Emmett Heidrick, and the club went into an instant slide that lasted until Rogers Hornsby arrived in 1916. With the exception of one or two players, and at that seldom the same ones for more than a year or two, the Cardinals could not even field what would pass for a decent minor league team during most of the period. Konetchy, who put in several seasons with the team, was probably its best all-purpose player prior to Hornsby.

THE BEST, THE WORST, AND THE WEIRDEST TEAMS BETWEEN 1901 AND 1919

• •

AMERICAN LEAGUE

THE BEST

1912 BOSTON RED SOX
W–105 L–47
Manager: Jake Stahl

Regular Lineup—1B, Jake Stahl; 2B, Steve Yerkes; 3B, Larry Gardner; SS, Heinie Wagner; RF, Harry Hooper; CF, Tris Speaker; LF, Duffy Lewis; C, Bill Carrigan; P, Joe Wood; P, Hugh Bedient; P, Buck O'Brien; P, Ray Collins; P, Sea Lion Hall

After winning 34 games in 1912, Wood was never again the same, and, curiously, all of the other Red Sox pitching mainstays that year suffered a similar fate. Following the 1915 season none of them ever won another game in the majors. But in 1912 Boston had by far the best and the deepest mound staff in the game. The team had only one flaw: It was weak up the middle, where Wagner and Yerkes were journeymen infielders at best—or, more accurately, it would have been weak if Speaker hadn't been behind them in center field. Speaker covered so much ground that he gave the club the equivalent of a fifth infielder, and Carrigan, the AL's top fielding catcher, was worth a sixth. In addition, Speaker hit .383, a club record until Ted Williams arrived, and only Ty Cobb's presence denied Tris the distinction of being the game's best hitter during the teens. The most complimentary thing said about Stahl as a manager was that he was unobtrusive but efficient. He didn't need to do much more in 1912, though, than fill out the lineup card. When the club started poorly the following season, Stahl was replaced by Carrigan, who in 1915 became the third player-manager in the Red Sox' brief history to win a flag. Perhaps the strongest testimony as to how good the 1912 Crimson Hose were was offered by John McGraw, who felt they beat the finest Giants club he ever managed in the World Series that fall, and in a manner that would later become highly uncharacteristic of a Red Sox team—by winning the deciding seventh game with a last-ditch rally in their final turn at bat.

THE WORST

1909 WASHINGTON SENATORS
W–42 L–110
Manager: Joe Cantillon

Regular Lineup—1B, Jiggs Donahue; 2B, Jim Delahanty; 3B, Wid Conroy; SS, George McBride; RF, Jack Lelivelt; CF, Clyde Milan; LF, George Browne; C, Gabby Street; P, Walter Johnson; P, Bob Groom; P, Dolly Gray; P, Charlie Smith

True, the 1915 and 1916 Philadelphia A's had worse W–L records, but we're talking here about major league teams and that just isn't what Connie Mack fielded in those years. The 1909 Senators, on the other hand, had two excellent pitchers in Johnson and Groom and the AL's finest fielding shortstop in McBride, who also had his career best season at the plate. But McBride's best was a .234 BA, and when Milan hit just .200, one of the lowest marks ever for a regular outfielder, Johnson and Groom got so little support that they lost 51 games between them. In fact, the Senators' offensive leader, utilityman Bob Unglaub, collected just 41 RBIs while Conroy led the club in runs with a mere 44. Cantillon was later a highly successful manager in the minor leagues, but his record with Washington probably wrecked his chances of ever getting another try in the majors. He was replaced in 1910 by Jimmy McAleer, who piloted the club to a 24½-game improvement, but the Senators were so far behind the pack in those years that even that gigantic gain brought them up only to seventh place. To illustrate just how far behind, prior to 1912 the team's best finish was sixth, with a 61–73 record (.455), back in 1901.

THE WEIRDEST

1906 CLEVELAND NAPS
W–89 L–64
Manager: Nap Lajoie

Regular Lineup—1B, Claude Rossman; 2B, Nap Lajoie; 3B, Bill Bradley; SS, Terry Turner; RF, Bunk Congalton; CF, Elmer Flick; LF, Jim Jackson; C, Harry Bemis; P, Otto Hess; P, Addie Joss; P, Bill Bernhard; P, Bob Rhoads

Lajoie's men (named after him) led the AL in batting, runs scored, fielding, complete games and ERA. Indeed, they won the team Triple Crown, a victory that in every other season since 1885 has assured a pennant. But Cleveland could do no better than third place, and it's impossible now to look back and figure out why. Backup catcher Nig Clarke hit .358, tying for the highest average in the AL among players in more than 50 games; the team turned 26 more double plays than the runner-up; Congalton hit .320; and Bradley and Turner combined with Lajoie and rookie Rossman to give Cleveland an infield second only to that of the Cubs in 1906. The one weak link was Jackson, who hit just .214, but Harry Bay, who played nearly as much, hit .275, and besides, every club that season—again excepting the Cubs—had at least one regular who contributed little offensive punch. Was the problem Lajoie? He's the easy culprit to cite since he never played on a pennant winner, let alone managed one. But a suspicion lurks that this team, already, in only its sixth season of existence, had the seeds of the doom that seems to hover perpetually over the franchise. Prior to expansion in 1961, Cleveland produced a steady flow of strong teams and great players but only three pennants. Since then, in the event you haven't noticed, its best finish was a distant third in 1968.

NATIONAL LEAGUE

THE BEST

1902 PITTSBURGH PIRATES
W–103 L–36
Manager: Fred Clarke

Regular Lineup—1B, Kitty Bransfield; 2B, Claude Ritchey; 3B, Tommy Leach; SS, Wid Conroy; RF, Honus Wagner; CF, Ginger Beaumont; LF, Fred Clarke; C, Harry Smith/Jack O'Connor; P, Jack Chesbro; P, Deacon Phillippe; P, Jesse Tannehill; P, Sam Leever; P, Ed Doheny

Was this team really better than the 1906 Cubs, winners of a record 116 games? Bet on it, but resign yourself to the fact that there's no way to prove it. It can't even be proven that in 1902 the Pirates were better than the AL flag-winning A's because there was no World Series play as yet owing to the war that was still raging between the two major leagues. Before the next season began, in fact, Pittsburgh lost Chesbro, Tannehill, and Conroy to the larcenous AL, forcing Clarke to move Wagner to shortstop and at last assign him a position he could call his own. Still, the Pirates were strong enough to cop their third consecutive flag with ease, though not by anywhere near the record 27½ games they'd finished ahead of second-place Brooklyn in 1902. The game has already entered the deadball era—Pittsburgh scored 250 fewer runs than league-leading Boston had just five years earlier but still topped the NL by a margin of 143 runs—and the Cubs already were beginning to assemble the super pitching staff and crew of base thieves that would spearhead them the remainder of the decade. But in 1902 the Pirates were still their equal in both departments and had in Wagner a player who may never have been equalled.

THE WORST

1905 BROOKLYN SUPERBAS
W–48 L–104
Manager: Ned Hanlon

Regular Lineup—1B, Doc Gessler; 2B, Charlie Malay; 3B, Emil Batch; SS, Phil Lewis; RF, Harry Lumley; CF, Johnny Dobbs; LF, Jimmy Sheckard; C, Lew Ritter; P, Harry McIntire; P, Doc Scanlan; P, Elmer Stricklett; P, Mal Eason; P, Oscar Jones

The two Docs couldn't even begin to cure the ills of this, the only Brooklyn team since 1875 to finish in the cellar. Hanlon was seemingly undermined by a pitching staff that looked adequate on paper but surrendered a league-leading 3.76 earned runs per game. What really did the club in, though, was awful fielding—25% more errors than Boston, the second most porous team in the NL, and one suspects a lot more that were called hits by incredulous scorers who simply couldn't believe this outfit's glovework could be as leaky as it seemed—and an anemic attack that was led by Batch with just 49 RBIs. A contender as recently as 1903, Brooklyn plummeted swiftly for a slew of reasons, but all appear linked to Hanlon. His skill in judging and inspiring players had so deteriorated that by 1905 the team had let slip through its fingers many of the more talented performers in the game and received practically nothing in exchange. When Brooklyn sent Gessler and Sheckard, two of its better hitters, to the Cubs the following season and got in return a pair of .230 men, Doc Casey and Billy Maloney, its fate was sealed until Wilbert Robinson was hired to manage it in 1914.

THE WEIRDEST

1917 CINCINNATI REDS
W–78 L–76
Manager: Christy Mathewson

Regular Lineup—1B, Hal Chase; 2B, Dave Shean; 3B, Heinie Groh; SS, Larry Kopf; RF, Tommy Griffith; CF, Edd Roush; LF, Greasy Neale; C, Ivy Wingo; P, Pete Schneider; P, Fred Toney; P, Mike Regan; P, Clarence Mitchell; P, Hod Eller

The most disparate collection of oddballs since, well, maybe the 1878 Cincinnati Red Stockings. The Reds leaped from seventh to fourth place with a blend of Chase, one of the all-time wheeler-dealers, and Mathewson, the era's greatest straight arrow, and would win the flag two years later—but only after both were gone. Around for Chase's amusement were volatile backup outfielder Sherry Magee; 20-game winner Schneider, another *bon vivant* who would become a famous minor league slugger after his arm went the following season; two future pro football Hall of Famers, Neale and sub outfielder Jim Thorpe; and Roush, one of the game's leading iconoclasts. Mathewson was in over his head with this club and knew it. The team didn't really come together until rollicking Pat Moran took over the reins at the beginning of the 1919 season and Jake Daubert was snared from Brooklyn to replace Chase. But Matty showed in his two and a half seasons at the Cincinnati helm that if his health hadn't given out after he was accidentally gassed while serving in World War I he might have been one of that extremely rare breed: a great pitcher who later became a successful manager. Under his tutelage both Roush and Groh, considered by some to be the best fielding third baseman ever, first emerged as stars. Shean, a .213 hitter who had been out of the majors since 1912, may have played a larger role on this team than has previously been credited to him. When he went to the Boston Red Sox the following season he was instrumental in bringing the Hub its last world championship team to date.

SPECIAL FEATURE TEAM: THE HITLESS WONDERS

1906 CHICAGO WHITE SOX
W-93 L-58
Manager: Fielder Jones

Regular Lineup—1B, Jiggs Donahue; 2B, Frank Isbell; 3B, Lee Tannehill/George Rohe; SS, George Davis; RF, Bill O'Neill/Patsy Dougherty; CF, Fielder Jones; LF, Eddie Hahn; C, Billy Sullivan; P, Frank Owen; P, Nick Altrock; P, Doc White; P, Ed Walsh; P, Roy Patterson; P, Frank Smith

It is no mystery how the 1906 White Sox came to be known as "The Hitless Wonders." Not only did they win the pennant despite finishing last in the AL in both BA and SA, but they defeated the vaunted Cubs, winners of an all-time record 116 games during the regular season, in the World Series while batting just .198. Everyone who has spent any time browsing through the stats for the 1906 season has a theory for how the Sox did it. The most often espoused explanation is that they locked up the pennant by going on a 19-game winning streak late in the season and then shut down the Cubs in the Series by playing superior defense. Problems sprout from every which way, however, when a closer look is taken at the archives. First off, the Sox' victory skein began in early August and by no means settled matters; in fact, Chicago did not manage to shake the second-place Yankees until the final week of the season. Next, the Sox had a poor World Series defensively, making 14 errors altogether and nine in the last two contests, both of which the team needed to win and did.

Then what is the reason the Sox triumphed? Well, another one that's heard a lot and that makes a fair amount of sense springs from the observation that Sox pitchers were the stingiest in the majors when it came to giving up walks, while the team's hitters paced the AL in accruing bases on balls. The trouble here is that even with all those free passes Chicago still had only the fifth-best on-base percentage in the AL and scored far fewer runs than either Cleveland or New York. And the Sox pitchers, though parsimonious with walks, were only fourth-best in the league in the fewest number of hits allowed and next to last in strikeouts, both of which departments are usually equally important barometers in gauging a team's probable success.

Several other notions that initially seem appealing also ultimately fail to account for how the Hitless Wonders did it, leaving us with only that fallback word for an explanation: intangibles. Or so, some 86 years after the fact, it would appear. Yet my hunch is that those who were paying close attention in 1906 spotted two ostensible reasons for the White Sox' unlikely victory, the manager–centerfielder and the shortstop. In two separate early-season transactions Chicago purchased Hahn and Dougherty from New York. The pair solidified what up until then had been a dreadful outfield that numbered O'Neill, a poor fielder with nothing much to offer on offense either, and Frank Hemphill, who batted .075 before being cut. Since Jones, from all reports, played a large role in the club's deals, he undoubtedly had a heavy responsibility in bringing Hahn and Dougherty on board. He also knew how to get the utmost out of the team's limited talents. All during the season he platooned Rohe and the weak-hitting Tannehill, frequently bringing in the latter as a late-inning defensive replacement. What's more, Jones was good with pitchers and a master at playing the deadball-era game. But probably his most crucial attribute, at least in 1906, was his readiness to go with the player who was hot. For the first three games of the World Series he spelled Davis, who was nursing an injury, with Tannehill. When Davis was in shape to return in the fourth game, he sat down Tannehill, his most brilliant fielder, in favor of Rohe, largely because Rohe had won the previous game with a three-run triple. It was a move that not many managers would have made in an era when defense was the hallmark, and it made a legend of both Rohe and the team.

That leaves Davis, a few steps slower at 35 but still with enough pop to lead the club in extra base hits and RBIs. Then, despite missing half the World Series, he led all hitters on both teams with six RBIs and tied with three other teammates for the most runs scored. Had Davis retired on that note he would almost certainly now be in the Hall of Fame.* Following the 1906 season, he had a career batting average of .306, at that point the best in history among middle infielders or third basemen (Davis began as a third baseman) who had played at least 1500 games in the majors. He also held the record for the most career hits by a switch hitter, a distinction that remained his until Mickey Mantle came along. The Hitless Wonders provided Davis with his only taste of being on a flag winner, and he made the most of it.

*Davis declined sharply after the 1906 season but still retired with credentials that ought to have long since earned his enshrinement in Cooperstown.

A LONG SEASON

. . . .

1909 SAN FRANCISCO SEALS
W-132 L-80
Manager: Danny Long

Regular Lineup—1B, Tom Tennant; 2B, Kid Mohler; 3B, Rollie Zeider; SS, Roy McArdle; RF, Heinie Melchior; CF, Doc Miller; LF, Ping Bodie; C, Claude Berry; Util, Nick Williams/Mundle Mondorff/Jimmy Lewis; P, Cack Henley; P, Frank Browning; P, Joe Corbett; P, Jack Ames

In 1903 the four teams that comprised the California State League—Los Angeles, San Francisco, Oakland and Sacramento—spirited Portland and Seattle away from the Pacific Northwest League to form a new circuit called the Pacific Coast League and bid for admission to organized baseball's National Association. Enraged by this act of piracy, Pacific Northwest League officials, vowing to crush the outlaw loop, renamed themselves the Pacific National League and planted competing teams in Los Angeles and San Francisco. Much to the surprise of Eastern observers, the fledgling PCL not only fended off the head-on challenge but earned acceptance as a bona fide minor league by the National Association. However, the struggle for survival had just begun. The new federation suffered from sparse financial backing in several of its cities and a severe competitive imbalance. In the PCL's initial season Los Angeles bolted away with the pennant, finishing 27½ games ahead of second-place Sacramento, and was the only team to break .500. In the process the Angels won an all-time organized-baseball record 133 games.

Finding the going too expensive, Sacramento was replaced in 1904 by Tacoma. Tacoma lasted for two years, then succumbed too and took down with it its sister Washington State team, Seattle. The defection of the two Northwest franchises, coupled with the great San Francisco earthquake in the spring of 1906, which destroyed the PCL headquarters and forced a three-week suspension of play, so rocked the league that it could muster only four teams in 1907 and again in 1908.

By 1909 the PCL was back up to six clubs, bolstered by the return of Sacramento and the addition of a second team in the Los Angeles area, the Vernon Villagers. In his dual role as loop president and owner of the San Francisco Seals, Cal Ewing predicted a banner season. Years later it was revealed that Ewing also owned a piece of the Oakland team, a conflict of interest that might have dulled the rivalry between the two Bay Area clubs had it been known at the time. As it was, the players and fans of both teams were at a fever pitch when the Oaks and Seals kicked off the 1909 season on March 30 at the Seals' new domicile, Recreation Park, built to replace the original Recreation Park, which also had been a casualty of the earthquake.

The Seals won the opening clash 2–1 with Browning prevailing over Oaks ace Jimmy Wiggs. It was but the first of 46 times the two teams would meet in 1909 as Ewing, in his exuberance over the league's improved prospects, expanded the PCL schedule so that it ran until the end of October. Well-played and exciting as the opener was, some in the crowd were disturbed that only three runs had been tallied. They hoped the low score was not a harbinger that the 1909 campaign would be a reprise of 1908, when there had been so little offense in the PCL that the batting leader, Babe Danzig of Los Angeles, had hit just .298. It would be a long season in more ways than one if that were to occur.

Seven months later, when the curtain descended on the afternoon of October 31, Seals fans had the following nuggets to treasure. Browning had won a PCL-record 16 straight games, four of them by shutouts and one a no-hitter. Henley had bested Wiggs 1–0 in the most brilliant pitching duel in PCL history, a 24-inning marathon on June 8 that Williams, playing in place of Bodie, had won with a single. Henley furthermore had been the league's top hurler with 31 victories and a .756 winning percentage, and the Seals had also had the league's top hitter in

Melchior. But most important, the club had won its first PCL pennant. If it had been a long season in San Francisco, it was only because the Seals were piloted by a man named Long.

Not until some while after the season, when the official stats were finally released, did PCL followers realize that for the second year in a row the loop had not a single .300 hitter. Melchior's winning BA rounded off to .298 but was actually slightly lower than Danzig's mark the previous year. Even more embarrassing, Mohler, who functioned as the Seals leadoff hitter and had been voted to the PCL All-Star team, was discovered to have hit a measly .193.[1] Yet San Francisco had been the league's most potent team, if only because its hitters didn't have to face Browning and Henley. But the Seals' twin mound mainstays were just two of the multitude of pitchers in the PCL who were enjoying themselves as no group of hurlers ever would again, for the deadball era had descended upon the Coast loop with a vengeance. If hitters in the PCL had been anemic in 1908 and even more overmatched in 1909, the 1910 season was saved from becoming an offensive travesty only by Bodie, who tagged 30 home runs to lure attention away from the fact that the loop's top batter, Hunky Shaw, a switch-hitting outfielder from Yakima, Washington, who had failed to stick with the Pirates two years earlier, finished at .281, the lowest average ever to lead a top minor league.[2]

Shaw played with the Seals in 1910, replacing Miller, who had been shipped to the Cubs and then speedily traded to the Braves. Zeider was also gone in 1910, called up by the White Sox, with whom the Seals had a loose working agreement, and Bodie was sold to the Pale Hose for delivery in 1911. Missing also on Opening Day in 1910 was Browning; the 5'5" righthander had been acquired by the Tigers.

By then Seals fans had begun to feel that the 1909 season had been too short in all. Their team slipped back into the pack, replaced by the Portland Beavers, who featured a pitching staff

1. Mohler was the last lefthander to play either second base or shortstop in the high minors. A steady .300 hitter earlier in his career before the deadball era took hold, he followed his .193 season in 1909 by batting .191 the next year for the Seals.
2. The PCL was not the only minor league affected when the deadball era reached its apex during the 1905–10 seasons. Each of the other two top minor leagues, the American Association and the International League, also lacked for a .300 hitter at least one season, and in 1906 Cleburne outfielder George Whiteman led the Texas League, then a Class B circuit, with a .281 BA, identical to Shaw's 1910 PCL-leading mark.

that in 1910 compiled 88 consecutive shutout innings to establish an all-time O.B. record.[3] And what would prove just as dis-
heartening in the years ahead, the PCL schedule was shaved after
the 1909 season. Never again would a team in any league play
enough games to have a realistic opportunity to break the Angels' record of 133 victories. The tragedy was that the Seals had
been on the brink of shattering the mark only to go into a tailspin after clinching the pennant. Facing last-place Vernon at
home in a season-ending series, San Francisco needed just two
victories to tie the Angels' record and three to break it. Instead
the Seals were blasted 12–3 by the Villagers on October 30 and
then squandered their final chance to earn at least a share of
the record by dropping the second half of a morning–afternoon
twin bill to close the season. At the time, of course, few in San
Francisco really cared. Records were still many years away from
becoming the obsession they are now. Winning the pennant was
what mattered most, although once that was achieved the Seals
set their sights on the next target. Despite having played 212
games in 216 days, the team did not disperse for a well-deserved
winter's rest as soon as the season ended. They reconvened the
next day at Recreation Park to begin a series of games against
a National League all-star squad that lasted deep into November.

3. During the skein the Beavers shut out opponents in nine straight games and parts
of two others. Bill Steen, Gene Krapp and Vean Gregg were the hurlers who did
most of the whitewash work. Gregg blanked Sacramento in both ends of a doubleheader on October 9, midway through the streak. Joining Cleveland the following
year, he won 20 or more games in each of his first three major league seasons and
then encountered arm trouble.

THE BABE'S FIRST
PENNANT WINNER

· ·

1914 PROVIDENCE GRAYS
W-95 L-59
Manager: Bill Donovan

Regular Lineup—1B Eddie Onslow; 2B, Dave Shean; 3B, Paddy Bauman; SS, Bunny Fabrique; RF, Al Platte; CF, Guy Tutwiler; LF, Ray Powell; C, Jack Onslow/ Brad Kocher; P, Carl Mays; P, Babe Ruth; P, Toots Shultz; P, Jack Bentley; P, Ralph Comstock; P, Bill Bailey; P, Red Oldham

The Grays were Ruth's third professional team, all in the space of the same season. He began the campaign with the Baltimore Orioles of the International League, owned and managed by Jack Dunn, was purchased by the Red Sox, and then sent back in August to the IL, this time to Providence, after a short stay in the Hub. The natural assumption is that Ruth must have needed more seasoning, but BoSox manager Bill Carrigan later admitted privately that there was another reason for his return to the minors. According to Carrigan, Ruth, though only 19, was already good enough for the majors, but Sox owner Joe Lannin, who also had an interest in the Providence club, dispatched Babe to the Grays in the hope he could give the financially troubled franchise a pennant. In any case, Providence, even prior to Ruth's arrival, was inordinately blessed with talent for a minor league team—especially in a season when there were three major leagues.* Every single member of the Grays' regular cast had either previously played in the majors or would do so before the decade was out.

In 1914, Shean topped the league in batting, Platte led it in runs and hits, and Mays had the most wins. Moreover, Tutwiler set an all-time loop mark that year for triples with 29, and the Grays had both the league's best batting average and highest fielding average. Yet, even with Ruth, they had a dogfight until the very last week of the season before they claimed the pennant, finishing three games ahead of Buffalo and four in front of Rochester. The Grays were only 10–12 versus the runner-up Bisons but made up the difference by massacring last-place Jersey City, taking 18 of the 22 games the clubs played against one another, while Buffalo was just 14–8 versus the cellar dwellers. A year later, with both Ruth and Mays gone to the Red Sox and Tutwiler injured much of the season, Providence slipped to second place, two games back of Buffalo. Falling attendance, coupled with other economic problems brought on by the nation's war effort, forced the team to leave the International League at the end of the 1917 season.

Ruth's IL stats in 1914 show that he hit .231, had only one home run—on September 5 at Toronto off Ellis Johnson—and fanned 26 times in 121 at bats. But the Babe won 22 games (14 with Baltimore and eight with Providence), more than any other pitcher in the IL except Mays. The club's main cogs on an everyday basis were Fabrique, Tutwiler, the Onslow brothers, Shean and Platte. In 1914, Shean was 31 years old and Platte just 24, with the best part of his career seemingly ahead of him. Yet Platte never again scaled the heights he did that season, although he played productively in the minors for another decade, while Shean clawed his way back to the majors three years later when he was 34. The Onslows also had long and meritorious careers in the minors, Eddie in particular. He held the Tigers' first base job for a while in 1912 when he was just 19 and fresh from having won the Southern Michigan League batting crown, but was hampered by a lack of power, a serious handicap for a first baseman even in the deadball era. Another IL first baseman in 1914, Wally Pipp of Rochester, was outhit by Onslow but won a post with the Yankees the following year after he led the loop in home runs and total bases and was second in triples to Tutwiler. Both Pipp and Buffalo's star outfielder, Frank Gilhooley, who paced the IL in 1914 with 62 stolen bases, would later be teammates of Ruth's in the majors, and Pipp would precede the

Babe as the AL's premier slugger. Bentley would later switch to first base and set the all-time IL single season record for the most hits before joining the New York Giants and returning to the mound to face Ruth in the 1923 World Series.

For winning the IL flag in 1914, Donovan was rewarded with the Yankees' dugout job the following year. He held it through the 1917 season, after which he was replaced by Miller Huggins.

*The Federal League operated as a third major league in 1914 and 1915.

A SHORT SEASON

● ●

1918 BINGHAMPTON BINGOS
W–85 L–38
Manager: Chick Hartman

Regular Lineup—1B, Polly McLarry; 2B, Chick Hartman; 3B, Eddie Zimmerman; SS, Leo Hanley; RF, Bill Kay; CF, Jim Riley; LF, Pete Knisley/Rabbit Oakes; C, Bill Fischer/John Haddock; P, Johnny Beckvermit; P, Luther Barnes; P, Festus Higgins; P, Sam Frock; P, John Verbout; P, Oscar Tuero; P, Mike Bill; P, Mysterious Walker

At the commencement of the 1918 season the International League was in such a state of chaos that its collapse was feared. Further eroding its already shaky underpinnings was an ever-increasing national focus on World War I. When it grew apparent early in the 1918 campaign that interest in the game had dwindled, the IL was expected to be one of the first minor leagues to have to suspend operations until the war ended. Instead the IL became the only minor league to survive until Labor Day, when Provost Marshal General Crowder's "work-or-fight" order, which classed baseball as nonessential to the war effort, went into effect, and Binghampton, a last-minute addition to the loop, played a lead role in its salvation.[1]

1. The IL was not only the lone minor league to finish as much of its season as the work-or-fight order would allow, it was the sole minor league to last out the month of July. Eight Class AA, Class A, and Class B leagues began the 1918 season. The Southern Association was the first casualty, surrendering on June 28. The Western

The Bingos had previously been a member of the New York State League, which had shut down following the 1917 season, and actually represented three adjoining cities—Binghampton, Endicott and Johnson City. Official home to the team was Johnson City, the site of Johnson Field, where Binghampton teams in several different minor leagues performed for more than half a century.[2] The park was named after club owner George F. Johnson, who also ran the Endicott-Johnson Shoe factory, one of the area's largest employers. Owing to its affiliation with Johnson's business concern, the team was alternately known as the Cobblers. By the close of the 1918 season, Binghampton had become a classic study in how minor league teams in a time of great stress are assembled and kept afloat. Knowing the Class B State League club would not be strong enough to compete in the Class AA IL, Johnson corraled Hartman from Denver in the Western League to do double duty as manager and second baseman and then garnered Zimmerman and several other experienced Class AA players to complement his State League nucleus of Haddock, Bill, Walter Ancker, Bill Irving, Pete Shields and Kay. A fixture in Binghampton since 1914, Kay was the team's best holdover player. Still, he was past 40 when the 1918 season began, and even Johnson must have worried that his star hitter would find IL pitching too much of a challenge. Indeed, expectations of any sort for the Bingos seemed unrealistic.

Hopes were roused immediately, though, when the club won its opening game on May 8, besting the defending IL champion Toronto Maple Leafs 3–2 in 17 innings. The Bingos swiftly became the talk of the league by running off nine straight victories before suffering their first defeat on May 18, a 1–0 heartbreaker in the second half of a doubleheader with those same Maple

---

League, Texas League, and Pacific Coast International League ceased play on July 7. The American Association closed down on July 21, the Eastern League quit the following day, and on July 24 the Pacific Coast League left the IL to carry on alone.

2. Johnson Field, like the Polo Grounds in New York, was an example of a park that had to be built to fit the already existing contours of a city. Because of the way the streets around the field were situated, left field was about 318 feet down the line while the right field barrier stood some 383 feet away, and a poke to dead center field, bizarrely, had to travel only 340 feet to go the distance. After watching a number of their young power hitters, who were supposedly being groomed at Binghampton to take advantage of the short rightfield porch in Yankee Stadium, change their strokes so they could hit the inviting center field target in Johnson Field, Yankees brass eventually shortened the right field fence. They could do nothing, however, about the center field barrier, which was bound by the street that ran behind it.

Leafs. Heading into June, Binghampton still held a comfortable lead over second-place Rochester despite losing Ancker, first baseman Shields and Gingras, the team's starting pitcher on Opening Day, to the army. In their stead, Johnson secured McLarry from Shreveport of the Texas League and recruited Fischer from his own shoe factory, where the former major league backstopper was working after being released for refusing to report to the Pittsburgh Pirates. McLarry made everyone forget Shields by winning the IL batting crown in 1918, and Fischer took the catching job away from Haddock, but the military draft would remain the club's Achilles heel all season. The pitching staff in particular was in constant turmoil, as only Frock and Higgins were assured of retaining their draft-deferred status. Frock was exempt because at 36 he was overage, and Higgins had been beaned earlier in his career, saddling him with constant headaches—he would die six years later of a brain hemorrhage.

Like most major and minor league clubs in 1918, the Bingos tried twilight games to enable fans who were involved in war work to attend, but the experiment was not a notable success. The team nevertheless did surprisingly well at the gate, thanks in part to clever promotion. A Soldiers and Sailors Bat and Ball Day on June 15 lured some 12,000 locals to Johnson Field to watch the "Beast of Berlin" (an effigy of the German Kaiser) hanged before the game began, but Johnson at that juncture needed no gimmicks. Two Monday mornings later the Bingos stood at 32–9 and were 7½ games up on Rochester. Sparked by McLarry's hitting and the mound work of Higgins, Barnes and Beckvermit—the latter won 14 of his first 15 decisions—the team maintained its torrid pace well into July. Still holding a 7½-game lead at midmonth, the Bingos then experienced their first slump of the season, losing all six games they played the week of July 14–20. Suddenly the club began feeling pressure from Toronto, which passed Rochester and ended the month only a few percentage points out of first place.

In early August the Bingos lost their grip on the top spot for the first time all season as the Maple Leafs continued to spurt. The two clubs then battled neck and neck for the remaining four weeks of the campaign, during which time the Bingos underwent so many personnel changes that Hartman seldom fielded the same lineup two days in a row. Oakes, who had been claimed by New London of the Eastern League earlier in the season, returned to Binghampton when that loop folded. Knisley mean-while had been acquired from Louisville to serve as an extra outfielder when the American Association went under and went on a hitting rampage that sewed up a regular garden post. Han-ley, a local product, took his .197 batting average to the bench when Frank O'Rourke, later a fine major league shortstop, also came to the Bingos from the New London club. But the most critical alterations in the team's makeup involved the two oldest veteran players, Frock and Kay. In August, Frock was dismissed by the Bingos when it surfaced that he had been secretly acting as a recruiting agent for a rival IL club, the Baltimore Orioles, who were out of contention in 1918 but looking to stockpile play-ers for the following season. Kay left the club in early August for personal reasons, forcing Hartman to put Knisley in his spot and return the weak-hitting Oakes to left field.

On the last Sunday morning of the season, September 1, Binghampton led Toronto by a scant six percentage points. When both clubs swept doubleheaders, Toronto from Buffalo and Binghampton from Baltimore, the Bingos held their slender edge going into the season's final day. Once again Binghampton squared off against Baltimore in a twin bill while Toronto was slated to play Buffalo another pair. After Verbout beat Balti-more's Rube Parnham in the opener, 2–1, the news reached Johnson Field that Toronto had also won its first game with Buffalo. That put the pennant all in the hands of Beckvermit. A win by him would cement first place for the Bingos regardless of what Toronto did in its second game. Facing Beckvermit was the Orioles' ace lefthander, Ralph Worrell, who, although still short of his twentieth birthday, had already won 24 games in the war-abbreviated season to lead all IL pitchers. With a 17–3 record, Beckvermit likewise had a pitching title of his own al-ready under lock and key—the winning percentage champion-ship. The game thus matched the IL's top two hurlers and promised to be a tight-fought mound duel. It was all of that as Beckvermit gave up solo runs in each of the first two innings and then shut the Orioles down cold. But those two tallies proved to be all that Worrell needed. Although he allowed nine hits on the day—three to Knisley alone—the Bingos managed to dent the plate just once, that in the fourth inning. When the Maple Leafs squeezed by Buffalo 5–4 in the nightcap of their twin bill, they snatched the IL pennant by two percentage points.

Deeply disappointed, Johnson replaced Hartman over the winter as the Bingos player-manager with former National League MVP Wildfire Schulte, but it was to no avail. The Baltimore Orioles emerged as the new IL power in 1919, winning their first of what would be an organized-baseball record seven straight pennants. Ironically, Worrell, the Orioles star in 1918, had no part in the triumph. His Labor Day victory over the Bingos in fact turned out to be the last professional game he ever pitched. Along with so many others, he died that winter in the great influenza epidemic.

Shrinking attendance cost the Bingos their IL franchise after the 1919 season. For the next two years Binghampton fielded an outlaw team and then joined the newly formed New York–Pennsylvania League in 1923. In 1938 the loop renamed itself the Eastern League, a title that had fallen vacant when the former Eastern League had collapsed during the early days of the Depression. Binghampton eventually became a Yankees farm team and remained a member of the Eastern League until 1968. The club had long since adopted a new nickname, calling itself the Triplets to signify that it represented not only Binghampton but also Endicott and Johnson City. In actuality, the franchise much preferred to be known as Tri-City rather than Binghampton. By any name, the Triplets were an Eastern League power until the very end. In their last season in organized baseball, they debuted one of the loop's most famous graduates, a twenty-one-year-old catcher from Kent State University named Thurman Munson.

ERA ALL-STAR TEAMS

● ●

AMERICAN LEAGUE		NATIONAL LEAGUE	
1B	Hal Chase	1B	Ed Konetchy
2B	Nap Lajoie	2B	Larry Doyle
3B	Home Run Baker	3B	Tommy Leach
SS	Ray Chapman	SS	Honus Wagner
OF	Ty Cobb	OF	Fred Clarke
OF	Tris Speaker	OF	Sherry Magee
OF	Joe Jackson	OF	Zach Wheat
C	Wally Schang	C	Johnny Kling
P	Walter Johnson	P	Pete Alexander
P	Cy Young	P	Christy Mathewson
UTIL	Eddie Collins	UTIL	Gavvy Cravath
MGR	Bill Carrigan	MGR	John McGraw
*	Sam Crawford	*	Harry Steinfeldt

MINOR LEAGUES

1B	Bunny Brief	C	Henri Rondeau
2B	Polly McLarry	P	Harry Vickers
3B	Herman Bronkie	P	Stoney McGlynn
SS	Dave Altizer	UTIL	Duke Kenworthy
OF	George Whiteman	MGR	Bill Clymer
OF	Johnny Beall	*	Jay Kirke
OF	Frank Huelsman		

*Best player who failed to make the team

LEG FOUR

1920–1941

TEAM NOTES AND RECORD HOLDERS: 1920–41

AMERICAN LEAGUE COMPOSITE STANDINGS

Number of Years Finishing in Each Position

Team	1	2	3	4	5	6	7	8	Aggregate
New York	12	6	3	0	0	0	1	0	1
Cleveland	1	3	6	7	1	3	1	0	2
Detroit	3	3	2	4	4	4	2	0	3
Washington	3	1	3	5	2	6	2	0	4
Philadelphia	3	4	2	0	2	1	3	7	5
Chicago	0	1	3	2	6	2	5	3	6
St. Louis	0	1	3	3	2	5	5	3	7
Boston	0	3	0	3	3	2	2	9	8

NEW YORK YANKEES

Pennants: 1921, 1922, 1923, 1926, 1927, 1928, 1932, 1936, 1937, 1938, 1939, 1941

Manager: Joe McCarthy, 1931–41, served eleven seasons with the club; Miller Huggins piloted the Yankees for twelve seasons (1918–29), but only ten were during this era.

Park: Polo Grounds, 1921–22
Yankee Stadium, 1923–present (opened on April 18, 1923)

Best Year: 1927 (110–44, .714)

Worst Year: 1925 (69–85, .448)

Top Rookie: Joe DiMaggio, 1936

Biggest Disappointment: Babe Ruth, 1925

Best Deal: Making Red Sox manager Ed Barrow their general manager at the close of the 1920 season; in the decade that followed he brought virtually every player of any value the Red Sox had to New York.

Worst Deal: Sending Wally Schang to the Browns in 1926 and leaving the club without a frontline catcher, forcing it to use thirty-five-year-old Hank Severeid, who was playing his last innings in the majors, in the World Series that year, which the Yankees lost.

Other:

1920—Become the first team in the century to top 100 homers when they club 115 and the first team to collect more homers than stolen bases

1923—Win third straight flag by 16-game margin; beat Giants in World Series to claim the franchise's first World Championship; become the first team ever to average less than one error a game

1925—Come in 7th, the club's worst finish between 1912 and 1966; pace majors in FA for record fourth straight year

1927—AL record (since broken) 110 wins; first team in ML history to total both 100 home runs and triples; register ML record .489 SA

1931—Score ML twentieth-century record 1067 runs; Lou Gehrig and Babe Ruth establish ML record for the most RBIs by two teammates (347)

1936—Win pennant by AL-record 19½ games; ML-record five players with 100 or more RBIs

1939—First AL team to win four straight pennants; first ML team to win four straight World Series

HITTING		PITCHING	
Batting Ave.	.393, Babe Ruth, 1923	Wins	27, Carl Mays, 1921
Slugging Ave.	.847, Babe Ruth, 1920	Losses	21, Sam Jones, 1925
Home Runs	60, Babe Ruth, 1927	Innings	337, Carl Mays, 1921
RBIs	184, Lou Gehrig, 1931	Games Started	38, Carl Mays, 1921
Total Bases	451, Babe Ruth, 1921	Complete Games	30, Carl Mays, 1921
Hits	231, Earle Combs, 1927	Strikeouts	194, Lefty Gomez, 1937
Runs	177, Babe Ruth, 1921	Bases on Balls	135, Monte Pearson, 1936
Doubles	52, Lou Gehrig, 1927	Winning Pct.	.839, Lefty Gomez, 1934
Triples	23, Earle Combs, 1927	ERA	2.28, Wilcy Moore, 1927*
Bases on Balls	170, Babe Ruth, 1923	Saves	19, Johnny Murphy, 1939
Stolen Bases	61, Ben Chapman, 1931	Shutouts	6, Carl Mays, 1920

*Tiny Bonham won the AL ERA crown in 1940 with a 1.90 mark, which is the club record for the period if you don't mind that he worked only 99 innings.

Lou Gehrig, playing for almost any other team, would hold club records for the period in just about every batting department. So, for that matter, would Joe DiMaggio, who instead holds none. Three Hall of Fame pitchers—Red Ruffing, Herb Pennock and Waite Hoyt—also are missing from the chart, which, in their cases, doesn't necessarily mean they were deprived of recognition here because they played for the Yankees. Indeed, the only Yankees pitcher from the period who was in any way deprived of deserved recognition was Mays. Chapman's contributions have also gone largely unrecognized. In 1930 he had 122 RBIs and scored 120 runs in addition to swiping a period-record 61 sacks.

CLEVELAND INDIANS

Pennants: 1920
Manager: Tris Speaker, 1920–26
Park: League Park
Municipal Stadium, 1932–present (opened on July 31, 1932); because their new park was so huge and crowds during the Depression and war years were seldom very big, the Indians continued to use League Park during the period as well, especially for weekday games
Best Year: 1920 (98–56, .636)
Worst Year: 1928 (62–92, .403)
Top Rookie: Tie between Wes Ferrell and Earl Averill, both in 1929
Biggest Disappointment: Jeff Heath's bust of a season in 1940 was more critical, but Carl Lind's descent in 1929 was swifter and just as painful to team fans
Best Deal: George Burns from the Red Sox, 1924
Worst Deal: Wes Ferrell to the Red Sox, 1934
Other:
1920—Star shortstop Ray Chapman becomes the only player ever to be killed in a major league game; the club nevertheless goes on to win the only ML pennant by a Cleveland team between 1876 and 1948
1923—Top majors in BA (.301) and runs with 888, also have the second-best staff ERA in the AL but somehow, despite all that, can finish no better than 3rd, 16½ games back of the Yankees
1926—Finish a strong 2nd, just three games behind pennant-winning Yankees
1929—On May 13 at League Park, the Tribe hosts the Yankees in the first game between two teams who both wear uniforms that have numbers on their backs
1932—First team to hire a former player (Jack Graney) to broadcast its games
1936—Only year between 1929 and 1941 that the club fails to finish in the first division and even at that has 80–74 record, one of the best ever by a second-division team
1940—Team is called the "Cry Babies" after an unsuccessful attempt to oust unpopular manager Ossie Vitt and loses the pennant to Detroit by a one-game margin

HITTING		PITCHING	
Batting Ave.	.388, Tris Speaker, 1920	Wins	31, Jim Bagby, 1920
Slugging Ave.	.644, Hal Trosky, 1936	Losses	19, Al Milnar, 1941
Home Runs	42, Hal Trosky, 1936	Innings	343, Bob Feller, 1941
RBIs	162, Hal Trosky, 1936	Games Started	44, George Uhle, 1923
Total Bases	405, Hal Trosky, 1936	Complete Games	32, George Uhle, 1926
Hits	232, Earl Averill, 1936	Strikeouts	261, Bob Feller, 1940
Runs	140, Earl Averill, 1931	Bases on Balls	208, Bob Feller, 1938
Doubles	64, George Burns, 1926	Winning Pct.	.938, Johnny Allen, 1937
Triples	20, Joe Vosmik, 1935 20, Jeff Heath, 1941	ERA	2.49, Stan Coveleski, 1920*
Bases on Balls	99, Earl Averill, 1934	Saves	7, Willis Hudlin, 1928
Stolen Bases	23, Lyn Lary, 1938	Shutouts	6, Orel Hildebrand, 1933
			6, Mel Harder, 1934
			6, Bob Feller, 1941

*Monte Pearson in 1933 led the AL with a 2.33 ERA but pitched just 135 innings.

It's nice to think that if the Indians had been in the NL during this period—or anyway not in the same circuit as the Yankees—they surely would have won several more pennants. But that probably isn't true. The Senators, Tigers and A's all put together mini-dynasties at junctures when the Yankees were in transition, so why didn't Cleveland? Well, for some of the same basic reasons probably that the Tribe continually fell short during the preceding era, only no one's ever quite been able to put his finger on what they are.

DETROIT TIGERS

Pennants: 1934, 1935, 1940
Manager: Ty Cobb, 1921–26
Park: Navin Field; renamed Briggs Stadium after team owner Frank Navin died in 1935 and the Briggs family assumed control of the club
Best Year: 1934 (101–53, .656)
Worst Year: 1931 (61–93, .396)
Top Rookie: Three-way tie among Hank Greenberg, 1933, Rudy York, 1937, and Barney McCosky, 1939
Biggest Disappointment: Al Wingo, 1926
Best Deal: Grabbing Mickey Cochrane from the A's, 1934
Worst Deal: Waiving Dixie Walker to Brooklyn, 1939
Other:

1921—AL record .316 team BA but manage to finish only 6th, eleven games under .500

1923—Team hits .300 or better for third year in a row

1924—Compile 86 wins, the most in any season between 1917 and 1933

1929—Release Harry Heilmann on waivers after he hits .344

1934—First pennant since 1909; three infield regulars play all 154 games, first baseman Hank Greenberg plays 153 games

1935—First World Championship team; set new ML record with .978 FA

1937—Top ML team BA of .292

1939—Set AL record (since tied) for the highest winning percentage by a second-division team (.526) when they finish 5th with 81 wins and just 73 losses

1940—Win flag by one game; top majors in runs and BA

HITTING		PITCHING	
Batting Ave.	.403, Harry Heilmann, 1923	Wins	24, Schoolboy Rowe, 1934
Slugging Ave.	.683, Hank Greenberg, 1938	Losses	21, Hooks Dauss, 1920
Home Runs	58, Hank Greenberg, 1938	Innings	316, Hooks Dauss, 1923
RBIs	183, Hank Greenberg, 1937	Games Started	39, Hooks Dauss, 1923
Total Bases	397, Hank Greenberg, 1937	Complete Games	26, Tommy Bridges, 1936
Hits	237, Harry Heilmann, 1921	Strikeouts	175, Tommy Bridges, 1936
			175, Bobo Newsom, 1940
Runs	144, Charlie Gehringer, 1930, 1936	Bases on Balls	137, Hal Newhouser, 1941
	144, Hank Greenberg, 1938		
Doubles	63, Hank Greenberg, 1934	Winning Pct.	.842, Schoolboy Rowe, 1940
Triples	19, Charlie Gehringer, 1929	ERA	2.83, Bobo Newsom, 1940
	19, Roy Johnson, 1931		
	19, Barney McCosky, 1940		
Bases on Balls	119, Hank Greenberg, 1938	Saves	17, Al Benton, 1940
Stolen Bases	33, Roy Johnson, 1931	Shutouts	6, Schoolboy Rowe, 1935

How can the Indians be ranked ahead of the Tigers here? For one thing, they had five more first-division finishes, and moreover Detroit had several very lean years in the twenties. Hitting was never the problem, but Dauss didn't assemble all those stamina records because he was on a roll. After he left, the Tigers for a long while consistently had one of the poorest team ERAs in the AL.

WASHINGTON SENATORS

Pennants: 1924, 1925, 1933
Manager: Bucky Harris, 1924–28, 1935–41
Park: Griffith Stadium
Best Year: 1933 (99–53, .651)
Worst Year: 1940 (64–90, .416)
Top Rookie: Monte Weaver, 1932
Biggest Disappointment: Roger Peckinpaugh, 1926; after being the AL MVP in 1925, he was never again a regular player.
Best Deal: Reobtaining Buddy Myer from the Red Sox in 1929
Worst Deal: Sending Bobo Newsom and Ben Chapman to the Red Sox, 1937
Other:

1920—Team generates some offense for a change, hitting .291 and scoring 723 runs, but worst staff ERA in the AL (4.17) spells a 6th-place finish

1924—First flag won by a Washington team in any major league

1926—Top the majors with a .292 team BA

1930—In the greatest hitting and scoring year in the twentieth century, are the only ML team with a staff ERA below 4.00 (3.96)

1932—Last ML team to make 100 or more triples in a season

1933—Last flag won by a Washington ML team; shortstop Joe Cronin finishes second in MVP balloting, the highest finish by a Washington player since 1931, when baseball writers began doing the voting

1934—Plummet from 99 wins in 1933 to just 66 and finish 7th, one of the biggest drops in history by a pennant winner

1936—Last first-division finish until 1943

1941—Shortstop Cecil Travis hits .359, second in the ML only to Ted Williams, who bats .406

HITTING		PITCHING	
Batting Ave.	.379, Goose Goslin, 1923	Wins	26, General Crowder, 1932
Slugging Ave.	.614, Goose Goslin, 1928	Losses	19, Ken Chase, 1939 19, Dutch Leonard, 1940
Home Runs	22, Zeke Bonura, 1938	Innings	327, General Crowder, 1932
RBIs	129, Goose Goslin, 1924	Games Started	39, General Crowder, 1932
Total Bases	329, Goose Goslin, 1925	Complete Games	25, Walter Johnson, 1921
Hits	227, Sam Rice, 1925	Strikeouts	162, Bump Hadley, 1930
Runs	127, Joe Cronin, 1930	Bases on Balls	146, Bobo Newsom, 1936
Doubles	45, Joe Cronin, 1933	Winning Pct.	.800, Stan Coveleski, 1925 .800, Earl Whitehill, 1933
Triples	20, Goose Goslin, 1925	ERA	2.51, Garland Braxton, 1928
Bases on Balls	102, Buddy Myer, 1934	Saves	22, Firpo Marberry, 1926
Stolen Bases	63, Sam Rice, 1920	Shutouts	6, Walter Johnson, 1924

The only time in history when it must have been fun, by and large, to be a follower of a Washington major league baseball team. Many of the batting records here, although modest in comparison to the ones players on other teams were setting during this period, are all-time Senators' marks. The club, after winning three pennants in a ten-season span, started to slide in the mid-thirties and contended seriously only one more time, in 1945, before abandoning Washington.

PHILADELPHIA ATHLETICS

Pennants: 1929, 1930, 1931
Manager: Connie Mack, 1920–41
Park: Shibe Park
Best Year: 1931 (107–45, .704)
Worst Year: 1920 (48–106, .312)
Top Rookie: Mickey Cochrane, 1925
Biggest Disappointment: Benny McCoy, 1940–41
Best Deal: The relationship Connie Mack established with Baltimore owner–manager Jack Dunn, which enabled the A's to purchase most of the minor league Orioles' great players in the mid-twenties.
Worst Deal: The manner in which Connie Mack dismantled his 1929–31 dynasty
Other:
  1920—Receive AL-record low 356 walks
  1921—Finish last for the AL-record seventh consecutive year
  1922—A's end all-time ML-record skein of 35 consecutive losing months when they have their first winning month since 1915
  1925—Gain 2nd place for best finish since 1914
  1927—A's hitters fan only 326 times all year, an AL record low
  1929—Win first flag since 1914 by 18 games; top majors in both FA and ERA
  1931—Franchise record .704 winning percentage
  1933—Come in 3rd, last time the club finishes that high under Connie Mack
  1936—Harry Kelley has a 15–12 record; rest of pitching staff is 38–88
  1941—Team finishes era in same spot where it began it—last place

HITTING		**PITCHING**	
Batting Ave.	.392, Al Simmons, 1927	Wins	31, Lefty Grove, 1931
Slugging Ave.	.749, Jimmie Foxx, 1932	Losses	25, Scott Perry, 1920
Home Runs	58, Jimmie Foxx, 1932	Innings	298, Eddie Rommel, 1923
RBIs	169, Jimmie Foxx, 1932	Games Started	40, George Caster, 1938
Total Bases	438, Jimmie Foxx, 1932	Complete Games	27, Lefty Grove, 1931, 1932
Hits	253, Al Simmons, 1925	Strikeouts	209, Lefty Grove, 1930
Runs	152, Al Simmons, 1930	Bases on Balls	139, George Earnshaw, 1930
Doubles	53, Al Simmons, 1926	Winning Pct.	.886, Lefty Grove, 1931
Triples	16, Bing Miller, 1929 16, Al Simmons, 1930	ERA	2.06, Lefty Grove, 1931
Bases on Balls	128, Max Bishop, 1929, 1930	Saves	9, Lefty Grove, 1927, 1930
Stolen Bases	35, Billy Werber, 1937	Shutouts	4, done by four different pitchers

For the ten years between 1925 and 1934 the A's were only a shade below the Yankees in the aggregate standings. During the other twelve seasons in the period they were generally the AL's worst team. That averages out to fifth place overall, and then only because none of the teams below them managed to capture a single pennant between 1920 and 1941, let alone three. I'll refrain from saying any more about what I think of Connie Mack as a manager and leave the chart to speak for what I think of Grove as a pitcher.

CHICAGO WHITE SOX

Pennants: None
Manager: Jimmy Dykes, 1934–41
Park: Comiskey Park
Best Year: 1920 (96–58, .623)
Worst Year: 1932 (49–102, .325)
Top Rookie: Earl Sheely, Bibb Falk and Johnny Mostil joined the club in 1921; all of them had good rookie seasons and remained good players for several seasons, but none was nearly good enough to help the club out of the hole into which it had been dumped by the Black Sox Scandal
Biggest Disappointment: Pat Caraway, 1931
Best Deal: Forking over around $100,000 to the A's in 1933 for Al Simmons, Jimmy Dykes and Mule Haas
Worst Deal: Giving Willie Kamm to Cleveland for Lew Fonseca, 1931
Other:

1920—Set twentieth-century record for a team playing a 154-game schedule by having four 20-game winners; also a record for the most 20-game winners by a team that failed to win a pennant

1922—In an effort to shed his miserly image, owner Charlie Comiskey shells out $125,000 for minor league third baseman Willie Kamm, a record purchase at the time

1926—Team finishes above .500 for the last time until 1936

1932—Set AL record for the lowest winning percentage by a 7th-place team (.325)

1938—Team's most promising young pitcher, Monte Stratton, loses a leg in an off-season hunting accident

1940—4th-place finish marks the first time since 1920 that team has finished in the first division two years in a row

1941—Staff notches 106 complete games to make the Sox the last ML team to collect 100 or more CGs

HITTING		PITCHING	
Batting Ave.	.388, Luke Appling, 1936	Wins	25, Red Faber, 1921
Slugging Ave.	.589, Joe Jackson, 1920	Losses	24, Pat Caraway, 1931
Home Runs	27, Zeke Bonura, 1934 27, Joe Kuhel, 1940	Innings	353, Red Faber, 1922
RBIs	138, Zeke Bonura, 1936	Games Started	39, Red Faber, 1920, 1921
Total Bases	336, Joe Jackson, 1920	Complete Games	32, Red Faber, 1921
Hits	222, Eddie Collins, 1920	Strikeouts	148, Red Faber, 1922
Runs	135, Johnny Mostil, 1925	Bases on Balls	147, Vern Kennedy, 1936
Doubles	43, Earl Sheely, 1925 43, Bibb Falk, 1926	Winning Pct.	.750, Monte Stratton, 1937
Triples	20, Joe Jackson, 1920	ERA	2.37, Thornton Lee, 1941
Bases on Balls	127, Lu Blue, 1931	Saves	18, Clint Brown, 1937, 1939
Stolen Bases	47, Eddie Collins, 1923	Shutouts	5, Ted Lyons, 1925 5, Monte Stratton, 1937

What team had five Hall of Fame players and three Hall of Famers who served as its manager at various times during the season and yet finished in last place? Right, the White Sox, but I'll let you figure out for yourself what year it happened. It's quite a comment on the quality of this club after 1922 that one of the Hall of Famers, Lyons, appears only once on the chart despite being one of the AL's better pitchers during most of the era. That Appling also appears just once on it is a comment too, but more on the type of hitter he was.

ST. LOUIS BROWNS

Pennants: None

Manager: Rogers Hornsby, 1933–37

Park: Sportsman's Park; began sharing it with the Cardinals in 1920

Best Year: 1922 (93–61, .604)

Worst Year: 1939 (43–111, .279)

Top Rookie: Harlond Clift, 1934

Biggest Disappointment: Tie between Ray Kolp and Dixie Davis, 1923; a combined 25–10 in 1922, they finished a combined 9–18 the following year, helping the club slide to fifth place

Best Deal: Acquiring Bobo Newsom from Boston, 1938; buying George McQuinn from the Yankees that year rates a close second

Worst Deal: Giving the Senators General Crowder and Heinie Manush for Goose Goslin, 1930; Goslin for Manush would have been about an even deal but the addition of Crowder made it a heist

Other:

1920—Top majors with .308 BA but finish below .500

1921—First team in ML history with three players who have 200 or more hits

1922—Finish 2nd, one game behind Yankees, with 93 wins, most ever by the team while it's based in St. Louis; become first team in history to have four players who have 100 or more RBIs

1928—3rd-place finish is the last time until 1942 that the club will finish that high

1930—5.07 staff ERA is worst in AL

1933—First basement finish since 1913

1935—Staff ERA of 6.24 is the worst in AL history

1939—Lose franchise record 111 games and set AL record for poorest home performance (18–59); come in last, AL record 64½ games out of 1st

1941—Win 70 games, the most since 1929

HITTING		PITCHING	
Batting Ave.	.420, George Sisler, 1920	Wins	27, Urban Shocker, 1922
Slugging Ave.	.632, George Sisler, 1920	Losses	24, Sam Gray, 1931
Home Runs	39, Ken Williams, 1922	Innings	348, Urban Shocker, 1922
RBIs	155, Ken Williams, 1922	Games Started	40, Bobo Newsom, 1938
Total Bases	399, George Sisler, 1920	Complete Games	31, Urban Shocker, 1921
			31, Bobo Newsom, 1938
Hits	257, George Sisler, 1920	Strikeouts	226, Bobo Newsom, 1938
Runs	145, Harlond Clift, 1936	Bases on Balls	192, Bobo Newsom, 1938
Doubles	51, Beau Bell, 1937	Winning Pct.	.808, General Crowder, 1928
Triples	20, Heinie Manush, 1928	ERA	2.71, Urban Shocker, 1920
Bases on Balls	126, Lu Blue, 1929	Saves	7, Hub Pruett, 1922
			7, Chad Kimsey, 1931
			7, Jack Knott, 1935
Stolen Bases	51, George Sisler, 1922	Shutouts	5, Urban Shocker, 1920

Ever wonder what would have happened if the Browns had won the pennant in 1922, making them, and not the Cardinals, the first St. Louis team to go over the top in this century? The Browns were a pretty good team all during the twenties, but after their Sportsman's Park co-tenants won a few flags, they began to give the appearance of an outfit that had thrown in the towel, an impression that not even Bill Veeck or the 1944 dream season could alter appreciably.

BOSTON RED SOX

Pennants: None
Manager: Joe Cronin, 1935–41
Park: Fenway Park
Best Year: 1938 (88–61, .591)
Worst Year: 1932 (43–111, .279)
Top Rookie: Ted Williams, 1939
Biggest Disappointment: Ed Morris, 1930–31; supposedly on the comeback trail that would have returned him to his 1928–29 form, he was murdered during spring training in 1932
Best Deal: Almost every trade the club made after Tom Yawkey took over the team was a good one, with the two most pivotal probably being getting Jimmie Foxx from the A's and Joe Cronin from the Senators
Worst Deal: Almost every trade the club made between 1920 and 1933 was a disaster, starting with the sale of Babe Ruth to the Yankees prior to the 1920 season
Other:
1921—Club finishes 5th, the last time until 1934 that it will come in that high
1928—Ed Morris and Jack Russell have combined 30–29 record; other pitchers are a combined 27–67
1929—Score fewest runs in majors (605) and hit fewest homers (28)
1931—Finish 6th to escape the cellar for the first time since 1924
1932—Set franchise record by losing 111 games; first last-place team in AL history to have the loop batting leader, Dale Alexander
1933—Tom Yawkey buys the team
1934—4th-place finish is the club's highest since 1918
1937—Finish 9½ games out of 1st, the closest that any AL team comes to the Yankees between 1936 and 1939
1940—Become the first team in ML history to go three years in a row without having a pitcher who works at least 200 innings
1941—Rookie Dick Newsome becomes the club's first pitcher since 1937 to hurl 200 or more innings in a season

HITTING		**PITCHING**	
Batting Ave.	.406, Ted Williams, 1941	Wins	25, Wes Ferrell, 1935
Slugging Ave.	.735, Ted Williams, 1941	Losses	25, Red Ruffing, 1928
Home Runs	50, Jimmie Foxx, 1938	Innings	322, Wes Ferrell, 1935
RBIs	175, Jimmie Foxx, 1938	Games Started	39, Howard Ehmke, 1923
Total Bases	398, Jimmie Foxx, 1938	Complete Games	31, Wes Ferrell, 1935
Hits	201, Joe Vosmik, 1938	Strikeouts	153, Lefty Grove, 1937
Runs	139, Jimmie Foxx, 1938	Bases on Balls	119, done by four different pitchers
Doubles	67, Earl Webb, 1931	Winning Pct.	.789, Lefty Grove, 1937
Triples	17, Harry Hooper, 1920	ERA	2.54, Lefty Grove, 1939
	17, Russ Scarritt, 1929		
Bases on Balls	145, Ted Williams, 1941	Saves	10, Wilcy Moore, 1931
Stolen Bases	40, Billy Werber, 1934	Shutouts	6, Lefty Grove, 1936

If your picture of the Red Sox during this era is of the team that vainly chased the Yankees in the late thirties, you'll be certain I made a dreadful miscalculation in determining the aggregate standings. The Red Sox were worse even than the Browns? For sure, and there was a long stretch of years when they were worse even than the Phillies or the Braves. In 1930, for instance, while every other AL team had at least one hitter who knocked in over 110 runs, Webb led the Red Sox with just 66 RBIs.

NATIONAL LEAGUE COMPOSITE STANDINGS

Number of Years Finishing in Each Position

Team	1	2	3	4	5	6	7	8	Aggregate
New York	7	5	5	0	3	2	0	0	1
St. Louis	5	5	3	3	3	3	0	0	2
Pittsburgh	2	5	5	6	3	1	0	0	3
Chicago	4	3	4	4	4	1	1	1	4
Brooklyn	2	2	2	2	2	10	2	0	5
Cincinnati	2	3	3	2	3	2	2	5	6
Boston	0	0	0	3	4	2	9	4	7
Philadelphia	0	0	0	1	1	2	6	12	8

NEW YORK GIANTS

Pennants: 1921, 1922, 1923, 1924, 1933, 1936, 1937
Manager: John McGraw, 1920–32
Park: Polo Grounds
Best Year: 1937 (95–57, .625)
Worst Year: 1932 (72–82, .468)
Top Rookie: Cliff Melton, 1937
Biggest Disappointment: Jack Bentley, 1925
Best Deal: Obtaining Irish Meusel from the Phillies, 1921
Worst Deal: Giving up Frankie Frisch for Rogers Hornsby, 1927; McGraw should have known he'd never be able to get along with Hornsby and wind up having to get rid of him too
Other:

1921—First NL team with three players who collect 100 or more RBIs

1922—First NL team to win a pennant without having a 20-game winner; last NL team to win back-to-back World Championships prior to 1975–76 Reds

1924—Win NL-record fourth straight flag, last three without a 20-game winner; outfielder Jimmy O'Connell banned for his part in a bribe offer to a Phillies player, the last active player to be barred for life from the game

1929—First ML team to use a public address system in its home park

1930—Team BA of .319 sets twentieth-century ML record

1932—Bill Terry replaces McGraw as manager, first managerial change by the club since 1902; team outscores its opponents 755–706 but finishes 6th with a 72–82 record

1934—Allow fewest runs in majors (583) and have best staff ERA in majors by a full half run but finish two games off the pace after dropping two straight games to the Dodgers on the closing weekend of the season

1937—Club wins 90 or more games for the fifth straight year and is the last in franchise history to claim back-to-back pennants

1940—Outscore opponents 663–659 but finish 6th, eight games below .500

HITTING		**PITCHING**	
Batting Ave.	.401, Bill Terry, 1930	Wins	26, Carl Hubbell, 1936
Slugging Ave.	.635, Mel Ott, 1929	Losses	17, Larry Benton, 1929
Home Runs	42, Mel Ott, 1929	Innings	313, Carl Hubbell, 1934
RBIs	151, Mel Ott, 1929	Games Started	37, Fred Toney, 1920 37, Fred Fitzsimmons, 1934
Total Bases	392, Bill Terry, 1930	Complete Games	28, Larry Benton, 1928
Hits	254, Bill Terry, 1930	Strikeouts	159, Carl Hubbell, 1937
Runs	139, Bill Terry, 1930	Bases on Balls	97, Roy Parmelee, 1935
Doubles	43, Bill Terry, 1931	Winning Pct.	.813, Carl Hubbell, 1936
Triples	20, Bill Terry, 1931	ERA	1.66, Carl Hubbell, 1933
Bases on Balls	118, Mel Ott, 1938	Saves	12, Dick Coffman, 1938
Stolen Bases	49, Frankie Frisch, 1921	Shutouts	10, Carl Hubbell, 1933

Terry set many all-time club records in 1930 and 1931, including the most doubles in a season. The total, which is quite low for an all-time record holder, tells you something about the Polo Grounds, the park in which the Giants played. Hits that in other places went for two bases often grew into inside-the-park home runs there. The pitching chart indicates that no Giants hurler during the period could complain of being overworked. Hubbell may be the only Hall of Famer from this era who never started more than 35 games in a season. Significantly, too, no members of the Giants pitching staff during their 1921–24 pennant string appear on the chart.

ST. LOUIS CARDINALS

Pennants: 1926, 1928, 1930, 1931, 1934
Manager: Frankie Frisch, 1933–38
Park: Robison Field, 1920
  Sportsman's Park, 1920–41; the Cards played their last game
  at Robison Field on June 6, 1920, beating the Cubs, 5–2, and
  then began using Sportsman's Park as tenants of the Browns;
  in their first game at Sportsman's, on July 1, 1920, they lost
  6–2 to the Pirates in ten innings
Best Year: 1931 (101–53, .656)
Worst Year: 1924 (65–89, .422)
Top Rookie: Johnny Mize, 1936
Biggest Disappointment: The Dean brothers; they won 49 games
  between them in 1934, 43 games between them in 1935, 29
  games between them in 1936, and then won only 16 more
  games between them for the club
Best Deal: Getting Bob O'Farrell from the Cubs, 1925; the following year he was the NL MVP
Worst Deal: Trading Jack Fournier to Brooklyn, 1923
Other:
  1921—Three Cardinals, Rogers Hornsby, Austin McHenry and
    Jack Fournier, finish 1–2–3 in the NL batting race
  1922—Austin McHenry dies of a brain tumor
  1926—First NL pennant by a St. Louis team; first pennant of
    the century by either St. Louis ML team
  1930—All eight regulars hit .300 or better; score twentieth-
    century NL-record 1004 runs; collect ML-record 373 doubles
  1933—Cards set post-1901 ML record for the highest winning
    percentage by a second-division team (.536) when they finish
    5th despite winning 82 games and losing only 71
  1934—Despite having a World Championship team, the club
    draws only 350,000 fans all year
  1939—Lead the majors with a .294 team BA
  1941—The Cooper brothers, the NL's most successful brother
    battery in this century, play together for the first of four
    straight seasons

HITTING		PITCHING	
Batting Ave.	.424, Rogers Hornsby, 1924	Wins	30, Dizzy Dean, 1934
Slugging Ave.	.756, Rogers Hornsby, 1925	Losses	20, Jesse Haines, 1920
Home Runs	43, Johnny Mize, 1940	Innings	324, Dizzy Dean, 1935
RBIs	154, Ducky Medwick, 1937	Games Started	37, Bill Doak, 1920 / 37, Jesse Haines, 1920 / 37, Ferdie Schupp, 1920
Total Bases	450, Rogers Hornsby, 1922	Complete Games	29, Dizzy Dean, 1935
Hits	250, Rogers Hornsby, 1922	Strikeouts	199, Dizzy Dean, 1933
Runs	141, Rogers Hornsby, 1922	Bases on Balls	127, Ferdie Schupp, 1920
Doubles	64, Ducky Medwick, 1936	Winning Pct.	.811, Dizzy Dean, 1934
Triples	20, Rogers Hornsby, 1920 / 20, Jim Bottomley, 1928	ERA	2.40, Ernie White, 1941
Bases on Balls	92, Johnny Mize, 1939	Saves	11, Dizzy Dean, 1936
Stolen Bases	48, Frankie Frisch, 1927	Shutouts	7, Dizzy Dean, 1934

Ernie who? Bet you were as surprised as I was by that one. The chart demonstrates why Dean isn't the record holder in complete games—he was used an awful lot in relief. By the time you finish thumbing through all the NL charts in this section, it ought to be firmly established in your mind who the greatest right-handed batter in history was. P.S. White was really a pretty good pitcher before his arm started troubling him.

PITTSBURGH PIRATES

Pennants: 1925, 1927
Manager: Pie Traynor, 1934–39
Park: Forbes Field
Best Year: 1925 (95–58, .621)
Worst Year: 1939 (68–85, .444)
Top Rookie: Paul Waner, 1926
Biggest Disappointment: Adam Comorosky, 1931
Best Deal: Obtaining Remy Kremer from Oakland of the Pacific Coast League, 1924; though 31 at the time, Kremer won 143 games for the club over the next decade
Worst Deal: Making the Cubs a gift of Kiki Cuyler, 1928
Other:

1925—First team to come back to win a World Series after being behind 3 games to 1

1927—Waner brothers have finest season in history by two brothers on the same team

1928—Team BA of .309 leads the majors by 13 points

1930—Last NL team to collect 100 or more triples in a season

1932—Owner Barney Dreyfuss dies and his widow takes control of the team; Pirates finish 2nd with 86–68 record, only four games out of 1st, despite being outscored 711–701

1934—Become the last ML team to play a home game on Sunday

1938—Lose pennant to Cubs after having a seemingly insurmountable lead; pivotal contest of the year is decided by Gabby Hartnett's "Homer in the Gloamin' "

1940—Pitching staff achieves only 49 complete games, a new NL-record low

1941—Pirates pitchers compile the fewest strikeouts in NL and team's fielders post the loop's worst FA but club nevertheless finishes a solid 4th

HITTING		**PITCHING**	
Batting Ave.	.385, Arky Vaughan, 1937	Wins	25, Johnny Morrison, 1923
			25, Burleigh Grimes, 1928
Slugging Ave.	.593, Kiki Cuyler, 1925	Losses	19, Wilbur Cooper, 1923
Home Runs	23, Johnny Rizzo, 1938	Innings	331, Burleigh Grimes, 1928
RBIs	131, Paul Waner, 1927	Games Started	38, Wilbur Cooper, 1921, 1923
			38, Lee Meadows, 1927
			38, Remy Kremer, 1930
Total Bases	366, Kiki Cuyler, 1925	Complete Games	29, Wilbur Cooper, 1921
Hits	237, Paul Waner, 1927	Strikeouts	143, Cy Blanton, 1937
Runs	144, Kiki Cuyler, 1925	Bases on Balls	110, Johnny Morrison, 1923
Doubles	62, Paul Waner, 1932	Winning Pct.	.789, Red Lucas, 1936
Triples	26, Kiki Cuyler, 1925	ERA	2.16, Babe Adams, 1920
Bases on Balls	119, Elbie Fletcher, 1940	Saves	7, Mace Brown, 1937, 1939, 1940
Stolen Bases	52, Max Carey, 1920	Shutouts	8, Babe Adams, 1920

The Pirates are the only team that established no club batting marks for the period during the 1929–31 hitters' feast. Cooper's bad luck exceeded that of even Vic Willis's. By the time the Pirates were back in contention, after years in the doldrums, Cooper was gone. Now you know, if you already didn't, who held the club home run record before Kiner came along. You probably didn't know, though, that Cuyler in 1925 had the best season of any Pirates player during the period.

CHICAGO CUBS

Pennants: 1929, 1932, 1935, 1938
Manager: Charlie Grimm, 1932–38
Park: Wrigley Field
Best Year: 1935 (100–54, .649)
Worst Year: 1921 (64–89, .418)
Top Rookie: Hack Miller, 1922
Biggest Disappointment: Chuck Klein, 1934–35
Best Deal: Getting Kiki Cuyler from Pittsburgh, 1928, for Sparky Adams and Pete Scott
Worst Deal: Giving the Cardinals three capable players and $185,000 for Dizzy Dean, 1938
Other:
1921—William Wrigley buys the team
1925—First cellar finish in franchise's 49-year existence
1928—Stay in race all season before finishing 3rd, just four games out; have best FA in majors (.975) and tie A's for fewest runs allowed (615)
1930—NL record .481 SA as Hack Wilson hits an NL-record 56 home runs, collects an all-time record 190 RBIs, and joins with Kiki Cuyler, who has 134 RBIs, to set an NL record for the most RBIs (324) by two teammates
1932—Staff ERA of 3.44 is the best in the majors
1935—Break open a close pennant race by setting ML record for the most consecutive games won (21) without a tie or a loss; become the first team to allow all its games to be broadcast
1938—Team FA of .978 is a new NL record
1941—Pattern of winning a pennant every three years, which began in 1929, is broken as team finishes 6th

HITTING		PITCHING	
Batting Ave.	.380, Rogers Hornsby, 1929	Wins	27, Pete Alexander, 1920
Slugging Ave.	.723, Hack Wilson, 1930	Losses	19, Larry French, 1938
Home Runs	56, Hack Wilson, 1930	Innings	363, Pete Alexander, 1920
RBIs	190, Hack Wilson, 1930	Games Started	40, Pete Alexander, 1920
Total Bases	423, Hack Wilson, 1930	Complete Games	33, Pete Alexander, 1920
Hits	229, Rogers Hornsby, 1929	Strikeouts	173, Pete Alexander, 1920
Runs	156, Rogers Hornsby, 1929	Bases on Balls	130, Sheriff Blake, 1929
Doubles	57, Billy Herman, 1935, 1936	Winning Pct.	.786, Lon Warneke, 1932
Triples	18, Billy Herman, 1939	ERA	1.91, Pete Alexander, 1920
Bases on Balls	105, Hack Wilson, 1930	Saves	8, Guy Bush, 1929 8, Charlie Root, 1938
Stolen Bases	43, Kiki Cuyler, 1929 43, George Grantham, 1923	Shutouts	9, Bill Lee, 1938

French is the only pitcher to set a club loss record for the period while playing on a pennant winner. The Cubs' best all-around player during this era is by no means an easy choice, but Billy Herman should be high on everyone's list. Picking the best pitcher is just as tough, although I can make the strongest argument for Root. Riggs Stephenson was unable to crack the chart but set a twentieth-century club record for the highest career batting average among players active five or more seasons in a Cubs uniform.

BROOKLYN DODGERS

Pennants: 1920, 1941
Manager: Wilbert Robinson, 1920–31
Park: Ebbets Field
Best Year: 1941 (100–54, .649)
Worst Year: 1937 (62–91, .405)
Top Rookie: Johnny Frederick, 1929
Biggest Disappointment: Ducky Medwick, 1940
Best Deal: Robbing the Phillies of Dolph Camilli, 1938
Worst Deal: Handing the Reds Ernie Lombardi, 1932
Other:

1920—Staff ERA of 2.62 is best in the majors; win pennant by seven-game margin

1924—Finish 2nd, only 1½ games out, with the top pitching tandem in the majors, Dazzy Vance and Burleigh Grimes; between them Vance and Grimes are 50–19, while the rest of the pitching staff is 42–43

1925—Owner Charlie Ebbets dies

1927—Score fewest runs in majors (541) and finish 6th despite 3.36 staff ERA, the best in NL

1928—Lead the majors with a 3.25 staff ERA but can finish no better than 6th

1930—Top majors with 13 shutouts and NL with 4.03 ERA

1932—Wilbert Robinson is replaced by Max Carey, the club's first managerial change since 1914; after being called the Robins during much of Robinson's tenure, Brooklyn again becomes the Dodgers

1935—Outfielder Len Koenecke is killed in a mid-air fight with the pilot of the plane he's chartered

1938—Larry McPhail is hired as general manager; club becomes the second in the majors to install lights in its home park

1941—Win pennant after a twenty-one-year drought, longest flagless spell in franchise's history; become the first team to wear plastic helmets after several key players are idled by beanings

HITTING		PITCHING	
Batting Ave.	.393, Babe Herman, 1930	Wins	28, Dazzy Vance, 1924
Slugging Ave.	.678, Babe Herman, 1930	Losses	19, Burleigh Grimes, 1925
			19, Watty Clark, 1929
			19, Van Lingle Mungo, 1936
Home Runs	35, Babe Herman, 1930	Innings	327, Burleigh Grimes, 1923
RBIs	130, Jack Fournier, 1925	Games Started	39, Kirby Higbe, 1941
	130, Babe Herman, 1930		
Total Bases	416, Babe Herman, 1930	Complete Games	33, Burleigh Grimes, 1923
Hits	241, Babe Herman, 1930	Strikeouts	262, Dazzy Vance, 1924
Runs	143, Babe Herman, 1930	Bases on Balls	132, Kirby Higbe, 1941
Doubles	52, Johnny Frederick, 1929	Winning Pct.	.889, Fred Fitzsimmons, 1940
Triples	22, Hy Myers, 1920	ERA	2.09, Dazzy Vance, 1928
Bases on Balls	119, Dolph Camilli, 1938	Saves	15, Jack Quinn, 1931
Stolen Bases	32, Max Carey, 1927	Shutouts	7, Whitlow Wyatt, 1941

Vance would probably average between 300 and 350 strikeouts a season if he were pitching now. Herman, on the other hand, would probably bat around .285. The Dodgers won the first and last pennants in the NL during this era and were saved from oblivion for most of the seasons in between by the presence of the three teams who finished below them in the aggregate standings—and especially by the Braves and Phillies. Bill Terry wasn't completely around the bend when he asked if Brooklyn was still in the league.

CINCINNATI REDS

Pennants: 1939, 1940
Manager: Jack Hendricks, 1924–29
Park: Crosley Field (name changed from Redlands Field after Powell Crosley bought the club)
Best Year: 1940 (100–53, .654)
Worst Year: 1934 (52–99, .344)
Top Rookie: Sammy Bohne, 1921
Biggest Disappointment: Ernie Lombardi and Frank McCormick, 1941; poor years by the two former MVPs probably cost the team, which had the best pitching and defense in the NL that year, a third consecutive flag
Best Deal: Snaring Ernie Lombardi from Brooklyn, 1932
Worst Deal: Sending Hughie Critz to the Giants for Larry Benton, 1930; Critz still had several years of good ball left in him, while Benton was never much help to the Reds
Other:
1923—Staff 3.21 ERA tops the majors by nearly half a run
1924—Manager Pat Moran dies in spring training of Bright's Disease; first baseman Jake Daubert dies after the season's over following routine surgery
1928—Sidney Weil buys the team
1930—Team scores the fewest runs in the NL (665) and ties for the lowest BA (.281)
1931—First cellar finish since 1901
1933—Finish last despite setting NL record for fewest walks allowed per game (1.72) by pitchers
1934—Powell Crosley buys the bankrupt club, which finishes last for the fourth straight year
1935—Team becomes the first in the majors to introduce night baseball
1938—Rise from last place to 4th in first year under manager Bill McKechnie
1940—Win pennant by 12 games, the largest margin of victory in the NL since 1931

HITTING		PITCHING	
Batting Ave.	.353, Bubbles Hargrave, 1926	Wins	27, Dolf Luque, 1923 27, Bucky Walters, 1939
Slugging Ave.	.577, Harry Heilmann, 1930	Losses	25, Paul Derringer, 1933
Home Runs	30, Ival Goodman, 1938	Innings	322, Dolf Luque, 1923
RBIs	128, Frank McCormick, 1939	Games Started	38, Eppa Rixey, 1922 38, Pete Donohue, 1925, 1926
Total Bases	312, Frank McCormick, 1939	Complete Games	31, Bucky Walters, 1939
Hits	209, Frank McCormick, 1938, 1939	Strikeouts	202, Johnny Vander Meer, 1941
Runs	115, Billy Werber, 1939	Bases on Balls	126, Johnny Vander Meer, 1941
Doubles	45, George Kelly, 1929	Winning Pct.	.826, Elmer Riddle, 1941
Triples	22, Jake Daubert, 1922	ERA	1.93, Dolf Luque, 1923
Bases on Balls	101, George Burns, 1923	Saves	9, Don Brennan, 1936
Stolen Bases	36, Edd Roush, 1920	Shutouts	6, Dolf Luque, 1923 6, Johnny Vander Meer, 1941

No, it wasn't Goodman who broke Sam Crawford's club home run record; it was someone on this chart, though, who was once a teammate of Crawford's. For those who feel Hargrave's bat title is tainted since he had only 326 at bats, you might prefer to consider Roush's .352 batting average in 1921 the true club high for the period. In any event, the Reds had precious few hitters of consequence between Roush's departure and McCormick's arrival. In 1930, while most other teams were scoring around 900 runs, Cincinnati tallied just 665 and had the only NL player, Hod Ford, who hit under .250 in 400 or more at bats.

BOSTON BRAVES

Pennants: None
Manager: Bill McKechnie, 1930–37
Park: Braves Field
Best Year: 1933 (83–71, .539)
Worst Year: 1935 (38–115, .248)
Top Rookie: Wally Berger, 1930
Biggest Disappointment: Ben Cantwell, 1935
Best Deal: Obtaining Ben Cantwell, Al Spohrer and two other players from the Giants for Joe Genewich, 1928
Worst Deal: Trading Rogers Hornsby to the Cubs, 1929
Other:

1920—Score fewest runs in the majors (523); avoid cellar finish by just half a game

1923—Christy Mathewson named club president

1924—Team tops the NL in FA and has decent pitching but finishes last when it has .256 BA, 19 points lower than the next worst hitting team, and scores 156 fewer runs than every other NL club

1928—Set NL record for the lowest winning percentage (.327) by a 7th-place team during a season in which a 154-game schedule is played

1930—Rookie star Wally Berger hits 38 home runs, still an NL frosh record; the rest of the team only hits 28 four-baggers as the club finishes last in the league in homers

1935—Club sets twentieth-century NL record for the lowest winning percentage (.248) and ML record for the poorest road performance (13–65); team is last in the NL in runs and SA despite having the league home run and RBI king, Wally Berger; Ben Cantwell has 4–25 pitching record, the poorest in this century by a pitcher in 25 or more decisions

1937—Braves become only team in this century to have two rookie 20-game winners, Lou Fette and Jim Turner

1938—In first year under Casey Stengel club finishes above .500 and is the only team besides the Yankees that Stengel ever manages in the majors to an over-.500 finish

1941—Become known as the Braves again after trying unsuccessfully for five years to change team nickname to the Bees

HITTING		PITCHING	
Batting Ave.	.387, Rogers Hornsby, 1928	Wins	20, done by four pitchers, two of them, Lou Fette and Jim Turner, in 1937
Slugging Ave.	.632, Rogers Hornsby, 1928	Losses	25, Ben Cantwell, 1935
Home Runs	38, Wally Berger, 1930	Innings	299, Joe Oeschger, 1920, 1921
RBIs	130, Wally Berger, 1935	Games Started	36, Joe Oeschger, 1921
Total Bases	341, Wally Berger, 1930	Complete Games	24, Jim Turner, 1937
Hits	206, Lance Richbourg, 1928	Strikeouts	112, Ed Brandt, 1931
Runs	114, Ray Powell, 1921	Bases on Balls	109, Ed Brandt, 1928
Doubles	44, Wally Berger, 1931	Winning Pct.	.667, Ben Cantwell, 1933 .667, Lou Fette, 1937
Triples	18, Ray Powell, 1921	ERA	2.38, Jim Turner, 1937
Bases on Balls	107, Rogers Hornsby, 1928	Saves	8, Bob Smith, 1936
Stolen Bases	24, Lance Richbourg, 1927	Shutouts	6, Lou Fette, 1937

The chart tells the whole story. With the exception of Hornsby and Berger, Richbourg and Powell were about the two best players the Braves had during this period. It's not as if they had overwhelming pitching either. Brandt's record strikeout total is shamefully low, even for the era. If you still question Hornsby's credentials, consider that he once held a *fourth* twentieth-century team batting average record—his .361 mark for the Giants in 1927 stood until Bill Terry broke it two years later.

PHILADELPHIA PHILLIES

Pennants: None
Manager: Burt Shotton, 1928–33
Park: Baker Bowl, 1920–38; Phillies lost the last game ever played in the Baker Bowl, 14–1, to the Giants on June 30, 1938 Shibe Park, 1938–41; the team became tenants of the Athletics officially on July 4, 1938, as it split a holiday doubleheader with the Braves
Best Year: 1932 (78–76, .506)
Worst Year: 1941 (43–111, .279)
Top Rookie: Curt Davis, 1934
Biggest Disappointment: Don Hurst, 1933; after setting the current NL record for the most RBIs by a first baseman (143) in 1932, he dropped to just 76 ribbies and was gone from the majors a year later
Best Deal: Getting Dolph Camilli from the Cubs for Don Hurst, 1934
Worst Deal: Tie between trading Bucky Walters to the Reds, 1938, and trading Dolph Camilli to the Dodgers, 1938
Other:
1920—Team receives twentieth-century ML record low 283 walks
1927—Staff ace Jack Scott becomes the last pitcher in major league history to hurl two complete games in one day
1928—Team has two standout rookies, Pinky Whitney and Chuck Klein, but nevertheless manages to win just 43 games
1929—5th-place finish is club's best since 1917; team has four players who have 200 or more hits each to set ML record
1930—Team has twentieth-century ML-record high 6.71 staff ERA, finishes a bad last despite scoring 944 runs
1932—Team comes in 4th for only first-division finish between 1918 and 1949
1935—Team's 228 errors are the most by far in the ML
1936—Team becomes the last to top 250 errors in a season (252)
1940—Team scores just 494 runs, by far the least in the ML
1941—Pitching staff turns in only 35 complete games, a new ML-record low

HITTING		PITCHING	
Batting Ave.	.398, Lefty O'Doul, 1929	Wins	19, Jumbo Elliott, 1931
			19, Curt Davis, 1934
Slugging Ave.	.687, Chuck Klein, 1930	Losses	22, Eppa Rixey, 1920
			22, Hugh Mulcahy, 1940
Home Runs	43, Chuck Klein, 1929	Innings	313, Jimmy Ring, 1923
RBIs	170, Chuck Klein, 1930	Games Started	37, Jimmy Ring, 1925
Total Bases	445, Chuck Klein, 1930	Complete Games	25, Eppa Rixey, 1920
Hits	254, Lefty O'Doul, 1929	Strikeouts	135, Wayne LaMaster, 1937
			135, Claude Passeau, 1937
Runs	158, Chuck Klein, 1930	Bases on Balls	120, Hugh Mulcahy, 1938
Doubles	59, Chuck Klein, 1930	Winning Pct.	.593, Phil Collins, 1930
Triples	15, Chuck Klein, 1932	ERA	2.84, Lee Meadows, 1920
Bases on Balls	116, Dolf Camilli, 1936	Saves	7, Syl Johnson, 1937
Stolen Bases	20, Chuck Klein, 1932	Shutouts	4, Hal Carlson, 1925

Right, Klein is the only player during this period to set club marks in both total bases and stolen bases. Collins's record winning percentage came with a last-place team; Davis won 19 as a rookie and was traded two years later; LaMaster's strikeout mark also came in his rookie season and, as it turned out, his only full season in the majors. Explanations abound for this team's protracted stay in the second division, and don't think after glancing at the chart, that poor hitting wasn't one of them. By the late thirties the Phils had the least punch of any team in the majors.

THE BEST, THE WORST AND THE WEIRDEST TEAMS BETWEEN 1920 AND 1941

• •

AMERICAN LEAGUE

THE BEST

1939 NEW YORK YANKEES
W–105 L–45
Manager: Joe McCarthy

Regular Lineup—1B, Babe Dahlgren; 2B, Joe Gordon; 3B, Red Rolfe; SS, Frank Crosetti; RF, Charlie Keller; CF, Joe DiMaggio; LF, George Selkirk/Tommy Henrich; C, Bill Dickey; P, Red Ruffing; P, Lefty Gomez; P, Bump Hadley; P, Atley Donald; P, Steve Sundra; P, Johnny Murphy; P, Marius Russo; P, Orel Hildebrand; P, Monte Pearson

No, I'm not being contrary when I call this team greater than the 1927 Murderers Row gang. By the end of the 1939 season rival American League club owners believed it too. Most of them despaired of ending the Yankees' overwhelming domination of the game after McCarthy piloted New York to a ludicrously easy fourth consecutive pennant and World Championship despite having only one pitcher, Ruffing, who hurled over 200 innings or won more than 13 games. The catch was that Marse Joe had seven other starters that year who were so superb that he had in effect an eight-man rotation, plus a reliever, Murphy, who could bail any of them out of trouble whenever it was necessary, which was seldom. Murphy appeared in just 38 games but rang up 19 saves, an amazing total for that time—the NL co-leaders in 1939 had just nine. More than that, the Yankees owned in Keller a rookie slugger so good that Henrich, the previous year's rookie sensation, couldn't keep his job. Man for man, the 1927 team fielded a better regular lineup, but its bench was weak and the competition was not nearly as strong as that provided in 1939 by the Red Sox, Indians, White Sox and Tigers. None seemed to have a prayer of overtaking the Yankees—ever— but in 1940 the Tigers somehow did, for that one year only, to break a string of what would otherwise have been eight consecutive pennants and might have gone as high as ten or twelve had the war not intervened. For their lengthy and virtually uncontested grip on the top rung, the 1936–39 Yankees rate the award as the era's best team, and the 1939 season was their apex. Not only did the club lead the majors in runs and homers, but it also had the best FA and its staff ERA was .77 runs lower than that of Cleveland, the second best team pitching-wise in the AL that year.

THE WORST

1937 ST. LOUIS BROWNS
W–46 L–108
Managers: Rogers Hornsby/Jim Bottomley

Regular Lineup—1B, Harry Davis; 2B, Tom Carey; 3B, Harlond Clift; SS, Bill Knickerbocker; RF, Beau Bell; CF, Sammy West; LF, Joe Vosmik; C, Rollie Hemsley; P, Orel Hildebrand; P, Jack Knott; P, Chief Hogsett; P, Jim Walkup; P, Julio Bonetti

The two former Cardinals stars Hornsby and Bottomley could do nothing to stir their slumbering cotenants of Sportsman's Park, mostly because no one in the Browns camp had the slightest notion of how to find and develop decent pitchers. A failing all during the club's 52-year sojourn in St. Louis, it reached its nadir in the mid-thirties. In 1936 the Browns finished seventh with a 6.24 staff ERA, the worst in AL history, but the A's had an ERA nearly as bad. The following year, though, St. Louis stood alone, with a 6.00 ERA that was 1.13 runs higher than any other AL team's, as the Browns exceeded even their own customarily low standards and thereby relegated an outfit with the AL's second-best club batting average to the cellar, behind an A's team that had finished there in 1936 and improved not one whit. Knott's 4.89 ERA looked so good in comparison to the figures that his hillmates produced that several AL teams coveted him, including the Yankees. But the Browns weren't altogether dumb; they wanted a quality replacement, and when they got Bobo Newsom from the Red Sox, they made him their mound ace in Knott's stead and catapulted all the way up to seventh place in 1938 as Newsom gave the club its lone twenty-game winner between 1930 and 1950. The shame was that the Browns knew all during the 1936 season that they were in dire need of pitching. So what was their only significant off-season move? They swapped Moose Solters and Ivy Andrews to Cleveland in a deal that in one fell swoop sheared the club of its RBI and ERA leaders.

THE WEIRDEST

1928 CHICAGO WHITE SOX
W-72 L-82
Managers: Ray Schalk/Lena Blackburne

Regular Lineup—1B, Bud Clancy; 2B, Bill Hunnefield; 3B, Willie Kamm; SS, Bill Cissell; RF, Alex Metzler; CF, Johnny Mostil; LF, Carl Reynolds/Bibb Falk; C, Buck Crouse/Moe Berg; P, Tommy Thomas; P, Ted Lyons; P, Red Faber; P, Ted Blankenship; P. Grady Adkins

This team included the only major league player who later became a spy (Berg), a rookie first baseman named Art "The Great" Shires who punched out his manager, Blackburne, not once but twice in 1929, and Mostil, back from a suicide attempt that had shelved him for almost the entire 1927 season. But that was only a small piece of what made it bizarre. By the late 1920s most of the other clubs had followed the Yankees' lead and begun playing longball. The White Sox, still yearning for the deadball era, were last in the majors in home runs and slugging average and first in stolen bases with 139, a total that would not be achieved again by any club until the war years. Despite their throwback attack, however, the White Sox remained mildly competitive, usually finishing around fifth, as they did in 1928. But they would not finish that high again until 1935. Their reactionary tactics finally caught up with them, beginning in 1929, when they dropped to seventh place, spared the cellar only because the Red Sox, playing in cozy Fenway Park, could produce only 28 homers and 605 runs. In 1928 Metzler and utilityman Bill Barrett tied for the White Sox's club lead in homers with three, and Kamm's 84 RBIs were 29 more than runner-up Metzler produced. Comiskey Park patrons saw shades of the Hitless Wonders and the days of Big Ed Walsh everywhere they looked, a vision that was heightened when Walsh's son joined the team's hill staff. And no, spacious Comiskey wasn't entirely the reason for this team's woeful lack of punch. In 1924, for instance, the White Sox had nearly twice as many homers as the pennant-winning Senators and were third in the AL in runs. Of course, the fact that the 1924 club finished last no doubt contributed to the notion of trying to turn back the calendar.

NATIONAL LEAGUE

THE BEST

1924 NEW YORK GIANTS
W–93 L–60
Managers: John McGraw; Hugh Jennings (during McGraw's illness)

Regular Lineup—1B, George Kelly; 2B, Frankie Frisch; 3B, Heinie Groh; SS, Travis Jackson; RF, Ross Youngs; CF, Hack Wilson; LF, Irish Meusel; C, Frank Snyder; P, Art Nehf; P, Virgil Barnes; P, Hugh McQuillan; P, Jack Bentley; P, Rosy Ryan

The only club in NL history to cop four consecutive pennants was so accustomed to winning by 1924 that it didn't start to take seriously the challenges mounted by Brooklyn and Pittsburgh until late in the race. Then, prior to a game with the seventh-place Phillies on the final weekend of the season, in what was either the dumbest bribe attempt ever or a bit of horseplay that backfired, depending on whose version of events was believed, sub outfielder Jimmy O'Connell offered Philadelphia shortstop Heinie Sand $500 not to play his best that day. Suspended and subsequently barred for life from the game, O'Connell had been a disappointment to the Giants after starring in the Coast League and seemingly wasn't missed. But the team was never again the same, although McGraw maintained that late-season injuries to Frisch and Groh were the reason rather than the O'Connell incident. Whatever the case, the Giants had five Hall of Famers in their regular lineup, plus a sixth, Bill Terry, on the bench, and it's conceivable that in Groh they had a seventh regular who was better than all of them except Frisch. McGraw possessed only one pitcher, Barnes, who labored more than 188 innings and had no one among the NL leaders in wins or complete games, but he juggled his staff so cleverly that eight men contributed heavily to the club's pennant run. When Washington took the seventh and deciding game of the World Series, however, on Earl Mc-Neely's dribbler that bounced over the head of 18-year-old rookie Freddie Lindstrom, Groh's replacement, the Giants' aura of invincibility was punctured beyond repair. The loss to the Senators, coming on the heels of a devastating defeat by the Yankees in the 1923 Series, agonized McGraw to the end of his life and added to the tarnish on what otherwise might have gone down in history as an ineffably grand dynasty.

THE WORST

1935 BOSTON BRAVES
W–38 L–115
Manager: Bill McKechnie

Regular Lineup—1B, Buck Jordan; 2B, Les Mallon; 3B, Pinky Whitney; SS, Bill Urbanski; RF, Randy Moore; CF, Wally Berger; LF, Hal Lee; C, Al Spohrer; P, Fred Frankhouse; P, Ben Cantwell; P, Bob Smith; P, Ed Brandt; P, Huck Betts; P, Danny MacFayden

McKechnie piloted virtually the same crew to fourth place in 1934, and the Braves' first serious contender since 1915 was anticipated in 1935. Owner Judge Fuchs was so confident of success that he stood pat, with the exception of adding 40-year-old Babe Ruth, and the result was an unmitigated disaster. Betts, a 17-game winner in 1934, slumped to just two wins, the lowest total in pre-expansion NL history for a hurler who pitched a minimum of 154 innings, and Cantwell, the NL winning percentage champ in 1933, had a 4–25 record. Berger topped the circuit in homers and RBIs, ostensibly a monumental feat considering that rival hurlers could so easily afford to pitch around him when the game was on the line—Whitney, the club's second-best RBI man, had 70 fewer ribbies than Berger. The problem for the Braves, and what saved Berger's stats, was that the game was seldom on the line when he came to bat. The Phillies, although they finished a poor seventh, wound up 26 games ahead of Boston, which was far and away the widest margin of victory Philadelphia enjoyed over a rival NL team at the end of any season between 1917 and 1950.

THE WEIRDEST

1930 CHICAGO CUBS
W–90 L–64
Managers: Joe McCarthy/Rogers Hornsby

Regular Lineup—1B, Charlie Grimm; 2B, Footsie Blair; 3B, Woody English; SS, Clyde Beck; RF, Kiki Cuyler; CF, Hack Wilson; LF, Riggs Stephenson; C, Gabby Hartnett; P, Pat Malone; P, Guy Bush; P, Charlie Root; P, Sheriff Blake; P, Bud Teachout; P, Bob Osborn

Five of the club's regulars—Stephenson, Wilson, Hartnett, English and Cuyler—hit .335 or better, but in this, the century's greatest season for batters, the Cubs actually found themselves short of offensive production after Hornsby was injured early in the season. Shorn of its top hitter after having opted to cut aging Norm McMillan, who could play anywhere in the infield, the club was forced to employ a keystone combination of Beck and Blair that provided an aggregate .255 batting average and ninety-three RBIs—only the lowly Reds and Red Sox got less hitting from their middle infielders in 1930—yet still finished just two games behind the pennant-winning Cardinals. Wilson set the NL home run record and the all-time RBI record that season, Hartnett had one of the best years ever by a catcher, and Malone was the NL's leading hurler. Had Hornsby not been disabled, or had the club kept McMillan at third base and put English at shortstop, McCarthy would probably have won his second straight pennant and not been driven to seek another job. The 1930 Cubs, spearheaded by Wilson, made history and also changed the course of it irrevocably. Would anyone else but McCarthy have been able to lead the Yankees out of the funk that blanketed them after Miller Huggins's death and into the greatest period of prosperity that any professional sports team has ever enjoyed? Possibly so, but probably not. Another good question is whether McCarthy would have allowed Wilson to disintegrate to a point where he followed up his record-shattering season with just 13 homers and 61 RBIs in 1931.

SPECIAL FEATURE TEAM: THE GAS HOUSE GANG

● ●

1934 ST. LOUIS CARDINALS
W-95 L-58
Manager: Frankie Frisch

Regular Lineup—1B, Ripper Collins; 2B, Frankie Frisch; 3B, Pepper Martin; SS, Leo Durocher; RF, Jack Rothrock; CF, Ernie Orsatti; LF, Joe Medwick; C, Spud Davis; P, Dizzy Dean; P, Paul Dean; P, Tex Carleton; P, Bill Hallahan; P, Bill Walker

Even Frisch was never certain who pinned the "Gas House Gang" tag on his team or when the colorful sobriquet first gripped the public imagination. Frank Graham, a writer for the *New York Sun,* is believed by many sources to have coined the nickname, but he did not really begin to call the Cardinals the Gas House Gang in print until 1935. If Graham truly was the originator of the label, then the 1934 team was never known as the Gas House Gang. And at best, the Cardinals won only one pennant during the stretch when they played the cut-and-slash, heart of the Depression brand of baseball that earned them a niche among the most famous teams in history.

That pennant was something special, though. When the final month of the 1934 season began, the Cardinals trailed the defending NL champion Giants by 4½ games and had been playing catchup ball ever since June 6. But a late surge that saw St. Louis win 21 of its last 28 contests brought the Gang dead even with New York on September 28. The Dean brothers then took

● ● 181 ● ●

turns defeating the last-place Reds on the closing weekend of the season while the Dodgers and their rookie manager Casey Stengel were knocking off the Giants twice, to the everlasting mortification of New York skipper Bill Terry, who had said, "Is Brooklyn still in the league?" when asked to assess the Dodgers' chances back in the spring.

In 1933 the Cardinals had finished fifth (albeit with the best record ever by a second-division team playing a 154-game schedule) despite leading the NL in both runs and stolen bases. The 1934 team continued to be the loop's top scoring and base-swiping outfit but struggled in the field—both Medwick and Martin paced the NL in errors. It had superior pitching, however, thanks to the arrival of Dizzy Dean's younger brother Paul, a 19-game winner as a rookie, and also benefitted from having Frisch at the helm from the outset of the season. In 1933 the Fordham Flash had not been appointed player–manager until July, too late for the Cardinals to rally after a 46–45 start under incumbent Gabby Street. The only other significant additions were Davis, an excellent hitter for a catcher who had been acquired in a winter trade with the Phillies, and Rothrock, up from the minors where he had been banished after eight mediocre years in the American League. In his first season with the Cards, Rothrock played in every game, scored 106 runs and led the NL in at bats. After suffering a decline at the plate the following season, he was swiftly returned to the minors.

Ironically, the Gas House Gang reached their pinnacle not in 1934 but a year later. With rookie ballhawk Terry Moore replacing Orsatti, the club led the NL in fielding. Tighter defense helped bring the Cardinals an extra victory, but it went for naught when the Cubs won a modern NL-record 21 straight games late in the season, although the slight gain did earn St. Louis the distinction of being one of the very few defending champions who improved on a winning performance, only to be dethroned anyway. After 1935 the Gas House Gang started to crumble, finishing third and fourth the next two seasons before tumbling all the way to sixth place in 1938. By then the press had ceased referring to the team by its famous nickname, and for good reason. When the club opened the 1939 season, only Medwick and Martin remained from the pennant winner of just five years earlier, and by the end of the following year they too were both gone.

The Gas House Gang was thus in many ways more the stuff of

legend than fact. Viewed as a great team by those who know them only by reputation, the 1934–38 Cardinals were actually not nearly as good as the Giants and Cubs of that same period. The Red Birds were not even a collection of tough characters, as might be imagined of a crew named for the denizens of a vaporous fuel establishment. What the Gas House Gang did have was élan, most of it centered in the scrappy Martin, the trigger-tempered Medwick and the torrentially colorful Dizzy Dean. When they left the team became known simply as the Cardinals again and, perhaps not coincidentally, seemed the better for it. Medwick and Dean each won an MVP Award while playing with the Cardinals but were on only one pennant winner. Stan Musial, who came along right after the Gas House Gang era ended, was on four pennant winners in his first four seasons with the club.

NO COMPETITION
FOR THE CATS

● ●

1924 FORT WORTH PANTHERS
W–109 L–41
Manager: Jakey Atz

Regular Lineup—1B, Big Boy Kraft; 2B, Eddie Palmer; 3B, Dugan Phelan; SS, Jackie Tavener; RF, Stump Edington; CF, Jack Calvo; LF, Ziggy Sears; C, John Bischoff/Possum Moore; P, Joe Pate; P, Paul Wachtel; P, Ralph Head; P, Augie Johns; P, Jim Middleton; P, Hank Hulvey

By 1924 the Class AA International League was up against it. The Baltimore Orioles, orchestrated by owner–manager Jack Dunn, were jogging to their sixth of what would be seven straight pennants with a team that was comprised of such future major league stars as Lefty Grove, Joe Boley, George Earnshaw, Tommy Thomas, and Twitchy Dick Porter. Playing a 168-game schedule, Baltimore finished 19 games ahead of second-place Toronto and provided further ammunition for observers who worried that the Orioles' pennant monopoly would soon spell the end of the IL if it were not brought to a halt. Reformers were hamstrung for the moment, however, by a ruling a few years earlier that exempted IL teams from organized baseball's draft system. Since all of the Orioles' key players were owned outright by Dunn and were not subject to being claimed by major league teams, he was free to keep them until he received an offer that was too attractive to refuse, as happened after the 1924 season when the Philadelphia Athletics paid $100,500 for Grove.

● ● **184** ● ●

The IL's plight was discussed and debated throughout the baseball community in 1924, but few outside the Southwest were aware that the Class A Texas League was faced with an even more troublesome problem. Although TL teams could have their top players drafted by Class AA and major league clubs, the Fort Worth Panthers had managed to assemble a dynasty that was every bit as spectacular as Baltimore's. Like the Orioles, the Cats claimed a sixth straight pennant in 1924 and would win a seventh the following year. Moreover, Fort Worth triumphed with an ease that made the 1924 IL flag race seem hotly contested in comparison.

Anticipating that the Cats would be impossible to beat over the long haul, the TL reverted to a split season in 1924 after playing a straight schedule the previous year, in the hope that someone might overtake Fort Worth if given two chances for the price of one. The first half-season opened on April 16 and ended on Independence Day eve with the Cats a cozy nine games ahead of second-place Houston. Rival TL clubs were thankful to begin the season afresh on the midsummer holiday, but their respite was short lived. Over the next sixty-three days the Cats bagged 58 victories against just 18 defeats to post a second-half winning percentage of .763. When the season terminated on September 14, Fort Worth led second-place Beaumont by 18 games and finished 22½ games up on the rest of the TL after the overall standings were computed. The Cats then climaxed their campaign by beating Southern Association champion New Orleans to capture their third Dixie Series in four years.

Fort Worth's secret to success was simple enough. The club's co-owners, W.K. Stripling and Paul LeGrave, sought out mature players who, for one reason or another, no longer had realistic prospects of playing in the majors, and paid them so handsomely that they were happy to stay in the TL. Many of the team's stars, although originally from other sectors of the country, took up permanent residence in Texas after their playing days were over. Among them were Wachtel, Johns, Edington, Phelan and Tavener. But none derived more benefit from playing for the Cats' dynasty than Kraft. A fearsome hitter and, contrary to his nickname, an agile fielder and baserunner—he led the Cats with 18 steals in 1924—Kraft had abandoned major league ambitions a decade earlier after bringing an unpopular suit against organized baseball over his sale to a minor league team in a lower classification than he believed his qualifications warranted. After hitting .349 in 1924 and setting TL records with 55 home runs (since broken), 414 total bases, and 196 RBIs (both of which still stand), Kraft retired from baseball at 37 and opened a highly lucrative car dealership in Fort Worth, where he continued to live comfortably until his death in 1958.

Wachtel and Pate were the club's twin mound aces. Between them they had a 52–18 record in 1924 as Pate led the TL in wins for the third time in five seasons and Wachtel added 22 more victories to a career TL total that would reach a loop-record 231 by the time he retired in 1930. Pate was acquired by the Athletics the following year. As a thirty-four-year-old rookie, he was a perfect 9–0 for the A's in 1926 before slipping back to the minors again. Wachtel had pitched briefly for the Dodgers in 1917, but his dream of returning to top company was ended in 1920 when his bread-and-butter pitch, the spitball, was prohibited in the majors except to a few hurlers who had already established their careers.

Also on the team were Deeby Foss, a backup third baseman who saw a fair amount of action because Phelan was in a year-long slump (he hit just .219, the poorest average in the league for a regular, but nevertheless topped the TL in walks), and former NL stolen-base king Bob Bescher. Brought to Fort Worth to compete for the left field job with Sears, who had a bad year in 1923, Bescher, at age 40, had little left, hitting just .197. However, his presence prodded Sears to bat .323, his finest season to date. After the 1928 campaign, Sears quit as a player and became an umpire in the TL. Later he was promoted to the National League and served there as an arbiter for twelve years, long enough to see his son Ken reach the majors as a catcher with the Yankees.

Atz, a banjo-hitting second baseman with the White Sox during the deadball era, was at midcareer as a manager in 1924. Notwithstanding his seven straight pennants with the Panthers, he never advanced beyond the TL and, indeed, spent the last part of his dugout sojourn with teams in the lower minors. Rather amazingly, the only member of the Cats' 1924 powerhouse who subsequently played or managed in the majors long enough to have qualified for a pension, if there had been any such thing in the 1920s, was Tavener. Although just 5'5" and 138 pounds, he had great range and hit with surprising clout. In 1928, his last of four seasons as Detroit's shortstop, Tavener had just 123 hits, but 44 of them were for extra bases, including 15 triples, good for fourth in the AL. Upon leaving the majors, he followed the same path as many of the Cats, returning to live in Fort Worth, where he had found more than fleeting recognition during his days of glory in Panther Park.

The complete 1924 TL standings, plus comments, follow:

Team	W	L	Pct.	GB
Fort Worth Panthers	101	49	.727	—
Houston Buffaloes	80	73	.523	22½
Beaumont Exporters	77	73	.513	24
Wichita Falls Spudders	77	74	.510	24½
San Antonio Missions	75	75	.500	26
Dallas Steers	75	79	.487	28
Galveston Cubs	61	93	.396	42
Shreveport Gassers	54	100	.351	49

After winning a seventh consecutive pennant in 1925, albeit by only twelve games, their smallest margin since 1919, the Panthers finally restored a measure of competition to the TL when they slipped to third the following year. Age, perhaps a trace of complacency, and the loss of Pate, the team's winningest pitcher, brought an end to a dynasty that has never been equaled since in the professional game.

HOW THE MINORS
MIRRORED THE
MAJORS IN THE YEAR
OF THE HITTER

• •

1930 MISSION REDS
W–91 L–110
Manager: Wade Killifer

Regular Lineup—1B, George Burns; 2B, John Monroe; 3B, Eddie Mulligan; SS, Bill Rodda; RF, Fuzzy Hufft; CF, Ernie Kelly; LF, Ike Boone/Harry Rosenberg; C, Bill Brenzel/Fred Hofman; P, Bert Cole; P, Herman Pillette; P, Dutch Lieber; P, Jack Knott; P, George Caster; P, Ted Pillette

In 1930, facing the Great Depression and a corresponding drop in attendance, baseball moguls on the q.t. juiced up the ball in the hope that an increase in scoring and hitting would keep the turnstiles clicking, and the result was an explosion that reverberated throughout all of organized baseball. Nowhere was the impact more deeply felt than in San Francisco, home at the time to not just one but *two* teams in the Pacific Coast League. The PCL played a split-season schedule for the third year in a row in 1930, and the Mission Reds, sharing San Francisco and Old Rec Park with the more established though not necessarily more popular San Francisco Seals, finished seventh overall in the eight-team loop and dead last in the second half of the campaign.

A year earlier the Reds had compiled the best record in the PCL and joined with the Seals to produce the first pennant race in O.B. history between two teams using the same ballpark.[1]

1. Two other PCL teams, the Los Angeles Angels and the Hollywood Stars, also did

When owner Herbert Fleishhacker realized that even if his team repeated its performance he would still lose money, he peddled Boone to the Brooklyn Dodgers after Boone launched the 1930 season by hitting .448 in the first 83 games. At that pace Boone would have established a record for the highest batting average in O.B. history, and while it's doubtful that he would have continued to hit at a .448 clip for the full season, in 1930 it was certainly well within the realm of possibility. Fleishhacker's Reds had a .305 team average that year as nine regular players in the PCL topped the .350 mark and two ex-big leaguers, Johnny Bassler and Hank Severeid, hit .368 and .367 respectively as the catching combo for the Hollywood Stars. Indeed, only one regular in the entire league hit below .264 as averages everywhere climbed into a stratosphere never reached before or since in O.B.[2] The PCL was actually one of the lighter-hitting leagues; playing a 210-game schedule, home run leader Dave Barbee of Hollywood had "just" 41 taters and Earl Sheely of the Seals led with 180 RBIs, ten fewer than Hack Wilson of the Cubs achieved that year playing a 154-game schedule.

Part of what made the Reds so intriguing in 1930 despite their losing record was where they played. Old Rec Park featured a right-field wall only 235 feet from the plate that was topped by a fifty-foot-high fence capable of reducing even the most gargantuan blasts to mere singles and making it possible, on occasion, for a rightfielder to pick a drive off the towering screen on the rebound, wheel and throw a batter out at first base. The park also had an eight-row section in the grandstand that was known to fans as "the Booze Cage," a sobriquet left over from pre-

---

this on several occasions. The original Hollywood franchise was actually located in Los Angeles and shared Wrigley Field with the Angels. Not until 1939, after a second Hollywood franchise had replaced Mission in the PCL, did the Stars move to Gilmore Field in Hollywood, the home they occupied until they left the PCL when the Dodgers and Giants moved to the West Coast.

2. In 1930, as is shown by the list that follows, only one regular player (400 or more at bats) hit below .250 in any of the Class AA or Class A minor leagues, the two highest classifications at the time.

League	Top Hitter	Worst Hitter
Pacific Coast	.403, Earl Sheely	.256, Bernie DiViveiros
International	.376, Ripper Collins	.265, Warren Cote
American Association	.380, Bevo Lebourveau	.268, Marty Hopkins
Southern Association	.380, Joe Hutcheson	.246, Ray Flaskamper
Texas	.379, Ox Eckhardt	.253, Art Whalen
Eastern	.346, Bill Dreesen	.268, Joe Maley
Western	.354, Woody Jensen	.255, Jack Nielson

Prohibition days when the 75¢ admission price included either a shot of whiskey, two bottles of beer, or a ham and cheese sandwich. Few patrons chose the sandwich. The clubhouses were in center field, inside a murky wooden cottage. Since there were only two showers in each clubhouse, it behooved players not to sit in front of their lockers after a game and savor their exploits if they wanted hot water.

But the Reds had a lot more perks to offer fans than their park, even after Boone departed. First baseman Burns, voted the American League MVP just four years earlier, hit .349; Monroe at second base clocked 241 hits, 28 homers and a .350 BA; and Hufft clubbed .356 with 37 homers and 178 RBIs. The pitching staff, for a minor league team, was highly respectable—Cole and both the Pillette brothers were among the top hurlers in the PCL—but in 1930 all except Herman, the elder Pillette, had off years. Near the end of the season, Fleishhacker, pinched still more by declining attendance and the aftershock of the previous fall's stock market crash, let Rosenberg, his most promising young player, go to the New York Giants. Rosenberg never panned out in the majors, the Dodgers made little use of Boone and none of the other Mission stars figured prominently in the big league history of the thirties. Knott and Caster, both of whom were secondary pitchers in 1930, were the only two Reds who later achieved even a modicum of success in top company. When Old Rec was torn down the following year, replaced by Seals Stadium, the Missions very soon became auxiliary residents of both the new park and San Francisco. The franchise survived in the Bay Area until 1938 when it was shifted to Hollywood, which in turn had lost its original franchise shortly after its fine 1930 season.

As an indication of how little regard was given to enormous hitting stats in 1930, shortstop Dud Lee, a .275 hitter and the weakest offensive performer on the championship Hollywood Stars, was voted the club's MVP. The Missions' MVP, according to many observers, was Mulligan, a fixture for years in the PCL but a bare .300 hitter in 1930.

FUN DOWN ON
THE FARM

• •

1933 COLUMBUS RED BIRDS
W–101 L–51
Manager: Ray Blades

Regular Lineup—1B, Mickey Heath; 2B, Burgess Whitehead; 3B, Lew Riggs; SS, Bernie Borgmann; RF, Jack Rothrock; CF, Hal Anderson; LF, Nick Cullop; C, Bill DeLancey; P, Paul Dean; P, Bill Lee; P, Bud Teachout; P, Jim Lindsey; P, Clarence Heise; P, Ralph Judd; P, Jim Winford

In 1933, while many major league teams still had at best a rudimentary farm system, the St. Louis Cardinals had not just one but two affiliates in the top echelons of the minors—Rochester in the International League and Columbus in the American Association. Both bore nicknames that indicated their allegiance: Rochester was called the Red Wings and Columbus the Red Birds. Rochester had for some time been the class of the International League, bagging four straight pennants before ceding the throne in 1932 to Newark, and in 1933 the Cardinals decided it was Columbus's turn to have a little fun.

The Red Birds began the campaign with Gordon Slade at short, Charlie Wilson at second and Art Shires at first. These three infield regulars and pitcher Jim Lindsey soon became embroiled in controversy and departed the club in early June under orders from AA president Thomas Hickey. Suspicion that the Cardinals were engaging in hanky-panky with regard to the amount and payment of the quartet's salaries caused Hickey to make Columbus lop them from the roster and find replacements. At the time Wilson was hitting .356, Slade .353 and Shires .313, while Lindsey had a 7–2 record, but Hickey's mandate nonetheless imposed little hardship on Columbus. Whitehead, the Red Birds' regular second baseman in 1932, and Borgmann were simply advanced to first-string roles, and Heath was shifted from Rochester to Columbus. All Lindsey's departure meant was more work for the other staff members.

Columbus took over the top spot on May 17 and was never dislodged the rest of the way. At the close of the regular season the Red Birds' record was 15½ games better than Minneapolis's 86–67 mark, which rated as the AA's second best overall. However, the two teams were considered dual pennant winners owing to a restructuring the AA underwent prior to the season in an attempt to combat flagging attendance. To prevent a runaway pennant winner and assure a meaningful postseason tournament, the loop split into two divisions, placing Columbus in the East and Minneapolis in the West. The experiment lasted two seasons and did little to spark attendance—nothing any of the minor leagues tried during the Depression seemed to help much, save night baseball. What it did provide, though, was a postseason tuneup for the Red Birds, who had seemed to lose some of their drive during the last weeks of the season. Blades's men revived to stop Minneapolis in the playoff and then tumble Buffalo, the IL champ, in the Little World Series five games to three.

The following year Cardinals general manager Branch Rickey summoned Dean, Whitehead, DeLancey and Rothrock to the parent club. Each of the four played an important role in bringing the NL flag to St. Louis and thereupon shared in the renown that came to the team after it was dubbed the Gas House Gang. Several other members of the Red Birds cast also made an impact in the majors. Slade was waived to Cincinnati, where he became the Reds regular shortstop in 1934. Riggs also was sold to the Reds a year later and held the Queen City third base slot for four years before giving way to Billy Werber. Blades, a former Cardinals outfielder and still a part-time player in 1933, returned to St. Louis as manager in 1939. After a strong second-place finish in his first season at the team's helm, he was fired when the Cardinals started poorly in 1940. But the best of all the Red Birds turned out to be Lee. Unable to crack the Cardinals' pitching rotation, he joined the Cubs in 1934 and

ranked among the NL's best pitchers during the next six seasons.

Also a member of the 1933 Red Birds was Mike Gonzalez, the
first Cuban-born catcher to fashion a successful career in the
majors. At 43 he was a backup to DeLancey and an aide
to Blades. And like Blades, he too later coached and managed
for the Cardinals. Columbus's most valuable player in 1933 was
Dean, Dizzy's brother, who paced the AA with 22 wins, 222
strikeouts and a 3.15 ERA, but Cullop was without a doubt the
team's best-known player—at least on the minor league level. A
failure in numerous big-league trials, including a lengthy one
with the 1931 Reds, Cullop compiled 420 home runs and 1857
RBIs in the minors, placing him high among the career leaders
on both lists. In 1933 he easily paced the Red Birds in every
major slugging department and led the AA in triples with 22.
Heath, another prolific slugger in the minors, ironically had
also been a teammate of Cullop's on the 1931 Reds. A highly
promising rookie at the time, he suffered an early-season injury
that effectively ended any chance he had at a major league career, although he continued to play in the minors for another
decade.

Heath hit just .231 in 1933 to make it all the more apparent to
him that he would never get back to the majors, but he nonetheless had a good time. So did everyone in the Ohio capital. The
1933 pennant was Columbus's first since the 1905–07 powerhouse had swept three straight. In 1934 Columbus repeated as
the East Division AA champ and again beat Minneapolis in the
postseason playoff for the loop title. After winning their third
pennant of the 1930s in 1937, the Red Birds went through a short
dry spell before regaining the top spot in 1941 under Burt Shotton. Though Columbus subsequently won three league playoff
championships, it never again won another pennant in the AA.
Part of the reason is that the city left the loop after the 1954
season and joined the International League, where it adopted a
new parent club, Pittsburgh, and a new nickname, the Jets.

ERA ALL-STAR TEAMS

AMERICAN LEAGUE

1B	Lou Gehrig
2B	Charlie Gehringer
3B	Harlond Clift
SS	Joe Sewell
OF	Babe Ruth
OF	Al Simmons
OF	Hank Greenberg
C	Mickey Cochrane
P	Lefty Grove
P	George Uhle
UTIL	Jimmie Foxx
MGR	Joe McCarthy
*	Joe DiMaggio

NATIONAL LEAGUE

1B	Johnny Mize
2B	Rogers Hornsby
3B	Pie Traynor
SS	Arky Vaughan
OF	Chuck Klein
OF	Paul Waner
OF	Mel Ott
C	Gabby Hartnett
P	Dazzy Vance
P	Carl Hubbell
UTIL	Joe Medwick
MGR	Bill McKechnie
*	Frankie Frisch

MINOR LEAGUES

1B	Buzz Arlett
2B	John Monroe
3B	Charlie English
SS	Ray French
OF	Ike Boone
OF	Smead Jolley
OF	Moose Clabaugh

C	Al Devormer
P	Tom Sheehan
P	Sam Gibson
UTIL	Lou Novikoff
MGR	Jack Dunn
*	Ox Eckhardt

*Best player who failed to make the team

LEG FIVE

1942–1960

TEAM NOTES AND RECORD HOLDERS: 1942–60

AMERICAN LEAGUE COMPOSITE STANDINGS

Number of Years Finishing in Each Position

Team	1	2	3	4	5	6	7	8	Aggregate
New York	13	1	4	1	0	0	0	0	1
Cleveland	2	6	2	5	2	2	0	0	2
Boston	1	3	5	5	1	1	3	0	3
Detroit	1	4	0	3	8	2	0	1	4
Chicago	1	2	5	2	2	5	1	1	5
St. Louis–Baltimore	1	1	2	0	1	5	6	3	6
Washington	0	2	0	1	4	1	5	6	7
Philadelphia–Kansas City	0	0	0	2	3	2	4	8	8

NEW YORK YANKEES

Pennants: 1942, 1943, 1947, 1949, 1950, 1951, 1952, 1953, 1955, 1956, 1957, 1958, 1960
Manager: Casey Stengel, 1949–60
Park: Yankee Stadium
Best Year: 1942 and 1954 (103–51, .669)
Worst Year: 1959 (79–75, .513)
Top Rookie: Gil McDougald, 1951
Biggest Disappointment: Fred Sanford, 1949
Best Deal: Getting Clete Boyer and Art Ditmar from their Kansas City cousins in 1957 along with Bobby Shantz tops even the Maris deal made after the 1959 season
Worst Deal: Giving Jackie Jensen to Washington in 1952
Other:
1943—Win seventh flag in eight years
1945—Dan Topping and Del Webb buy the club from Jake Ruppert's heirs
1947—Tie AL record by winning 19 straight games
1949—Win it all despite giving up an AL record 812 walks
1953—Become the first team in history to win five straight pennants and the only team ever to win five straight World Championships; 18-game winning streak is longest in AL since 1947
1954—Post .669 winning percentage, highest in AL history by a 2nd-place team
1958—Win fourth straight pennant and ninth in the past ten years; sprint to 25–6 start and lead AL by record 17 games on August 2
1959—Club has lowest winning percentage (.513) since 1925
1960—Rebound after a year away from the top to lead the majors in runs, home runs and wins, only to lose World Series to the Pirates despite compiling record .338 team BA; end regular season with 15-game winning streak to cop flag by eight games after leading AL by just .002 percentage points before the streak began

HITTING		PITCHING	
Batting Ave.	.353, Mickey Mantle, 1956	Wins	21, done by four different pitchers, including Vic Raschi three times
Slugging Ave.	.705, Mickey Mantle, 1956	Losses	13, Monk Dubiel, 1944
			13, Bill Bevens, 1946, 1947
			13, Bob Turley, 1955
Home Runs	52, Mickey Mantle, 1956	Innings	275, Vic Raschi, 1949
RBIs	155, Joe DiMaggio, 1948	Games Started	37, Vic Raschi, 1949
Total Bases	376, Mickey Mantle, 1956	Complete Games	24, Allie Reynolds, 1952
Hits	205, Snuffy Stirnweiss, 1944	Strikeouts	210, Bob Turley, 1955
Runs	138, Tommy Henrich, 1948	Bases on Balls	179, Tommy Byrne, 1949
Doubles	42, Tommy Henrich, 1948	Winning Pct.	.833, Spud Chandler, 1943
Triples	22, Snuffy Stirnweiss, 1945	ERA	1.64, Spud Chandler, 1943
Bases on Balls	146, Mickey Mantle, 1947	Saves	27, Joe Page, 1949
Stolen Bases	55, Snuffy Stirnweiss, 1945	Shutouts	7, Whitey Ford, 1958
			7, Allie Reynolds, 1951

Apart from Raschi, the 21 game winners were Tiny Bonham, Ed Lopat and Bob Turley, and there were several others who won 20 in a season. The thing that tells you just how dominant the Yankees were in this era is that almost all of them, while winning 20 games, lost fewer than ten. In fact, as the chart suggests, it was a cause for alarm when *any* Yankee pitcher between 1942 and 1960 lost in double figures. You're welcome to make of it what you will that DiMaggio appears only once on the chart for this era and not at all in the previous one.

CLEVELAND INDIANS

Pennants: 1948, 1954
Manager: Lou Boudreau, 1942–50
Park: League Park, 1942–46 (final game played on September 21, 1946)
　Municipal Stadium, 1942–present; following the 1946 season, the club began playing all of its home games here
Best Year: 1954 (111–43, .721)
Worst Year: 1946 (68–86, .442)
Top Rookie: Gene Bearden, 1948
Biggest Disappointment: Gene Bearden, 1949
Best Deal: Getting Joe Gordon from the Yankees for Allie Reynolds, 1947; it was one of the very few deals in history that helped both clubs tremendously without hurting either appreciably
Worst Deal: Tie between giving up Minnie Minoso and more for Lou Brissie, 1951, and trading Rocky Colavito for Harvey Kuenn prior to the 1960 season
Other:
　1942—Team finishes in the first division for the second straight year with a sub-.500 record
　1945—Bill Veeck buys the club; team plays only 147 games, fewest by any club since 154-game schedule was adopted
　1948—First ML team to draw over 2,000,000 fans; win AL record low nine one-run games but nevertheless become reigning World Champions as the club bags the team Triple Crown and defeats Boston in the only AL pennant playoff game in history
　1949—Set new ML record by making only 103 errors
　1950—Finish 4th in the AL with a better record than the NL pennant-winning Phillies
　1952—Become the only team in ML history with three 20-game winners and the league home run and RBI leaders not to win a pennant
　1954—Set AL record for the highest winning percentage (.721) and most wins (111)
　1957—Herb Score is nearly killed by a line drive to the face and is never again an effective pitcher
　1959—Club leads AL race for a while in September, the last time to date that it has ever led after July

HITTING		PITCHING	
Batting Ave.	.355, Lou Boudreau, 1948	Wins	26, Bob Feller, 1946
Slugging Ave.	.613, Al Rosen, 1953	Losses	17, Early Wynn, 1957
Home Runs	43, Al Rosen, 1953	Innings	371, Bob Feller, 1946
RBIs	145, Al Rosen, 1953	Games Started	42, Bob Feller, 1946
Total Bases	367, Al Rosen, 1953	Complete Games	36, Bob Feller, 1946
Hits	204, Dale Mitchell, 1948	Strikeouts	348, Bob Feller, 1946
Runs	123, Al Smith, 1955	Bases on Balls	154, Herb Score, 1955
Doubles	45, Lou Boudreau, 1944, 1947	Winning Pct.	.767, Bob Lemon, 1954
Triples	23, Dale Mitchell, 1949	ERA	2.18, Bob Feller, 1946
Bases on Balls	106, Les Fleming, 1942	Saves	19, Ray Narleski, 1955
Stolen Bases	28, George Case, 1946	Shutouts	10, Bob Feller, 1946 10, Bob Lemon, 1948

As great as Feller's 1946 season was, he was on his way to an even better one in 1947 before he hurt his arm. Rosen also might have had better seasons than his 1953 gem if he hadn't wrecked his finger the following year. And Score ... well, why go on? This team was hexed, and still is, and no better explanation for its bizarre history has ever been offered. My vote for the Indians' best player during this era goes to Larry Doby. Although he didn't make the chart, he's the runner-up in several hitting departments and was second as a centerfielder only to one other Indian: Tris Speaker.

BOSTON RED SOX

Pennants: 1946
Manager: Joe Cronin, 1942–47
Park: Fenway Park
Best Year: 1946 (104–50, .675)
Worst Year: 1960 (65–89, .422)
Top Rookie: Walt Dropo, 1950
Biggest Disappointment: Walt Dropo, 1951
Best Deal: Getting Jackie Jensen from Washington, 1954
Worst Deal: Shipping Sam Mele and Mickey Harris to Washington for Walt Masterson, 1949
Other:

1946—First flag since 1918; team gains 33 games over the previous year's finish, a record for a pennant winner that is greatly diminished by the fact that 1945 was a war year

1949—Club becomes the only team in history to lose two consecutive pennants by a one-game margin

1950—Club scores ML-record 625 runs at home and is the last team to score over 1000 runs (1027) or hit over .300 (.302)

1954—Set AL records for the lowest winning percentage by a first-division team (.448) and the most games finished behind the pennant winner by a first-division team (42)

1955—First baseman Harry Agganis dies of a pulmonary embolism

1958—Finish above .500 for the last time until 1967

1960—Club ends the era with the poorest staff ERA in the majors (4.62)

HITTING		PITCHING	
Batting Ave.	.388, Ted Williams, 1957	Wins	25, Boo Ferriss, 1946 25, Mel Parnell, 1949
Slugging Ave.	.731, Ted Williams, 1957	Losses	16, Frank Sullivan, 1960
Home Runs	43, Ted Williams, 1949	Innings	295, Mel Parnell, 1949
RBIs	159, Ted Williams, 1949 159, Vern Stephens, 1949	Games Started	35, Boo Ferriss, 1946 35, Tex Hughson, 1946 35, Frank Sullivan, 1955
Total Bases	368, Ted Williams, 1949	Complete Games	27, Mel Parnell, 1949
Hits	208, Johnny Pesky, 1946	Strikeouts	172, Tex Hughson, 1946
Runs	150, Ted Williams, 1949	Bases on Balls	134, Mel Parnell, 1949
Doubles	44, Ted Williams, 1948	Winning Pct.	.806, Boo Ferriss, 1946
Triples	11, Dom DiMaggio, 1950 11, Bobby Doerr, 1950 11, Jackie Jensen, 1956	ERA	2.26, Tex Hughson, 1944
Bases on Balls	162, Ted Williams, 1947	Saves	27, Ellis Kinder, 1953
Stolen Bases	22, Jackie Jensen, 1954	Shutouts	6, Boo Ferriss, 1946 6, Tex Hughson, 1946 6, Ellis Kinder, 1949

The charts should tell you that the Red Sox during the period consistently had better teams than Cleveland did—on paper, anyway. But since great individual stats are seldom enough by themselves to produce pennants, Boston won just one.

DETROIT TIGERS

Pennants: 1945
Manager: Steve O'Neill, 1943–48
Park: Briggs Stadium
Best Year: 1950 (95–59, .617)
Worst Year: 1952 (50–104, .325)
Top Rookie: Tie between Dick Wakefield, 1943, and Harvey Kuenn, 1953
Biggest Disappointment: Dick Wakefield, 1946–49
Best Deal: Garnering Steve Gromek and Ray Boone from Cleveland, 1953
Worst Deal: Presenting the White Sox with Billy Pierce, 1949
Other:

1942—Lead the majors with 671 pitching strikeouts as no hurler in the AL has more than 113

1945—Break St. Louis Browns' year-old ML record by taking the pennant with only 88 wins and a .575 winning percentage

1946—Top the majors with 94 complete games

1948—Become the last major league team with the sole exception of the Cubs to install lights in its park

1951—Suffer first sub-.500 season since 1942

1952—Finish in last place for the first time in franchise history, thus ending the team's record for being the only one of the 16 franchises that began the 1901 season never to finish in the basement

1953—Despite abysmal 5.25 staff ERA, which results in opponents scoring 923 runs, nearly an era record, team sneaks into 6th place at the wire

1956—Win 82 games, the most by any Detroit team between 1951 and 1961

1960—Trade manager Jimmy Dykes to Cleveland for the Tribe's manager Joe Gordon, the only such swap in ML history

HITTING		**PITCHING**	
Batting Ave.	.353, Harvey Kuenn, 1959	Wins	29, Hal Newhouser, 1944
Slugging Ave.	.604, Hank Greenberg, 1946	Losses	20, Art Houtteman, 1952
Home Runs	44, Hank Greenberg, 1946	Innings	352, Dizzy Trout, 1944
RBIs	133, Vic Wertz, 1949	Games Started	40, Dizzy Trout, 1944
Total Bases	327, Al Kaline, 1956	Complete Games	33, Dizzy Trout, 1944
Hits	218, George Kell, 1950	Strikeouts	275, Hal Newhouser, 1946
Runs	121, Al Kaline, 1955	Bases on Balls	142, Paul Foytack, 1956
Doubles	56, George Kell, 1950	Winning Pct.	.763, Hal Newhouser, 1944
Triples	11, done by five different players	ERA	1.81, Hal Newhouser, 1945
Bases on Balls	137, Roy Cullenbine, 1947	Saves	10, Art Houtteman, 1948
			10, Hank Aguirre, 1960
Stolen Bases	19, Al Kaline, 1960	Shutouts	8, Hal Newhouser, 1949

The Tigers didn't want to pay Greenberg what he felt he was worth and passed him on to Pittsburgh in 1947. At the end of the 1947 season they cut Cullenbine, replacing him with George Vico. That kind of maneuvering helps explain why they won only one pennant despite having a generous sprinkling of fine players all during the period. The fact that Newhouser spread his club record achievement over four different seasons fosters the impression that he wasn't just a wartime fluke. Rather, two of his peak years came while the war was in progress.

CHICAGO WHITE SOX

Pennants: 1959
Manager: Jimmy Dykes, 1942–46
Park: Comiskey Park
Best Year: 1954 and 1959 (94–60, .610)
Worst Year: 1948 (51–101, .336)
Top Rookie: Luis Aparicio, 1956
Biggest Disappointment: Pat Seerey, 1949
Best Deal: Picking the A's pocket of Nellie Fox, 1950
Worst Deal: Trading Ed Lopat to the Yankees, 1948
Other:

1943—Play ML-record 43 doubleheaders

1945—In last wartime season put together the AL's second-weirdest team of the era, one that tops the loop in BA while finishing last in the majors in homers and has two of the AL's top batters, Tony Cuccinello (.308) and Johnny Dickshot (.302), both of whom are released after the season ends and never play another game in the majors

1948—Only cellar finish between 1935 and 1970

1950—Steal just 19 bases, the fewest in the majors

1951—Hire Paul Richards as manager, almost immediately become known as the "Go-Go White Sox" and top the majors with 99 steals

1954—Club has best season since 1920, sets AL record for the most games finished behind pennant winner (17) by a team with a .600 or better winning percentage

1955—Frank "Trader" Lane resigns as the team's general manager

1959—Bill Veeck buys the club, brings the first pennant in forty years to South Side fans

1960—Become the first team to put names on the backs of its uniforms and also the first to employ an exploding scoreboard

HITTING		PITCHING	
Batting Ave.	.328, Luke Appling, 1943	Wins	22, Early Wynn, 1959
Slugging Ave.	.535, Minnie Minoso, 1954	Losses	20, Eddie Smith, 1942 20, Bill Wight, 1948
Home Runs	29, Gus Zernial, 1950 29, Eddie Robinson, 1951	Innings	276, Billy Pierce, 1956
RBIs	117, Eddie Robinson, 1951	Games Started	37, Early Wynn, 1959
Total Bases	304, Minnie Minoso, 1954	Complete Games	21, Billy Pierce, 1956
Hits	201, Nellie Fox, 1954	Strikeouts	192, Billy Pierce, 1956
Runs	119, Minnie Minoso, 1954	Bases on Balls	137, Billy Pierce, 1950
Doubles	40, Don Kolloway, 1942	Winning Pct.	.842, Sandy Consuegra, 1954
Triples	18, Minnie Minoso, 1954	ERA	1.97, Billy Pierce, 1955
Bases on Balls	108, Ferris Fain, 1953	Saves	18, Harry Dorish, 1953
Stolen Bases	56, Wally Moses, 1943 56, Luis Aparicio, 1959	Shutouts	7, Billy Pierce, 1953

After examining the chart and the aggregate standings, you might think Chicago's only pennant during the period came in 1954. And you'd be forgiven, at least here, because the 1954 crew, from an offensive standpoint anyway, was probably the best one the White Sox assembled between 1921 and 1983. Question: Who's the only White Sox player to hit .320 or better twice since 1942? Name him and you'll know whom I rate the club's best player in this era.

BALTIMORE ORIOLES

Pennants: 1944
Manager: Paul Richards, 1955–60
Park: Sportsman's Park (St. Louis), 1942–53
  Memorial Stadium (Baltimore), 1954–60
Best Year: 1944 and 1960 (89–65, .578)
Worst Year: 1951 (51–102, .338)
Top Rookie: Vern Stephens, 1943
Biggest Disappointment: Roy Sievers, 1950–53
Best Deal: Acquiring Clint Courtney from the Yankees, 1952
Worst Deal: Tie between giving the Indians Vic Wertz for Bob Chakales, 1954, and giving the Senators Roy Sievers for Gil Coan, 1954
Other:
  1944—Team wins only flag while franchise is based in St. Louis, sets record (since broken) for the lowest winning percentage by a pennant winner (.578)
  1945—Last St. Louis Browns team to break .500 mark (.536)
  1946—Club wins 66 games, the last time it will win that many while it's based in St. Louis
  1950—Club hires a hypnotist in an unsuccessful effort to rid its players of a defeatist complex as it loses 96 games
  1951—Bill Veeck buys team, tries everything to perk up both its attendance and performance, including hiring midget Eddie Gaedel to pinch hit in a game against the Tigers
  1953—Club suffers ML-record 20 straight losses at home, finishes last in its final season in St. Louis
  1954—Franchise moves to Baltimore, becomes known as the Orioles
  1958—Lee McPhail becomes the team's general manager and president
  1960—2nd-place finish is only the second time since 1922 that the franchise has finished so high

HITTING		**PITCHING**	
Batting Ave.	.329, Al Zarilla, 1948	Wins	20, Ned Garver, 1951
Slugging Ave.	.499, Walt Judnich, 1942	Losses	21, Fred Sanford, 1948
			21, Don Larsen, 1954
Home Runs	27, Chet Laabs, 1942	Innings	260, Ned Garver, 1950
	27, Jeff Heath, 1947		
RBIs	109, Vern Stephens, 1944	Games Started	35, Bob Turley, 1954
Total Bases	270, Vern Stephens, 1945	Complete Games	24, Ned Garver, 1951
Hits	207, Bob Dillinger, 1948	Strikeouts	185, Bob Turley, 1954
Runs	110, Bob Dillinger, 1948	Bases on Balls	181, Bob Turley, 1954
Doubles	39, Harlond Clift, 1942	Winning Pct.	.731, Nels Potter, 1944
Triples	13, Bob Dillinger, 1949	ERA	2.19, Hoyt Wilhelm, 1959
Bases on Balls	106, Harlond Clift, 1942	Saves	16, George Zuverink, 1956*
Stolen Bases	34, Bob Dillinger, 1947	Shutouts	4, Sig Jakucki, 1944
			4, Milt Pappas, 1959

*In 1944 George Caster had twelve saves, the club's all-time best while the franchise was in St. Louis.

Shame on you if you've never heard of Bob Dillinger. He may have been the greatest good-hit no-field third baseman in the game's history. Zarilla's 1948 season, following on the heels of a .224 one in 1947, was the kind of thing that kept Brownie fans from suicide. You just never knew when someone like Zarilla or Garver, without giving any previous inkling that it was coming, might fashion a neat year.

WASHINGTON SENATORS

Pennants: None
Manager: Ossie Bluege, 1943–47; Bucky Harris, 1950–54
Park: Griffith Stadium
Best Year: 1945 (87–67, .565)
Worst Year: 1949 (50–104, .325)
Top Rookie: Irv Noren, 1950
Biggest Disappointment: Harlond Clift, 1943–45; had he had anything left at all the Senators almost undoubtedly would have won the pennant in 1945
Best Deal: Many good ones to choose from; check out how they got Bob Porterfield, Jackie Jensen, Roy Sievers, and Jeff Heath; but the best is still the way they got Jim Lemon for, literally, next to nothing
Worst Deal: Giving Mickey Vernon and Early Wynn to Cleveland, 1949; the Indians later gave Vernon back dirt cheap but kept Wynn
Other:
1943—Finish 2nd, best showing since 1933
1944—Set AL record with last-place finish only 25 games out of 1st place
1945—Last Washington team to finish as high as 2nd place and nearly become the first twentieth-century team to rise from last place to 1st the next year
1950—Finish 5th, ML-record 25 games behind the 4th-place team
1952—Club finishes above .500 for the last time while it's based in Washington
1956—Chuck Stobbs (3.60) is only starter to post an ERA under 5.27 as club compiles 5.33 staff ERA, the poorest in the majors, and also tops majors in errors; opponents as a result score era-record 924 runs
1957—Shortened dimensions of park result in Roy Sievers hitting 26 home runs at home, a Griffith Stadium record; Sievers in addition becomes the first Washington player to top the AL in home runs
1960—Club wins 73 games in its final season in Washington, best showing since 1953

HITTING		PITCHING	
Batting Ave.	.353, Mickey Vernon, 1946	Wins	22, Bob Porterfield, 1953
Slugging Ave.	.579, Roy Sievers, 1957	Losses	20, Chuck Stobbs, 1957
Home Runs	42, Roy Sievers, 1957 42, Harmon Killebrew, 1959	Innings	274, Pete Ramos, 1960
RBIs	115, Mickey Vernon, 1953	Games Started	37, Pete Ramos, 1958
Total Bases	331, Roy Sievers, 1957	Complete Games	24, Bob Porterfield, 1953
Hits	207, Mickey Vernon, 1946	Strikeouts	185, Camilio Pascual, 1959
Runs	114, Eddie Yost, 1950	Bases on Balls	122, Walt Masterson, 1948
Doubles	51, Mickey Vernon, 1946	Winning Pct.	.708, Dutch Leonard, 1945
Triples	15, Stan Spence, 1942 15, Pete Runnels, 1954	ERA	2.12, Roger Wolff, 1945
Bases on Balls	151, Eddie Yost, 1956	Saves	18, Dick Hyde, 1958
Stolen Bases	61, George Case, 1943	Shutouts	9, Bob Porterfield, 1953

At a glance, this club looks as though it should have been much stronger during the period than the St. Louis-Baltimore entry. The fault for it being weaker probably belongs to the Griffiths, who saw no reason not to do things like keep Clark's nephew Sherry Robertson on the payroll for years since the club wasn't going anywhere anyway. Robertson may be the worst player in history to spend ten seasons in the majors. Yost was the club's most valuable player during the fifties, and Porterfield, for a couple of years anyway, was its finest pitcher.

KANSAS CITY ATHLETICS

Pennants: None
Manager: Connie Mack, 1942–50
Park: Shibe Park (Philadelphia), 1942–54
  Municipal Stadium (Kansas City), 1955–67
Best Year: 1948 (84–70, .545)
Worst Year: 1943 and 1946 (49–105, .318)
Top Rookie: Alex Kellner, 1949
Biggest Disappointment: Jim Finigan, 1955–56
Best Deal: Buying Hank Majeski from the Yankees, 1946
Worst Deal: Letting Roger Maris go to the Yankees, 1960
Other:
  1943—Team ties its own AL record by losing 20 straight games
  1947—Break .500 for the first time since 1933
  1948—Franchise's final first-division finish while it's based in
    Philadelphia
  1949—Set ML record by turning 217 double plays; tie AL rec-
    ord set by the 1939 Tigers for the highest winning percent-
    age (.526) by a second-division team during a season in which
    a 154-game schedule is played; record five pitchers issue 100
    or more walks
  1950—A's finish in basement in the team's final year under
    Connie Mack with 5.49 staff ERA, the poorest in the majors
    since 1939
  1951—Jimmy Dykes becomes the first man other than Mack
    to manage the team
  1954—Team finishes last in its final year in Philadelphia
  1955—Team finishes a heady 6th its first year in Kansas City
  1958—.474 winning percentage is team's best while in Kansas
    City
  1960—Pitchers Ray Herbert and Buddy Daley are a combined
    30–31 for the last-place A's; the rest of the staff is 28–65

HITTING		**PITCHING**	
Batting Ave.	.344, Ferris Fain, 1951	Wins	24, Bobby Shantz, 1952
Slugging Ave.	.592, Bob Cerv, 1958	Losses	22, Art Ditmar, 1956
Home Runs	38, Bob Cerv, 1958	Innings	280, Bobby Shantz, 1952
RBIs	125, Gus Zernial, 1951	Games Started	37, Harry Byrd, 1953
Total Bases	305, Bob Cerv, 1958	Complete Games	27, Bobby Shantz, 1952
Hits	190, Vic Power, 1955	Strikeouts	152, Bobby Shantz, 1952
Runs	128, Eddie Joost, 1949	Bases on Balls	141, Phil Marchildon, 1947
Doubles	43, Ferris Fain, 1952	Winning Pct.	.774, Bobby Shantz, 1952
Triples	12, Elmer Valo, 1949	ERA	2.48, Bobby Shantz, 1952
Bases on Balls	149, Eddie Joost, 1949	Saves	18, Tom Gorman, 1955*
Stolen Bases	17, Spook Jacobs, 1954	Shutouts	5, Bobby Shantz, 1952

*The record for the most saves by an A's pitcher while the club was in Philadelphia is 12, jointly held by Joe Berry (1944) and Russ Christopher (1947).

The A's are the only team that was rotten when the franchise was transferred and remained rotten right up till the time it was transferred again to Oakland. To illustrate how bad it got: The 1957 A's were the first club in history that didn't have a single pitcher good enough to work enough innings to qualify as an ERA leader. It's not as if they made up for it in other areas either. Jacobs was the last Athletics player in the period to steal more than ten bases in a season.

NATIONAL LEAGUE COMPOSITE STANDINGS

Number of Years Finishing in Each Position

Team	1	2	3	4	5	6	7	8	Aggregate
Brooklyn-L.A.	7	5	4	1	0	0	2	0	1
St. Louis	4	5	4	1	2	1	2	0	2
Boston-Milwaukee	3	5	2	4	0	3	2	0	3
New York-San Francisco	2	1	5	1	6	2	0	2	4
Cincinnati	0	1	2	3	4	6	3	0	5
Philadelphia	1	0	2	3	4	1	2	6	6
Pittsburgh	1	2	0	4	1	1	5	5	7
Chicago	1	0	1	1	4	3	5	4	8

LOS ANGELES DODGERS

Pennants: 1947, 1949, 1952, 1953, 1955, 1956, 1959
Manager: Walter Alston, 1954–60
Park: Ebbets Field (Brooklyn),1942–57; in the last game at Ebbets, on September 24, 1957, Danny McDevitt of the Dodgers blanked the Pirates, 3–0
Roosevelt Stadium (Jersey City, New Jersey), 1956–57; the Dodgers played a number of their home games across the river during their last two seasons in Brooklyn
Los Angeles Coliseum, 1958–60
Best Year: 1953 (105–49, .682)
Worst Year: 1944 (63–91, .409)
Top Rookie: Jackie Robinson, 1947
Biggest Disappointment: Bobby Morgan, 1950
Best Deal: Pirating Billy Cox, Preacher Roe and Gene Mauch from the Pirates, 1948
Worst Deal: Leaving Roberto Clemente unprotected, enabling Pittsburgh to draft him, 1955
Other:
1942—104 wins ties ML record for the most victories by an also-ran
1943—Only ML team to score over 700 runs
1946—Lose to Cardinals, 2 games to 0, in first-ever pennant playoff series
1947—Set new NL attendance record; garner NL record 732 walks
1951—Lose pennant playoff series to the Giants on Bobby Thomson's "Shot Heard 'Round the World"; become the only team in NL history to lose two consecutive flags on the last day of the season
1952—106 errors is new NL record low
1953—Tie ML record when six players score 100 or more runs
1955—Open season with ten consecutive wins to set new ML record; conclude season by winning first World Championship in franchise history
1958—Franchise moves to Los Angeles, sets new ML attendance record in its first year on the West Coast
1959—Take first flag by a West Coast team by beating the Braves in a pennant playoff series; set new ML record for the lowest winning percentage by a flag winner (.564)

HITTING		PITCHING	
Batting Ave.	.357, Dixie Walker, 1944	Wins	27, Don Newcombe, 1956
Slugging Ave.	.647, Duke Snider, 1954	Losses	16, Hal Gregg, 1944
Home Runs	43, Duke Snider, 1956	Innings	280, Ralph Branca, 1947
RBIs	142, Roy Campanella, 1953	Games Started	37, Carl Erskine, 1954
Total Bases	378, Duke Snider, 1954	Complete Games	20, Don Newcombe, 1950
Hits	203, Jackie Robinson, 1949	Strikeouts	246, Don Drysdale, 1960
Runs	132, Pee Wee Reese, 1949 132, Duke Snider, 1953	Bases on Balls	137, Hal Gregg, 1944
Doubles	43, Augie Galan, 1944	Winning Pct.	.880, Preacher Roe, 1951
Triples	17, Jim Gilliam, 1953	ERA	2.36, Curt Davis, 1942
Bases on Balls	148, Eddie Stanky, 1945	Saves	24, Jim Hughes, 1954
Stolen Bases	50, Maury Wills, 1960	Shutouts	6, Johnny Podres, 1957

No one season by either a hitter or a pitcher stands out during the period above all others. Moreover, there are eighteen different names on the chart and every record figure is solid. If those are the marks of a great team, then the Dodgers were the best in this area. Yet we all know there was one better. The panel isn't foolish enough to try and name this club's top player and pitcher for the period. It would be tough even to select an All-Star team. Where, for example, would you put Jim Gilliam? And whom would you leave out to include him?

ST. LOUIS CARDINALS

Pennants: 1942, 1943, 1944, 1946
Manager: Eddie Dyer, 1946–50
Park: Sportsman's Park; shared with the Browns until 1954 when the club became its sole occupant, and renamed Busch Stadium prior to the 1954 season
Best Year: 1942 (106–48, .688)
Worst Year: 1955 (68–86, .442)
Top Rookie: Johnny Beazley, 1942
Biggest Disappointment: Eddie Kazak, 1950; by a narrow margin over Eddie Yuhas, 1953
Beat Deal: Obtaining Curt Flood from Cincinnati, 1958
Worst Deal: Sending Johnny Mize to the Giants, 1942
Other:

1942—Fire Branch Rickey as general manager—he moved to Brooklyn to take a similar job with the Dodgers; set franchise record with .688 winning percentage and become the first team since the 1926 Cardinals to beat the Yankees in a World Series

1943—Team BA of .279 leads the majors by 17 points

1944—Top the majors in BA, FA, ERA and runs; become the last NL team to sweep three straight pennants

1946—Top the NL in BA, FA, ERA and runs but are nevertheless tied with the Dodgers at the end of the regular season and forced to undergo a playoff in order to claim the pennant

1949—Steal NL-record low 17 bases; lose pennant on the last day of the season

1950—Host first opening night game in ML history

1953—Augie Busch buys the club when previous owner Fred Saigh is forced to sell it after being sentenced to the federal pen for income tax evasion

1957—Finish 2nd with a team not expected to be a contender as McDaniel brothers provide the spark

1959—Come in 7th but only 16 games out of 1st

HITTING		PITCHING	
Batting Ave.	.376, Stan Musial, 1948	Wins	22, Mort Cooper, 1942, 1944
Slugging Ave.	.702, Stan Musial, 1948	Losses	16, Harvey Haddix, 1955
			16, Murray Dickson, 1947, 1948
Home Runs	39, Stan Musial, 1948	Innings	282, Larry Jackson, 1960
RBIs	131, Stan Musial, 1948	Games Started	38, Larry Jackson, 1960
Total Bases	429, Stan Musial, 1948	Complete Games	24, Mort Cooper, 1943
Hits	230, Stan Musial, 1948	Strikeouts	225, Sam Jones, 1958
Runs	135, Stan Musial, 1948	Bases on Balls	114, Vinegar Bend Mizell, 1953
Doubles	53, Stan Musial, 1953	Winning Pct.	.810, Ted Wilks, 1944
Triples	20, Stan Musial, 1943, 1946	ERA	1.78, Mort Cooper, 1942*
Bases on Balls	107, Stan Musial, 1949	Saves	26, Lindy McDaniel, 1960
Stolen Bases	26, Red Schoendienst, 1945	Shutouts	10, Mort Cooper, 1942

*Howie Pollet led the NL in 1943 with a 1.75 ERA but pitched only 118 innings.

What's there to say? Too bad Musial wasn't a better base thief? There aren't even some nice surprises on the list of runner-up recordholders. Musial, as you might imagine, in almost every major batting department also had the second-best season of any Cardinals player during the period. Naming the club's top pitcher for this era makes for a very tough call. It narrows down to a choice between two southpaws who both just missed cracking the chart—Harry Brecheen and Howie Pollet.

MILWAUKEE BRAVES

Pennants: 1948, 1957, 1958
Manager: Billy Southworth, 1946–49, 1950–51
Park: Braves Field (Boston), 1942–52
  County Stadium (Milwaukee), 1953–60
Best Year: 1957 (95–59, .617)
Worst Year: 1942 (59–89, .399)
Top Rookie: Alvin Dark, 1948
Biggest Disappointment: Willard Marshall, 1950
Best Deal: Three way tie—Tommy Holmes from the Yankees, 1942; Bob Elliott from the Pirates, 1947; Lew Burdette and cash from the Yankees for Johnny Sain, 1951
Worst Deal: Giving the Cardinals Red Barrett and some $60,000 for Mort Cooper, 1945; Barrett went on to win 23 games that year while Cooper proved to be pretty well shot
Other:
  1943—Finish 6th despite having one of the best mound staffs in the majors as team scores the fewest runs in the majors and is last in the NL in BA, OBP and SA
  1945—Team is second in the ML in homers and has in Tommy Holmes the only player since the end of the deadball era to be a league leader both in home runs and fewest strikeouts
  1946—Group headed by Lou Perini buys the club
  1947—Team wins 86 games, its best showing since 1916, and leads NL in BA for the first time since 1877
  1948—Team claims its second and last twentieth century pennant while the franchise is based in Boston
  1952—Draw 281,278 fans and abandon Boston
  1953—First franchise shift since 1903; club sets new ML attendance record its first year in Milwaukee and soars from 7th to 2nd
  1958—Club become the first NL team to lose a World Series after leading 3 games to 1
  1959—Bid to become the first NL team since the 1942–44 Cardinals to win three straight pennants falls short when the club is beaten by the Dodgers in a pennant playoff series

HITTING		PITCHING	
Batting Ave.	.355, Hank Aaron, 1959	Wins	24, Johnny Sain, 1948
Slugging Ave.	.636, Hank Aaron, 1959	Losses	21, Jim Tobin, 1942
Home Runs	47, Eddie Mathews, 1953	Innings	315, Johnny Sain, 1948
RBIs	135, Eddie Mathews, 1953	Games Started	39, done by four different pitchers
Total Bases	367, Tommy Holmes, 1945	Complete Games	28, Jim Tobin, 1942, 1944
			28, Johnny Sain, 1948
Hits	224, Tommy Holmes, 1945	Strikeouts	191, Warren Spahn, 1950
Runs	125, Tommy Holmes, 1945	Bases on Balls	122, Vern Bickford, 1950
Doubles	47, Tommy Holmes, 1945	Winning Pct.	.767, Warren Spahn, 1953
Triples	15, Billy Bruton, 1956	ERA	2.10, Warren Spahn, 1953
Bases on Balls	131, Bob Elliott, 1948	Saves	15, Don McMahon, 1959
Stolen Bases	35, Sam Jethroe, 1951	Shutouts	7, Warren Spahn, 1951

Holmes's season in 1945 was the most outstanding one in this century by a Boston Braves player. All of his entries on the chart are twentieth century Boston Braves records. Lew Burdette, the Braves' best pitcher during the era apart from Spahn, is one of the four pitchers tied for the most starting assignments. The others are Spahn, Sain and Bickford. In 1950, his peak season, Bickford had 19 wins by early September and then tried and failed six times to get his 20th. Tobin never won 20 either. In 1942, despite hurling 28 complete games, he won just 12.

SAN FRANCISCO GIANTS

Pennants: 1951, 1954
Manager: Leo Durocher, 1948–55
Park: Polo Grounds (New York), 1942–57
  Seals Stadium (San Francisco), 1958–59
  Candlestick Park, 1960-present; first game on April 12, 1960
Best Year: 1954 (97–57, .630)
Worst Year: 1943 (55–98, .359)
Top Rookie: Bill Voiselle, 1944
Biggest Disappointment: Mel Ott, 1943; batted .234, had just 47 RBIs and hit no home runs on the road all year
Best Deal: Acquiring Alvin Dark and Eddie Stanky in a block-buster deal with the Braves, 1950
Worst Deal: Sending Red Schoendienst to Milwaukee, 1957
Other:
  1943—Finish last for the first time since 1915
  1946—Second cellar finish in four years; team completes its poorest four-year stretch since 1899–1902
  1947—Hit 221 home runs, new ML record and still the NL mark
  1951—Win pennant on Bobby Thomson's three-run homer in historic pennant playoff series with Brooklyn after being 13½ games out of first place as late as August 11
  1954—Sweep Indians in the World Series to register one of the biggest upsets in professional sports history
  1957—Club finishes a bad 6th its last year in New York
  1958—Giants host first ML game in history on the West Coast, beating the Dodgers 8–0 on April 15 to open the season
  1959—Lead NL race by two games with eight to play and then wind up finishing four games out of 1st by dropping seven of last eight games
  1960—Have second-best ERA in NL and are third in loop in runs but nevertheless finish 5th, with poor fielding being the leading culprit; team makes the most errors in the majors and has the lowest FA

HITTING		PITCHING	
Batting Ave.	.347, Willie Mays, 1958	Wins	23, Sal Maglie, 1951 23, Larry Jansen, 1951
Slugging Ave.	.667, Willie Mays, 1954	Losses	19, Dave Koslo, 1946
Home Runs	51, Johnny Mize, 1947 51, Willie Mays, 1955	Innings	313, Bill Voiselle, 1944
RBIs	138, Johnny Mize, 1947	Games Started	41, Bill Voiselle, 1944
Total Bases	382, Willie Mays, 1955	Complete Games	24, Bill Voiselle, 1944
Hits	212, Willie Mays, 1954	Strikeouts	209, Sam Jones, 1959
Runs	137, Johnny Mize, 1947	Bases on Balls	118, Bill Voiselle, 1944
Doubles	43, Willie Mays, 1959	Winning Pct.	.833, Hoyt Wilhelm, 1952
Triples	20, Willie Mays, 1957	ERA	2.30, Johnny Antonelli, 1954
Bases on Balls	144, Eddie Stanky, 1950	Saves	19, Marv Grissom, 1954
Stolen Bases	40, Willie Mays, 1956	Shutouts	6, Johnny Antonelli, 1954, 1956 6, Jack Sanford, 1960

Mays had 128 home runs in his first three full seasons as a major leaguer but only 321 RBIs. He's the greatest slugger in history who was never an RBI leader. That's a very small bone to pick, though, in what was otherwise a career of amazing productivity and consistency. Antonelli and Voiselle are the most prominent hurlers on the chart largely because they each had one great season, but Maglie was the club's best pitcher during the era.

CINCINNATI REDS

Pennants: None
Manager: Bill McKechnie, 1942–46; Birdie Tebbetts, 1954–58
Park: Crosley Field
Best Year: 1956 (91–63, .591)
Worst Year: 1945 (61–93, .396)
Top Rookie: Frank Robinson, 1956
Biggest Disappointment: Ray Jablonski, 1955
Best Deal: Robbing the Phillies of Ken Raffensberger, 1947
Worst Deal: Sending Hank Sauer and Frankie Baumholtz to the Cubs for Peanuts Lowrey and Harry Walker, 1949
Other:

1943—2nd-place finish is club's highest between 1941 and 1961

1944—Last above-.500 finish until 1956; pace majors in complete games, fewest walks allowed and fewest strikeouts by batters but lackadaisical offense that scores the second-fewest runs in the NL consigns team to a distant 3rd-place finish

1946—Lose ML-record 41 one-run games

1949—Ken Raffensberger and Herm Wehmeier have combined 29–29 record; rest of hill staff is 33–63

1951—Ken Raffensberger and Ewell Blackwell have combined 32–32 record; rest of hill staff is 36–54; club finishes last in the NL in batting

1955—Club finishes in the second division for the eleventh straight year, a stretch made all the more extraordinary by the fact that it never once finishes in the cellar

1956—Team wins 91 games, most since 1940, and clubs 221 home runs to tie the NL record and the then-existing ML record

1960—Set twentieth-century record which endures until 1991 for the fewest wins (67) and the lowest winning percentage (.435) by a team destined to win a pennant the next year

HITTING			PITCHING	
Batting Ave.	.326, Ted Kluszewski, 1954	Losses	23, Bucky Walters, 1944
Slugging Ave.	.642, Ted Kluszewski, 1954	Losses	19, Howie Fox, 1949 19, Ken Raffensberger, 1950
Home Runs	49, Ted Kluszewski, 1954	Innings	289, Johnny Vander Meer, 1943
RBIs	141, Ted Kluszewski, 1954	Games Started	38, Ken Raffensberger, 1949
Total Bases	368, Ted Kluszewski, 1954	Complete Games	27, Bucky Walters, 1944
Hits	205, Vada Pinson, 1959	Strikouts	193, Ewell Blackwell, 1947
Runs	131, Vada Pinson, 1959	Bases on Balls	162, Johnny Vander Meer, 1943
Doubles	47, Vada Pinson, 1959	Winning Pct.	.742, Bucky Walters, 1944
Triples	12, Vada Pinson, 1960	ERA	2.32, Joe Beggs, 1946
Bases on Balls	94, Augie Galan, 1947 94, Johnny Temple, 1957	Saves	20, Frank Smith, 1954
Stolen Bases	32, Vada Pinson, 1960	Shutouts	6, Bucky Walters, 1944 6, Ewell Blackwell, 1946, 1947 6, Ken Raffensberger, 1952

For some reason it took the Reds nearly forty years to come up with a slugger like Kluszewski who could exploit the inviting dimensions of Crosley Field. Pinson, after his first five seasons, looked like a sure bet to make the Hall of Fame. Raffensberger wins the Vic Willis Award for this period. With a better team he probably would have had four or five 20-win seasons rather than none. Beggs was a bullpen ace who set his ERA record in the only year he was used chiefly as a starter.

PHILADELPHIA PHILLIES

Pennants: 1950
Manager: Eddie Sawyer, 1948–52, 1958–60
Park: Shibe Park; became its sole occupant in 1955 when the A's moved to Kansas City
Best Year: 1950 (91–63, .591)
Worst Year: 1942 (42–109, .278)
Top Rookie: Richie Ashburn, 1948
Biggest Disappointment: Stretch Schultz, 1947
Best Deal: Getting Eddie Waitkus from the Cubs, 1948
Worst Deal: Sending Ken Raffensberger to the Reds for Al Lakeman, 1947
Other:

1942—Score just 394 runs; finish last in the NL in fielding despite having the first player in ML history, outfielder Danny Litwhiler, to go through an entire season without making an error; set NL record with fifth straight last-place finish

1943—Play NL record 43 doubleheaders

1944—Carpenter family takes over the team after its previous owner, Bill Cox, is banned for betting on games; team known as the Blue Jays in 1944–45

1949—Club wins 81 games, the most since 1917

1950—Second pennant in franchise history is accompanied by 91 wins, the club's best showing since 1916; team beaten four straight games in the World Series by the Yankees in most competitive postseason sweep in history

1952—Robin Roberts is 28–7; rest of mound staff is 59–60

1954—Lead majors with 78 complete games, 29 of them by Robin Roberts and 21 by Curt Simmons

1958—First cellar finish since 1947

1960—Manager Eddie Sawyer let go one game into the season; club finishes last for the third straight year under his replacement, Gene Mauch

HITTING		**PITCHING**	
Batting Ave.	.371, Harry Walker, 1947*	Wins	28, Robin Roberts, 1952
Slugging Ave.	.551, Del Ennis, 1950	Losses	22, Robin Roberts, 1957
Home Runs	32, Stan Lopata, 1956	Innings	347, Robin Roberts, 1953
RBIs	126, Del Ennis, 1950	Games Started	41, Robin Roberts, 1953
Total Bases	328, Del Ennis, 1950	Complete Games	33, Robin Roberts, 1953
Hits	221, Richie Ashburn, 1951	Strikeouts	198, Robin Roberts, 1953
Runs	111, Richie Ashburn, 1954	Bases on Balls	114, Rube Melton, 1942
Doubles	40, Del Ennis, 1948	Winning Pct.	.800, Robin Roberts, 1952
Triples	16, Harry Walker, 1947*	ERA	2.59, Robin Roberts, 1952
Bases on Balls	125, Richie Ashburn, 1954	Saves	22, Jim Konstanty, 1950
Stolen Bases	32, Richie Ashburn, 1948	Shutouts	6, Robin Roberts, 1951
			6, Curt Simmons, 1952

*Includes only Walker's stats that year with the Phillies.

A mediocre to bad team for most of the period that was shot to greatness one season when all of its young players came through and caught the Dodgers by surprise. Roberts, with a better supporting cast, would have been a cinch 350-game winner. Ashburn, at his peak in an era when there were many great glovemen playing center field, may have been the best of them all. Lopata is one of the very few catchers to hold a club era home-run record; he also had a .535 SA in 1956.

PITTSBURGH PIRATES

Pennants: 1960
Manager: Frankie Frisch, 1942–46
Park: Forbes Field
Best Year: 1960 (95–59, .617)
Worst Year: 1952 (42–112, .273)
Top Rookie: Danny O'Connell, 1950
Biggest Disappointment: Bob Chesnes, 1949
Best Deal: Bagging Smokey Burgess, Don Hoak and Harvey Haddix from Cincinnati, 1959
Worst Deal: Getting virtually nothing of value from the Braves in return for Bob Elliott, 1947
Other:

1944—2nd-place finish and 90 wins are club's best showing between 1928 and 1960

1947—4.68 staff ERA, the poorest in the majors, dooms club to a tie for last place

1948—Only first-division finish between 1946 and 1958

1953—5.33 staff ERA; reliever Johnny Hetki (3.95) is only hurler of consequence with an ERA under 4.53

1954—Lose 100 or more games for the third consecutive season under new general manager Branch Rickey

1955—Club is last for fourth consecutive season; Bob Friend and Vern Law have a combined 24–19 record, the rest of the hill staff is 36–75

1959—First time since 1945 that the club finishes above .500 two years in a row

1960—Club wins its first pennant in 33 years and defeats the Yankees in the only seven-game World Series to be decided by a home run on the last pitch

HITTING		PITCHING	
Batting Ave.	.334, Bill Virdon, 1956*	Wins	22, Bob Friend, 1958
Slugging Ave.	.658, Ralph Kiner, 1949	Losses	21, Murray Dickson, 1952
Home Runs	54, Ralph Kiner, 1949	Innings	314, Bob Friend, 1956
RBIs	127, Ralph Kiner, 1947, 1949	Games Started	42, Bob Friend, 1956
Total Bases	361, Ralph Kiner, 1947, 1949	Complete Games	25, Rip Sewell, 1943
Hits	186, Stan Rojek, 1948 186, Dick Groat, 1960	Strikeouts	183, Bob Friend, 1960
Runs	124, Ralph Kiner, 1951	Bases on Balls	116, Johnny Lindell, 1953*
Doubles	41, Vince DiMaggio, 1943	Winning Pct.	.947, Roy Face, 1959
Triples	19, Johnny Barrett, 1944	ERA	2.54, Rip Sewell, 1943
Bases on Balls	137, Ralph Kiner, 1951	Saves	24, Roy Face, 1960
Stolen Bases	28, Johnny Barrett, 1944	Shutouts	5, Rip Sewell, 1942 5, Max Butcher, 1944

*Includes only Virdon's and Lindell's stats with the Pirates. Both of them spent part of their record seasons with other clubs.

Dick Groat, who hit .325 in 1960, had the highest average during the period among players who were with the Pirates for an entire season. Friend rates as the club's best pitcher in this era and Kiner as its best player. Friend had some competition from Sewell and Face, among others; Kiner had almost none, although Roberto Clemente, by the end of the period, was beginning to show signs that he was a bit more than a .270-hitting outfielder with a great arm.

CHICAGO CUBS

Pennants: 1945
Manager: Charlie Grimm, 1944–49
Park: Wrigley Field
Best Year: 1945 (98–56, .636)
Worst Year: 1956 and 1960 (60–94, .390)
Top Rookie: Ernie Banks, 1954
Biggest Disappointment: Dick Drott, 1958–60
Best Deal: Snagging Hank Sauer and Frankie Baumholtz from Cincinnati, 1949
Worst Deal: Sending Eddie Stanky to Brooklyn for Bob Chipman, 1944
Other:

1942—Club wins just 68 games, its poorest showing since 1925
1945—Last pennant in franchise history
1946—Last first-division finish until 1967
1948—Club finishes in the cellar for the first time since 1925
1950—Last team in ML history to make over 200 errors (201) in a season playing a 154-game schedule
1952—Only .500 finish between 1947 and 1963
1954—Even with rookie star Ernie Banks, the club has a poorer record than it did in 1953
1957—Rookies Moe Drabowsky and Dick Drott are a combined 28–26; other pitchers go 34–66
1959—Ernie Banks plays on his best team prior to expansion when the Cubs win 74 game and tie for 5th
1960—Sink to 7th place, only one game out of cellar, as team gives up 776 runs, the most in the majors, and also has the worst ERA in the majors (4.35)

HITTING		PITCHING	
Batting Ave.	.355, Phil Cavarretta, 1945	Wins	22, Hank Wyse, 1945
Slugging Ave.	.614, Ernie Banks, 1958	Losses	20, Bob Rush, 1950 20, Sam Jones, 1955 20, Glen Hobbie, 1960
Home Runs	47, Ernie Banks, 1958	Innings	278, Claude Passeau, 1942 278, Hank Wyse, 1945
RBIs	143, Ernie Banks, 1958	Games Started	36, Bob Anderson, 1959 36, Glen Hobbie, 1960
Total Bases	379, Ernie Banks, 1958	Complete Games	24, Claude Passeau, 1942
Hits	197, Phil Cavarretta, 1944	Strikeouts	198, Sam Jones, 1955
Runs	119, Ernie Banks, 1958	Bases on Balls	185, Sam Jones, 1955
Doubles	37, Don Johnson, 1944	Winning Pct.	.688, Hank Wyse, 1945
Triples	15, Phil Cavarretta, 1944	ERA	2.40, Ray Prim, 1945*
Bases on Balls	116, Richie Ashburn, 1960	Saves	13, Turk Lown, 1956 13, Don Elston, 1959
Stolen Bases	23, Tony Taylor, 1959	Shutouts	7, Hi Bithorn, 1943

*In 1945 Hank Borowy led the NL with a 2.14 ERA but pitched only 122 innings.

Apart from Banks, the Cubs were a disaster from 1946 through the end of the period. Johnny Schmitz was probably their best pitcher, but even he had only a couple of good years. Exclude Banks and Cavarretta's two wartime seasons and you'd find yourself looking at the era's most abysmal hitting chart.

THE BEST, THE WORST
AND THE WEIRDEST
TEAMS BETWEEN 1942
AND 1960

• •

AMERICAN LEAGUE

THE BEST

1954 CLEVELAND INDIANS
W–111 L–43
Manager: Al Lopez

Regular Lineup—1B, Vic Wertz; 2B, Bobby Avila; 3B, Al Rosen; SS, George Strickland; RF, Dave Philley; CF, Larry Doby; LF, Al Smith; C, Jim Hegan; P, Early Wynn; P, Bob Lemon; P, Mike Garcia; P, Bob Feller; P, Art Houtteman; P, Ray Narleski; P, Don Mossi; P, Hal Newhouser

The Tribe won an AL-record 111 games mainly because they had to in order to hold off the Yankees, who triumphed every year but one between 1949 and 1958 and who, in 1954, won 103 games in their own right and were quite possibly the best team Casey Stengel ever managed. It's easy, in retrospect, to say the Indians were a fluke team that got hot and had a bushel of luck, but that wasn't at all the case. Cleveland actually started very slowly, suffered a critical early season injury to Rosen and received a career year only from Avila. Lemon, Wynn and Garcia all had numerous other seasons that were just as good, Rosen declined markedly after breaking his finger and was never the same player, and Philley and Wertz had, by their standards, putrid years. What lifted this team to such towering heights were Doby,

• • 231 • •

two rookie relievers—Narleski and Mossi—and its chief cata-
lyst, Hegan, considered by many, and not just in Cleveland, to
have been the era's slickest defensive catcher and its shrewdest
handler of pitchers. That the Indians never won again is not a
blemish on their achievement but rather can be attributed to
the demoralizing Series defeat the Giants handed them, the sudden and permanent slippage of several key players like Rosen
and Avila, and the general run of fate that has perennially
haunted the franchise. In 1955 Herb Score, the most heralded
young pitcher to appear since Feller, arrived from Indianapolis
to take up the slack after Feller's fade left the team in need of
a fourth starter, and for a time seemed destined for a career
that even Feller himself would have envied. An all too brief time,
just as the 1954 season was, for Clevelanders, an all too brief
payoff for their fifty-three-year wait for the Tribe to finally take
its turn at being the game's dominant team.

THE WORST

1945 PHILADELPHIA ATHLETICS
W–52 L–98
Manager: Connie Mack

Regular Lineup—1B, Dick Siebert; 2B, Irv Hall; 3B, George Kell; SS, Eddie Busch;
RF, Hal Peck; CF, Bobby Estalella; LF, Charlie Metro/Bill McGhee; C, Buddy Rosar;
P, Bobo Newsom; P, Russ Christopher; P, Jesse Flores; P, Luther Knerr; P, Don
Black; P, Joe Berry; P, Steve Gerkin

Granted, there were so many bad teams during the war years
it's somewhat unfair to single out just one of them—it's even a
bit nasty to hit on a wartime team at all—and I'll concede too
that I'm always primed to be hard on Mack. But the man deserved it. To saddle a decent pitching staff, for a war year anyway, with a collection of hitters who produced only 494 runs,
the fewest by any AL team since the abbreviated 1919 season,
was either criminally stubborn or senile, depending on your view
of Mack's operation of the franchise in those years. Kell, a rookie
in 1945, led the club in RBIs with all of 56, and Busch and Hall
were busy setting a record by playing in their second consecutive season as a keystone combination without either of them
hitting a single home run. There were dozens of draft-deferred
players in the high minors who could have beefed up this team,
but Mack, either a masochist or a misanthrope (again depending

on your own psychological slant on the man), preferred to torture his pitchers and the citizens of Philadelphia with a crew of stiffs. Perhaps he felt secure because the Phillies that year were just as ghastly. But they at least offered their followers a final look at the likes of Jimmie Foxx, Gus Mancuso and Ben Chapman in major league games, whereas Mack's assemblage had all the drawing power of a factory-league team. The A's, deservedly, brought up the rear of the AL in 1945 not only in the standings but also in attendance. Gerkin, undeservedly, was winless in twelve decisions despite compiling a 3.62 ERA, which exactly matched the team's figure and was only .26 runs higher than the league ERA.

THE WEIRDEST

1953 BOSTON RED SOX
W–84 L–69
Manager: Lou Boudreau

Regular Lineup—1B, Dick Gernert; 2B, Billy Goodman; 3B, George Kell; SS, Milt Bolling; RF, Jimmy Piersall; CF, Tom Umphlett; LF, Hoot Evers; C, Sammy White; P, Mel Parnell; P, Mickey McDermott; P, Sid Hudson; P, Skinny Brown; P, Willard Nixon; P, Ellis Kinder

Any Red Sox fans (and there no doubt were some) who were so devastated by the team's third successive failure, in 1950, to nab a pennant that was ripe for the taking that they stayed away from all thoughts of baseball for the next two seasons would have felt like they'd missed about ten years' worth of developments if they came out to a game in Fenway Park in 1953. During the short intervening period Boston had cleaned house to a greater extent than any contender in history save for the 1914 A's. Goodman was the lone regular holdover from the 1950 powerhouse, although Ted Williams returned from the air corps late in the campaign. Yet the new bunch, different as they were from the sluggers to which Red Sox fans had grown accustomed, finished a solid fourth, creating hope that the club indeed knew what it was doing. Still more rookie talent arrived the following year in the persons of Tom Brewer, Frank Sullivan, Harry Aganis, Ted Lepcio and Billy Consolo. But the original batch of rookies, excepting Piersall, all fell flat on their fannies, and the second wave, after showing considerable early promise, also failed to pan out for the most part. It would be more than a

decade yet before another club youth movement finally produced a winner. In 1953, though, for that one year, the Red Sox
seemed to be on to something precious. No one knew at the time
how their heretofore uninspired farm system had suddenly become the most fertile in the majors, and no one ever did really
figure out why so many of the players it produced bloomed bril-
liantly in their first couple of major league seasons, only to
wither away quickly thereafter.

NATIONAL LEAGUE

THE BEST

1953 BROOKLYN DODGERS
W–105 L–49
Manager: Chuck Dressen

Regular Lineup—1B, Gil Hodges; 2B, Jim Gilliam; 3B, Billy Cox; SS, Pee Wee
Reese; RF, Carl Furillo; CF, Duke Snider; LF, Jackie Robinson; C, Roy Campanella;
P, Carl Erskine; P, Russ Meyer; P, Billy Loes; P, Preacher Roe; P, Clem Labine;
P, Jim Hughes; P, Johnny Podres

After triumphing in a close race the previous year, Brooklyn
clinched the flag in 1953 on September 12, the earliest date that
an NL club ever ended matters in a 154-game schedule. The
Dodgers scored 955 runs, 187 more than the second-highest-
scoring NL team that year, and had one of the deepest hill staffs
in NL history, even after losing their ace, Don Newcombe, to the
army. Dressen had the luxury of spreading the work among ten
pitchers, all of whom had winning records. Erskine, the staff
leader, was the only member required to labor more than 200
innings, and Loes led the club in losses with just eight. But hitting was where the Dodgers really excelled, although some
would argue that their fielding was a still greater forte—or even
their base running. The fact was that the Dodgers towered above
the rest of the league in 1953. They finished 13 games ahead of
the second-place Braves, newly transplanted to Milwaukee, and
would probably have won more games than any NL club since
World War II had there been the necessary impetus. That came
in the World Series that fall, and once again, as always up to
that point, the Dodgers failed their followers. Brooklyn lost in

six games to the Yankees when Erskine was battered in two of the three contests he started and none of the club's second-line hurlers stepped forward to take up the slack. But the Series loss was the team's lone black mark and should not keep it from being ranked among the greatest nines. Even in defeat the Dodgers made history. They were the first Series loser to hit .300 or better.

THE WORST

1952 PITTSBURGH PIRATES
W–42 L–112
Manager: Billy Meyer

Regular Lineup—1B, Tony Bartirome; 2B, Johnny Merson; 3B, Pete Castiglione; SS, Dick Groat; RF, Gus Bell; CF, Bobby Del Greco/Catfish Metkovich; LF, Ralph Kiner; C, Joe Garagiola; P, Murray Dickson; P, Howie Pollet; P, Ted Wilks; P, Bob Friend; P, Woody Main; P, Paul LaPalme; P, Cal Hogue; P, Ron Kline

The Pirates had crept into seventh place in 1951 after finishing last in 1950 and seemed poised to improve another notch or two the following year. Instead they finished 22½ games behind the seventh-place Braves, the last NL team to play in Boston. Branch Rickey loaded the club with former Cardinals like Pollet, Wilks, and Garagiola, many of whom he'd signed before leaving St. Louis for the general manager's job in Brooklyn, but their championship habits failed to rub off on the rest of his crew. Panicked, he then embarked on a youth program that would ensure Pittsburgh a club-record four consecutive cellar finishes. Dickson, in 1952, became the only Pirates hurler in this century to lose 20 games in a season but was also the lone staff member to win more than seven; the experience of pitching for this team may have been part of what turned him into a recluse after he left baseball. The club was so awful that Kiner amassed just 87 RBIs despite hitting 37 home runs—stats like that, though relatively common now, were unheard of in the 1950s—and utility infielder Clem Koshorek and Bartirome, two rookies who appealed to Rickey but to no one else, collected 31 RBIs and no home runs between them in a combined 677 at bats. Meyer, naturally, was made the scapegoat, but his replacement, Fred Haney, who would win two pennants with Milwaukee later in the decade, fared no better over the next three seasons. The real culprit was Rickey, whose reputation as one of the canniest judges of player talent was in shreds by the time he left the Pittsburgh organization.

THE WEIRDEST

1949 ST. LOUIS CARDINALS
W-96 L-58
Manager: Eddie Dyer

Regular Lineup—1B, Nippy Jones; 2B, Red Schoendienst; 3B, Eddie Kazak; SS, Marty Marion; RF, Stan Musial; CF, Chuck Diering; LF, Enos Slaughter; C, Del Rice/Joe Garagiola; P, Howie Pollet; P, Harry Brecheen; P, Al Brazle; P, George Munger; P, Ted Wilks; P, Gerry Staley

Winners of four pennants in five years during the mid-forties, the Cardinals were still rated the team to beat as late as 1949. They lost the flag on the last day of the season but were lucky to come that close given the two weak spots—third base and center field—that their normally superb farm system would remain unable to shore up until the mid-fifties. In an effort to replace aging Terry Moore, the Cardinals were forced to employ a long string of marginal fly chasers like Diering and Erv Dusak and eventually resorted even to trying Musial, a fine outfielder but without the range or the arm to handle the center garden. To replace Whitey Kurowski, whose shoulder blew out in 1948, Dyer and his successor Marion experimented with four different regular hot cornermen in four seasons, ranging from Yankees castoff Billy Johnson to career minor leaguer Don Lang. Kazak, who showed evidence in 1949 of being the solution, was injured after being selected to the All-Star squad as a rookie and never recovered his early form. The mystery to Cardinals followers—and indeed to everyone who has studied the team's plight in those years—is why St. Louis continually ignored Don Richmond, a third baseman on its Rochester farm team with an erratic glove but impeccable minor league hitting credentials, or else (and this is not so mysterious, considering that the Cards were one of the last teams to integrate) didn't recruit one of the many fine black outfielders and third basemen such as Willie Mays and Hank Thompson, who were ready and waiting for the chance. Surely somebody like Ray Dandridge, not needed by the Giants after they landed Thompson, could have provided a couple of years of solid third base for the Cardinals in that period, even at his advanced age, and probably another flag or two.

SPECIAL FEATURE
TEAM: THE WHIZ KIDS

• •

1950 PHILADELPHIA PHILLIES
W–91 L–63
Manager: Eddie Sawyer

Regular Lineup—1B, Eddie Waitkus; 2B, Mike Goliat; 3B, Willie Jones; SS, Granny Hamner; RF, Del Ennis; CF, Richie Ashburn; LF, Dick Sisler; C, Andy Seminick; P, Robin Roberts; P, Curt Simmons; P, Jim Konstanty; P, Bob Miller; P, Bubba Church; P, Russ Meyer; P, Ken Heintzelman

In 1949 Meyer, a righthander, and Heintzelman, a southpaw, each won 17 games to spark the Phillies into third place, the team's highest finish since 1917. Between them Meyer and Heintzelman had a dazzling 34–18 record while the rest of the Phils hill crew won 47 games and lost 55. For the club to advance another notch or two in 1950, the formula was simple. Its lefty-righty tandem had to have another strong year and some rookie pitchers had to develop.

The Phillies' top righty-lefty tandem indeed did come through in a big way in 1950, only it did not consist of Meyer and Heintzelman. That pair crashed to a dreadful combined record of 12–20. And while two rookie hurlers, Miller and Church, were helpful, compiling 19 wins between them, it was the sudden development of Konstanty, a thirty-three-year-old reliever, that was largely responsible for the team's rocketing to the top of the pack. Konstanty logged 16 victories in 1950, saved 22 other wins and justly became the first fireman to bag an MVP award. Roberts and Simmons meanwhile emerged as the team's new righty-lefty tandem and accounted for 37 wins. Among them, Konstanty and the two main starters combined for 53 victories and just 26 defeats. With Ennis, Seminick and Sisler all enjoying career years and Goliat chipping in 13 homers and 64 RBIs in his only season as a regular, the Phillies shot to a huge lead as the season entered the home stretch and were still a seemingly safe seven games in front with only a week and a half to go.

Then it all began to turn sour. Miller came up with a bum arm and Church was hit in the face by a line drive. With Simmons having been summoned to active military service on September 10, Roberts was suddenly the team's only healthy and effective starter. To increase Sawyer's panic, Seminick was hobbled by an ankle injury in a home plate collision with Monte Irvin of the Giants. Still, the Phillies opened the final weekend of the season two games ahead of the Dodgers with just two to play. A 7–3 loss on Saturday forced Sawyer to call on Roberts to make his third start in five days the following afternoon at Ebbets Field. Opposing Roberts was Don Newcombe. Both were shooting for their 20th wins. A pennant playoff series seemed a certainty when Brooklyn tied the game 1–1 on a fluke home run by Pee Wee Reese and then began teeing off on Roberts in the bottom of the ninth. But Ashburn threw the potential game-winning run out at the plate, and Roberts proceded to retire both Carl Furillo and Gil Hodges with the bases jammed. In the top of the tenth Sisler pumped a three-run homer into the seats to give the Phils their first flag since 1915.

When the Whiz Kids were swept by the Yankees in the World Series, they were called the Fizz Kids by some members of the media. In truth, Philadelphia hung tough in all four games and needed only crisper fielding and a couple of key hits to have reversed the outcome. But the following year the team could no longer duck the Fizz Kids label. Simmons was still in the military service, Miller's arm failed to come around, Meyer and Heintzelman continued to disappoint, and Konstanty descended once again to mediocrity. That left Sawyer with only two reliable pitchers, Roberts and Church. The pair boasted a 36–26 record between them, but when the other hill member combined for a 37–55 mark, the Phillies plummeted to fifth place and were never again a serious contender during the 1950s.

What prevented the Whiz Kids from becoming a dynasty is

surprisingly easy to understand. The Phillies were a young team in 1950—thus the Whiz Kids tag—but they were not really all that much younger than the Dodgers and the Giants, their two principal competitors that year. Brooklyn's pitching staff was actually the same average age (27) as that of the Phillies, and New York's regular lineup matched the Phillies' average age of 26. More than that, the Phillies, for all their youth, had no rookies in 1950 apart from Church and Miller who ever developed into helpful players, and during the next two seasons their farm system delivered no useful rookies at all. The Giants and the Dodgers meanwhile unveiled Willie Mays and Joe Black, the NL's premier rookies in 1951 and 1952. That both were black, as was Sam Jethroe of the Boston Braves, the 1950 Rookie of the Year, was lost on the Phillies and their owner, Bob Carpenter. Not until 1957 would Carpenter deign to recruit a black player, thereby making the Phillies the last NL team to integrate.

The Whiz Kids handle may thus have been something of a misnomer. Some preferred to call Sawyer's 1950 bunch the "Fighting Phillies," withal a much more accurate nickname perhaps, though the club was not so much scrappy as tenacious. Unlike a Phillies team of 14 years later, which curiously was about the same average age and also had a manager who had never been much of a player, the 1950 crew did not wilt when their seemingly insurmountable lead began to melt like snow in July during the closing days of the season. They hung on to win. And in as gutsy a fashion as can be imagined.

THE WARTIME GAME IN THE MINORS

•••••••••••••••••••••••••••••••••••••

1945 TOLEDO MUD HENS
W-69 L-84
Manager: Ollie Marquardt

Regular Lineup—1B, Ed Ignasiak; 2B, Bobby Wren, 3B, Steve Collins; SS, Dick Kimble; RF, George Corona; CF, Fred Reinhart; LF, Don Smith/Bob Okrie; C, Russ Lyons/Jim Crandall; Util, Nick Polly/Blackstone Thompson; P, Cliff Fannin; P, John Whitehead; P, Jim Mains; P, Al LaMacchia; P, Ned Graver; P, Earl Smalling; P, Elwood Knierim; P, John Miller

Once upon a time Toledo had been home to the first major league team to break the color barrier. In 1884 the Toledo Blue Stockings were ushered into the American Association, then a major league, and allowed to bring with them Mose Walker, their catcher from the previous year when they had played in the Northwestern League. Walker and his brother Welday, who also saw duty with the Blue Stockings in 1884, were the only two acknowledged black Americans to perform in the majors prior to Jackie Robinson in 1947. Toledo lost its franchise when the AA cut back to eight teams in 1885 but returned to the loop for the 1890 season. As in 1884, when the AA had expanded to twelve clubs in an attempt to thwart the insurgent Union Association, the circumstances that gave Toledo a second window of opportunity in the majors were unusual. Between the Players League rebellion and the defection of the Cincinnati franchise to the National League, the AA was left with only two teams that were west of the Ohio River—St. Louis and Louisville. To help keep down travel expenses, the loop took on both Toledo and Columbus. Mose Walker meanwhile had continued to play in the minors, though not with Toledo, until 1889 when the color barrier, which had been clandestinely imposed on major league teams after the 1884 season, began to be practiced throughout professional baseball.

A member of the Western League (the forerunner of the American League) after its second taste of major league ball, Toledo switched to the Inter State League in 1897 and later returned to the reorganized Western League for the 1901 season before becoming a charter member of the new American Association, which was revived in 1902 as a minor league. Along with the change in scenery came one of the truly great team nicknames: Toledo was now known as the Mud Hens.

By 1945 the Mud Hens had been in the AA for forty-four years but had won only one pennant, back in 1927 under a peppery young manager named Casey Stengel. A strong second-place finish in 1944 had fueled hopes of a second pennant come 1945, but the realists in the Mud Hens' camp knew they were dashed when four of the best players on the 1944 club—Babe Martin, Len Schulte, Joe Schultz and lefty fireballer Earl Jones—were missing at the beginning of the 1945 campaign. All had been called up by the St. Louis Browns, with whom the Mud Hens had a working agreement. It was a match made by someone with a perverse sense of justice, for the Browns too had won only one pennant in their long history, that just the previous year, and consequently were hellbent on retaining their first-ever occupancy of the American League penthouse in 1945. The parent club's ambitions naturally took precedence, thus the theft of Jones, Martin, Schulte and Schultz. Also absent in 1945 were sixteen-game winner Bill Seinsoth and outfielder Bill Burgo. Standing in for the departed sextet were Collins, Lyons, Crandall, Okrie, Thompson, Polly (acquired in mid-season from Louisville for pitcher Harry Kimberlin) and nineteen-year-old Garver, the Browns' most promising farmhand.

Garver proved to be unready for the AA and spent part of the season with Elmira in the Eastern League, but the Mud Hens had to make do all year with the others for the lack of anyone better. All suffered from the team's most common malady in 1945—a failure to deliver with men on base. The Mud Hens led the AA in runners stranded. Marquardt's charges had some other sizable weaknesses too, principally pitching, fielding and hitting in general, but none of the other AA clubs were in much better shape. By the last year of wartime baseball the ranks of qualified players had been so thinned by the military draft that even teams in the majors were glad for whatever they could get. As an example of how short the Mud Hens were of top-grade talent, Fannin was the only man on the club's roster all season who would play a substantial amount in the majors after the war. In 1945 he led Toledo in every major pitching department—wins, strikeouts, ERA, and winning percentage. At that, he had a rather unimposing 11–9 record. Whitehead, a taciturn Texan who had once been a decent pitcher with the White Sox but was long past his best days in 1945, was the only other Mud Hen in enough innings to qualify as an ERA leader and also tied for second on the club in wins with eight.

At the plate the team was not quite as lackluster. Wren, Reinhart, Polly and Corona all hit over .300, and Ignasiak was third in the league in RBIs with 102. After Ignasiak, though, the drop to the next most productive Mud Hen was an alarming one. Collins knocked home a mere 55 runs. Then came Reinhart with 52 and Wren and Kimble with 49 apiece.

Toledo thus was a thoroughly mediocre outfit in 1945, and we need not belabor the reasons for its sixth-place finish by citing any more meager stats. Actually, about the only stat that is of much interest anyway is that the Mud Hens had the best record in the league against the pennant-winning Milwaukee Brewers, gaining an even split of the 22 games the teams played. That kind of thing did not go unnoticed in Toledo in 1945. God knows, there was precious little else about that last wartime season that folks along the Maumee River had to cheer.

Why then are we lavishing all this attention on the 1945 Toledo Mud Hens? Because they were a typical team during a hard time in what had been one of the three best minor leagues prior to the war and would become so again as soon as the following season. When the Mud Hens opened for business in 1946, most of their wartime cast was gone. They had been good ballplayers, all of them, but not first caliber. Each had some major flaw—no fastball (Smalling); a gaping hole in his swing (Ignasiak); zero power (Reinhart)—that would have prevented him from playing even in the high minors in a normal year. But 1945 was far from normal. It was a year in which teams everywhere in the country had to make do, and the Mud Hens did well enough to accomplish what has always been the foremost objective of a minor league franchise. They got through the season. They carried on.

Before we let them go, let's call the roll of the 1945 Mud Hens' individual leaders.

HITTING	PITCHING
Batting Average—.316, Bobby Wren	Wins—11, Cliff Fannin
Slugging Average—.418, Bobby Wren	Losses—12, John Whitehead
Home Runs—12, Ed Ignasiak	Innings—161, Cliff Fannin
RBIs—102, Ed Ignasiak	Games Started—23, John Whitehead
Total Bases—219, Ed Ignasiak	Complete Games—13, Cliff Fannin
Hits—160, Fred Reinhart	Strikeouts—126, Cliff Fannin
Runs—80, Bobby Wren	Bases on Balls—79, Cliff Fannin
Doubles—28, Fred Reinhart	Winning Pct.—.550, Cliff Fannin
Triples—11, Ed Ignasiak	ERA—3.41, Cliff Fannin
Bases on Balls—79, Ed Ignasiak	Appearances—37, Elwood Knierim
Stolen Bases—14, Bobby Wren	Shutouts—2, Cliff Fannin
	2, John Miller
	2, Al LaMacchia

FIREWORKS IN
THE DELL

• •

1949 NASHVILLE VOLUNTEERS
W-95 L-57
Manager: Rollie Hemsley

Regular Lineup—1B, Tookie Gilbert; 2B, Buster Boguskie; 3B, Floyd Fogg; SS, Harold Quick; RF, Bob Borkowski; CF, Paul Maudlin; LF, Babe Barna; C, Carl Sawatski; P, Bobo Holloman; P, Garman Mallory; P, Frank Marino; P, Ben Wade; P, Tony Jacobs; P, Cookie Cuccurullo

The Vols, a perennial Southern Association power during the late forties and early fifties, copped their second straight flag in 1949 and then cruised through the postseason playoffs to take the overall league championship as well. Playing in Sulphur Dell, the oldest park in organized baseball at the time, Nashville customarily dusted the competition by corraling a couple of savvy lefty pull hitters who could thrive on the Dell's short (about 262 feet down the line) right-field fence.* In 1949, the club was car-

---

*The list of all-time Southern Association hitting record holders drives home just how influential the Dell was throughout the loop's history.

Batting Average	416,	Hugh Hill Nashville	1902[1]
Home Runs	64,	Bob Lennon, Nashville	1954[2]
RBIs	182,	Chuck Workman, Nashville	1948
Total Bases	447,	Bob Lennon, Nashville	1954
Runs	155,	Jay Partridge, Nashville	1930
Hits	236,	Wilbur Goode, Atlanta	1925
Doubles	65,	Joe Dwyer, Nashville	1936
Triples	28,	Gil Coan, Chattanooga	1945

ried chiefly by Barna (.341 with 42 homers and 138 RBIs), Gilbert (.334 with 33 homers and 122 RBIs), and Sawatski, who had the best overall season at the plate of any catcher in the majors or the high minors since World War II when he stroked .360 with an SA-top 45 homers and 153 RBIs. Borkowski, a righthanded hitter and the loop's leading batter with a .376 average, in contrast had 78 RBIs and just nine homers.

A Cubs farm team at the time, Nashville furnished the parent club with Sawatski and Borkowski the following year and the Giants with Gilbert, who had been on loan to the Vols in 1949. None of the three ever did much in higher company, nor did any of the Vols pitchers, although Holloman pitched a no-hitter for the Browns four years later in his first major league start (which also turned out to be his lone complete game in the majors). Mallory, the club's ace, had a 20–4 record but a suspiciously high 3.89 ERA that proved a more accurate barometer of his ability when he skidded to 4–12 in 1950 after being promoted to Los Angeles in the Pacific Coast League. At the opposite end of the spectrum, Cuccurullo, who pitched briefly with the Pirates during the war years, finished in 1949 with a lusterless 6–11 record and a terminally terrible 6.69 ERA. The rest of the SA was well stocked, however, with both former and future major league hurlers, including Bobo Newsom, Hugh Mulcahy, Johnny Podjany, Joe Krakauskas, Earl Caldwell, Hi Bithorn, Johnny Klippstein, Willard Nixon, Art Fowler, Pete Wojey and Jim Bagby, Jr. Probably the Vols' top player, and the SA's as well, was Barna, a disappointment a few years earlier with the Giants. In 1951 Barna led the SA in hitting. That same season Jack Harshman, a lefty-swinging first baseman with Nashville, by then a Giants' farm team, paced the loop with 47 home runs. Two years later, after failing to hit in the majors, Harshman switched to pitching and led the SA with 23 wins. The league in those years was full of odd success stories like Harshman's, but this was one of the last that ended in a substantial major league career. Moreover, the 1949 season was the last time the Vols won an SA pennant in the company of Mobile, Memphis, Chat-

1. Like every Nashville player on the list, Hill was a lefthanded hitter. The only two other .400 hitters in SA history were also lefty-hitting Vols, Phil Weintraub in 1934 and Les Fleming in 1941.
2. Broke the former mark of 50 set in 1930 by Jim Poole of Nashville, who prior to 1948 also held the SA RBI record with 167, likewise in 1930. Poole too was, of course, a lefthanded hitter.

tanooga, Atlanta, New Orleans, Birmingham and Little Rock, the cast of teams that had been intact by then for more than two generations (except for a short period just prior to World War II when Knoxville spelled Mobile) in what was the most stable of all the minor leagues. The SA, after Atlanta deserted to become a major league city and several other longtime minor league strongholds like New Orleans dropped out of organized baseball altogether, combined forces with some of the teams from the old Sally League to form the Southern League in 1972, a circuit that presently includes only Memphis, Chattanooga and Birmingham from the period when the SA was in its heyday.

TOUGH TEAM
IN TINSELTOWN

• •

1953 HOLLYWOOD STARS
W-106 L-74
Manager: Bobby Bragan

Regular Lineup—1B, Dale Long; 2B, Monte Basgall; 3B, Gene Handley; SS, Jack Phillips; RF, Ted Beard; CF, Tom Saffell; LF, Lee Walls; C, Eddie Malone/Bobby Bragan; P, George O'Donnell; P, Jim Walsh; P, Red Munger; P, Lloyd Hittle; P, Gordy Maltzberger; P, Mel Queen; P, Harry Fisher; P, Japhet Lynn

Going to a baseball game in Los Angeles lacked the cachet in 1953 that it has now. Certainly you were not apt to find yourself seated alongside Marilyn Monroe at Wrigley Field, home of the Los Angeles Angels, or behind John Wayne at Gilmore Field, where the Hollywood Stars held court. What you were guaranteed, though, was seeing a brand of professional baseball that was deemed neither major league nor minor league.

In 1953 the Pacific Coast League celebrated its second season as an Open Classification circuit, a limbo designation reluctantly conceded to it by organized baseball after PCL moguls had fought bitterly ever since the close of World War II to gain major league status. The chief accoutrement of the Open Classification rating was that the eight PCL teams were prohibited from using players on option from major league teams. As a result of this restriction, all the clubs except Los Angeles, which retained its affiliation with the Chicago Cubs on a curtailed basis, severed official connections with major league organizations and determined to go it alone. Most, however, quietly engineered informal working agreements, knowing that on their own they would be unable to hire enough good players to stay competitive. Hollywood, for one, struck a bargain with Pittsburgh that had a curious resolution in 1953. While the Pirates were the worst team in the majors for the second year in a row, the Stars were in the process of becoming the PCL's first repeat pennant winner since 1944. Odd as that may seem, there was actually little mystery about it. After finishing last in 1950 and seventh in 1951, Pittsburgh had elected to go with youth and jettisoned most of its older players, either releasing them outright or peddling them to minor league clubs cheaply in return for other considerations. Hollywood was the chief beneficiary of the Pirates' housecleaning effort. The Stars not only got quality performers like Saffell, Beard, Basgall and Fisher who were just a hair short of having major league talent, but also garnered several players who could still be considered prospects, albeit rapidly aging ones.

Long, Phillips and O'Donnell were three such members of the 1953 Stars. At twenty-seven Long had already labored ten seasons in the minors sandwiched around a couple of undistinguished major league trials. Despite winning the PCL's MVP award in 1953, he was destined to spend the 1954 season in Hollywood before he finally earned another shot that he parlayed into a nine-year hitch in the majors. Phillips was a strange one, a big rawboned first baseman who had so little power that the Yankees tried to convert him into a shortstop in the late forties. The experiment failed, but Bragan remembered it and installed Phillips at short when John O'Neil was traded to Oakland early in the 1953 season. Phillips handled the position so well that he was voted the PCL's MVP the following year, making him the third Star in a row to cop the prize (in 1952 Johnny Lindell, a pitcher turned outfielder turned pitcher again, had won). When Phillips was acquired in 1955, however, by the Tigers, who already had Harvey Kuenn at short, he was returned to first base, where his shortage of power again hampered him from ever claiming the job on a fulltime basis. O'Donnell was the Stars' staff bellwether in 1953. His 20 wins got him a long test in 1954 with the Pirates that he ultimately flunked. A finesse pitcher who needed considerable offensive and defensive help to win, he was 3–9 for a Pittsburgh team that excelled in giving its hurlers as little support as possible.

Also with the Stars in 1953 was Frank Kelleher, a former two-time PCL home run champ. Nearing thirty-seven, Kelleher marked his eighth season with the club by leading it in hitting while serving as a spare outfielder. At the other end of the ladder was Walls, the youngest player on the team. Just turned twenty, he bid observers to look askance at the PCL's Open Classification system, for it was plain that he was a Pirates farmhand through and through who had been sent to Hollywood for grooming. The obvious hypocrisy underlying the arrangements that brought Walls and other budding future major leaguers to PCL teams in 1952 and 1953 resulted in a radical restructuring of the Open Classification concept. Prior to the 1954 season the rule that PCL clubs could not take players on option was rescinded, and each was allowed to have a maximum of five optionees on its roster.

Hollywood rooters could not have cared less, of course, about how their team had been assembled. An alarming number seemed no longer to care much about seeing their team play either. Attendance in 1953 at Gilmore Field was down some 36,500 from the 1952 total, an average of 406 patrons a game, a significant amount when the typical crowd was only around 3000. The PCL as a whole, though technically not a minor league at the time, was suffering from the same problem that every minor league did in the early fifties. Six of the eight PCL teams showed a drop in 1953 in attendance despite an exceptional competitive balance throughout the league.[1] The last-place Sacramento Solons finished only 31 games behind the Stars, and sixth-place San Diego ended up a mere five games out of third. Sacramento furthermore had the pleasure of probably costing second-place Seattle the pennant. The Solons won 16 of the 31 games the two clubs played but lost 17 of 23 to Hollywood.[2] Meanwhile the Stars were triumphing with a collection of players who functioned well as a unit but seemed little better than mediocre individually. Among the regulars only Beard hit above .273 (.286), and Long was the lone Star to pace the PCL in a major

1. In 1953, as an illustration, San Francisco drew just 175,459 fans, the club's smallest attendance since 1936, the peak of the Depression.

2. The PCL schedule-maker in 1953 had no easy task. Each team played 180 games, 33 versus Opponent A (its arch rival), 30 against Opponent B (its next most hated foe), 28 against Opponents C and D, 23 against Opponent E, 22 against Opponent F, and 20 against Opponent G. To reduce the schedule-maker's headaches and cut operating costs, the league dispensed with an All-Star game and postseason playoffs and abbreviated the second games of doubleheaders to seven innings.

hitting or pitching department, winning both the home run and RBI crowns. As a team, the Stars were fifth in BA, tied for fourth in FA and had no players among the top ten hitters or ERA qualifiers.

In 1954 Hollywood squandered a chance to win a third straight pennant by losing a one-game playoff to San Diego, made necessary when the two teams ended the regular season in a first-place tie. Two years later Bragan retired as a player and moved up to the dugout post in Pittsburgh, stripping the Stars of the PCL's top manager, and at the conclusion of the 1957 season Gilmore Field was forced to close its doors as the Hollywood franchise folded, an unpublicized casualty of the Dodgers' move to Los Angeles. The Stars' departure, along with those of the Los Angeles Angels and San Francisco Seals, caused a massive upheaval in the PCL. Indeed, the loop soon became the PCL in name only. All of the circuit's eight cities in 1953 except Sacramento truly were situated on or very near the Pacific coast, but within a decade the PCL found itself with franchises in places like Arkansas and Tulsa, Oklahoma. Today only Portland remains from the eight teams that comprised the loop in the last season that the Stars reigned as its champs.

ERA ALL-STAR TEAMS

AMERICAN LEAGUE

1B	Mickey Vernon
2B	Joe Gordon
3B	Al Rosen
SS	Lou Boudreau
OF	Ted Williams
OF	Mickey Mantle
OF	Joe DiMaggio
C	Yogi Berra
P	Bob Feller
P	Bob Lemon
UTIL	Minnie Minoso
MGR	Casey Stengel
*	Nellie Fox

NATIONAL LEAGUE

1B	Stan Musial
2B	Red Schoendienst
3B	Eddie Mathews
SS	Ernie Banks
OF	Willie Mays
OF	Duke Snider
OF	Ralph Kiner
C	Roy Campanella
P	Robin Roberts
P	Warren Spahn
UTIL	Jackie Robinson
MGR	Billy Southworth
*	Pee Wee Reese

MINOR LEAGUES

1B	Rocky Nelson
2B	Jack Cassini
3B	Ray Dandridge
SS	Jack Wallaesa
OF	Al Pinkston
OF	Earl Rapp
OF	Jack Graham

C	Bill Raimondi
P	Eddie Erautt
P	George Bamberger
UTIL	Luke Easter
MGR	Ben Geraghty
*	Frank Carswell

*Best player who failed to make the team

LEG SIX

1961–1976

TEAM NOTES AND RECORD HOLDERS: 1961-76

AMERICAN LEAGUE

Number of Years Finishing in Each Position

Team	1	2	3	4	5	6	7	8	9	10	11	12	Aggregate
Baltimore	4	3	5	1	1	1	1	0	0	0	0	0	1
Detroit	1	1	5	3	1	1	1	0	0	1	1	1	2
Minnesota	1	4	2	0	1	2	4	1	1	0	0	0	3
New York	5	0	2	0	2	3	2	0	1	1	0	0	4
Boston	2	0	2	1	4	2	1	2	2	0	0	0	5
Kansas City–Oakland	3	2	0	3	0	1	1	1	2	3	0	0	6
Chicago	0	4	0	3	1	0	2	0	3	1	0	2	7
Kansas City	0	1	0	2	0	0	0	3	1	1	0	0	8
Los Angeles–California	0	0	1	0	2	2	1	6	2	1	0	1	9
Cleveland	0	0	1	0	4	3	1	3	0	1	1	2	10
Washington–Texas	0	0	0	1	0	2	2	3	2	3	1	2	11
Seattle–Milwaukee	0	0	0	0	0	0	0	0	0	0	4	4	12

Statisticians would probably recoil from the method I used to determine the aggregate standings for the period, and my own subjective instincts tell me the Tigers were not the second-best club and the A's should be marked higher for their renascence after moving to Oakland. But it will take a better mathematical mind than mine to devise a scheme that can figure out how much more finishing ninth in a ten-team league should be worth than finishing eleventh in a twelve-team one, to cite just one of the many problems here that boggle me and at the same time are not my fascination. So I'll just share the aggregate standings for both the ten-team and the twelve-team spans during the period and then exit to the room that holds the toys that do interest me.

AGGREGATE STANDINGS: 1961–68

1. Detroit
2. Baltimore
3. Minnesota
4. Chicago
4. New York
6. Cleveland
7. Boston
8. Los Angeles–California
9. Kansas City–Oakland
10. Washington

AGGREGATE STANDINGS: 1969–76

1. Baltimore
2. Oakland
3. Boston
4. New York
5. Minnesota
6. Kansas City
7. Detroit
8. Chicago
9. California
10. Washington–Texas
11. Cleveland
12. Seattle–Milwaukee

I'm obliged, though, to point out that the first-place team, by my system, in every season since 1969 is the league pennant winner but the second-place team isn't always the winner of the other division. What I think is a more sensible way, especially for the seasons since 1977 when all the teams, in the AL at least, began facing one another virtually the same number of times each season, is to designate the team with the second-best over-all record as the second-place team and so on down the line. When that's done, as an example, Detroit, the AL East winner in 1972, slips to third behind Chicago, the second-place club in the AL West. This method had little influence on the aggregate standings for the 1969–76 period but, as you might expect, played havoc with the standings from 1977 to the present.

BALTIMORE ORIOLES

Pennants: 1966, 1969, 1970, 1971, 1973 (D)*, 1974 (D)
Manager: Earl Weaver, 1968–76
Park: Memorial Stadium
Best Year: 1969 (109–53, .673)
Worst Year: 1967 (76–85, .472)
Top Rookie: Wally Bunker, 1964
Biggest Disappointment: Curt Blefary, 1968
Best Deal: Obtaining Frank Robinson from Cincinnati, 1966
Worst Deal: Shipping Davey Johnson, Pat Dobson and more to Atlanta, 1973
Other:
- 1961—Club leads the AL with a 3.22 ERA but finishes a distant 3rd when it scores fewer runs than every team but the 9th-place A's and the 10th-place expansion Senators
- 1962—Club again has the best ERA in the AL (3.69) but tumbles to 7th when none of its young pitchers can win more than 12 games
- 1963—Make just 99 errors to become first team in history to make less than 100 in a season
- 1964—Make less than 100 errors for second year in a row and set new ML FA record (.985) that is tied by 1980 Orioles but otherwise lasts until 1988
- 1966—Second pennant in the franchise's sixty-six-year history is followed by its first World Championship
- 1967—Team finishes below .500 for the last time until 1986
- 1969—109 wins set ML record for the most by any team since division play began
- 1971—Win third straight pennant; become the first team since the 1942–44 Cardinals to win 100 or more games three years in a row and the only flag winner in ML history to have four 20-game winners
- 1974—Pace AL with .562 winning percentage, the lowest to top either major league since the beginning of division play in 1969
- 1976—Led the AL in FA for the third straight year

*D = division winner only

HITTING		PITCHING	
Batting Ave.	.318, Merv Rettenmund, 1971	Wins	24, Mike Cuellar, 1971
			24, Dave McNally, 1970
Slugging Ave.	.646, Jim Gentile, 1961	Losses	18, Pat Dobson, 1972
Home Runs	49, Frank Robinson, 1966	Innings	323, Jim Palmer, 1975
RBIs	141, Jim Gentile, 1961	Games Started	40, Dave McNally, 1969, 1970
			40, Mike Cuellar, 1970
			40, Jim Palmer, 1976
Total Bases	367, Frank Robinson, 1966	Complete Games	25, Jim Palmer, 1975
Hits	194, Brooks Robinson, 1974	Strikeouts	202, Dave McNally, 1968
Runs	122, Frank Robinson, 1966	Bases on Balls	133, Mike Torrez, 1975
Doubles	38, Brooks Robinson, 1961	Winning Pct.	.805, Dave McNally, 1971
Triples	12, Paul Blair, 1967	ERA	1.95, Dave McNally, 1968
Bases on Balls	118, Ken Singleton, 1975	Saves	27, Stu Miller, 1963
Stolen Bases	57, Luis Aparicio, 1964	Shutouts	10, Jim Palmer, 1975

The chart reflects just how strong the Orioles really were from 1961 to 1976. The individual record holders, particularly in the batting departments, are spread out over the entire sixteen-year period. The chart also points up something that's already been forgotten: that Dave McNally for several years was probably the best pitcher on the strongest mound staff any team has had since expansion occurred. Few outside of Baltimore are likely to remember either that for a number of years Bob Boyd and Rettenmund jointly held the club batting-average record (Bob Nieman hit .322 in 1956 but in only 388 at bats).

DETROIT TIGERS

Pennants: 1968, 1972 (D)

Manager: Mayo Smith, 1967–70

Park: Tiger Stadium; name changed from Briggs Stadium when John Fetzer assumed control of the team in 1961

Best Year: 1968 (103–59, .636)

Worst Year: 1975 (57–102, .358)

Top Rookie: Mark Fidrych, 1976

Biggest Disappointment: Norm Cash, 1962; his BA dropped 118 points, the most ever by a defending batting titlist

Best Deal: Obtaining Norm Cash from Cleveland for Steve Demeter; the deal was made prior to the 1960 season but didn't really begin to impact until the expansion era began

Worst Deal: Letting Phil Regan go to the Dodgers for Dick Tracewski, 1966

Other:

1961—101 wins ties franchise record

1963—Only sub-.500 finish between 1961 and 1969

1968—Win pennant easily with top scoring unit and stingiest defense in the AL; top two pitchers, Denny McLain and Mickey Lolich, have combined 48–15 record

1969—Finish 19 games back of division champ Baltimore despite winning 90 games; third straight season of 90 or more wins marks the first and only time since 1907–09 that the team has enjoyed such a stretch of success

1972—Win division by ½-game margin when games postponed by strike at the beginning of the season are not made up

1975—Go winless in 19 straight games, the longest losing skein in the AL since 1943

1976—Rookie Mark Fidrych has 19–9 record and is the only starting pitcher to win more games than he loses

HITTING		**PITCHING**	
Batting Ave.	.361, Norm Cash, 1961	Wins	31, Denny McLain, 1968
Slugging Ave.	.662, Norm Cash, 1961	Losses	21, Mickey Lolich, 1974
Home Runs	45, Rocky Colavito, 1961	Innings	376, Mickey Lolich, 1971
RBIs	140, Rocky Colavito, 1961	Games Started	45, Mickey Lolich, 1971
Total Bases	354, Norm Cash, 1961	Complete Games	29, Mickey Lolich, 1971
Hits	193, Norm Cash, 1961	Strikeouts	308, Mickey Lolich, 1971
Runs	129, Rocky Colavito, 1961	Bases on Balls	158, Joe Coleman, 1974
Doubles	41, Al Kaline, 1961	Winning Pct.	.838, Denny McLain, 1968
Triples	14, Jake Wood, 1961	ERA	1.96, Denny McLain, 1968
Bases on Balls	124, Norm Cash, 1961	Saves	38, John Hiller, 1973
Stolen Bases	58, Ron LeFlore, 1976	Shutouts	9, Denny McLain, 1969

On the surface, the chart seems unrepresentative because all the batting marks except one were set in an expansion year. But it's also true that the Tigers had a very powerful attack that season and a lot less punch subsequently, even in the two years when they won a pennant (1968) and a division title (1972). Of much greater significance is the fact that of all the franchises that have been in existence since 1901, only the Tigers have had the majority of their all-time pitching records established since expansion occurred. Six of the eleven era records listed above are all-time club marks, including two—starts and strikeouts— by Lolich, who may have been the Vic Willis of his time in that he pitched for some good teams but his peak seasons came while he was toiling for poor ones.

MINNESOTA TWINS

Pennants: 1965, 1969 (D), 1970 (D)
Manager: Sam Mele, 1961–66
Park: Metropolitan Stadium; park hosted the first ML game in the state of Minnesota on April 21, 1961, with the expansion Senators beating the former Senators, 5–3
Best Year: 1965 (102–60, .630)
Worst Year: 1961 (70–90, .438)
Top Rookie: Tony Oliva, 1964
Biggest Disappointment: Dave Boswell, 1970
Best Deal: Snatching Mudcat Grant from Cleveland, 1964
Worst Deal: Selling Jim Kaat to the White Sox, 1973
Other:

1961—Franchise moves from Washington to Minnesota

1962—First above-.500 team since 1953

1963—Hit 225 home runs, top the majors in runs and have six players with 20 or more homers to tie the record of the 1961 Yankees; best winning percentage (.565) since 1945

1965—Franchise record 102 wins and first pennant since 1933

1967—Lead AL race by one game with two to play but finish one game back of Red Sox after dropping final two contests to them in Fenway Park

1969—Are swept by the Orioles in the first AL Championship Series

1970—Lose second consecutive ALCS to the Orioles in three straight games; team is managed by Bill Rigney after Billy Martin is canned despite winning the division the previous year

1973—Lead AL in batting and outscore opponents 738–692 but barely manage to achieve a .500 finish

1976—Top the AL in runs and BA but finish last in fielding

HITTING		PITCHING	
Batting Ave.	.364, Rod Carew, 1974	Wins	25, Jim Kaat, 1966
Slugging Ave.	.606, Harmon Killebrew, 1961	Losses	20, Pete Ramos, 1961
Home Runs	49, Harmon Killebrew, 1964, 1969	Innings	325, Bert Blyleven, 1973
RBIs	140, Harmon Killebrew, 1969	Games Started	42, Jim Kaat, 1965
Total Bases	374, Tony Oliva, 1964	Complete Games	25, Bert Blyleven, 1973
Hits	218, Rod Carew, 1974	Strikeouts	258, Bert Blyleven, 1973
Runs	126, Zoilo Versalles, 1965	Bases on Balls	127, Jim Hughes, 1975
Doubles	45, Zoilo Versalles, 1965	Winning Pct.	.773, Bill Campbell, 1976
Triples	13, Zoilo Versalles, 1965 13, Cesar Tovar, 1970	ERA	2.47, Camilo Pascual, 1963
Bases on Balls	1945, Harmon Killebrew, 1969	Saves	34, Ron Perranoski, 1970
Stolen Bases	49, Rod Carew, 1976	Shutouts	9, Bert Blyleven, 1973

Had the Twins won the pennant in 1967 instead of falling one game short and not stumbled in the LCS's in both 1969 and 1970, they would have laid strong claim to being the AL's top club during this period. Killebrew's best overall season, like those of many sluggers during the era, came in an expansion year, but unlike Cash and Gentile, for two, he had several others that were nearly as good. Oliva appears only once on the chart but was without question one of the AL's top offensive stars all during the era, and Tovar, although his talents were concealed somewhat by those of his slugging teammates and then superseded by Carew's, also rates very high.

NEW YORK YANKEES

Pennants: 1961, 1962, 1963, 1964, 1976
Manager: Ralph Houk, 1961–63, 1966–73
Park: Yankee Stadium, 1961–73, 1976-present
   Shea Stadium, 1974–75; shared Shea with the Mets for two
   seasons while Yankee Stadium was being renovated
Best Year: 1961 (109–53, .673)
Worst Year: 1966 (70–89, .440)
Top Rookie: Thurman Munson, 1970
Biggest Disappointment: Tom Tresh, 1966–68
Best Deal: Finessing Cleveland out of Graig Nettles, 1973
Worst Deal: Sending Stan Bahnsen to the White Sox for Rich
   McKinney, 1972
Other:
1961—Set record in very first year of expansion era for most
   wins (109) by a team on a 162-game schedule; collect ML-
   record 240 home runs and have record six players with 20
   or more home runs
1964—CBS buys the club; tie own record by winning fifth
   straight pennant; have now won 15 pennants in the past 18
   seasons
1965—First second-division finish since 1925
1966—First cellar finish since 1912, albeit with the highest ever
   winning percentage (.440) by an AL basement dweller
1968—Set post-deadball ML low with .214 team BA
1972—Win 92 games, fourth most in the majors, but nevertheless finish 15 games behind Baltimore in the AL East
1973—Shipping magnate George Steinbrenner buys the club
1975—Billy Martin hired as manager, replacing Bill Virdon
1976—Win flag to end club's longest pennant drought since
   1901–20

HITTING

Batting Ave.	.348, Elston Howard, 1961		
Slugging Ave.	.687, Mickey Mantle, 1961		
Home Runs	61, Roger Maris, 1961		
RBIs	142, Roger Maris, 1961		
Total Bases	366, Roger Maris, 1961		
Hits	209, Bobby Richardson, 1962		
Runs	132, Mickey Mantle, 1961		
Doubles	38, Tony Kubek, 1961 38, Bobby Richardson, 1962 38, Chris Chambliss, 1975		
Triples	8, Mickey Rivers, 1976		
Bases on Balls	126, Mickey Mantle, 1961		
Stolen Bases	43, Mickey Rivers, 1976		

PITCHING

Wins	25, Whitey Ford, 1961
Losses	20, Mel Stottlemyre, 1966
Innings	328, Catfish Hunter, 1975
Games Started	39, done by five different pitchers
Complete Games	30, Catfish Hunter, 1975
Strikeouts	217, Al Downing, 1964
Bases on Balls	120, Al Downing, 1964
Winning Pct.	.862, Whitey Ford, 1961
ERA	2.05, Stan Bahnsen, 1968
Saves	35, Sparky Lyle, 1972
Shutouts	7, Catfish Hunter, 1975

Stottlemyre is Lolich's chief competition for the era's Vic Willis Award. Besides Rivers, only five other Yankees during the period—Horace Clarke, Bill Robinson, Jerry Kenney, Roy White and Bobby Murcer—were able to collect as many as seven triples in a season. If Mantle's and Maris's expansion-aided 1961 season is eliminated from consideration, Thurman Munson rates as the club's most productive player here, with White and Murcer being his main challengers. Just two years after expansion had inflated hitting stats, the club won the 1963 pennant with only one regular, Howard (.287), able to post a BA above .271.

BOSTON RED SOX

Pennants: 1967, 1975
Manager: Eddie Kasko, 1970–73
Park: Fenway Park
Best Year: 1975 (95–65 .594)
Worst Year: 1965 (62–100 .383)
Top Rookie: Fred Lynn, 1975
Biggest Disappointment: Chuck Schilling, 1962
Best Deal: The trade that brought Dick Stuart from Pittsburgh, 1963
Worst Deal: Giving the Yankees Sparky Lyle for Danny Cater, 1972
Other:

1963–Bill Monbouquette and reliever Dick Radatz are a combined 35–16; rest of staff is 41–69

1965—Lose 100 games for the first time since 1932

1966—Eighth consecutive sub-.500 finish; come in only half a game ahead of the last-place Yankees

1967—Rise from 9th place to 1st is the biggest gain by a pennant winner since the 1899 Brooklyn Superbas

1969—Pace the majors with 197 home runs

1972—Lose division race to Detroit by ½ game

1974—Top AL in runs but are the only team except for the two division cellar finishers not to have at least one player with 80 or more RBIs

1975—Allow 709 runs, the most of any flag winner during the era

1976—End era with tenth straight above-.500 finish; lead AL with 134 homers, the lowest total to lead the loop in a season when a full schedule was played since 1949

HITTING		PITCHING	
Batting Ave.	.331, Fred Lynn, 1975	Wins	22, Jim Lonborg, 1967
			22, Luis Tiant, 1974
Slugging Ave.	.622, Carl Yastrzemski, 1967	Losses	18, Bill Monbouquette, 1965
			18, Dave Morehead, 1965
Home Runs	44, Carl Yastrzemski, 1967	Innings	311, Luis Tiant, 1974
RBIs	121, Carl Yastrzemski, 1967	Games Started	39, Jim Lonborg, 1967
Total Bases	360, Carl Yastrzemski, 1967	Complete Games	25, Luis Tiant, 1974
Hits	189, Carl Yastrzemski, 1967	Strikeouts	246, Jim Lonborg, 1967
Runs	125, Carl Yastrzemski, 1970	Bases on Balls	121, Don Schwall, 1962
Doubles	47, Fred Lynn, 1975	Winning Pct.	.727, Ray Culp, 1968
Triples	10, Lu Clinton, 1962	ERA	1.91, Luis Tiant, 1972
Bases on Balls	119, Carl Yastrzemski, 1969	Saves	29, Dick Radatz, 1964
Stolen Bases	54, Tommy Harper, 1973	Shutouts	7, Luis Tiant, 1974

A string of poor teams in the early sixties prevented Boston from finishing higher in the aggregate standings. Yaz's huge season in 1967 deprived several other sluggers like Rico Petrocelli, George Scott, Dick Stuart and Tony Conigliaro from a place on the chart, but apart from Yaz, Reggie Smith was actually the club's biggest offensive asset during the period. To illustrate at what a low ebb the Red Sox were when expansion occurred in 1961, they finished next to last in the AL in home runs that year, behind even the expansion Washington Senators, and as late as 1966, the year before they won a pennant, Jose Santiago led the pitching staff in wins with 12.

OAKLAND ATHLETICS

Pennants: 1971 (D), 1972, 1973, 1974, 1975 (D)
Manager: Dick Williams, 1971–73
Park: Municipal Stadium (Kansas City), 1960–67
  Oakland Coliseum (Oakland), 1968–present
Best Year: 1971 (101–60, .627)
Worst Year: 1964 (57–105, .352)
Top Rookie: Jim Nash, 1966
Biggest Disappointment: Manny Jiminez, 1963
Best Deal: Obtaining Ken Holtzman from the Cubs, 1972
Worst Deal: Giving Manny Trillo to the Cubs, 1975
Other:
  1965—Finish last for the second consecutive year and the third
    season in the last five despite the presence of two expansion
    teams in the league
  1967—End 13-season stay in Kansas City with AL-record 24th
    last-place finish; 3.68 ERA, which is the worst in the AL,
    would have been the best in the majors in 1930
  1968—Franchise moves to Oakland; top AL with .240 BA, the
    lowest in ML history by a loop leader
  1971—Win AL West to give the franchise its first title of any
    kind since 1931
  1972—Hold off pesky Detroit team in LCS to win franchise's
    first pennant since 1931 and then win its first World Cham-
    pionship since 1930 by beating the Reds in the World Series
  1973—First team in AL history to win a pennant without a 20-
    game winner or a .300 hitter
  1974—Become the last team to win three straight World
    Championships
  1975—Become only team since division play began in 1969 to
    win five straight division titles
  1976—Set AL record with 341 stolen bases; become first team
    in 20th century to have three players with 50 or more steals

HITTING		PITCHING	
Batting Ave.	.308, Norm Siebern, 1962 .308, Claudell Washington, 1975	Wins	25, Catfish Hunter, 1974
Slugging Ave.	.608, Reggie Jackson, 1969	Losses	20, Orlando Pena, 1963
Home Runs	47, Reggie Jackson, 1969	Innings	318, Catfish Hunter, 1974
RBIs	118, Reggie Jackson, 1969	Games Started	41, Catfish Hunter, 1974
Total Bases	334, Reggie Jackson, 1969	Complete Games	24, Vida Blue, 1971
Hits	193, Jerry Lumpe, 1962	Strikeouts	301, Vida Blue, 1971
Runs	123, Reggie Jackson, 1969	Bases on Balls	112, Blue Moon Odom, 1969
Doubles	39, Joe Rudi, 1974 39, Reggie Jackson, 1975	Winning Pct.	.808, Catfish Hunter, 1973
Triples	15, Gino Cimoli, 1962	ERA	1.82, Vida Blue, 1971
Bases on Balls	118, Sal Bando, 1970	Saves	32, Jack Aker, 1966
Stolen Bases	75, Bill North, 1976	Shutouts	8, Vida Blue, 1971

Washington collected 182 hits in 1975 to set an Oakland club record that stood until 1988. The following year Phil Garner set the Oakland club record for triples when he bagged 12. In the A's last year in Kansas City they finished last but were only 29½ games behind the pennant-winning Red Sox, and one has to wonder what would have happened if the franchise hadn't moved, as most of the pieces that formed the great Oakland teams in the early seventies were already in place. Blue's 301 K's are not a club record, of course, or even a club southpaw record, but they made him the only 300-K pitcher who never before or after his big season had as many as 200 K's.

CHICAGO WHITE SOX

Pennants: None
Manager: Al Lopez, 1961–65, 1968
Park: Comiskey Park
Best Year: 1964 (98–64, .605)
Worst Year: 1970 (56–106, .346)
Top Rookie: Tommy Agee, 1966
Biggest Disappointment: Pete Ward, 1965–69
Best Deal: Obtaining Chet Lemon from Oakland, 1975
Worst Deal: Swapping Bill Robinson to the Phillies for a minor
league catcher, 1972
Other:
  1964—Lead majors with 2.72 ERA; finish 2nd just one game
    behind Yankees
  1965—Third straight 2nd-place finish
  1966—Allow AL record low 2.63 runs per game at home; finish
    fourth despite AL best 2.68 ERA as team hits .231, worst in
    majors
  1967—Finish 4th again with .225 team BA as no Sox regular
    can hit above .241
  1968—End skein of 18 consecutive finishes above .500; last AL
    team to date to average fewer than three runs per game
    while playing a full schedule
  1970—Finish last for the first time since 1948
  1971—Third baseman Bill Melton becomes the first White Sox
    player ever to lead the AL in home runs
  1972—2nd-place finish is the team's highest prior to 1983 un-
    der the two-division format
  1974—For the first time in history the team leads the AL in
    home runs with 135
  1975—Follow breakthrough year by finishing next to last in
    AL in both homers and runs

HITTING		PITCHING	
Batting Ave.	.316, Jorge Orta, 1974	Wins	24, Wilbur Wood, 1972, 1973
Slugging Ave.	.603, Dick Allen, 1972	Losses	21, Stan Bahnsen, 1973
Home Runs	37, Dick Allen, 1972	Innings	377, Wilbur Wood, 1972
RBIs	113, Dick Allen, 1972	Games Started	49, Wilbur Wood, 1972
Total Bases	305, Dick Allen, 1972	Complete Games	22, Wilbur Wood, 1971, 1974
Hits	187, Floyd Robinson, 1962	Strikeouts	215, Gary Peters, 1967
Runs	98, Tommy Agee, 1966	Bases on Balls	117, Stan Bahnsen, 1973
Doubles	45, Floyd Robinson, 1962	Winning Pct.	.731, Joel Horlen, 1967
Triples	12, Tom McCraw, 1968	ERA	1.88, Joel Horlen, 1964
Bases on Balls	99, Dick Allen, 1972	Saves	27, Hoyt Wilhelm, 1964
Stolen Bases	53, Luis Aparicio, 1963	Shutouts	8, Wilbur Wood, 1972

Good pitching throughout the period saved this club from finishing near the bottom in the aggregate standings. As it was, Chicago ended the sixties with less going for it than most of the four new expansion teams. Agee's club runs mark exemplifies the White Sox' main problem all during the era—they just couldn't put enough tallies on the board. Determining who the team's most productive player was for this period isn't easy. Apart from Allen, who only gave the club two and a half seasons, Carlos May is probably as good a choice as any. On the other hand, there are plenty of good pitchers to select from, with Wood ranking as the best.

KANSAS CITY ROYALS (1969–76)

Pennants: 1976 (D)
Manager: Bob Lemon, 1970–72; handled the club just a few days
longer than Jack McKeon, 1973–75
Park: Municipal Stadium, 1969–72
Royals Stadium, 1973–present; first game on April 10, 1973
Best Year: 1975 (91–71, .562)
Worst Year: 1970 (65–97, .401)
Top Rookie: Lou Piniella, 1969
Biggest Disappointment: Harmon Killebrew; hit .199 as the
club's DH, virtually killing any chance the Royals had of overtaking the A's in 1975
Best Deal: Getting Amos Otis from the Mets, 1970
Worst Deal: Giving Lou Piniella to the Yankees for Lindy Mc-
Daniel, 1974
Other:
1969—First-year expansion team; finish 4th in six-team
division
1970—End ML-record skein of most consecutive losses to one
team (23) by beating the Orioles
1971—First time team finishes above .500
1974—Last sub-.500 finish until 1983
1975—First AL expansion team to win as many as 90 games
(91)
1976—Win division title to become the first AL expansion team
to qualify for postseason play; lose the only LCS to go the
limit and be decided by a home run in the winning team's
last at bat when Yankees first baseman Chris Chambliss hits
a solo four-bagger off reliever Mark Littell

HITTING		PITCHING	
Batting Ave.	.333, George Brett, 1976	Wins	22, Steve Busby, 1974
Slugging Ave.	.547, John Mayberry, 1975	Losses	19, Paul Splittorff, 1974
Home Runs	34, John Mayberry, 1975	Innings	292, Steve Busby, 1974
RBIs	106, John Mayberry, 1975	Games Started	38, Steve Busby, 1974
Total Bases	303, John Mayberry, 1975	Complete Games	20, Steve Busby, 1974
Hits	215, George Brett, 1976	Strikeouts	206, Bob Johnson, 1970
Runs	94, George Brett, 1976	Bases on Balls	105, Steve Busby, 1973
Doubles	40, Amos Otis, 1976	Winning Pct.	.682, Dennis Leonard, 1975
Triples	14, George Brett, 1976	ERA	2.08, Roger Nelson, 1972
Bases on Balls	122, John Mayberry, 1973	Saves	23, Ted Abernathy, 1971
Stolen Bases	52, Amos Otis, 1971	Shutouts	6, Roger Nelson, 1972

Competitive almost from the moment of their inception, the Royals probably would have gone over the top earlier if they hadn't run into bad luck with Nelson and Busby. As just one illustration of how much talent the club had in comparison to its sister expansion franchises, Lou Piniella, arguably the Royals' most productive all-around player during the period, didn't make the chart despite leading the AL in doubles one year and hitting over .300 several times. Hal McRae, who hit .332 in 1976 and had 38 doubles the previous year, also missed earning a spot.

CALIFORNIA ANGELS

Pennants: None
Manager: Billy Rigney, 1961–68
Park: Wrigley Field, 1961
  Dodger Stadium, 1962–65; shared with the Los Angeles Dodgers and known as Chavez Ravine for AL games
  Anaheim Stadium, 1966–present; first game April 19, 1966
Best Year: 1962 and 1970 (86–76, .531)
Worst Year: 1968 (67–95, .414)
Top Rookie: Buck Rodgers, 1962
Biggest Disappointment: Ken Hunt, 1962
Best Deal: Theft of Nolan Ryan from the Mets, 1972
Worst Deal: Swapping Leon Wagner to Cleveland, 1964
Other:
  1961—Begin life as the Los Angeles Angels; finish 8th only ½ game out of 7th, in new 10-team league in initial season
  1962—Ascend to 3rd place; lead AL as late as July 4
  1965—Become the California Angels
  1967—Achieve third first-division finish in first seven seasons; win first team crown by leading AL in FA
  1968—Suffer club record 95 losses and sink to 8th place
  1972—Score fewest runs in the AL (454) despite finishing fifth in loop in batting as team's hitters draw the fewest walks in the majors; last AL team to date to average fewer than three runs per game, albeit while playing an abbreviated schedule
  1974—Have worst record in the league for the first time and finish last in the AL West; Nolan Ryan sets AL record for the most wins (22) by a pitcher with a last-place team
  1976—Pitching staff paces AL in complete games and strikeouts, but team finishes ten games below .500 with the lowest BA in the AL and the fewest runs scored

HITTING		**PITCHING**	
Batting Ave.	.329, Alex Johnson, 1970	Wins	22, Clyde Wright, 1970
			22, Nolan Ryan, 1974
Slugging Ave.	.517, Leon Wagner, 1961	Losses	19, George Brunet, 1967
			19, Clyde Wright, 1973
			19, Frank Tanana, 1974
Home Runs	37, Leon Wagner, 1962	Innings	333, Nolan Ryan, 1974
RBIs	107, Leon Wagner, 1962	Games Started	41, Nolan Ryan, 1974
Total Bases	306, Leon Wagner, 1962	Complete Games	26, Nolan Ryan, 1973, 1974
Hits	202, Alex Johnson, 1970	Strikeouts	383, Nolan Ryan, 1973
Runs	115, Albie Pearson, 1962	Bases on Balls	202, Nolan Ryan, 1974
Doubles	34, Bob Rodgers, 1962	Winning Pct.	.690, Dean Chance, 1964
Triples	13, Jim Fregosi, 1968	ERA	1.65, Dean Chance, 1964
	13, Mickey Rivers, 1975		
Bases on Balls	96, Albie Pearson, 1961	Saves	27, Minnie Rojas, 1967
Stolen Bases	70, Mickey Rivers, 1975	Shutouts	11, Dean Chance, 1964

Ryan and Chance dominate the chart, but the Angels had a number of fine pitchers during their first sixteen years of existence. In contrast, after they left cozy Wrigley Field, where home runs came easily, they very seldom had much pop. Excluding Johnson, the Angels in this period never had anyone who was even a mild contender for a batting title, and their home run leader as late as 1976 was Bobby Bonds with just ten.

CLEVELAND INDIANS

Pennants: None
Manager: Birdie Tebbetts, 1963–66
Park: Municipal Stadium
Best Year: 1965 (87–75, .537)
Worst Year: 1971 (60–102, .370)
Top Rookie: Chris Chambliss, 1971
Biggest Disappointment: Charlie Spikes, 1975–77
Best Deal: Getting Gaylord Perry and Frank Duffy from the Giants, 1972
Worst Deal: Trading Jim Perry to the Twins for Jack Kralick, 1963
Other:
1961—Lead AL in hits and BA but are only sixth in runs scored as team's hitters draw the fewest walks in the loop
1965—Win 87 games for best season between 1960 and 1991
1966—Last time the team finishes above .500 two years in a row
1967—Pitching staff notches AL-record 1189 strikeouts
1969—Finish with worse record than even the two new expansion teams to end club's AL-record skein of fifty-four years without coming in last; Luis Tiant becomes first Cleveland hurler since 1901 to lose 20 games
1971—Three years after having had the best staff ERA in the AL, club has the worst (4.38)
1972—Club's topsy-turvy pattern that will soon become its hallmark becomes more pronounced as mound staff has third-best ERA in AL after having had the worst the previous year
1974—Special "10¢ Beer Night" on June 4 culminates when fans become so riotous the game is forfeited to Texas
1975—Team has the first black manager in ML history, Frank Robinson

HITTING		PITCHING	
Batting Ave.	.322, Jimmy Piersall, 1961	Wins	24, Gaylord Perry, 1972
Slugging Ave.	.524, Boog Powell, 1975	Losses	20, Luis Tiant, 1969
Home Runs	31, Leon Wagner, 1972	Innings	344, Gaylord Perry, 1973
RBIs	108, Rocky Colavito, 1965	Games Started	41, Gaylord Perry, 1973
Total Bases	288, Tony Horton, 1969	Complete Games	29, Gaylord Perry, 1972, 1973
Hits	178, Tito Francona, 1961	Strikeouts	325, Sam McDowell, 1965
Runs	101, Dick Howser, 1964	Bases on Balls	153, Sam McDowell, 1971
Doubles	34, Rico Carty, 1976	Winning Pct.	.700, Luis Tiant, 1968
Triples	8, Tito Francona, 1961	ERA	1.60, Luis Tiant, 1968
Bases on Balls	95, Ken Harrelson, 1969	Saves	21, Dave LaRoche, 1976
Stolen Bases	40, Jose Cardenal, 1968	Shutouts	9, Luis Tiant, 1968

The chart makes it painfully clear that the Indians had pretty good pitching all during the period but just about zero offense. Almost all the club batting marks are embarrassingly low, and to make it worse, the bulk of them were set by players who had just one good season, if that, in a Cleveland uniform. Further pain will be created in Cleveland when it's noted that Francona, the only name to appear more than once on the hitting chart, already had his best years behind him by 1961. Horton, on the other hand, seemingly had his peak years still ahead of him when he had to be institutionalized in 1970 and became yet another Indian who had his promising career tragically short-circuited.

TEXAS RANGERS

Pennants: None
Manager: Gil Hodges, 1963–67
Park: Griffith Stadium, 1961
  DC Stadium, 1962–71; known as Robert F. Kennedy Stadium, 1968–71
  Arlington Stadium (Texas), 1972–present
Best Year: 1969 (86–76, .531)
Worst Year: 1963 (56–106, .346)
Top Rookie: Mike Hargrove, 1974
Biggest Disappointment: Denny McLain, 1971
Best Deal: Getting Frank Howard and more from the Dodgers, 1965
Worst Deal: Giving up Ed Brinkman, Joe Coleman, and Aurelio Rodriguez for Denny McLain, 1971
Other:
  1961—Begin life as the Washington Senators; finish tied for last with Kansas City
  1966—Achieve highest finish to date, a heady 8th
  1969—Under rookie manager Ted Williams club has its best year while based in Washington
  1971—Last in AL East in final year in Washington
  1972—Club celebrates move to Texas by finishing last in the AL and losing an AL expansion-team record 15 straight games; team BA is a dismal .217 and staff ERA is also AL's worst
  1974—Gain franchise-record 27 games over 1973 finish under new manager Billy Martin; become the first Rangers team to break .500
  1976—Club is done in by a weak bullpen crew for the second year in a row, finishes ten games below .500 with the fewest saves in the AL

HITTING		PITCHING	
Batting Ave.	.310, Chuck Hinton, 1962	Wins	25, Ferguson Jenkins, 1974
Slugging Ave.	.574, Frank Howard, 1969	Losses	22, Denny McLain, 1971
Home Runs	48, Frank Howard, 1969	Innings	328, Ferguson Jenkins, 1974
RBIs	126, Frank Howard, 1970	Games Started	41, Jim Bibby, 1974
			41, Ferguson Jenkins, 1974
Total Bases	340, Frank Howard, 1969	Complete Games	29, Ferguson Jenkins, 1974
Hits	175, Frank Howard, 1969	Strikeouts	225, Ferguson Jenkins, 1974
Runs	111, Frank Howard, 1969	Bases on Balls	113, Jim Bibby, 1974
Doubles	33, Jeff Burroughs, 1974	Winning Pct.	.676, Ferguson Jenkins, 1974
Triples	12, Chuck Hinton, 1963	ERA	2.17, Mike Paul, 1972
Bases on Balls	132, Frank Howard, 1970	Saves	27, Darold Knowles, 1970
Stolen Bases	51, Dave Nelson, 1972	Shutouts	6, Ferguson Jenkins, 1974
			6, Bert Blyleven, 1976

What's probably the most interesting thing here is that all but two of the franchise's offensive records for the period were established while the club was in Washington, while almost all the pitching records were set after it moved to Dallas–Fort Worth. Something you might find equally interesting—and I won't deprive you of the fun of discovering it for yourself—is determining who the expansion Senators' offensive leaders and most productive player would have been if they hadn't had Howard. Or, for that matter, Hinton. Washington fans deserved a lot better after suffering for two and a half decades with the original Senators, only to lose them just when they became a decent team again.

MILWAUKEE BREWERS (1969–76)

Pennants: None
Manager: Del Crandall, 1972–75
Park: Sicks Stadium (Seattle), 1969; park was previously used
by the Seattle Rainiers of the Pacific Coast League
County Stadium (Milwaukee), 1970–present; previously the
home of the NL Milwaukee Braves
Best Year: 1974 (76–86, .469)
Worst Year: 1969 (64–98, .395)
Top Rookie: Pedro Garcia, 1973
Biggest Disappointment: Pedro Garcia, 1974–76
Best Deal: Obtaining George Scott from Boston in a multiplayer
trade, 1972
Worst Deal: Swapping Lou Piniella to Kansas City, 1969
Other:
1969—Begin life as the Seattle Pilots; finish last in the AL West
division
1970—Franchise moved to Milwaukee but remains in AL West
division
1972—Transferred to AL East division after Washington franchise is moved to Dallas–Fort Worth and placed in AL West
1975—4.34 staff ERA is the poorest in the AL
1976—Score fewest runs in AL (570) and finish last in AL East;
club is so desperate for punch that it employs Hank Aaron
(.229) most of the season as its DH and sticks with young
outfielder Gorman Thomas, who for the second year in a row
hits below .200

HITTING		**PITCHING**	
Batting Ave.	.306, George Scott, 1973	Wins	20, Jim Colborn, 1973
Slugging Ave.	.522, Tommy Harper, 1970	Losses	20, Clyde Wright, 1974
Home Runs	36, George Scott, 1975	Innings	314, Jim Colborn, 1973
RBIs	109, George Scott, 1975	Games Started	38, Jim Slaton, 1973, 1976
Total Bases	318, George Scott, 1975	Complete Games	22, Jim Colborn, 1973
Hits	185, George Scott, 1973	Strikeouts	169, Marty Pattin, 1971
Runs	104, Tommy Harper, 1970	Bases on Balls	106, Pete Broberg, 1975
Doubles	36, George Scott, 1974	Winning Pct.	.625, Jim Colborn, 1973
Triples	8, Bob Coluccio, 1973 8, Johnny Briggs, 1974	ERA	2.81, Bill Travers, 1976
Bases on Balls	95, Tommy Harper, 1969	Saves	31, Ken Sanders, 1971
Stolen Bases	73, Tommy Harper, 1969	Shutouts	5, Marty Pattin, 1971

Few people remember how truly awful this franchise was during its first eight years of existence—unless they happen to live in Seattle or Milwaukee. Scott and Harper played roughly the same role here that Howard and Hinton did for the expansion Senators; you can, if you're not exhausted from the last such experience, pick up some thrills along the way while learning who the runners-up were in all the batting departments. The club's pitching, on the other hand, was not all that bad, especially for an expansion team. Colborn in 1973 had the kind of year that might have won the Cy Young Award if he'd pitched for a contender.

NATIONAL LEAGUE

Number of Years Finishing in Each Position

Team	1	2	3	4	5	6	7	8	9	10	11	12	Aggregate
Cincinnati	5	3	1	3	2	0	1	1	0	0	0	0	1
Los Angeles	4	2	4	2	0	1	1	2	0	0	0	0	2
San Francisco	1	5	2	4	0	0	1	1	1	1	0	0	3
Pittsburgh	1	3	4	1	0	5	1	1	0	0	0	0	4
St. Louis	3	2	0	0	2	4	3	1	0	1	0	0	5
New York	2	0	0	0	3	2	0	0	2	6	0	0	6
Milwaukee–Atlanta	0	1	1	1	5	1	2	2	0	1	2	0	7
Chicago	0	0	3	1	2	0	3	3	2	1	1	0	8
Philadelphia	0	2	0	3	1	1	3	1	0	2	2	1	9
Houston	0	0	1	0	1	2	1	3	5	1	0	1	10
Montreal	0	0	0	0	0	0	1	1	2	1	2	1	11
San Diego	0	0	0	0	0	0	0	0	1	1	2	4	12

AGGREGATE STANDINGS: 1961–68

1. San Francisco
2. Los Angeles
3. St. Louis
4. Cincinnati
5. Pittsburgh
6. Milwaukee–Atlanta
7. Philadelphia
8. Chicago
9. Houston
10. New York

AGGREGATE STANDINGS: 1969–76

1. Cincinnati
2. Pittsburgh
3. Los Angeles
4. New York
5. San Francisco
6. St. Louis
7. Chicago
8. Houston
9. Atlanta
10. Philadelphia
11. Montreal
12. San Diego

CINCINNATI REDS

Pennants: 1961, 1970, 1972, 1973 (D), 1975, 1976
Manager: Sparky Anderson, 1970–76
Park: Crosley Field, 1961–70
  Riverfront Stadium, 1970–present; first game, June 30, 1970, was lost by the Reds to Atlanta, 8–2, at night
Best Year: 1975 (108–54, .667)
Worst Year: 1966 (76–84, .475)
Top Rookie: Johnny Bench, 1968
Biggest Disappointment: Joey Jay, 1963–64; a season from him like the one he had in 1962 would have meant the pennant both years
Best Deal: Obtaining Joe Morgan as part of a mammoth trade with Houston, 1972
Worst Deal: Trading Frank Robinson cost the Reds dearly, but at least they got something for him, namely a pitcher who won over 200 games (Milt Pappas); for Cesar Tovar, whom they sent to the Twins in 1965, all they received was Jerry Arrigo, who won 27 games in five seasons with the Reds
Other:
  1961—Bill Dewitt becomes the new owner; win first flag since 1940
  1964—Manager Fred Hutchinson dies of cancer; club loses the pennant on the final day of the season when it's beaten by Philadelphia
  1968—Lead majors in team BA by 21 points but also have the poorest ERA in the NL and finish 4th
  1969—Top majors in runs for the second straight year
  1973—Have best record in majors (99–63) but lose LCS to underdog Mets
  1975—Win franchise-record 108 games and first World Championship since 1940
  1976—Leave NL-record 1328 men on base in the process of netting second consecutive pennant and World Championship; become first NL team since 1921–1922 Giants to win back-to-back World Series

HITTING		PITCHING	
Batting Ave.	.348, Pete Rose, 1969	Wins	23, Bob Purkey, 1962 23, Jim Maloney, 1962
Slugging Ave.	.624, Frank Robinson, 1962	Losses	19, Sammy Ellis, 1966
Home Runs	45, Johnny Bench, 1970	Innings	293, Jack Billingham, 1973
RBIs	148, Johnny Bench, 1970	Games Started	40, Jack Billingham, 1973
Total Bases	380, Frank Robinson, 1962	Complete Games	18, Bob Purkey, 1962
Hits	230, Pete Rose, 1973	Strikeouts	265, Jim Maloney, 1963
Runs	134, Frank Robinson, 1962	Bases on Balls	110, Jim Maloney, 1965
Doubles	51, Frank Robinson, 1962	Winning Pct.	.821, Bob Purkey, 1962
Triples	14, Vada Pinson, 1963	ERA	1.99, Gary Nolan, 1972
Bases on Balls	132, Joe Morgan, 1975	Saves	37, Clay Carroll, 1972
Stolen Bases	67, Joe Morgan, 1973, 1975	Shutouts	7, Jack Billingham, 1973

Four all-time club batting marks were set during this period—hits, runs, doubles and bases on balls. Billingham's seven shutouts are also an all-time club record. Although he never won 20 games or posted the dazzling stats that Maloney, Nolan and Purkey did, he was the staff workhorse for a six-year span and probably ranks second only to Maloney as the club's top pitcher for the era. Bench has to be considered the best player. He may, in fact, be the best player the Reds have ever had.

LOS ANGELES DODGERS

Pennants: 1963, 1965, 1966, 1974
Manager: Walter Alston, 1961–76
Park: Los Angeles Coliseum, 1961
   Dodger Stadium, 1962–present; first game on April 10, 1962, resulted in a 6–3 loss to the Reds
Best Year: 1974 (102–60, .630)
Worst Year: 1967 (73–89, .451)
Top Rookie: Ted Sizemore, 1969
Biggest Disappointment: Billy Grabarkewitz, 1971
Best Deal: Getting Jim Wynn from Houston for Claude Osteen, 1974; the Dodgers later got Dusty Baker from Atlanta for Wynn
Worst Deal: Surrendering Ron Perranoski, Johnny Roseboro and Bob Miller to the Twins for Mudcat Grant and Zoilo Versalles, 1968
Other:
   1965—Win second World Championship in three years—the first NL team to accomplish this since the 1942–44 Cardinals
   1966—Swept in the World Series by the Orioles; go scoreless for a WS record 33 consecutive innings after scoring a solo run in the third inning of the opener
   1967—Suffer a 22-game drop in wins and fall from 1st to 7th
   1968—Team hits only 67 homers; leader Len Gabrielson, is only player on the club to hit as many as ten; Dodgers hit one more homer than Houston but score fewest runs in NL, a meager 470
   1973—Finish with 95 wins, the third-highest total in the majors, but trail Reds in NL West by 3½ games
   1974—Break eight-year drought without a postseason appearance, franchise's longest since 1921–40
   1976—Allow fewest runs in NL and 90 less than pennant-winning Reds but finish 10 games back of Cincinnati largely because the Reds outscore them by a whopping 249 runs

HITTING		**PITCHING**	
Batting Ave.	.346, Tommy Davis, 1962	Wins	27, Sandy Koufax, 1966
Slugging Ave.	.560, Frank Howard, 1962	Losses	18, Claude Osteen, 1968
Home Runs	32, Jim Wynn, 1974	Innings	336, Sandy Koufax, 1965
RBIs	153, Tommy Davis, 1962	Games Started	42, Don Drysdale, 1963, 1965
Total Bases	356, Tommy Davis, 1962	Complete Games	27, Sandy Koufax, 1965, 1966
Hits	230, Tommy Davis, 1962	Strikeouts	382, Sandy Koufax, 1965
Runs	130, Maury Wills, 1962	Bases on Balls	108, Stan Williams, 1961
Doubles	47, Wes Parker, 1970	Winning Pct.	.842, Ron Perranoski, 1963*
Triples	16, Willie Davis, 1970	ERA	1.73, Sandy Koufax, 1966
Bases on Balls	110, Jim Wynn, 1975	Saves	24, Jim Brewer, 1970
Stolen Bases	104, Maury Wills, 1962	Shutouts	11, Sandy Koufax, 1963

* In 1966 Phil Regan had a .933 WP but just fourteen wins.

All of Wills's and Tommy Davis's records came during an expansion year. Wynn played just two seasons with the Dodgers and had one good one and one bad one, yet set a period record in each—and with numbers that aren't exactly overwhelming. His marks more than suggest that the Dodgers weren't a great offensive team during the era. Actually, there were quite a few seasons when they were downright putrid. In 1966, a pennant year, LA ranked next to last in runs and was led in RBIs by Jim Lefebvre with 74; the following year Ron Fairly was the club's RBI king with 55; and in 1968 catcher Tom Haller's 53 RBIs paced the club, and Fairly was second with 43.

SAN FRANCISCO GIANTS

Pennants: 1962, 1971 (D)
Manager: Charlie Fox, 1970–74
Park: Candlestick Park
Best Year: 1962 (103–62, .624)
Worst Year: 1972 (69–86, .445)
Top Rookie: Gary Matthews, 1973
Biggest Disappointment: Ron Bryant, 1974
Best Deal: Getting Harvey Kuenn from Cleveland for Willie
  Kirkland and Johnny Antonelli, 1961
Worst Deal: Almost every trade the club made after the Kuenn
  one was a catastrophe; total up what the Giants got for Gay-
  lord Perry, Orlando Cepeda, Felipe Alou, George Foster and
  Matty Alou and you'll no longer be mystified why this team
  achieved so little during this era with so much talent
Other:
  1961—Top NL in runs but can't catch the Reds when no starter
    is able to win more than 13 games
  1962—Win pennant playoff series to give the club its first flag
    in San Francisco and send the Dodgers to their third playoff
    series defeat in the past 17 seasons
  1964—Juan Marichal is 21–8 but loses time to an injury; the
    rest of the hill staff is 69–64 as the club loses the flag by a
    three-game margin
  1968—Fourth straight 2nd-place finish
  1971—Lose 8½-game late-season bulge by dropping 16 of last
    24 contests but hold on to win NL West by one game over
    the Dodgers
  1972—First sub-.500 season since 1957
  1973—Last season above .500 until 1978
  1975—Gary Matthews leads the club in homers with just 12
  1976—Bobby Murcer and Gary Matthews hit 43 homers be-
    tween them; the rest of the club hits only 42

HITTING		PITCHING	
Batting Ave.	.320, Willie McCovey, 1969	Wins	26, Juan Marichal, 1968
Slugging Ave.	.656, Willie McCovey, 1969	Losses	18, Ray Sadecki, 1968
Home Runs	52, Willie Mays, 1965	Innings	329, Gaylord Perry, 1970
RBIs	142, Orlando Cepeda, 1961	Games Started	42, Jack Sanford, 1963
Total Bases	382, Willie Mays, 1962	Complete Games	30, Juan Marichal, 1968
Hits	200, Bobby Bonds, 1970	Strikeouts	248, Juan Marichal, 1963
Runs	134, Bobby Bonds, 1970	Bases on Balls	124, John D'Acquisto, 1974
Doubles	39, Willie McCovey, 1970	Winning Pct.	.806, Juan Marichal, 1966
Triples	10, done by four different players	ERA	1.98, Bob Bolin, 1968
Bases on Balls	137, Willie McCovey, 1970	Saves	21, Frank Linzy, 1965
Stolen Bases	48, Bobby Bonds, 1970	Shutouts	10, Juan Marichal, 1965

The era's best NL team on offense—don't forget they had people like Dave Kingman, Gary Matthews and Gary Maddox for a while too—and they had enough good middle infielders and pitchers like Marichal, Perry and Sanford to rank among the best defensively as well. Yet they won only one pennant and one division title. Why? The better question might be how many Cy Young Awards would Marichal have gotten if the Giants had won more. Chances are the answer would still be none. They had it in for him. They must have. From every angle, he was the top pitcher of the era. In both leagues.

PITTSBURGH PIRATES

Pennants: 1970 (D), 1971, 1972 (D), 1974 (D), 1975(D)
Manager: Danny Murtaugh, 1961–64, 1967, 1970–71, 1973–76
Park: Forbes Field, 1961–70
  Three Rivers Stadium, 1970–present; the Pirates opened their new park on July 16, 1970, by losing to the Reds, 3–2
Best Year: 1971 (97–65, .599)
Worst Year: 1963 (74–88, .457)
Top Rookie: Al Oliver, 1969
Biggest Disappointment: Steve Blass, 1972
Best Deal: Acquiring Matty Alou from the Giants, 1966
Worst Deal: Giving the Yankees Willie Randolph, Dock Ellis and Ken Brett for Doc Medich, 1976
Other:
  1961—Suffer 20-game drop after winning flag in 1960 and finish 6th
  1966—Second straight season with 90 or more wins
  1968—Steve Blass and reliever Ron Kline have a combined 30–11 record; rest of staff is 50–71
  1970—.549 winning percentage wins NL East and is the lowest in history to this point to qualify for postseason play
  1971—First team to wear form-fitting double-knit uniforms; share with Orioles the distinction of playing the first World Series night game
  1972—Lose NLCS to the Reds on a ninth-inning wild pitch by reliever Bob Moose in the fifth and deciding game
  1973—Stay in the NL East race until the last weekend of the season with 80–82 record
  1975—Fourth NLCS loss since 1970 prevents the club from winning what could have been five pennants in a six-year span

HITTING		PITCHING	
Batting Ave.	.357, Roberto Clemente, 1967	Wins	19, Dock Ellis, 1971 19, Steve Blass, 1972
Slugging Ave.	.646, Willie Stargell, 1973	Losses	19, Bob Friend, 1961
Home Runs	48, Willie Stargell, 1971	Innings	280, Bob Veale, 1964
RBIs	125, Willie Stargell, 1971	Games Started	38, Bob Friend, 1963 38, Bob Veale, 1964
Total Bases	342, Roberto Clemente, 1966	Complete Games	15, Jim Rooker, 1974 15, Jerry Reuss, 1975
Hits	231, Matty Alou, 1969	Strikeouts	276, Bob Veale, 1965
Runs	106, Willie Stargell, 1973	Bases on Balls	124, Bob Veale, 1964
Doubles	43, Willie Stargell, 1973	Winning Pct.	.750, Steve Blass, 1968
Triples	14, Roberto Clemente, 1965 14, Don Clendenon, 1965	ERA	2.05, Bob Veale, 1968
Bases on Balls	87, Willie Stargell, 1974	Saves	30, Dave Giusti, 1971
Stolen Bases	58, Frank Taveras, 1976	Shutouts	7, Bob Veale, 1965 7, Steve Blass, 1968

It's certainly worth pondering why the only team that set no period batting records in 1930 also set none in 1962 when expansion produced a similar hitting deluge. And if you can explain that, then figure out how the Pirates managed to hang tough all during this era without a single 20-game winner. Start with Giusti. He wasn't the whole reason, but he was definitely the club's top pitcher for the period.

ST. LOUIS CARDINALS

Pennants: 1964, 1967, 1968
Manager: Red Schoendienst, 1965–76
Park: Sportsman's Park, 1961–66 (known as Busch Stadium after 1953)
Busch Memorial Stadium, 1966–present; the Cards beat the Braves 4–3 in 12 innings on May 12, 1966, in the opening game in their new park
Best Year: 1967 (101–60, .627)
Worst Year: 1976 (72–90, .444)
Top Rookie: Dick Hughes, 1967
Biggest Disappointment: Joe Hague, 1971, with Dick Hughes, 1968, a close second
Best Deal: Pilfering Lou Brock from the Cubs, 1964
Worst Deal: Sending Steve Carlton to the Phillies for Rick Wise, 1972
Other:
1963—Finish second, stay in the race until the final week
1964—Win first flag in eighteen years; allow most runs (652) of any NL pennant winner during the era
1968—Falter after leading Tigers 3 games to 1 in the World Series and fail in bid to become first NL team since the 1921–22 Giants to win back-to-back World Championships
1970—First sub-.500 season since 1959
1971—Finish at 90–72, the club's best season during the seventies
1972—Are second in NL in batting and lead majors with 64 complete games but finish six games below .500 because decent hitting and pitching still don't keep team from being outscored 600–568
1975—Top NL in BA but are outscored by opponents, 689–662, and finish at 82–80
1976—Hit ML-low 63 home runs; rookie third baseman Hector Cruz leads the club with 13 four-baggers and is also the RBI leader with 71 despite hitting just .228

HITTING		**PITCHING**	
Batting Ave.	.363, Joe Torre, 1971	Wins	23, Bob Gibson, 1970
Slugging Ave.	.555, Joe Torre, 1971	Losses	19, Steve Carlton, 1970
Home Runs	37, Orlando Cepeda, 1967	Innings	314, Bob Gibson, 1969
RBIs	137, Joe Torre, 1971	Games Started	36, Bob Gibson, 1964, 1965
			36, Steve Carlton, 1971
Total Bases	352, Joe Torre, 1971	Complete Games	28, Bob Gibson, 1968, 1969
Hits	230, Joe Torre, 1971	Strikeouts	274, Bob Gibson, 1970
Runs	126, Lou Brock, 1971	Bases on Balls	119, Bob Gibson, 1961
Doubles	46, Lou Brock, 1968	Winning Pct.	.767, Bob Gibson, 1970
Triples	14, Lou Brock, 1968	ERA	1.12, Bob Gibson, 1968
Bases on Balls	76, Lou Brock, 1971	Saves	22, Al Hrabosky, 1975
Stolen Bases	118, Lou Brock, 1974	Shutouts	13, Bob Gibson, 1968

The chart kind of forces the greatness of Torre's 1971 season on you, doesn't it? In many ways it was as good as Musial's 1948 season, and in some ways it may even have been better. Who else since 1948 has collected 230 hits and over 130 RBIs in the same season? Only Tommy Davis, and he did it in an expansion year. Gibson's 1968 season also forces its greatness on you now. At the time, of course, it helped force some major readjustments to be made in the balance between hitters and pitchers.

NEW YORK METS (1962–76)

Pennants: 1969, 1973
Manager: Gil Hodges, 1968–71
Park: Polo Grounds, 1962–63
  Shea Stadium, 1964–present; the Mets inaugurated Shea by losing 4–3 to Pittsburgh on April 17, 1964
Best Year: 1969 (100–62, .617)
Worst Year: 1962 (40–120, .250)
Top Rookie: Jerry Koosman, 1968
Biggest Disappointment: Don Hahn, 1971–74
Best Deal: Getting Jerry Grote from Houston, 1966; he almost immediately began to pull together the team's mound staff and was heavily responsible for the quick development of its many talented young pitchers
Worst Deal: Tie between giving Nolan Ryan to California, 1972, and Amos Otis to Kansas City, 1970
Other:
  1962—Set twentieth-century ML record with 120 losses in first season
  1963—Set twentieth-century ML record by losing 22 straight games on the road; become last club to make 200 or more errors (210)
  1965—Lose over 100 games for fourth straight year; set ML record for most losses during a four-year period (452)
  1966—Lose less than 100 games for first time in franchise history and likewise escape the cellar for the first time
  1967—Use NL-record 54 players in a vain effort to avoid cellar; rookie Tom Seaver is 16–13 and rest of team's pitchers are 45–88
  1968—Team's batters fan 1203 times to set new ML record
  1969—First NL team since Brooklyn in 1899 to rise from 9th place to a pennant the following season
  1972—Manager Gil Hodges dies of a heart attack during spring training
  1973—Set ML record for the lowest winning percentage by a pennant winner (.509) and become first team to win a pennant without a 20-game winner, a .300 hitter or a 100 RBI man
  1974—Finish below .500 for the first time since 1968

HITTING		PITCHING	
Batting Ave.	.340, Cleon Jones, 1969	Wins	25, Tom Seaver, 1969
Slugging Ave.	.515, Don Clendenon, 1970	Losses	24, Roger Craig, 1962 24, Jack Fisher, 1965
Home Runs	37, Dave Kingman, 1976	Innings	291, Tom Seaver, 1970
RBIs	105, Rusty Staub, 1975	Games Started	36, Jack Fisher, 1965 36, Tom Seaver, 1970, 1973, 1975
Total Bases	298, Tommy Agee, 1970	Complete Games	21, Tom Seaver, 1970
Hits	191, Felix Millan, 1975	Strikeouts	289, Tom Seaver, 1971
Runs	107, Tommy Agee, 1970	Bases on Balls	116, Nolan Ryan, 1971
Doubles	37, Felix Millan, 1975	Winning Pct.	.781, Tom Seaver, 1969
Triples	9, Charlie Neal, 1962	ERA	1.76, Tom Seaver, 1971
Bases on Balls	95, Bud Harrelson, 1970	Saves	27, Tug McGraw, 1972
Stolen Bases	31, Tommy Agee, 1970	Shutouts	7, Jerry Koosman, 1968 7, Jon Matlack, 1974

Many of the club offensive records you see here, anemic as they are, endured until the mid-eighties, and two of them still remain on the books. Offense, in the event you haven't been paying attention, until very recently has never been one of the Mets' strong points. Hard as it may be to believe, they have never had a player who collected as many as 100 walks in a year. Or one who hit more than ten triples. Pitching is a whole other story.

ATLANTA BRAVES

Pennants: 1969 (D)
Manager: Lum Harris, 1968–72
Stadium: County Stadium (Milwaukee), 1961–65
　Fulton County Stadium (Atlanta), 1966–present; in the first ML game since 1884 played south of the Mason-Dixon line, the Braves lost 3–2 to Pittsburgh in 11 innings on April 12, 1966
Best Year: 1969 (93–69, .574)
Worst Year: 1975 (67–94, .416)
Top Rookie: Earl Williams, 1971
Biggest Disappointment: Andy Messersmith, 1976–77
Best Deal: Fleecing the Yankees of Clete Boyer, 1967
Worst Deal: Sending Rico Carty to Texas for Jim Panther, 1972
Other:
　1961—Top NL in homers for the third consecutive year
　1964—Finish 5th but just five games out of 1st; top majors runs with 803
　1965—In final season in Milwaukee set NL record by having six players with 20 or more homers
　1966—Shift to Atlanta to become first NL franchise in this century to move twice; pace NL in runs and homers but finish only 5th
　1967—First sub-.500 season since 1952
　1969—Win 93 games, until 1991 the most by the club since its move to Atlanta
　1973—Lead NL in BA but also have the loop's worst ERA (4.25) and finish below .500, this despite being the only team in ML history with three players who hit 40 or more home runs
　1975—Finish tied for last in NL in BA and next to last in runs scored
　1976—Leftfielder Jim Wynn hits just .207 but nevertheless leads the team in runs, homers and RBIs

HITTING		PITCHING	
Batting Ave.	.366, Rico Carty, 1970	Wins	24, Tony Cloninger, 1965
Slugging Ave.	.669, Hank Aaron, 1971	Losses	18, Phil Niekro, 1969
Home Runs	47, Hank Aaron, 1971	Innings	302, Phil Niekro, 1974
RBIs	122, Hank Aaron, 1966	Games Started	39, Phil Niekro, 1974 39, Carl Morton, 1975
Total Bases	355, Felipe Alou, 1966	Complete Games	22, Warren Spahn, 1962, 1963
Hits	219, Ralph Garr, 1971	Strikeouts	195, Phil Niekro, 1974
Runs	127, Hank Aaron, 1962	Bases on Balls	119, Tony Cloninger, 1965
Doubles	37, Hank Aaron, 1967 37, Felipe Alou, 1968	Winning Pct.	.767, Warren Spahn, 1963
Triples	17, Ralph Garr, 1974	ERA	1.87, Phil Niekro, 1967
Bases on Balls	127, Jim Wynn, 1976	Saves	27, Cecil Upshaw, 1969
Stolen Bases	35, Ralph Garr, 1973	Shutouts	7, Warren Spahn, 1963

How many of you in Milwaukee applauded when Upshaw set an all-time Braves record for saves after the club moved to Atlanta? Any hands go up? No, you care about the records set in a Milwaukee suit, and those living in Atlanta feel the opposite. Here then are the all-time Milwaukee or Atlanta records set during the period that aren't on the chart: Atlanta—Niekro, 23 wins, 1969, 6 shutouts, 1974; Alou, 122 runs, 1966. Milwaukee—Billy O'Dell, 18 saves, 1965; Aaron, 31 stolen bases, 1963; Eddie Mathews, 124 bases on balls, 1963.

CHICAGO CUBS

Pennants: None
Manager: Leo Durocher, 1966–71
Park: Wrigley Field
Best Year: 1969 (92–70, .568)
Worst Year: 1962 and 1966 (59–103, .364)
Top Rookie: Billy Williams, 1961
Biggest Disappointment: Rich Nye, 1968–69; had he been able to match his 1967 rookie performance, the club might well have won the NL East in 1969
Best Deal: Plucking Ferguson Jenkins from the Phillies, 1966
Worst Deal: Turning over Lou Brock to the Cardinals, 1964
Other:

1961—Club is managed by eight coaches, an experiment that lasts for four seasons

1962—Finish 9th, seven games behind the expansion Colt .45s

1965—Leo Durocher hired as manager to bring an end to the experiment that had the club being run by committee

1966—Finish last to allow the grateful Mets to escape the basement for the first time

1967—Club's 87 wins are the most since 1945

1969—Bleacher Bums make their debut as club leads the NL East for most of the season before folding and finishing 2nd

1973—Below .500 for the first time since 1966

1775—Tie for third in the NL in runs scored but finish 12 games below .500 with the worst staff ERA in the majors (4.57), attributable mostly to an abysmal bullpen that features Darold Knowles with a 5.83 ERA and Oscar Zamora with a 5.07 ERA

HITTING		PITCHING	
Batting Ave.	.354, Bill Madlock, 1975	Wins	24, Larry Jackson, 1964 24, Ferguson Jenkins, 1971
Slugging Ave.	.606, Billy Williams, 1972	Losses	22, Dick Ellsworth, 1966 22, Bill Bonham, 1974
Home Runs	37, Ernie Banks, 1962 37, Billy Williams, 1972	Innings	325, Ferguson Jenkins, 1969
RBIs	129, Billy Williams, 1970	Games Started	42, Ferguson Jenkins, 1969
Total Bases	373, Billy Williams, 1970	Complete Games	30, Ferguson Jenkins, 1971
Hits	205, Billy Williams, 1970	Strikeouts	274, Ferguson Jenkins, 1970
Runs	137, Billy Williams, 1970	Bases on Balls	109, Bill Bonham, 1974, 1975
Doubles	39, Billy Williams, 1964, 1965	Winning Pct.	.708, Milt Pappas, 1972
Triples	14, Don Kessinger, 1970	ERA	2.11, Dick Ellsworth, 1963
Bases on Balls	96, Ron Santo, 1967, 1968, 1969	Saves	31, Ted Abernathy, 1965
Stolen Bases	34, Jose Cardenal, 1975	Shutouts	7, Ferguson Jenkins, 1969

The chart doesn't leave much doubt who the Cubs' top hitter and pitcher were during the period. It's not as if either Williams or Jenkins lacked for competition, though. Every name on the chart was an important contributor to the club's rise in the mid-sixties, and among those not on it, Glen Beckert hit .342 one season and Bill Hands started just one fewer game than Jenkins in 1969 while winning 20. Yet the Cubs ended the period still looking for their first title of any kind since 1945. Worse still, they came close just once, in 1969.

PHILADELPHIA PHILLIES

Pennants: 1976 (D)
Manager: Gene Mauch, 1961–68
Park: Shibe Park, 1961–70
   Veterans Stadium, 1971–present; first game on April 10, 1971, resulted in a 4–1 victory over the Expos
Best Year: 1976 (101–61, .623)
Worst Year: 1961 (47–107, .305)
Top Rookie: Dick Allen, 1964
Biggest Disappointment: Mike Anderson, 1971–75
Best Deal: Getting Steve Carlton from the Cardinals, 1972
Worst Deal: Giving the Cubs Ferguson Jenkins, 1966
Other
   1961—Lose twentieth-century ML record 23 straight games
   1964—Lose flag after leading by 6½ games with 12 to play; first time since 1915–17 that club finishes above .500 three years in a row
   1966—Top NL in FA and complete games
   1971—Allow expansion Expos to escape the NL East cellar for the first time
   1972—Second straight NL East cellar finish; Steve Carlton sets twentieth-century record when he wins 46% of team's 59 victories
   1973—Finish last but trail division-winning Mets by just 11½ games
   1975—First season above .500 since 1967
   1976—Win 100 or more games for the first time in franchise history; club's three regular outfielders all hit .304 or better; third baseman Mike Schmidt wins third consecutive NL home run crown after becoming the first Phillie since 1933 to lead in four-baggers two years earlier

HITTING		PITCHING	
Batting Ave.	.330, Gary Maddox, 1976	Wins	27, Steve Carlton, 1972
Slugging Ave.	.632, Dick Allen, 1966	Losses	20, Steve Carlton, 1973
Home Runs	40, Dick Allen, 1966	Innings	346, Steve Carlton, 1972
RBIs	120, Greg Luzinski, 1975	Games Started	41, Jim Bunning, 1966
			41, Steve Carlton, 1972
Total Bases	352, Dick Allen, 1964	Complete Games	30, Steve Carlton, 1972
Hits	213, Dave Cash, 1975	Strikeouts	310, Steve Carlton, 1972
Runs	125, Dick Allen, 1964	Bases on Balls	136, Steve Carlton, 1974
Doubles	40, Johnny Callison, 1966	Winning Pct.	.741, Steve Carlton, 1976
	40, Dave Cash, 1975		
Triples	16, Johnny Callison, 1965	ERA	1.97, Steve Carlton, 1972
Bases on Balls	106, Mike Schmidt, 1974	Saves	22, Dick Selma, 1970
Stolen Bases	39, Larry Bowa, 1974	Shutouts	8, Steve Carlton, 1972

In 1972, when Carlton was 27–10, the Phils played only 156 games owing to the players' strike at the beginning of the season and won just 59 of them. The following year the club played a full 162-game schedule and improved to 71 wins while Carlton's record slipped to 13–20. But Carlton's career was full of things like that. How many other pitchers have been the staff work-horse on a pennant winner yet posted a losing record? Happened in the past ten years. Look it up.

HOUSTON ASTROS (1962–76)

Pennants: None

Manager: Harry Walker, 1968–72

Park: Colt Stadium, 1962–64

Astrodome, 1965–present; first domed stadium in the majors was inaugurated on April 12, 1965, when the Phillies beat the Astros, 2–0

Best Year: 1972 (84–69, .549)

Worst Year: 1975 (64–97, .398)

Top Rookie: Joe Morgan, 1965

Biggest Disappointment: Howie Goss, 1963

Best Deal: Obtaining Joe Niekro from Atlanta for $35,000, 1975

Worst Deal: The huge trade with the Reds that cost the club Joe Morgan, 1972, with the deal that gave Mike Cuellar to the Orioles in 1969 a not too distant second

Other:

1962—Begin life as the Colt .45s; finish 8th, 24 games ahead of the 10th-place Mets, the team's sister expansion club

1963—Play first Sunday night home game in ML history

1965—Change team nickname to Astros

1968—Finish in the cellar for the first time

1969—Set ML record with 1221 pitching strikeouts

1971—Play ML-record 75 one-run games

1972—Hit 134 home runs to set new club record

1973—Tie still-existing club record by hitting 134 home runs for the second year in a row

1975—Pitcher Don Wilson commits suicide; team finishes last in NL

1976—Gain 15½ games over 1975 finish in first full season under manager Bill Virdon

HITTING		PITCHING	
Batting Ave.	.333, Rusty Staub, 1967	Wins	20, Larry Dierker, 1969
			20, J. R. Richard, 1976
Slugging Ave.	.537, Cesar Cedeno, 1972, 1973	Losses	20, Dick Farrell, 1962
Home Runs	37, Jim Wynn, 1967	Innings	305, Larry Dierker, 1969
RBIs	107, Jim Wynn, 1967	Games Started	40, Jerry Reuss, 1973
Total Bases	300, Cesar Cedeno, 1972	Complete Games	20, Larry Dierker, 1969
Hits	185, Greg Gross, 1974	Strikeouts	235, Don Wilson, 1969
Runs	117, Jim Wynn, 1972	Bases on Balls	151, J. R. Richard, 1976
Doubles	44, Rusty Staub, 1967	Winning Pct.	.652, Larry Dierker, 1972
Triples	14, Roger Metzger, 1973	ERA	2.22, Mike Cuellar, 1966
Bases on Balls	148, Jim Wynn, 1969	Saves	29, Fred Gladding, 1969
Stolen Bases	58, Cesar Cedeno, 1976	Shutouts	6, Dave Roberts, 1973

Not one of the luckier teams, particularly with its pitchers. Two of the names on the chart are long since dead, Dierker's wing was gone by the time he was thirty, and Richard had just turned thirty when he had his stroke. Then there was Jim Umbricht. It looks as if a case can be made that Houston has become the Cleveland of the National League. Had Wynn played for the Cubs or the Phillies during his prime, or the Braves or the Reds—or almost any other team in the majors—a case would now be being made to get him into the Hall of Fame, if he were not already there.

MONTREAL EXPOS (1969–76)

Pennants: None
Manager: Gene Mauch, 1969–76
Park: Jarry Park
Best Year: 1974 (79–82, .491)
Worst Year: 1969 (52–110, .321)
Top Rookie: Carl Morton, 1970
Biggest Disappointment: Coco Laboy, 1970
Best Deal: Obtaining Ken Singleton, Mike Jorgensen and Tim Foli from the Mets for Rusty Staub, 1972
Worst Deal: Sending Ken Singleton and Mike Torrez to the Orioles for Dave McNally and Rich Coggins, 1975
Other:
   1969—Beat the Cardinals 8–7 on April 14 in the first NL game ever played outside the USA; lose expansion team record 20 straight games
   1971—With help from the Phillies, escape the NL East cellar for the first time
   1975—Finish tied with the Cubs for last in the NL East with a better record than three NL West teams
   1976—Finish in NL East cellar, the club's last basement finish until 1991; lose 107 games as Woody Fryman has a 13–13 record and every other pitcher on the staff has a losing record

HITTING		PITCHING	
Batting Ave.	.311, Rusty Staub, 1971	Wins	18, Carl Morton, 1970
Slugging Ave.	.526, Rusty Staub, 1969	Losses	22, Steve Rogers, 1974
Home Runs	30, Rusty Staub, 1970	Innings	295, Bill Stoneman, 1971
RBIs	103, Ken Singleton, 1973	Games Started	39, Bill Stoneman, 1971
Total Bases	289, Rusty Staub, 1969, 1971	Complete Games	20, Bill Stoneman, 1970
Hits	186, Rusty Staub, 1971	Strikeouts	251, Bill Stoneman, 1971
Runs	100, Ken Singleton, 1973	Bases on Balls	146, Bill Stoneman, 1971
Doubles	36, Tim Foli, 1976	Winning Pct.	.652, Mike Torrez, 1974 .652, Dale Murray, 1975
Triples	9, Willie Davis, 1974	ERA	2.81, Steve Renko, 1973
Bases on Balls	123, Ken Singleton, 1973	Saves	31, Mike Marshall, 1973
Stolen Bases	50, Larry Lintz, 1974	Shutouts	5, Bill Stoneman, 1969

Lintz was a semi-regular in 1974, but in 1976 he stole 31 bases for the A's while collecting just one official at bat. Murray in 1975 led the Expos staff with 15 wins, all of them in relief. That same year another Expos reliever, Don DeMola, was cut after appearing in 60 games, the second most in history by a pitcher playing in his last major league season. Back then, once you got past Staub and Singleton, you tended to note that kind of thing if you were an Expos fan.

SAN DIEGO PADRES (1969–76)

Pennants: None
Manager: Preston Gomez, 1969–72
Park: Jack Murphy Stadium; opened on April 8, 1969, the Padres beating the Astros 2–1 in a night game
Best Year: 1976 (73–89, .451)
Worst Year: 1969 (52–110, .321)
Top Rookie: Butch Metzger, 1976
Biggest Disappointment: Dave Roberts, 1974–76
Best Deal: Getting Willie McCovey from the Giants, 1974
Worst Deal: Sending Pat Dobson to Baltimore, 1971
Other:

1969—In first season score 114 fewer runs than every other team in the NL and post .225 BA

1970—Last in no major NL team departments except the most important one—wins

1971—Worst record in the NL for the third year in a row; last team to date to score fewer than 500 runs (486) while playing a full schedule

1974—.229 BA and 541 runs scored are both the poorest in the NL

1975—After six consecutive last-place finishes in the NL West, escape the division cellar for the first time

1976—Dave Winfield leads the club in homers with 13; runner-up Doug Rader hits only nine as club nets just 64 four-baggers

HITTING		**PITCHING**	
Batting Ave.	.318, Cito Gaston, 1970	Wins	22, Randy Jones, 1976
Slugging Ave.	.543, Cito Gaston, 1970	Losses	22, Randy Jones, 1974
Home Runs	38, Nate Colbert, 1970, 1972	Innings	315, Randy Jones, 1976
RBIs	111, Nate Colbert, 1971	Games Started	40, Randy Jones, 1976
Total Bases	317, Cito Gaston, 1970	Complete Games	25, Randy Jones, 1976
Hits	186, Cito Gaston, 1970	Strikeouts	231, Clay Kirby, 1971
Runs	92, Cito Gaston, 1970	Bases on Balls	122, Steve Arlin, 1972
Doubles	36, Johnny Grubb, 1975	Winning Pct.	.625, Randy Jones, 1975
Triples	10, Willie Davis, 1976	ERA	2.10, Dave Roberts, 1971
Bases on Balls	96, Willie McCovey, 1974	Saves	16, Butch Metzger, 1976
Stolen Bases	37, Enzo Hernandez, 1974	Shutouts	6, Fred Norman, 1972 6, Randy Jones, 1975

Don't feel totally devastated if you don't recall Gaston's great season. A lot of people in San Diego don't either. In 1970 he also had 29 homers and 93 RBIs. As a team, the Padres hit 172 homers that season, third best in the league. They still finished last owing to poor pitching. The following year Roberts had the second-lowest ERA in the NL and Kirby had the tenth lowest. They still finished last owing to poor hitting. Gaston? He hit .228.

THE BEST, THE WORST AND THE WEIRDEST TEAMS BETWEEN 1961 AND 1976

● ●

NATIONAL LEAGUE

THE BEST

1976 CINCINNATI REDS
W-102 L-60
Manager: Sparky Anderson

Regular Lineup—1B, Tony Perez; 2B, Joe Morgan; 3B, Pete Rose; SS, Dave Concepcion; RF, Ken Griffey; CF, Cesar Geronimo; LF, George Foster; C, Johnny Bench; P, Gary Nolan; P, Pat Zachry; P, Fred Norman; P, Jack Billingham; P, Don Gullett; P, Pedro Borbon; P, Rawley Eastwick; P, Santo Alcala

With the sole exception of Griffey, nobody on the club had a career year in 1976 and Bench had a terrible one. Yet the Reds lazed through the regular season, came wide awake to demolish the Phillies in the LCS and then handed the Yankees one of the most embarrassingly one-sided World Series defeats ever. Cincinnati did it with a lineup that had no soft spots, an adequate bench and the only pitching staff in history that had seven men who each won eleven or more games. Nolan and Gullett, when healthy, were the team's two most effective hurlers, but neither, although not yet thirty, was ever again completely sound, and several other members of the hill crew are forgotten names a mere sixteen years later. For that one season, though, all of them glistened like jewels with the benefit of the strongest regular lineup since expansion behind them. Two of its members are already in the Hall of Fame; Rose is a lock to become the third if and when he is reinstated; Perez and Concepcion both still stand an excellent chance of being enshrined; and Foster, at the time, looked as if he'd one day be yet a sixth strong candidate from the team.

THE WORST

1966 CHICAGO CUBS
W-59 L-103
Manager: Leo Durocher

Regular Lineup—1B, Ernie Banks; 2B, Glenn Beckert; 3B, Ron Santo; SS, Don Kessinger; RF, Billy Williams; CF, Adolfo Phillips; LF, Byron Browne; C, Randy Hundley; P, Dick Ellsworth; P, Ken Holtzman; P, Ferguson Jenkins; P, Bill Hands; P, Cal Koonce; P, Bob Hendley; P, Curt Simmons

The Mets during those years had several seasons that were poorer than the Cubs' 1966 campaign, but New York could be excused because it was an expansion team. Durocher had absolutely no excuse for steering this club to the distinction of being the first to allow the Mets to escape the cellar, although he pleaded dozens. The regular lineup and the pitching staff were both studded with Hall of Famers and All-Stars, and several of them, most notably Santo and Beckert, had terrific individual seasons. But against that, Ellsworth set the club record for pitching losses and Browne for batters' strikeouts. Moreover, Durocher, who prided himself on putting together teams that had loads of Dusty Rhodeses and other interesting spare parts flooding the bench, left himself with only two .220 hitters, George Altman and John Boccabella, to call on when his regulars needed spelling. Hundley, who set an NL rookie record when he caught 149 games, was the chief victim of the club's shortsightedness. He worked 612 games behind the plate in his first four seasons and was a burnout before he turned twenty-eight.

THE WEIRDEST

1973 NEW YORK METS
W-82 L-79
Manager: Yogi Berra

Regular Lineup—1B, John Milner; 2B, Felix Millan; 3B, Wayne Garrett; SS, Bud Harrelson; RF, Rusty Staub; CF, Don Hahn; LF, Cleon Jones; C, Jerry Grote; P, Tom Seaver; P, Jerry Koosman; P, Jon Matlack; P, George Stone; P, Tug McGraw; P, Ray Sadecki; P, Harry Parker

The only pennant winner to triumph without a .300 hitter, a 20-game winner, or a player who had at least 80 RBIs, this team came within a hair of winning the World Series as well. Many maintain that the Mets had to get every break in the world just to win their division, which was so densely packed in 1973 that the fifth-place Cubs were in the race until the last week and so mediocre that New York was the only team to break .500. And while all of that is true, the Mets nonetheless defeated a very good Cincinnati team in the LCS entirely on merit and nearly dethroned what may be the last team ever to sweep three straight World Championships, the 1972–74 Oakland A's. Seaver got the Cy Young Award and was the only Mets player to receive more than token MVP consideration—he finished eighth in the balloting—but Berra may have been the team's most valuable asset. Never a great inspirational leader, he made up for it with patience and the shrewd manipulation of his material, particularly the pitching staff and most especially Stone and Parker, who had a combined 20–7 record. Berra's achievement in 1973 was conceivably the best managing job during the 1970s, if not since expansion.

AMERICAN LEAGUE

THE BEST

1970 BALTIMORE ORIOLES
W-108 L-54
Manager: Earl Weaver

Regular Lineup—1B, Boog Powell; 2B, Davey Johnson; 3B, Brooks Robinson; SS, Mark Belanger; RF, Frank Robinson; CF, Paul Blair; LF, Don Buford; C, Ellie Hendricks; P, Jim Palmer; P, Mike Cuellar; P, Dave McNally; P, Dick Hall; P, Pete Richert; P, Eddie Watt

Weaver tried all season, without success, to find a reliable fourth starter, but his bullpen was so strong that it more than compensated for—and even masked—the club's lone weak spot. What's more, Palmer, Cuellar, and McNally compiled an aggregate 68–27 record, enabling the Orioles to make a mockery of the AL East race for the second year in a row. Indeed, except for the strike-shortened 1972 season, the club won every year between 1969 and 1974. The Orioles' five division titles brought only one World Championship, however, that in 1970, when they needed just five games in the World Series to dispatch the Reds. On that count alone the 1970 team qualifies as Weaver's best. Its 108 wins, the most since 1954 by an AL team in a nonexpansion year, clinches its ranking as the era's best as well.

THE WORST

1964 KANSAS CITY ATHLETICS
W-57 L-105
Managers: Eddie Lopat/Mel McGaha

Regular Lineup—1B, Jim Gentile; 2B, Dick Green; 3B, Ed Charles; SS, Wayne Causey; RF, Rocky Colavito; CF, Nelson Mathews; LF, Manny Jiminez/George Alusik; C, Doc Edwards; P, Orlando Pena; P, Diego Segui; P, John O'Donoghue; P, Moe Drabowsky; P, John Wyatt; P, Wes Stock

After vying for three years with the expansion Washington Senators for the AL cellar, the A's finally hit rock bottom in 1964 and remained there for three of their last four seasons in Kansas City. Horrendous pitching would probably have doomed them to another dozen or so losses had it not been for Wyatt and Stock, who between them saved 25 of the club's 57 victories and won 15 others. The two were also the only A's hurlers with ERAs below 4.00 as Kansas City won two legs of the flip side of the team Triple Crown in 1964, finishing last in fielding and ERA. Lopat, accustomed to being associated with winners, could tolerate the ineptitude for only two months before he jumped ship and left McGaha to ride out the rest of the storm. By the time the A's abandoned Kansas City, they had run through three more managers. Apart from Wyatt and Stock, the team's lone bright spots in 1964 were the slugging of Colavito, Causey's continued emergence as one of the AL's better infielders after he'd fizzled as a bonus baby with the Orioles almost a decade earlier, and rookie Green, the only key member of the 1964 cast who was still a part of the troupe when the franchise hit the jackpot in the early 1970s.

THE WEIRDEST

1966 NEW YORK YANKEES
W-70 L-89
Managers: Johnny Keane/Ralph Houk

Regular Lineup—1B, Joe Pepitone; 2B, Bobby Richardson; 3B, Clete Boyer: SS, Horace Clarke; RF, Roger Maris; CF, Mickey Mantle; LF, Tom Tresh; C, Elston Howard; P, Mel Stottlemyre; P, Jim Bouton; P, Pete Ramos; P, Steve Hamilton; P, Fritz Peterson; P, Al Downing; P, Fred Talbot; P, Hal Reniff; P, Dooley Womack

Just about everybody loved it when this club finished tenth and last, albeit by just half a game, but no one ever exactly understood how it happened. The team was awash with dissension, to be sure. And it didn't help that Howard was about through, Mantle and Maris were slipping fast, and Tresh had completely lost the batting stroke that had made him one of the AL's most promising young hitters just two years earlier. Yet the Yankees still finished seventh in hitting, tied for seventh in fielding and tied for fifth in ERA. Actually, they brought up the rear in only one significant department, the final standings. The Yankees of the previous two decades had contrived to win practically every year despite usually finishing in the middle of the pack in team stats. The 1966 team was so uncharacteristic that it defied belief. Of-

ten before, when the Yankees had won, it was a puzzle after-
wards how they'd done it. Now that they had finished in last
place for the first time in half a century, there was the same
puzzle. Houk, who moved down from the front office to run the
team after it grew painfully clear that Keane was out of his
element among free spirits like Mantle, Ford and Pepitone,
thought he had a handle on the problem. But if he did it never
showed up in the standings. The club was 12 games below .500
when Keane was given the gate and finished 19 games under the
break-even point. After winning three pennants in his first three
years as a manager (1961–63), Houk returned to the dugout in
1966 for seventeen years without ever winning another.

SPECIAL FEATURE
TEAM: THE
MIRACLE METS

• •

1969 NEW YORK METS
W-100 L-62
Manager: Gil Hodges

Regular Lineup—1B, Ed Kranepool; 2B, Ken Boswell; 3B, Wayne Garrett; SS, Bud Harrelson; RF, Ron Swoboda; CF, Tommie Agee; LF, Cleon Jones; C, Jerry Grote; P, Tom Seaver; P, Jerry Koosman; P, Gary Gentry; P, Don Cardwell; P, Ron Taylor; P, Jim McAndrew; P, Cal Koonce; P, Tug McGraw; P, Nolan Ryan

The Mets stirred hopes of a miracle for the first time in July 1969 by twice taking two parts of a three-game series with the then first-place Cubs and coming from behind several times before beating the Giants in a thrilling extra-inning game at Shea Stadium, but the fantasy seemed dead when a slump in early August dropped Hodges's men 9½ games back of Chicago. The Bruins then went into an even worse tailspin that left them only 2½ games in front when they journeyed to New York on September 8 for a two-game set. By the evening of September 10 the Amazing Mets were in first place by scant percentage points, and the margin had swelled to eight full games when the season closed some three weeks later. After sweeping the Atlanta Braves in the first-ever NLCS, the Mets were momentarily derailed in the World Series opener by Baltimore's Mike Cuellar but then granted the Orioles just 17 hits and five runs while bagging the next four games. When Hodges awakened on the morning of October 16 and pinched himself, he remembered that whatever

he had been dreaming could not have been nearly as improbable
as the scene the previous afternoon at Shea when Koosman retired the final Orioles batter to make the Mets, a perennial door-
mat during the first seven years of their existence, the World
Champions in their eighth campaign.

No team has ever quite matched the miracle of 1969. In the
years since other unlikely clubs—the 1987 Twins and the 1988
Dodgers leap instantly to mind—have claimed World Championships, but all of them pulled it off because a stronger opponent suffered key injuries or was psychologically devastated by
a stunning twist of fortune. The 1969 Mets needed no particular
breaks and knocked off their postseason rivals so convincingly
that their win, in hindsight, seems less an upset than a failure
to recognize that they were a good team in the making that was
converted into a winner more quickly than anyone believed possible through skillful managing and a thoroughly unique chain
of circumstances.

In 1969, with the addition of four new expansion teams, both
major leagues were divided into two divisions. The realignment
put the Mets, a ninth-place club in 1968, into what was now
essentially a six-team circuit and virtually guaranteed, with the
expansion Montreal Expos in their division, that the worst they
could finish was fifth. The Mets received a further morale boost
when they were left almost untouched by the draft to stock the
new teams while their division rivals were all stripped of at least
one player who figured prominently in the events of 1969. The
Cubs lost Bill Stoneman, a fine young pitcher, to the Expos; the
Phillies furnished the Expos with their keystone combo of Gary
Sutherland and Bobby Wine; the San Diego Padres plucked Clay
Kirby, an outstanding pitching prospect, from the Cardinals; and
the Expos relieved the Pirates of Don Clendenon, their regular
first sacker, and then traded him during the 1969 season to the
Mets. Who did the Mets lose during all this? No one of any great
value. Not one player who had been even remotely in the club's
plans for 1969 except spare outfielder Larry Stahl.

The reason the Mets were able to protect all their key players
from the expansion draft was that they had precious few players
who looked attractive to the new clubs. In 1968 Harrelson hit
.219, Agee batted .217 and had just 17 RBIs, Kranepool swatted
.231 with 20 RBIs, sub Jerry Buchek hit .182 and fanned 53 times
in just 192 at bats, and the team as a whole scored the fewest
runs in the majors and had the lowest slugging average. What

the Mets did have in abundance, though, were promising young pitchers, and in 1969 each and every one of them made a valuable contribution. Moreover, because of their youth—Koosman at twenty-six was the oldest starter—they all grew stronger as the summer wore on while older pitching staffs in the league were tiring.

Pitching was not the only factor in the Mets' success, however, or even the most critical one. Agee, Jones, Seaver and sub outfielder Art Shamsky all had career years in 1969. Shamsky exemplified the one place where the Mets were lucky: their bench. Whenever Hodges needed a replacement, one suddenly and unexpectedly rose to the occasion. In the LCS, Shamsky subbed for Swoboda and led the team with a .538 BA. Then in the World Series, when Hodges spelled Boswell, Al Weis, a .215 hitter during the regular season, stepped in and rapped .455 with a big home run in the final game. Clendenon meanwhile platooned with Kranepool after his acquisition from the Expos. In the LCS, when the Braves went exclusively with righthanders, the righty slugger rode the bench all the way. But against the Orioles, who started lefties Mike Cuellar and Dave McNally in four of the five games, Clendenon was more than ready. Despite sitting out Game 3 of the World Series, when the Orioles went with righty Jim Palmer, Clendenon led all hitters in home runs and RBIs.

Hodges platooned all that season at every position but center and left field, where Agee and Jones were just too much better than anyone else he had. It resulted in lackluster individual and team stats—the Mets paced the NL in no major departments and led their division only in fielding—but created an esprit that few other teams have ever achieved. Each member of the 1969 club felt, rightly, that he had played a vital hand in the team's triumph.

The Amazing Mets then perpetrated something that was nearly as extraordinary as their World Championship victory. For the next three seasons, 1970–72, they won exactly the same number of games each year (83), a feat in itself that no other team has ever accomplished, and then won a second pennant in 1973 while boasting only 82 victories, the fewest ever by a flag winner.

THE GREAT
TEXAS LEAGUE
HARBINGER

• •

1961 AMARILLO SONICS
W-90 L-50
Managers: Sheriff Robinson/Steve Souchock

Regular Lineup—1B, Charlie Buheller; 2B, Don Brummer; 3B, Mike Mathiesen; SS, Phil Linz; RF, Jack Davis; CF, Joe Pepitone; LF, Dick Berardino; C, Joe Miller/ Dick Windle; P, Jim Bouton; P, Jack Cullen; P, Paul Erickson; P, Bill Drummond; P, Bob Lasko; P, Rudy Stowe; P, Tom McNulty

The Texas League, just a few years after reaching its zenith in attendance and overall level of play, by 1961 had pared its schedule to 140 games and cut back to six teams after losing the Houston and the Dallas–Fort Worth franchises to the International League. In a further attempt to rekindle fan interest that had been dampened by a combination of televised major league games in Texas League cities, the general malaise that pervaded the high minors after the majors began moving franchises into former minor league bastions, and the disinterest in the minor league product that ensued when it was announced that major league ball would come to Texas for the first time the next year, in Houston, the TL experimented by playing an interlocking schedule with the six-team Mexican League. The setup called for every club to play four games with each of the teams in its "sister" circuit. It was a noble effort, but it proved to be a failure in 1961 as all the TL clubs with the exception of Austin, which split its 24 games outside the loop, demolished their ML rivals.

Pennant-winning Amarillo was the most successful, compiling a 19–5 record against Mexican clubs, and the Tulsa Oilers, which finished in second place, were only a notch less dominant. The experiment was also a flop at the gate—stateside anyway—as only Tulsa drew over 100,000 patrons that season and the TL teams had a total attendance that was a mere third the size of the ML's.

Yet no league with a Yankees farm team that had three players like Linz, Pepitone and Bouton could have a season that was not in some way memorable. In 1961, Linz led the TL in hitting, Pepitone was second in total bases and Bouton was third in strikeouts. More important, the trio had already manifested the traits—outspokenness, unconventionality and irreverence—that would soon put them at the forefront of the new breed of Yankees and, in fact, of ballplayers in general. Two members of the Sonics who never made the parent club—Brummer and Miller— also possessed these same un-Yankeelike traits. Brummer in particular made even Pepitone seem laid back and unassuming. But the team as a whole also pointed up, although only in retrospect, the reason that the great Yankees dynasty of the 1950s and early 1960s ultimately came unraveled. Amarillo had a glaring absence of talented young black players—as, for that matter, did Richmond in the International League, the Yankees' other affiliate at the time in the high minors. Much the same thing could be said, actually, about most of the other American League teams. In contrast, the National League by 1961 was already adorned with many good young black players and the following year would begin to move sharply ahead of the junior circuit when blacks like Hank Aaron, Willie Mays, Tommy Davis, Willie McCovey, Maury Wills, Vada Pinson, Frank Robinson and Roberto Clemente led it in virtually every major offensive department while the AL had an all-white crew of hitting leaders with the sole exception of Chicago's Floyd Robinson, who was tops in doubles.

The Amarillo club reflected—again only in retrospect—a second weakness that would come to haunt the Yankees a few years later: Other than Bouton, none of the team's young pitchers was ever of any help to the parent club. The best, off his 1961 performance, looked to be Stowe, who had a glittering 14–1 record. But he never matured. The only TL pitcher, as it turned out, who ever did much in the majors—again apart from Bouton— was an Austin reliever who had a 4–4 record in 51 appearances.

His inauspicious season in 1961 notwithstanding, he presently has the record for the most wins in the majors by a Texas League graduate. His name: Phil Niekro.

ERA ALL-STAR TEAMS

	AMERICAN LEAGUE		NATIONAL LEAGUE
1B	Harmon Killebrew	1B	Willie McCovey
2B	Rod Carew	2B	Joe Morgan
3B	Brooks Robinson	3B	Dick Allen
SS	Luis Aparicio	SS	Maury Wills
OF	Frank Robinson	OF	Roberto Clemente
OF	Carl Yastrzemski	OF	Lou Brock
OF	Tony Oliva	OF	Hank Aaron
C	Thurman Munson	C	Johnny Bench
P	Jim Palmer	P	Juan Marichal
P	Catfish Hunter	P	Bob Gibson
UTIL	Frank Howard	UTIL	Willie Stargell
MGR	Earl Weaver	MGR	Walter Alston
*	Al Kaline	*	Pete Rose/Sandy Koufax
RELIEF	Sparky Lyle	RELIEF	Dave Giusti

* Best player who failed to make the team

LEG SEVEN

1977–1991

TEAM NOTES AND RECORD HOLDERS: 1977–91

NATIONAL LEAGUE

Number of Years Finishing in Each Position

Team	1	2	3	4	5	6	7	8	9	10	11	12	Aggregate
Los Angeles	4	1	3	2	0	0	0	3	1	1	0	0	1
Philadelphia	1	2	2	3	2	0	0	0	1	2	1	1	2
St. Louis	2	2	2	0	1	4	1	0	1	0	2	0	3
Cincinnati	0	1	0	3	2	2	2	3	1	0	1	0	4
Montreal	3	0	1	2	3	1	0	1	1	2	1	0	5
Pittsburgh	1	2	1	1	2	2	1	0	1	2	0	2	6
Houston	1	0	1	1	3	1	1	3	2	0	1	1	7
San Francisco	0	2	0	2	2	3	1	0	4	0	0	1	8
New York	1	3	2	1	0	0	0	1	0	1	3	3	9
San Diego	0	2	0	0	0	1	4	2	1	1	2	2	11
Chicago	1	0	1	1	1	2	1	2	1	3	1	1	10
Atlanta	1	1	1	0	0	1	1	1	0	3	2	4	12

The standings indicate that the two NL divisions have been about equal in strength since 1977. Interestingly, though, as opposed to the AL, where most of the teams that were weak at the beginning of the era have remained weak throughout, the lower half of the NL standings has undergone a constant reshuffling during the period. Five years ago, for instance, the Cubs were in last place, the Mets next to last and the Astros all the way up in the fourth spot. What that could mean is that things in the NL turn around more rapidly than they do in the AL. It could also mean, of course, that in the NL teams can't hold it together as long. In any event, it seems a fair statement to make that the NL has been much more evenly balanced during the era than the AL. All of its clubs have won at least one division title since 1977 and ten teams have won more than one.

LOS ANGELES DODGERS

Pennants: 1977, 1978, 1981, 1983 (D), 1985 (D), 1988
Manager: Tommy Lasorda, 1977–91
Park: Dodger Stadium
Best Year: 1977 (98–64, .605)
Worst Year: 1986 and 1987 (73–89, .451)
Top Rookie: Fernando Valenzuela, 1981
Biggest Disappointment: Dave Goltz, 1980
Best Deal: Obtaining Pedro Guerrero from Cleveland for Bruce Ellingsen; deal made in 1974 while Guerrero was still in the minors and didn't really begin to make itself felt until 1980
Worst Deal: Sending Rick Sutcliffe and Jack Perconte to Cleveland, 1982
Other:

   1977—Only team in history to have four players with 30 or more home runs

   1978—First team to draw over 3,000,000 in a season

   1979—Play ML-record eleven consecutive errorless games in May

   1982—Set new ML attendance record with 3,608,881

   1983—Have lowest staff ERA in majors (3.10) and top NL in homers with 146

   1985—Pace majors with 2.96 staff ERA and 21 shutouts

   1986—Avoid finishing in NL West cellar by just half a game

   1987—Score fewest runs in majors (635) and finish 16 games under .500 with pitching staff that notches the most complete games in the NL and is only .04 runs from having the best ERA in the majors

   1988—Become first and only team in eighties to win two World Championships

   1989—Outscore opponents 554–536 and lead majors with 2.95 staff ERA but finish six games under .500

   1991—Have best home record in majors (54–27) but sub-.500 road performance contributes heavily to team's inability to hang on to top rung in season's final week

HITTING		PITCHING	
Batting Ave.	.338, Pedro Guerrero, 1987	Wins	23, Orel Hershiser, 1988
Slugging Ave.	.577, Pedro Guerrero, 1985	Losses	17, Fernando Valenzuela, 1984
Home Runs	33, Steve Garvey, 1977 33, Pedro Guerrero, 1985	Innings	285, Fernando Valenzuela, 1982
RBIs	115, Steve Garvey, 1977	Games Started	37, Fernando Valenzuela, 1982 37, Jerry Reuss, 1982
Total Bases	322, Steve Garvey, 1977	Complete Games	20, Fernando Valenzuela, 1986
Hits	210, Steve Sax, 1986	Strikeouts	242, Fernando Valenzuela, 1986
Runs	112, Brett Butler, 1991	Bases on Balls	124, Fernando Valenzuela, 1987
Doubles	43, Steve Sax, 1986	Winning Pct.	.864, Orel Hershiser, 1985
Triples	9, Steve Garvey, 1978	ERA	2.03, Orel Hershiser, 1985
Bases on Balls	108, Brett Butler, 1991	Saves	28, Jay Howell, 1989
Stolen Bases	56, Steve Sax, 1983	Shutouts	8, Fernando Valenzuela, 1981 8, Orel Hershiser, 1988 8, Tim Belcher, 1989

Most people outside of Los Angeles and Brooklyn aren't fond of the Dodgers, and even in Brooklyn not everyone likes them. But you can't not like this team's year-in, year-out excellence. Much was made of the fact that in 1986 the Dodgers had to struggle to escape their first cellar finish since 1905, but even at that they finished with the ninth-best record in a 12-team league.

PHILADELPHIA PHILLIES

Pennants: 1977 (D), 1978 (D), 1980, 1983
Manager: Danny Ozark, 1977–79
Park: Veterans Stadium
Best Year: 1977 (101–61, .623)
Worst Year: 1988 (65–96, .404)
Top Rookie: Juan Samuel, 1985
Biggest Disappointment: Ricky Jordan, 1990
Best Deal: Snagging John Denny from Cleveland, 1982
Worst Deal: Giving the Cubs Ryne Sandberg, 1982
Other:

1977—Tie year-old franchise record with 101 wins
1978—Lose NL-record third straight LCS in three years
1980—Win first World Championship in franchise history
1981—Carpenter family sells the team
1983—Win flag with oldest regular lineup in the majors
1984—Finish at .500 or above for franchise-record tenth straight season
1985—First sub-.500 finish since 1974
1986—Last time team finishes above .500 in 1980s
1989—Finish last in NL East for second year in a row and have poorest ERA in NL (4.04)
1991—Tie post-1893 club record by reeling off 13 consecutive wins; beat Cubs out for 3rd place in NL East by fraction of a percentage point

HITTING		PITCHING	
Batting Ave.	.331, Pete Rose, 1979	Wins	24, Steve Carlton, 1980
Slugging Ave.	.644, Mike Schmidt, 1981	Losses	16, Steve Carlton, 1983
			16, Kevin Gross, 1987
			16, Shane Rawley, 1988
Home Runs	48, Mike Schmidt, 1980	Innings	304, Steve Carlton, 1980
RBIs	130, Greg Luzinski, 1977	Games Started	38, Steve Carlton, 1980, 1982
Total Bases	342, Mike Schmidt, 1980	Complete Games	19, Steve Carlton, 1982
Hits	208, Pete Rose, 1979	Strikeouts	286, Steve Carlton, 1980, 1982
Runs	114, Mike Schmidt, 1977	Bases on Balls	128, Jose De Jesus, 1991
Doubles	46, Von Hayes, 1986	Winning Pct.	.760, John Denny, 1983
Triples	19, Juan Samuel, 1984	ERA	2.37, John Denny, 1983
Bases on Balls	128, Mike Schmidt, 1983	Saves	40, Steve Bedrosian, 1987
Stolen Bases	72, Juan Samuel, 1984	Shutouts	6, Steve Carlton, 1982

For a team that never once attained even the first division in the aggregate standings of any period since the last century, the Phillies made a remarkable turnaround during the current era before falling to the bottom of the heap again. Would they ever have accomplished it without expansion, free agency and a new stadium? We'll never know. Carlton nearly made the chart in another pitching department—walks. He gave up 90 in 1980 to rank third behind De Jesus and Kevin Gross (94 in 1986). His era record for losses was established, bizarrely, in a season when he pitched on a pennant winner.

ST. LOUIS CARDINALS

Pennants: 1982, 1985, 1987
Manager: Whitey Herzog, 1980–90
Park: Busch Stadium
Best Year: 1985 (101–61, .623)
Worst Year: 1990 (70–92, .432)
Top Rookie: Vince Coleman, 1985
Biggest Disappointment: Willie McGee, 1986; suffered 99-point drop in BA, largest in NL history by a defending batting champ
Best Deal: Tie between obtaining Ozzie Smith from San Diego, • 1982, and Jack Clark from San Francisco, 1985
Worst Deal: Making the Mets a gift of Keith Hernandez, 1983
Other:

1978—.426 winning percentage is team's poorest since 1924; finish just three games out of NL cellar

1981—Post best winning percentage in NL East (.578) but fail to qualify for postseason play

1982—Post lowest winning percentage (.568) to top NL since the beginning of division play in 1969

1983—First defending World Champion to finish below .500 since the 1966–67 Orioles

1985—Set twentieth-century NL record with sixth season of 100 or more wins

1987—Win flag despite being only team in majors to hit fewer than 100 home runs; first pennant winner in ML history without a pitcher who worked at least 200 innings; have eight pitchers who win at least eight games but none who win more than eleven

1988—For the third time in the eighties finish below .500 after winning the pennant the previous year

1990—Finish last in NL East for the first time since division play began in 1969

1991—Play 15 consecutive errorless games to tie ML record set by 1975 Reds

HITTING		PITCHING	
Batting Ave.	.353, Willie McGee, 1985	Wins	21, John Tudor, 1985 21, Joaquin Andujar, 1985
Slugging Ave.	.597, Jack Clark, 1987	Losses	19, Jose DeLeon, 1990
Home Runs	35, Jack Clark, 1987	Innings	275, John Tudor, 1985
RBIs	117, Pedro Guerrero, 1989	Games Started	38, Joaquin Andujar, 1985
Total Bases	313, Keith Hernandez, 1979	Complete Games	14, John Tudor, 1985
Hits	216, Willie McGee, 1985	Strikeouts	208, Jose DeLeon, 1988
Runs	121, Vince Coleman, 1987	Bases on Balls	100, John Denny, 1979
Doubles	48, Keith Hernandez, 1979	Winning Pct.	.741, Bob Forsch, 1977
Triples	19, Garry Templeton, 1979	ERA	1.93, John Tudor, 1985
Bases on Balls	136, Jack Clark, 1987	Saves	47, Lee Smith, 1991
Stolen Bases	110, Vince Coleman, 1985	Shutouts	10, John Tudor, 1985

Up until 1990 the Cardinals had seemed to be borrowing a few pages from the Dodgers' book on how to assemble a team. It had been a long, long time since they'd had a really bad season or been completely out of the hunt for longer than a couple of years. They had been doing it, too, without a real staff leader ever since Gibson retired, unlike the Dodgers, who always manage to find a Valenzuela or a Hershiser or a Koufax or a Sutton as the need arises. Ozzie Smith, not even close to making the chart, has been the team's best player during the period. Lee Smith's 47 saves in 1991 not only broke Bruce Sutter's club mark of 45 but set a new NL record.

CINCINNATI REDS

Pennants: 1979 (D), 1990
Manager: Pete Rose, 1984–89
Park: Riverfront Stadium
Best Year: 1981 (66–42, .611)
Worst Year: 1982 (61–101, .377)
Top Rookie: Chris Sabo, 1988
Biggest Disappointment: Duane Walker, 1982–85; Gary Redus, 1982–85; Paul Householder, 1982–83; this trio of young outfielders was expected to replace Ken Griffey, Dave Collins and George Foster, all of whom were lost to free agency or the threat of it following the 1981 season; when they failed to develop the team came apart
Best Deal: Bagging Tom Seaver from the Mets, 1977
Worst Deal: The team's failure to get with the times and pay its players what they were worth until so many had been lost to free agency that the club's morale was shot
Other:
  1977—First NL team to make fewer than 100 errors in a season (95)
  1978—Sparky Anderson canned as manager after second straight second-place finish in NL West
  1979—Club wins division in first year under John McNamara
  1981—Reds compile best record in the majors but fail to qualify for postseason play
  1982—By one-game margin, club escapes becoming first team since 1914–15 Philadelphia A's to have the worst record in the majors just one year after it had the best
  1985—Finish second in NL West in first full season under Pete Rose
  1987—Pitching staff sets all-time record for fewest complete games in a season (7)
  1988—Fourth consecutive 2nd-place finish in NL West
  1989—Pete Rose banned for betting on baseball games; club finishes 12 games below .500
  1990—Set ML record for the lowest winning percentage (.561) by a team in first place for the entire season; become first team in ML history to sweep a World Series against a team that won the previous year's World Series in a sweep
  1991—Follow world championship season by skidding, with no good excuse, to 14 games below .500 and posting .457 winning percentage, the poorest ever by reigning World Series winner.

HITTING		**PITCHING**	
Batting Ave.	.320, George Foster, 1977	Wins	23, Danny Jackson, 1988
Slugging Ave.	.631, George Foster, 1977	Losses	18, Bruce Berenyi, 1982
			18, Jeff Russell, 1984
Home Runs	52, George Foster, 1977	Innings	274, Mario Soto, 1983
RBIs	149, George Foster, 1977	Games Started	39, Tom Browning, 1986
Total Bases	388, George Foster, 1977	Complete Games	18, Mario Soto, 1983
Hits	204, Pete Rose, 1977	Strikeouts	274, Mario Soto, 1982
Runs	124, George Foster, 1977	Bases on Balls	104, Mario Soto, 1985
Doubles	51, Pete Rose, 1978	Winning Pct.	.727, Tom Seaver, 1979*
Triples	11, Mariano Duncan, 1990	ERA	2.35, Tom Seaver, 1977
Bases on Balls	117, Joe Morgan, 1977	Saves	39, John Franco, 1988
Stolen Bases	80, Eric Davis, 1986	Shutouts	6, Danny Jackson, 1988

*Seaver had a league-leading .875 WP in the strike-shortened 1981 season but compiled only fourteen wins, one short of the necessary number; his ERA in 1977 reflects only his work with the Reds—among those who pitched a full season with the club, Jose Rijo has the top mark (2.39 in 1988).

After looking at the chart, you'd be sure, if you didn't know better, that the Reds must have at least won their division in 1977. If they'd had Soto back then, they almost certainly would have. Foster's 1977 season was so monstrous that he set a number of all-time club records that are unlikely ever to be bettered.

MONTREAL EXPOS

Pennants: 1981 (D)
Manager: Buck Rodgers, 1985–91
Park: Olympic Stadium, 1977–present; first game on April 15, 1977, the Phils beating the Expos 7–2
Best Year: 1979 (95–65, .594)
Worst Year: 1991 (71–90, .441)
Top Rookie: Andre Dawson, 1977
Biggest Disappointment: Ross Grimsley, 1979; had he come anywhere near approaching his 1978 performance, the Expos would have won the NL East with ease
Best Deal: Getting Tony Perez from Cincinnati, 1977; he almost instantly helped make the club respectable
Worst Deal: Giving Texas Pete Incaviglia, 1986
Other:

1979—Lead majors with 3.14 ERA and win ninety-five games, most by club to date

1981—Lose LCS to Dodgers after returning home from LA with a 2–1 lead in games

1983—Finish over .500 for fifth consecutive year

1986—Finish under .500 for the last time until 1991

1990—Post top ERA in NL (3.37); for fourth consecutive year under Buck Rodgers finish at .500 or better with a team not expected to do much

1991—Begin campaign as the only NL franchise to go through the entire current era without having had at least one truly bad team, then proceed to finish in division basement; team forced to play last weeks of the season on the road after a section of Olympic Stadium collapses

HITTING		**PITCHING**	
Batting Ave.	.334, Tim Raines, 1986	Wins	20, Ross Grimsley, 1978
Slugging Ave.	.553, Andre Dawson, 1981	Losses	16, Steve Rogers, 1977
Home Runs	32, Andre Dawson, 1983	Innings	302, Steve Rogers, 1977
RBIs	123, Tim Wallach, 1987	Games Started	40, Steve Rogers, 1977
Total Bases	343, Andre Dawson, 1983	Complete Games	19, Ross Grimsley, 1978
Hits	204, Al Oliver, 1982	Strikeouts	206, Steve Rogers, 1977
Runs	133, Tim Raines, 1983	Bases on Balls	118, Floyd Youmans, 1986
Doubles	46, Warren Cromartie, 1979	Winning Pct.	.783, Bryn Smith, 1985
Triples	13, Rodney Scott, 1980	ERA	2.39, Mark Langston, 1989*
	13, Tim Raines, 1985		2.39, Dennis Martinez, 1991
	13, Mitch Webster, 1986		
Bases on Balls	97, Tim Raines, 1983	Saves	41, Jeff Reardon, 1985
Stolen Bases	97, Ron LeFlore, 1980	Shutouts	5, Steve Rogers, 1979, 1983
			5, Dennis Martinez, 1991

*Includes only Langston's ERA with the Expos in 1989.

Any team that was willing to let Dawson go elsewhere for nothing more than a draft choice had to have other priorities more important at the time than winning the pennant. Rogers gave the club his entire career and as a result holds most of the team's career pitching marks. Most of the club's career hitting records are held by Dawson and Raines, but Wallach must still merit a lot of consideration for the most valuable Expo during the current era despite his 1991 tailspin.

PITTSBURGH PIRATES

Pennants: 1979, 1990 (D), 1991 (D)
Manager: Chuck Tanner, 1977–85
Park: Three Rivers Stadium
Best Year: 1979 and 1991 (98–64, .605)
Worst Year: 1985 (57–104, .354)
Top Rookie: Johnny Ray, 1982; the Pirates continue to be the only one of the original 16 franchises that has never had a Rookie of the Year Award winner
Biggest Disappointment: Dave Parker, 1981–83
Best Deal: Reobtaining Mike Easler from Boston, 1979
Worst Deal: Sending Rick Langford, Tony Armas and Mitch Page to Oakland, 1977
Other:
  1978—Finish 2nd in NL East for third year in a row
  1979—Become first team to win two World Series after trailing 3 games to 1; the other such victory came in 1925 against Washington
  1981—First sub-.500 finish since 1973
  1984—Finish last in NL East despite posting loop's best ERA (3.11) and allowing fewest runs in majors (567)
  1985—Local group buys the club and installs Syd Thrift as general manager; team suffers first basement finish since 1955; Rick Reuschel is 14–8 with a 2.27 ERA; rest of hill staff is 43–96
  1986—Pirates have worst record in NL for second straight year
  1988—Win 85 games, the most since 1979
  1990—First postseason appearance since 1979; 95 wins are second most in the majors
  1991—Top NL in BA and runs but falter in LCS for the second year in a row when team's three best hitters—Andy Van Slyke, Bobby Bonilla and Barry Bands—once again all come up empty

HITTING		**PITCHING**	
Batting Ave.	.341, Bill Madlock, 1981	Wins	22, Doug Drabek, 1990
Slugging Ave.	.585, Dave Parker, 1978	Losses	19, Jose DeLeon, 1985
Home Runs	33, Barry Bonds, 1990	Innings	254, Rick Rhoden, 1986
RBIs	120, Bobby Bonilla, 1990	Games Started	35, Rick Rhoden, 1982, 1985
			35, Larry McWilliams, 1983
Total Bases	340, Dave Parker, 1978	Complete Games	12, Rick Rhoden, 1986
Hits	215, Dave Parker, 1977	Strikeouts	182, Bert Blyleven, 1978
Runs	112, Bobby Bonilla, 1990	Bases on Balls	103, Don Robinson, 1982
Doubles	45, Dave Parker, 1979	Winning Pct.	.800, John Candelaria, 1977
Triples	15, Andy Van Slyke, 1988	ERA	2.27, Rick Reuschel, 1985
Bases on Balls	107, Barry Bonds, 1991	Saves	34, Jim Gott, 1988
Stolen Bases	96, Omar Moreno, 1980	Shutouts	5, Doug Drabek, 1989

Blyleven holds the record for appearing on the charts of the most different teams during the same era. Free agency—and the specter of it—are what's made his feat possible, of course, but it shouldn't take away any of the luster from one of the most quietly outstanding careers in recent years. That the Pirates chose not to hold on to him—or Parker—or Candelaria—or a number of other players who were close to their caliber goes a fair amount of the way toward explaining why the franchise fell into such disrepair during the mid-eighties and may again in another couple of years.

HOUSTON ASTROS

Pennants: 1980 (D), 1986 (D)
Manager: Bill Virdon, 1977–82
Park: Astrodome
Best Year: 1986 (96–66, .593)
Worst Year: 1991 (65–97, .401)
Top Rookie: Jeff Bagwell, 1991
Biggest Disappointment: Charlie Kerfeld, 1987, 0–2 with a 6.67 ERA and no saves after going 11–2 with seven saves and a 2.59 ERA in 1986
Best Deal: Getting Kevin Bass and Frank DiPino from the Brewers for Don Sutton, 1982
Worst Deal: Giving the Cardinals Joaquin Andujar for Tony Scott, 1981
Other:

1977—Jose Cruz finishes third in BA, the only Astro during the current era to finish among the NL's top three hitters

1979—Finish 1½ games out of first in NL West; become last team to hit more triples in a season than home runs

1980—Win NL West for first time by defeating Dodgers in the only division playoff game to date in NL; pitcher J. R. Richard's career is ended by a stroke

1981—Allow just 331 runs, the fewest in majors, and compile the lowest staff ERA in majors (2.66) but lose division playoff to Dodgers in five games

1984—Finish 12 games behind division-winning San Diego despite outscoring the Padres and allowing fewer runs than the Padres

1986—Set club record for wins with 96

1988—Finish 5th in NL West with .506 winning percentage as every West team but Atlanta wins more than half its games

1990—Score fewest runs in majors (573) and have NL's lowest BA

1991—Youth movement loads team with bumper rookie crop but can't prevent first cellar finish since 1975

HITTING		**PITCHING**	
Batting Ave.	.315, Jose Cruz, 1978	Wins	21, Joe Niekro, 1979
Slugging Ave.	.498, Bob Watson, 1977	Losses	17, Bob Knepper, 1987
Home Runs	34, Glenn Davis, 1989	Innings	292, J. R. Richard, 1979
RBIs	110, Bob Watson, 1977	Games Started	38, J. R. Richard, 1979
			38, Joe Niekro, 1979, 1983, 1984
			38, Bob Knepper, 1986
Total Bases	287, Kevin Bass, 1986	Complete Games	19, J. R. Richard, 1979
Hits	195, Enos Cabell, 1978	Strikeouts	313, J. R. Richard, 1979
Runs	101, Enos Cabell, 1977	Bases on Balls	141, J. R. Richard, 1978
Doubles	38, Bob Watson, 1977	Winning Pct.	.692, Mike Scott, 1985
Triples	13, Jose Cruz, 1985	ERA	1.69, Nolan Ryan, 1981
Bases on Balls	93, Joe Morgan, 1980	Saves	33, Dave Smith, 1986
Stolen Bases	65, Gerald Young, 1988	Shutouts	5, Joe Niekro, 1979, 1982
			5, Mike Scott, 1986, 1988
			5, Bob Knepper, 1986

It says something important that no club era hitting records were set in 1986 when the Astros had their best season ever and also something important, but quite different, that no pitching records were set in 1980, the only other season the club won a division title. A pretty good team throughout the era, at least until recently, Houston has always been just a player or two short of being very good. How many of you expected to see Bass's name on the chart at all, let alone for the most total bases?

SAN FRANCISCO GIANTS

Pennants: 1987 (D), 1989
Manager: Roger Craig, 1986–91
Park: Candlestick Park
Best Year: 1989 (92–70, .568)
Worst Year: 1985 (62–100, .383)
Top Rookie: Will Clark, 1986
Biggest Disappointment: David Green, 1985
Best Deal: Obtaining Kevin Mitchell, Craig Lefferts and Dave
  Dravecky from San Diego, 1987
Worst Deal: Shipping Jack Clark to the Cardinals, 1985
Other:
  1978—89 wins is team's best showing since 1971
  1979—Finish 20 games under .500 as top hurler, Vida Blue,
    has 5.01 ERA after posting 2.79 ERA in 1978
  1981—Become first team in NL history to have a black man-
    ager, Frank Robinson
  1982—Team is outscored 687–673 but finishes 12 games above
    .500 and remains in division race until the last weekend of
    the season
  1985—Finish in NL West cellar for second year in a row; lose
    100 games for only time in franchise history
  1987—Win division without a pitcher who works more than
    186 innings or has more than 13 victories; nevertheless lead
    majors with 3.68 staff ERA
  1989—First pennant since 1962; suffer most one-sided World
    Series loss in history
  1990—Fifth consecutive year above .500 is longest such skein
    since 1958–71
  1991—Second-worst staff ERA in NL dooms team to the sec-
    ond division

HITTING		**PITCHING**	
Batting Ave.	.333, Will Clark, 1989	Wins	20, Mike Krukow, 1986
Slugging Ave.	.635, Kevin Mitchell, 1989	Losses	17, Mark Davis, 1984 17, Dave LaPoint, 1985
Home Runs	47, Kevin Mitchell, 1989	Innings	260, Bob Knepper, 1978
RBIs	125, Kevin Mitchell, 1989	Games Started	38, Jim Barr, 1977
Total Bases	345, Kevin Mitchell, 1989	Complete Games	16, Bob Knepper, 1978
Hits	192, Brett Butler, 1990	Strikeouts	178, Mike Krukow, 1986
Runs	109, Brett Butler, 1988	Bases on Balls	111, Vida Blue, 1979
Doubles	46, Jack Clark, 1978	Winning Pct.	.680, Rick Reuschel, 1989
Triples	11, Larry Herndon, 1980 11, Robby Thompson, 1989	ERA	2.25, Atlee Hammaker, 1983
Bases on Balls	105, Darrell Evans, 1978	Saves	30, Greg Minton, 1982
Stolen Bases	58, Bill North, 1979	Shutouts	6, Bob Knepper, 1978

The Giants' record during the current era is perhaps the best evidence of the present parity in the NL. Their wild swings for years made it hard for their followers to know whether they were watching a bad team or a good one. The truth is that until lately the Giants were neither. They were a bad good team some years and a good bad team other years. Mitchell's big 1989 season wiped Jack Clark's name almost totally off the chart. The pitching half of the chart helps to explain why the team has struggled so much. No Giants hurler has had a truly outstanding season since Ron Bryant in 1973.

NEW YORK METS

Pennants: 1986, 1988 (D)
Manager: Davey Johnson, 1984–90
Park: Shea Stadium
Best Year: 1986 (108–54, .667)
Worst Year: 1979 (63–99, .389)
Top Rookie: Dwight Gooden, 1984
Biggest Disappointment: Darryl Strawberry, 1989; although, as far as many Mets fans are concerned, he disappointed every year he was with the club
Best Deal: Snagging Gary Carter from the Expos, 1985
Worst Deal: Giving the Expos Jeff Reardon in 1981 for Ellis Valentine
Other:
1979—Finish last in NL East for third straight year
1983—Second consecutive last-place finish in NL East and fifth in seven years
1984—Finish 18 games over .500 despite being outscored 676–652
1985—Dwight Gooden and Ron Darling have combined 40–10 record; rest of the mound staff is 58–54; club's .602 winning percentage is its best since 1969 and marks the first and only time to date that both the Mets and the Yankees have played .600 or better ball in the same season
1986—Begin season with losing record, 1962–85 inclusive, against every NL team but the Padres; win division by post-expansion record 21½ games; 108 wins tie post-expansion NL record
1987—Nelson Doubleday, Jr., buys the club
1988—Lead NL in every important team department except BA before being surprised in LCS by underdog Dodgers
1990—For seventh consecutive year finish either 1st or 2nd in the NL East; score most runs in majors (775) for the first time in franchise history
1991—Mid-season slump swiftly plummets team out of contention and to poorest year since 1983

HITTING		PITCHING	
Batting Ave.	.328, Dave Magadan, 1990	Wins	24, Dwight Gooden, 1985
Slugging Ave.	.583, Darryl Strawberry, 1987	Losses	20, Jerry Koosman, 1977
Home Runs	39, Darryl Strawberry, 1987, 1988	Innings	276, Dwight Gooden, 1985
RBIs	117, Howard Johnson, 1991	Games Started	35, done by four different pitchers
Total Bases	319, Howard Johnson, 1989	Complete Games	16, Dwight Gooden, 1985
Hits	183, Keith Hernandez, 1985	Strikeouts	276, Dwight Gooden, 1984
Runs	108, Darryl Strawberry, 1988 / 108, Howard Johnson, 1991	Bases on Balls	114, Ron Darling, 1985
Doubles	41, Howard Johnson, 1989	Winning Pct.	.870, David Cone, 1988
Triples	10, Mookie Wilson, 1984	ERA	1.53, Dwight Gooden, 1985
Bases on Balls	97, Keith Hernandez, 1984 / 97, Darryl Strawberry, 1987	Saves	33, John Franco, 1990
Stolen Bases	58, Mookie Wilson, 1982	Shutouts	8, Dwight Gooden, 1985

Although he hasn't yet developed into the player that the Mets and everybody else expected him to be, Strawberry still managed to break many of the club's career and season batting records before he departed for LA—if only because he didn't have to shoot for any targets that you could call terribly difficult. Gooden, on the other hand, now seems a long shot to break any of his own all-time club marks, let alone Seaver's. One thing the Mets have had plenty of in recent years is great pitchers' winning percentages. In addition to Cone's mark, there was Gooden's .857 WP in 1985 and Ojeda's NL-top .783 WP a year later. In setting a new club RBI mark in 1991 Johnson added to the case he's making as not only the Mets' best current player but their best ever.

SAN DIEGO PADRES

Pennants: 1984
Manager: Dick Williams, 1982–85
Park: Jack Murphy Stadium
Best Year: 1984 (92–70, .568)
Worst Year: 1979 (68–93, .422)
Top Rookie: Benito Santiago, 1987
Biggest Disappointment: Shawn Abner, 1988–91
Best Deal: Getting George Hendrick from Cleveland, 1977
Worst Deal: Trading Ozzie Smith to the Cardinals for Garry Templeton, 1982
Other:
  1978—Break .500 mark for the first time in franchise history
  1980—First team in NL history with three players who have 50 or more stolen bases
  1981—Hit fewest homers in majors, 32 in 110 games; team leader Joe Lefebvre, with eight, is only player on club with more than four dingers
  1983—Finish at .500 mark for second year in a row for first time in franchise history
  1984—Become first second-wave expansion team to win a flag in NL
  1987—Finish last in NL despite finishing seventh in team BA, tenth in FA, and tenth in ERA
  1990—Finish 12 games below .500 despite scoring the same number of runs as opponents (673)
  1991—End season as only NL club that has a losing record, 1969–91 inclusive, against every rival team in the league

HITTING		**PITCHING**	
Batting Ave.	.370, Tony Gwynn, 1987	Wins	21, Gaylord Perry, 1978
Slugging Ave.	.558, Dave Winfield, 1979	Losses	18, Bob Shirley, 1977
Home Runs	34, Dave Winfield, 1979	Innings	263, Randy Jones, 1979
RBIs	118, Dave Winfield, 1979	Games Started	39, Randy Jones, 1979
Total Bases	333, Dave Winfield, 1979	Complete Games	13, Eric Show, 1988
Hits	218, Tony Gwynn, 1987	Strikeouts	179, Bruce Hurst, 1989
Runs	119, Tony Gwynn, 1987	Bases on Balls	100, Bob Shirley, 1977
Doubles	42, Terry Kennedy, 1982	Winning Pct.	.778, Gaylord Perry, 1978
Triples	13, Tony Gwynn, 1987	ERA	2.60, Ed Whitson, 1990
Bases on Balls	132, Jack Clark, 1989	Saves	44, Mark Davis, 1989
Stolen Bases	70, Alan Wiggins, 1984	Shutouts	4, Bruce Hurst, 1990

The Padres were the team that was most often cited during the mid-eighties by those who believe that once a club reaches the top nowadays all its motivation seems to drain away almost immediately. The argument is tough to counter, but it doesn't go far enough. The decline in motivation doesn't only occur on the field. It extends, as has clearly happened in the Padres' case, throughout the entire organization. An interesting note: In 1984–85, when the club had its best two-year stretch to date, just one era mark was set, by Wiggins for stolen bases.

CHICAGO CUBS

Pennants: 1984 (D), 1989 (D)

Manager: Don Zimmer, 1988–91, served for 45 more games than Herman Franks, 1977–79

Park: Wrigley Field; in 1988 the Cubs lost the distinction of being the only team in the majors to play all day games at home when lights were installed in Wrigley

Best Year: 1984 (96–65, .596)

Worst Year: 1980 (64–98, .395)

Top Rookie: Jerome Walton, 1989

Biggest Disappointment: Mike Bielecki, 1990

Best Deal: Fleecing the Phillies of Ryne Sandberg, 1982

Worst Deal: Sending Manny Trillo and Greg Gross to the Phils, 1979

Other:

1977—Only .500 finish between 1973 and 1984

1978—Tie for NL lead in BA and collect most hits in NL but net only 72 homers, fewer than every NL team but Houston

1979—Hit 135 home runs, nearly double team's 1978 total, after acquiring Dave Kingman, the NL's four-bagger champ

1982—Pitching staff notches just nine complete games and is the first in history to collect fewer than ten (1981 season excepted)

1983—For second year in a row compile only nine complete games, the fewest in the majors; Dick Ruthven with five is the only hurler to achieve more than one CG

1984—First postseason appearance in thirty-nine years; become only NL team to lose an LCS after leading 2 games to 0 in a best three-of-five series

1985—Owing mostly to injuries, 19 pitchers figure in at least one decision; Dennis Eckersley is the only hurler in enough innings (169) to be an ERA qualifier

1988—Set new ML record by going forty-three consecutive years without winning a pennant

1989—Win NL East with top team BA in loop but have no individual leaders in major hitting or pitching departments

1991—Club has pitcher among loop's top five in strikeout for the first time since 1979 when Greg Maddux is second in NL

HITTING		PITCHING	
Batting Ave.	.324, Bill Buckner, 1980	Wins	20, Rick Reuschel, 1977
Slugging Ave.	.613, Dave Kingman, 1979	Losses	16, Ray Burris, 1977
Home Runs	49, Andre Dawson, 1987	Innings	263, Greg Maddux, 1991
RBIs	137, Andre Dawson, 1987	Games Started	39, Ray Burris, 1977
Total Bases	353, Andre Dawson, 1987	Complete Games	12, Rick Sutcliffe, 1987
Hits	201, Bill Buckner, 1982	Strikeouts	198, Greg Maddux, 1991
Runs	116, Ryne Sandberg, 1990	Bases on Balls	106, Rick Sutcliffe, 1987
Doubles	41, Bill Buckner, 1980 41, Rafael Palmeiro, 1988	Winning Pct.	.941, Rick Sutcliffe, 1984*
Triples	19, Ryne Sandberg, 1984	ERA	2.79, Rick Reuschel, 1977
Bases on Balls	103, Gary Matthews, 1984	Saves	37, Bruce Sutter, 1979
Stolen Bases	54, Ryne Sandberg, 1985	Shutouts	4, Rick Reuschel, 1977

*Includes only Sutcliffe's stats with the Cubs in 1984.

It's got to be more than coincidence that the Cubs and the Red Sox, which play in the two quirkiest parks in the majors, have both gone eons now without winning a World Championship. Why that's so, though, is a puzzle. The Giants for years played in the quirkiest park of all, the Polo Grounds, and won several championships. In any case, the pitching half of the chart makes it clear why the Cubs have had problems during most of the current era. Reuschel is second to Sutcliffe in complete games, with nine in 1978, and Sutcliffe's second in K's, with 174 in 1987, to point up even more sharply the glaring absence in recent years of a staff leader.

ATLANTA BRAVES

Pennants: 1982 (D), 1991
Manager: Bobby Cox, 1978–81, 1990–91
Park: Atlanta County Stadium
Best Year: 1991 (94–68, .580)
Worst Year: 1988 (54–106, .338)
Top Rookie: David Justice, 1990
Biggest Disappointment: Bruce Sutter and Zane Smith, 1988; Smith continued to disappoint in a big way in 1989
Best Deal: Fiddling the Tigers out of John Smoltz in return for Doyle Alexander, 1987
Worst Deal: Handing Cleveland Brook Jacoby and Brett Butler for Len Barker, 1983
Other:
  1977—Relief pitcher Danny Frisella killed in a dune buggy accident; first cellar finish for the franchise since 1935
  1979—Finish last in NL West for fourth year in a row
  1980—Break .500 for the first time since 1974
  1982—Start season with NL-record 13 straight wins; hang on to win division by one game
  1983—Finish above .500 for last time to date
  1985—Staff ERA of 4.19 is NL's poorest; ML-low nine complete games
  1988—.338 winning percentage is franchise's worst since 1935; 54 wins are the fewest by an NL team during the '80s
  1990—Third consecutive season with worst record in NL
  1991—First team in modern ML history to win a pennant after posting the worst record in its league the previous year; seem poised to become the first franchise to win world championships in three different cities before dropping the final two games of the World Series in extra innings

HITTING		PITCHING	
Batting Ave.	.319, Terry Pendleton, 1991	Wins	21, Phil Niekro, 1979
Slugging Ave.	.580, Dale Murphy, 1987	Losses	20, Phil Niekro, 1977, 1979
Home Runs	44, Dale Murphy, 1987	Innings	342, Phil Niekro, 1979
RBIs	121, Dale Murphy, 1983	Games Started	44, Phil Niekro, 1979
Total Bases	332, Dale Murphy, 1984, 1985	Complete Games	23, Phil Niekro, 1979
Hits	192, Gary Matthews, 1978	Strikeouts	262, Phil Niekro, 1977
Runs	131, Dale Murphy, 1983	Bases on Balls	164, Phil Niekro, 1977
Doubles	37, Chris Chambliss, 1980 37, Dion James, 1987	Winning Pct.	.810, Phil Niekro, 1982
Triples	13, Brett Butler, 1983	ERA	2.55, Tom Glavine, 1991
Bases on Balls	117, Jeff Burroughs, 1977	Saves	30, Gene Garber, 1982
Stolen Bases	72, Otis Nixon, 1991	Shutouts	4, Phil Niekro, 1978 4, Tom Glavine, 1989

Niekro had the kind of year in 1979 that was reminiscent of the ones Boston Braves pitchers frequently had in the early part of the century. His easy delivery and seemingly tireless arm might have granted him 50 starts—or even 60—if he'd been active back then. Unless you're from Atlanta, you might be surprised to find Burroughs on the chart (he's also the runner-up in home runs, with 41 in 1977). But he actually had two very solid seasons with the Braves before reverting to the form that caused the Rangers to think his 1974 MVP season had been an aberration. Nixon's 72 thefts in his drug-abbreviated 1991 season set a twentieth century franchise record. That the Braves' "dream year" was a total team effort shows in how few era records were set in 1991, by far the club's best season since 1958.

AMERICAN LEAGUE

Number of Years Finishing in Each Position

Team	1	2	3	4	5	6	7	8	9	10	11	12	13	14	Aggregate
Boston	3	1	3	2	1	0	1	1	0	1	0	1	0	1	1
New York	2	2	0	2	0	2	2	1	1	2	1	0	0	0	2
Detroit	2	1	2	1	3	0	1	1	0	1	1	0	1	1	3
Kansas City	1	1	4	1	3	2	0	3	0	0	0	0	0	0	4
Baltimore	1	1	1	2	2	3	2	1	1	0	0	0	0	1	5
Milwaukee	1	1	2	2	1	1	0	3	0	0	0	3	0	1	6
Oakland	0	1	2	1	1	1	2	0	1	1	4	0	1	0	7
Toronto	3	1	0	0	1	0	1	1	3	2	0	2	1	0	8
California	0	3	1	2	2	1	0	0	0	1	0	1	1	3	9
Chicago	2	1	0	0	0	0	1	1	5	0	1	1	2	1	10
Minnesota	0	2	1	0	1	1	1	1	0	2	4	1	1	0	11
Texas	0	0	0	2	1	3	1	1	1	1	1	1	3	0	12
Cleveland	0	0	0	0	0	0	1	2	2	4	3	0	0	3	13
Seattle	0	0	0	0	0	0	0	0	3	0	4	2	2	4	14

The chart amply proves that even despite the A's recent run of success the East has been much the better of the two divisions since 1977. Five of the seven East division teams would have played in one more LCS during the period than they did if the clubs with the two best records had participated each year rather than the two division winners. That the worm has turned is demonstrated by the Angels' last-place finish in the West in 1991 while compiling a .500 record.

BOSTON RED SOX

Pennants: 1986, 1988 (D), 1990 (D)
Manager: Ralph Houk, 1981–84
Park: Fenway Park
Best Year: 1978 (99–64, .607)
Worst Year: 1983 (78–84, .481)
Top Rookie: Dave Stapleton, 1980
Biggest Disappointment: Butch Hobson, 1980
Best Deal: Getting Dave Henderson and Spike Owen from Seattle, 1986
Worst Deal: Sending Ferguson Jenkins to Texas, 1978
Other:

1978—Lead AL East by 14 games on July 17, only to wind up blowing it and losing the division title in a one-game playoff with the Yankees

1981—519 runs lead majors in strike-shortened season

1983—First sub-.500 finish since 1961

1984—Lead majors with .283 BA, seven points better than the next best hitting team

1986—Team loses seventh and deciding game of the World Series for the fourth time in its last four Series appearances

1988—Set new AL record by going fifty-seven straight years without finishing in last place; win division by one game over Tigers

1990—Set new ML record by losing eighth consecutive LCS game; lead majors in team BA for twentieth century record fourth year in a row

1991—Hobbled by familiar lack of mound depth and uncharacteristically mediocre home record (43–38); slip to fourth in team BA

HITTING		PITCHING	
Batting Ave.	.368, Wade Boggs, 1985	Wins	24, Roger Clemens, 1986
Slugging Ave.	.637, Fred Lynn, 1979	Losses	16, Mike Torrez, 1980
Home Runs	46, Jim Rice, 1978	Innings	282, Roger Clemens, 1987
RBIs	139, Jim Rice, 1978	Games Started	36, Mike Torrez, 1978, 1979
			36, Roger Clemens, 1987
Total Bases	406, Jim Rice, 1978	Complete Games	18, Roger Clemens, 1987
Hits	240, Wade Boggs, 1985	Strikeouts	256, Roger Clemens, 1987
Runs	128, Wade Boggs, 1988	Bases on Balls	121, Mike Torrez, 1979
Doubles	51, Wade Boggs, 1989	Winning Pct.	.882, Bob Stanley, 1978
Triples	15, Jim Rice, 1977, 1978	ERA	1.93, Roger Clemens, 1990
Bases on Balls	125, Wade Boggs, 1988	Saves	40, Jeff Reardon, 1991
Stolen Bases	30, Jerry Remy, 1978	Shutouts	8, Roger Clemens, 1988

The Red Sox are proof that you don't have to steal bases to win. In 1990 when they took the division, Ellis Burks led the club with nine thefts. Had the Sox caught the Yankees in 1977, held them off in 1978 and done just a shade better in the three seasons when they slipped to eighth overall in the AL, they would occupy the top spot in the aggregate standings for the era by a wide margin. As it is, they've easily been the loop's best club during the past decade. But in all that time they've never quite been good enough.

NEW YORK YANKEES

Pennants: 1977, 1978, 1980 (D), 1981
Manager: Billy Martin, 1977–78, 1979, 1983, 1985, 1988
Park: Yankee Stadium
Best Year: 1980 (103–59, .636)
Worst Year: 1990 (67–95, .414)
Top Rookie: Dave Righetti, 1981
Biggest Disappointment: Steve Kemp, 1983
Best Deal: Obtaining Rickey Henderson from the A's, 1985
Worst Deal: Giving the Cardinals Willie McGee for Bob Sykes, 1982
Other:

1978—Win second consecutive World Championship, the last team to accomplish this

1980—Fire Dick Howser after he wins 103 games and the division title in his first year at the club's helm

1981—Roar back to win division playoff and then LCS after finishing below .500 in second half of split season, but team's reputation for turning it on only when needed is shredded when it loses the World Series to the Dodgers in six games after leading 2 games to 0

1983—Ron Guidry, Dave Righetti, Ray Fontenot and Goose Gossage post a combined 56–24 record; the rest of the mound staff is 35–47

1985—Top the majors in runs with 839

1988—Three straight last-inning losses to the Tigers result in Billy Martin being fired as the club's manager for the fifth time

1989—Club ends the decade of the eighties with the best composite record in the AL for the past ten years but only one pennant and two division crowns

1990—Team's winning percentage (.414) is its lowest since 1912

1991—Winning percentage of .438 gives Yankees poorest back to back seasons in franchise history

HITTING		PITCHING	
Batting Ave.	.352, Don Mattingly, 1986,	Wins	25, Ron Guidry, 1978
Slugging Ave.	.597, Reggie Jackson, 1980	Losses	19, Tim Leary, 1990
Home Runs	41, Reggie Jackson, 1980	Innings	274, Ron Guidry, 1978
RBIs	145, Don Mattingly, 1985	Games Started	36, Tommy John, 1980
Total Bases	388, Don Mattingly, 1986	Complete Games	21, Ron Guidry, 1983
Hits	238, Don Mattingly, 1986	Strikeouts	248, Ron Guidry, 1978
Runs	146, Rickey Henderson, 1985	Bases on Balls	120, Phil Niekro, 1985
Doubles	53, Don Mattingly, 1986	Winning Pct.	.893, Ron Guidry, 1978
Triples	11, Willie Randolph, 1977	ERA	1.74, Ron Guidry, 1978
Bases on Balls	119, Willie Randolph, 1980	Saves	46, Dave Righetti, 1986
Stolen Bases	93, Rickey Henderson, 1988	Shutouts	9, Ron Guidry, 1978

Between them Mattingly and Henderson set three all-time club records in 1986, for hits, doubles and stolen bases (Henderson broke the latter in 1988). Guidry collected three all-time club marks in 1978, for strikeouts, winning percentage and shutouts; and Righetti, of course, shattered the ML record for saves in 1986. Dave Winfield, one of the club's best players during the period, is missing altogether from the chart despite having posted numbers that would have made his name the dominant one on the charts of many other teams had he signed with them rather than the Yankees. It's a strong possibility, in any case, that when we're distant enough from the current era to evaluate what went on in it, Winfield will turn out to have been its top free-agent acquisition.

DETROIT TIGERS

Pennants: 1984, 1987 (D)
Manager: Sparky Anderson 1980–91
Park: Tiger Stadium
Best Year: 1984 (104–58, .642)
Worst Year: 1989 (59–103, .364)
Top Rookie: Lou Whitaker, 1978
Biggest Disappointment: Ricky Peters, 1981
Best Deal: Signing Japanese leagues refugee Cecil Fielder, 1990
Worst Deal: Ticketing Ron LeFlore for Montreal, 1980
Other:

1978—Finish 5th in AL East with 86–76 record

1981—Have top FA in majors and make just 67 errors, ML-record low made somewhat meaningless by the fact that the schedule is abbreviated by a long midseason strike

1984—Get off to a 26–4 start, the best start by a team in this century

1987—Top majors in runs and homers in the year of the home run

1988—Sag to eighth in runs in the AL and sixth in homers

1989—Franchise-record 103 losses; 4.53 staff ERA is the worst in the majors

1990—Score second-most runs in AL but finish below .500 as staff ERA of 4.39 is again the worst in the AL

1991—Threaten until mid-September to be first team since 1906 White Sox to win a title despite being last in BA; finish second in AL in runs even though last in batting; in Rob Deer (.179) have poorest-hitting regular outfielder since 1886

HITTING		PITCHING	
Batting Ave.	.343, Alan Trammell, 1987	Wins	20, Jack Morris, 1983, 1986
Slugging Ave.	.592, Cecil Fielder, 1990	Losses	18, Fernando Arroyo, 1977
			18, Doyle Alexander, 1989
			18, Jack Morris, 1990
Home Runs	51, Cecil Fielder, 1990	Innings	294, Jack Morris, 1983
RBIs	132, Cecil Fielder, 1990	Games Started	38, Dan Petry, 1983
Total Bases	339, Cecil Fielder, 1990	Complete Games	20, Jack Morris, 1983
Hits	212, Ron LeFlore, 1977	Strikeouts	232, Jack Morris, 1983
Runs	126, Ron LeFlore, 1978	Bases on Balls	110, Jack Morris, 1985
Doubles	42, Lance Parrish, 1983	Winning Pct.	.724, Jack Morris, 1986
Triples	13, Larry Herndon, 1982	ERA	2.88, Jeff Robinson, 1988
Bases on Balls	101, Mickey Tettleton, 1991	Saves	32, Willie Hernandez, 1984
Stolen Bases	78, Ron LeFlore, 1979	Shutouts	6, Jack Morris, 1986

The chart makes you wonder what kind of magic the Tigers worked in 1984. Though it was the only year during the period that the club won a pennant, Hernandez was the lone man to set an era record that season. Morris has easily been Detroit's top pitcher since 1977, but the team's best player is up for grabs. It might be Parrish or Trammell—or it might have been LeFlore if he had remained with the club a couple more years. Be that as it may, the Tigers are the lone AL team to have set no new all-time individual season hitting or pitching records during the current era.

KANSAS CITY ROYALS

Pennants: 1977 (D), 1978 (D), 1980, 1984 (D), 1985
Manager: Dick Howser, 1981–86
Park: Royals Stadium
Best Year: 1977 (102–60, .630)
Worst Year: 1990 (75–86, .466)
Top Rookie: Kevin Seitzer, 1987
Biggest Disappointment: Mark Davis, 1990–91
Best Deal: Snagging Darrell Porter and Jim Colborn from the Brewers, 1977
Worst Deal: Sending Danny Jackson to the Reds for Kurt Stillwell, 1988
Other:

1977—Become first expansion team ever to top the majors in wins, with 102

1978—Set ML record by losing third straight LCS to the same team, the Yankees

1980—First AL expansion team to win a pennant

1985—First AL expansion team to win a World Championship

1986—Manager Dick Howser is discovered to be suffering from an inoperable brain tumor; Bo Jackson becomes the first Heisman Trophy winner since Vic Janowicz to play in the majors

1987—Finish 2nd in division despite scoring the fewest runs in the AL; Dick Howser dies

1989—Win 92 games despite scoring the fewest runs of any team in the AL West

1990—Narrowly keep record for never finishing in the cellar intact by edging out the Twins by 1½ games for the bottom spot in the AL West

1991—Release Bo Jackson prior to the season when team doctors posit that he's suffering from a career-ending hip ailment; become first team to occupy cellar in its division as late as August while playing better than .500 ball

HITTING		**PITCHING**	
Batting Ave.	.390, George Brett, 1980	Wins	23, Bret Saberhagen, 1989
Slugging Ave.	.664, George Brett, 1980	Losses	18, Larry Gura, 1983 18, Mark Gubicza, 1987 18, Danny Jackson, 1987
Home Runs	36, Steve Balboni, 1985	Innings	295, Dennis Leonard, 1978
RBIs	133, Hal McRae, 1977	Games Started	40, Dennis Leonard, 1978
Total Bases	363, George Brett, 1979	Complete Games	21, Dennis Leonard, 1978
Hits	230, Willie Wilson, 1980	Strikeouts	244, Dennis Leonard, 1977
Runs	133, Willie Wilson, 1980	Bases on Balls	120, Mark Gubicza, 1987
Doubles	54, Hal McRae, 1977	Winning Pct.	.800, Larry Gura, 1978
Triples	21, Willie Wilson, 1985	ERA	2.16, Bret Saberhagen, 1989
Bases on Balls	121, Darrell Porter, 1979	Saves	45, Dan Quisenberry, 1983
Stolen Bases	83, Willie Wilson, 1979	Shutouts	5, Dennis Leonard, 1977, 1979

Everybody on the hitting half of the chart, with the exception of Porter, is also the club's all-time record holder. Gura is one of only a handful of pitchers to appear as both his club's winning percentage and loss leader in the same era. Brett's injury-ridden year in 1980 caused him to be the only player in history to set all-time club batting and slugging average marks in the same season and yet have none of his other hitting stats from that year set even a period record. The chart makes a good case for Leonard as the franchise's best pitcher to date.

BALTIMORE ORIOLES

Pennants: 1979, 1983
Manager: Earl Weaver, 1977–82, 1985–86
Park: Memorial Stadium (new Camden Yards park to open in 1992)
Best Year: 1979 (102–57, .642)
Worst Year: 1988 (54–107, .355)
Top Rookie: Cal Ripken, Jr., 1982
Biggest Disappointment: John Shelby, 1984
Best Deal: Getting Rudy May, Rick Dempsey, Scott McGregor and Tippy Martinez from the Yankees; although the deal was made midway through the 1976 season, its major repercussions were felt during the current era
Worst Deal: Sending Doug DeCinces to the Angels, 1982
Other:

1977—Lead AL in FA and majors in complete games and double plays but score far fewer runs than either the Red Sox or the Yankees, the other two AL East contenders, and finish 2½ out of 1st

1980—Finish 2nd in AL East with second-best record in the majors

1982—Blow chance to tie for the division crown by losing to the Brewers on the last day of the season

1986—Finish last in AL East for the first time since division play began; hit ML-record low 13 triples

1987—Surrender ML-record 226 home runs; winning percentage of .414 is the franchise's lowest since 1955

1988—Begin season by losing AL-record 21 straight games; .335 winning percentage is the franchise's worst since 1939

1989—Set AL record for the greatest improvement by a cellar dweller by gaining 32½ games over previous year's finish; narrowly miss becoming the first last-place team to win a division crown the following year

1991—Orioles help prove that one player can't make much difference as Cal Ripken has the greatest offensive season ever by an AL shortstop, but the club still loses 95 games

HITTING		PITCHING	
Batting Ave.	.328, Ken Singleton, 1977	Wins	25, Steve Stone, 1980
Slugging Ave.	.566, Cal Ripken, Jr., 1991	Losses	17, Mike Boddicker, 1985
Home Runs	35, Ken Singleton, 1979	Innings	319, Jim Palmer, 1977
RBIs	124, Eddie Murray, 1985	Games Started	40, Mike Flanagan, 1978
Total Bases	368, Cal Ripken, Jr., 1991	Complete Games	22, Jim Palmer, 1977
Hits	211, Cal Ripken, Jr., 1983	Strikeouts	193, Jim Palmer, 1977
Runs	121, Cal Ripken, Jr., 1983	Bases on Balls	101, Steve Stone, 1980
Doubles	47, Cal Ripken, Jr., 1983	Winning Pct.	.781, Steve Stone, 1980
Triples	10, Phil Bradley, 1989	ERA	2.77, Mike Boddicker, 1983
Bases on Balls	107, Ken Singleton, 1977 107, Eddie Murray, 1984	Saves	37, Greg Olson, 1990
Stolen Bases	37, Al Bumbry, 1979	Shutouts	6, Jim Palmer, 1978

Looking at the chart, you'd be led to think that Ripken, in 1983, and 1991, had the best seasons of any Orioles player during the period and that Singleton and Murray were about equally valuable to the club—and all of that might not be far from the truth. Certainly Singleton never quite got the recognition he deserved and Murray has yet to have the kind of gigantic season you'd expect from a superstar. In any event, the Orioles were the second-best team in the majors during the first decade of the present period. Their bad luck—and the Yankees' too, for that matter—was that they were in the same division as the best team.

MILWAUKEE BREWERS

Pennants: 1982
Manager: Tom Trebelhorn, 1986–91
Park: County Stadium
Best Year: 1979 (95–66, .590)
Worst Year: 1984 (67–94, .416)
Top Rookie: Tie between Teddy Higuera and Ernest Riles, both in 1985
Biggest Disappointment: Billy Jo Robidoux, 1985–87
Best Deal: Garnering Rollie Fingers, Ted Simmons and Pete Vuckovich from the Cardinals, 1981
Worst Deal: Letting Darrell Porter get away to Kansas City, 1977
Other:

1978—Top majors in home runs, BA, OBP and SA; break .500 for the first time in franchise history

1982—Win first LCS in history that's played between two expansion teams after rallying from two-game deficit to beat the Angels

1984—Finish last in the AL two years after winning the pennant

1987—Set AL record by beginning the season with 13 straight wins

1988—Staff ERA of 3.45 is topped only by flag-winning A's

1990—Have poorest FA in AL after finishing tied for last in FA in 1989

1991–Late surge pulls team over .500 and nearly into contention, but Trebelhorn is nevertheless axed when the season ends

HITTING		PITCHING	
Batting Ave.	.352, Cecil Cooper, 1980	Wins	22, Mike Caldwell, 1978
Slugging Ave.	.578, Robin Yount, 1982	Losses	18, Danny Darwin, 1985
Home Runs	45, Gorman Thomas, 1979	Innings	293, Mike Caldwell, 1978
RBIs	126, Cecil Cooper, 1983	Games Started	36, Lary Sorensen, 1978
Total Bases	367, Robin Yount, 1982	Complete Games	23, Mike Caldwell, 1978
Hits	219, Cecil Cooper, 1980	Strikeouts	240, Ted Higuera, 1987
Runs	136, Paul Molitor, 1982	Bases on Balls	102, Pete Vuckovich, 1982
Doubles	49, Robin Yount, 1980	Winning Pct.	.750, Pete Vuckovich, 1982*
Triples	16, Paul Molitor, 1979	ERA	2.37, Mike Caldwell, 1978
Bases on Balls	98, Gorman Thomas, 1979	Saves	33, Dan Plesac, 1989
Stolen Bases	45, Paul Molitor, 1987	Shutouts	6, Mike Caldwell, 1981

*Vuckovich had a .778 WP in the abbreviated 1981 season but posted only fourteen wins.

Ask someone to name all the people in the past forty years who have hit .350 and chances are Cooper's name will be mentioned last, if at all. In any event, he and Yount rate as the top players on a club that turned the corner in the late seventies, hung close to the top for quite a while, slipped back, came on again briefly and is now once more on the upswing. Not a bad course to have followed for a team that was the AL's worst in the last era.

OAKLAND ATHLETICS

Pennants: 1981 (D), 1988, 1989, 1990
Manager: Tony La Russa, 1986–91
Park: Oakland Coliseum
Best Year: 1988 (104–58, .642)
Worst Year: 1979 (54–108, .333)
Top Rookie: Mark McGwire, 1987
Biggest Disappointment: Matt Keough, 1979–82
Best Deal: Getting Dave Stewart and Dennis Eckersley in separate acquisitions, 1986 and 1987, for a combined total, in personnel, of three minor leaguers
Worst Deal: Sending Rickey Henderson to the Yankees, 1985; although getting him back in 1989 helped to atone for the blunder
Other:

1979—Set Oakland club record with 108 losses

1980—In first year under Billy Martin team plays what's known as "Billyball," which includes working young pitchers to the hilt; the short-term result is 94 complete games by A's hurlers, the most in the majors since 1946; the long-term result is all of the young pitchers soon become burnouts

1981—Charlie Finley sells the club to Levis' jeans magnates; team has most wins in the majors (37) prior to the strike and finishes with second-best overall record in the majors

1985—Staff leads majors in complete games and AL in fewest walks allowed but has only the eleventh-best ERA in the league

1988—Staff tops the AL in ERA for the first of three straight years

1990—Win flag with lowest team BA in the AL West; set record for current era with 306 wins over a three-year period

1991—Sag to distant 4th in AL West with attack that features Mark McGuire whose .201 BA is the lowest in 103 years by a first baseman with enough plate appearances to be a batting title qualifier

HITTING		PITCHING	
Batting Ave.	.336, Carney Lansford, 1989	Wins	27, Bob Welch, 1990
Slugging Ave.	.618, Mark McGwire, 1987	Losses	20, Brian Kingman, 1980
Home Runs	49, Mark McGwire, 1987	Innings	290, Rick Langford, 1980
RBIs	124, Jose Canseco, 1988	Games Started	38, Vida Blue, 1977
Total Bases	347, Jose Canseco, 1988	Complete Games	28, Rick Langford, 1980
Hits	187, Jose Canseco, 1988	Strikeouts	205, Dave Stewart, 1987
Runs	120, Jose Canseco, 1988	Bases on Balls	108, Jose Rijo, 1986
Doubles	35, Jose Canseco, 1987	Winning Pct.	.818, Bob Welch, 1990
Triples	10, Luis Polonia, 1987	ERA	2.32, Steve McCatty, 1981
Bases on Balls	117, Rickey Henderson, 1980	Saves	48, Dennis Eckersley, 1990
Stolen Bases	130, Rickey Henderson, 1982	Shutouts	4, Steve McCatty, 1981
			4, Dave Stewart, 1990

Canseco set a host of Oakland club records in his 1988 MVP season, including, rather amazingly, the one for most hits. Until lately the A's have had incredibly little to show for the flock of talented young players they've come up with during the current era. Figure out what happened to all those great kid pitchers the team had a decade ago and who was responsible for it happening—no, Billy Martin wasn't the only culprit—and you have the reason this club floundered for so long in a division it ought to have dominated all during the eighties.

TORONTO BLUE JAYS

Pennants: 1985 (D), 1989 (D), 1991 (D)
Manager: Bobby Cox, 1982–85
Park: Exhibition Stadium, 1977–89
  Skydome, 1989–present; first game on June 5, 1989, Milwaukee 5, Toronto 3
Best Year: 1985 (99–62, .615)
Worst Year: 1979 (53–109, .327)
Top Rookie: Alfredo Griffin, 1979
Biggest Disappointment: Phil Huffman, 1979; 5.77 ERA and 6–18 record as a rookie starter, failed even to make the team in 1980
Best Deal: Talking Cleveland out of Alfredo Griffin, 1979
Worst Deal: Talking themselves into shipping Doyle Alexander to Atlanta, 1986
Other:
  1979—Suffer 109 losses, most by any AL team since expansion
  1981—37–69 record is worst in majors
  1983—Break .500 for the first time in franchise history (89–73)
  1985—Lose LCS after leading 3 games to 1 in first year LCSes are made best four-of-seven affairs
  1987—Squander seemingly safe lead in last week of season and lose division to Tigers on final day of season in 1–0 game to Detroit lefty Frank Tanana
  1989—Inaugurate new stadium by winning division and setting new AL attendance record
  1990—Become first team in ML history to draw over 4,000,000; score 68 more runs than Boston and give up three less runs but nevertheless lose the division to Boston in final weekend of the season; mound staff sets new ML record low for complete games with just six
  1991—Extend current record for the longest skein—now six years—having a winning record both at home and on the road; set new ML attendance record of 4,001,526

HITTING		PITCHING	
Batting Ave.	.322, Tony Fernandez, 1987	Wins	18, Dave Stieb, 1990
Slugging Ave.	.605, George Bell, 1987	Losses	18, Jerry Garvin, 1977 18, Phil Huffman, 1979
Home Runs	47, George Bell, 1987	Innings	288, Dave Stieb, 1982
RBIs	134, George Bell, 1987	Games Started	40, Jim Clancy, 1982
Total Bases	369, George Bell, 1987	Complete Games	19, Dave Stieb, 1982
Hits	213, Tony Fernandez, 1986	Strikeouts	198, Dave Stieb, 1984
Runs	111, George Bell, 1987	Bases on Balls	128, Jim Clancy, 1980
Doubles	41, Tony Fernandez, 1988	Winning Pct.	.750, Dave Stieb, 1990
Triples	17, Tony Fernandez, 1990	ERA	2.48, Dave Stieb, 1985*
Bases on Balls	119, Fred McGriff, 1988	Saves	34, Tom Henke, 1987
Stolen Bases	60, Dave Collins, 1984	Shutouts	5, Dave Stieb, 1982

*In 1986 Mark Eichhorn had a 1.72 ERA in 157 innings, just five short of the necessary number; he also had 166 strikeouts.

Second only to the Royals as the most successful expansion franchise to date, the Blue Jays have built mainly through the free-agent draft and have been so skillful at it that they took just one year longer than the Royals to reach the top of their division. Stieb has obviously been the club's best pitcher to date, but picking its best player makes for a very tough call. I like Fernandez, but Roberto Alomar may be the choice by 1994 or so.

CALIFORNIA ANGELS

Pennants: 1979 (D), 1982 (D), 1986 (D)
Manager: Gene Mauch, 1981–82, 1985–87
Park: Anaheim Stadium
Best Year: 1982 (93–69, .574)
Worst Year: 1980 (65–95, .406)
Top Rookie: Wally Joyner, 1986
Biggest Disappointment: Dave Frost, 1980
Best Deal: Acquiring John Candelaria from Pittsburgh, 1985
Worst Deal: Handing Jason Thompson to Pittsburgh, 1981
Other:

1978—First above-.500 finish since 1970; free-agent outfielder Lyman Bostock is slain

1979—Win first division crown and post two consecutive seasons above .500 for the first time in franchise history

1982—93 wins set new club record; become the only AL team to lose a best-of-five LCS after winning the first two games

1985—Turn 202 double plays to top majors; lose division by scant one-game margin to Royals owing to season-long failure to develop a reliable starting rotation

1986—Score the most runs of any team in AL West and draw the most walks of any team in majors; lose LCS in seven games to Red Sox after being just one strike away from winning the series in five games

1989—Finish 3rd in AL West with third-best record in the league

1991—First team ever to finish in division cellar even while posting an even .500 winning percentage; Jim Abbott, Mark Langston and Chuck Finley are a combined 55–28, but other pitchers go 26–53

HITTING		PITCHING	
Batting Ave.	.339, Rod Carew, 1983	Wins	19, Nolan Ryan, 1977
			19, Mark Langston, 1991
Slugging Ave.	.548, Doug DeCinces, 1982	Losses	19, Kurt McCaskill, 1991
Home Runs	39, Reggie Jackson, 1982	Innings	299, Nolan Ryan, 1977
RBIs	139, Don Baylor, 1979	Games Started	37, Nolan Ryan, 1977
Total Bases	333, Don Baylor, 1979	Complete Games	22, Nolan Ryan, 1977
Hits	188, Carney Lansford, 1979	Strikeouts	341, Nolan Ryan, 1977
Runs	120, Don Baylor, 1979	Bases on Balls	204, Nolan Ryan, 1977
Doubles	42, Doug DeCinces, 1982	Winning Pct.	.773, Bert Blyleven, 1989
	42, Johnny Ray, 1988		
Triples	13, Devon White, 1989	ERA	2.40, Chuck Finley, 1990
Bases on Balls	106, Brian Downing, 1987	Saves	46, Brian Harvey, 1991
Stolen Bases	56, Gary Pettis, 1985	Shutouts	7, Frank Tanana, 1977

It tells something about the team, but more perhaps about the division in which it played, that California won the AL West three times in an eight-year span without a pitcher who won more than 18 games in a season during that time. The club's best player for the period has been Downing, and Bobby Grich, although not on the chart, grades out to have been the second best. Ryan, still a terrific pitcher some dozen years after the Angels assumed he had at most a couple of good seasons left and so let him become a free agent, ranks as the team's biggest mistake of the current era.

CHICAGO WHITE SOX

Pennants: 1983 (D)
Manager: Tony La Russa, 1979–86
Park: Comiskey Park, 1977–90
New Comiskey Park, 1991–present; opening game on April 18, 1991, resulted in a 16–0 shellacking at the hands of Detroit
Best Year: 1983 (99–63, .611)
Worst Year: 1989 (69–92, .429)
Top Rookie: Ron Kittle, 1983
Biggest Disappointment: Ken Kravec, 1980
Best Deal: Getting LaMarr Hoyt and Oscar Gamble from the Yankees for Bucky Dent, 1977
Worst Deal: Sending Tony Bernazard to Seattle, 1983
Other:
1977—Win 90 games but finish just third in AL West
1981—Bill Veeck sells the club, saying he's unable to keep up financially with owners like George Steinbrenner and Ray Kroc; team finishes above .500 but has only 23–30 record in second half of the strike-divided season.
1983—Win division by AL postexpansion record 20-game margin; top AL in runs; become only team during the eighties with two 20-game winners (LaMarr Hoyt and Rich Dotson) to fail to win the pennant
1986—Last in AL in BA, SA and runs
1988—Last in AL in runs and FA
1989—First AL West cellar finish since 1976
1990—Win 94 games, 25 more than in 1989, and finish with third-best record in the majors, behind only the A's and the Pirates

	HITTING		**PITCHING**
Batting Ave.	.318, Chet Lemon, 1979 .318, Frank Thomas, 1991	Wins	24, LaMarr Hoyt, 1983
Slugging Ave.	.553, Frank Thomas, 1991	Losses	18, LaMarr Hoyt, 1984
Home Runs	37, Carlton Fisk, 1985	Innings	261, LaMarr Hoyt, 1983
RBIs	113, Harold Baines, 1985	Games Started	36, LaMarr Hoyt, 1983
Total Bases	318, Harold Baines, 1984	Complete Games	15, Jack McDowell, 1991
Hits	198, Harold Baines, 1985	Strikeouts	198, Floyd Bannister, 1985
Runs	99, Chet Lemon, 1977	Bases on Balls	111, Ken Kravec, 1979
Doubles	44, Chet Lemon, 1979 44, Ivan Calderon, 1990	Winning Pct.	.759, Rich Dotson, 1983
Triples	13, Lance Johnson, 1991	ERA	2.64, Britt Burns, 1981
Bases on Balls	138, Frank Thomas, 1991	Saves	57, Bobby Thigpen, 1990
Stolen Bases	77, Rudy Law, 1983	Shutouts	4, Rich Dotson, 1981 4, Britt Burns, 1983, 1985 4, Tom Seaver, 1984

Fisk is the only catcher to hold a share of a team's all-time season home run record. Baines is a sound choice as the club's best player during the current era, but no pitcher jumps out of the pack. Burns is probably as good a candidate as any. The fact is that Chicago has lacked a real staff leader ever since Wilbur Wood departed. McDowell nevertheless was the only hurler to set a club era CG mark in 1991. Thomas meanwhile shattered the Sox's all-time walk record in his first full season and showed promise of soon becoming the club's finest all-around player since Minnie Minoso.

MINNESOTA TWINS

Pennants: 1987, 1991
Manager: Tom Kelly, 1987–91
Park: Metropolitan Stadium, 1977–81
  Humphrey Metrodome, 1982–present; first game on April 6, 1982, Seattle 11, Minnesota 7
Best Year: 1991 (95–67, .586)
Worst Year: 1982 (60–102, .370)
Top Rookie: Kent Hrbek, 1982
Biggest Disappointment: Dave Engle, 1985
Best Deal: Heisting Tom Brunansky from the Angels, 1982
Worst Deal: Giving Frank Viola to the Mets, 1989
Other:
  1979—Team finishes above .500 for the last time until 1987
  1982—Have poorest ERA in the majors, steal the fewest bases and lose the most games
  1984—Carl Pohlad buys the club from the Griffith family; team is second in the AL West with 81–81 record
  1987—Set new AL record for lowest winning percentage (.525) by a pennant winner; set ML record for lowest road winning percentage (.375) by a pennant winner
  1988—Become first AL team to draw 3,000,000; set new ML record for fewest errors (84) and highest FA (.986)
  1990—Finish last in the AL West just three years after winning the World Championship
  1991—Win club-record 16 straight games; become first AL team since inception of division play in 1969 to cop a title after bringing up the rear of its division the previous year; repeat first-ever feat of 1987 by winning a World Series despite losing every contest played on the road.

HITTING		PITCHING	
Batting Ave.	.388, Rod Carew, 1977	Wins	24, Frank Viola, 1988
Slugging Ave.	.570, Rod Carew, 1977	Losses	18, Geoff Zahn, 1980 18, Allan Anderson, 1990
Home Runs	34, Kent Hrbek, 1987	Innings	303, Dave Goltz, 1977
RBIs	121, Kirby Puckett, 1988	Games Started	39, Dave Goltz, 1977
Total Bases	365, Kirby Puckett, 1986	Complete Games	19, Dave Goltz, 1977
Hits	239, Rod Carew, 1977	Strikeouts	215, Bert Blyleven, 1986
Runs	128, Rod Carew, 1977	Bases on Balls	101, Bert Blyleven, 1987
Doubles	45, Kirby Puckett, 1989	Winning Pct.	.774, Frank Viola, 1988
Triples	16, Rod Carew, 1977	ERA	2.45, Allan Anderson, 1988
Bases on Balls	95, Chili Davis, 1991	Saves	42, Jeff Reardon, 1988 42, Rick Aguilera, 1991
Stolen Bases	28, Dan Gladden, 1988	Shutouts	5, Geoff Zahn, 1980

Take away the 1987, 1988 and 1991 seasons and the Twins during this period have been almost a mirror image of the Phillies in the early thirties, with Puckett in the role of Chuck Klein, loads of good intermediate sluggers, constant changes at catcher and the two middle infield positions, and a host of starting pitchers who produce decent seasons now and then but mostly just surrender tons of home runs and compile huge ERAs. The one guy who doesn't fit into the comparative picture is Gladden; the Phils didn't have anyone quite like him. And what makes it even more odd is that they should have, because he's definitely a throwback type of player.

TEXAS RANGERS

Pennants: None
Manager: Bobby Valentine, 1986–91
Park: Arlington Stadium
Best Year: 1977 (94–68, .580)
Worst Year: 1985 (62–99, .385)
Top Rookie: Bump Wills, 1977
Biggest Disappointment: George Wright, 1985
Best Deal: Getting Rafael Palmeiro from the Cubs for Mitch Williams, 1989
Worst Deal: Sending Ron Darling and Walt Terrell to the Mets for Lee Mazzilli, 1982
Other:

1978—Team finishes above .500 two years in a row for the first time in franchise history

1979—Third straight above-.500 finish; team plays ML-record 135 night games

1983—Give up the fewest runs in the majors (609) and score 639 runs but somehow finish eight games below .500

1985—Second straight AL West cellar finish, behind even the expansion Mariners

1986—Finish second in AL West with 87 wins

1987—Finish tied for last in AL West but post .463 winning percentage

1990—For only the second time in franchise history finish above .500 for two years in a row.

1991—Win club-record 14 straight games; finish 3rd in division with first team since 1982 Brewers to have three 200-hit men; top majors with 829 runs

HITTING		PITCHING	
Batting Ave.	.341, Julio Franco, 1991	Wins	18, Ferguson Jenkins, 1978
			18, Charlie Hough, 1987
Slugging Ave.	.543, Ruben Sierra, 1989	Losses	16, Charlie Hough, 1985, 1988
Home Runs	30, Pete Incaviglia, 1986	Innings	285, Charlie Hough, 1987
	30, Ruben Sierra, 1987		
RBIs	119, Ruben Sierra, 1989	Games Started	40, Charlie Hough, 1987
Total Bases	344, Ruben Sierra, 1989	Complete Games	18, Jon Matlack, 1978
Hits	210, Mickey Rivers, 1980	Strikeouts	301, Nolan Ryan, 1989
Runs	115, Rafael Palmeiro, 1991	Bases on Balls	143, Bobby Witt, 1986
Doubles	49, Rafael Palmeiro, 1991	Winning Pct.	.692, Ferguson Jenkins, 1978
Triples	14, Ruben Sierra, 1989	ERA	2.27, Jon Matlack, 1978
Bases on Balls	113, Toby Harrah, 1985	Saves	38, Jeff Russell, 1989
Stolen Bases	52, Bump Wills, 1978	Shutouts	5, Bert Blyleven, 1977

All of the hitting marks, with the exception of those for SA, home runs, walks and RBIs (which all belong to Frank Howard), are franchise records. The same isn't true of the pitching marks, however, as the Rangers have gone quite a long spell now without a 20-game winner or a real take-charge mound leader. Hough rates as the club's top pitcher during the era, but that shouldn't be true a few years hence, assuming a couple of the talented young hoses now with the Rangers develop as hoped. With all that, the Rangers are still the only one of the original or second-wave expansion teams that has never won a title of any kind.

CLEVELAND INDIANS

Pennants: None
Manager: Pat Corrales, 1983–87
Park: Municipal Stadium
Best Year: 1986 (84–78, .519)
Worst Year: 1991 (57–105, .352)
Top Rookie: Sandy Alomar, Jr., 1990
Biggest Disappointment: Cory Snyder, 1987–90
Best Deal: Getting Brook Jacoby and Brett Butler from the Braves, 1984
Worst Deal: Trading Jay Bell to Pittsburgh for Felix Fermin, 1989
Other:
  1979—Only above-.500 finish between 1977–86 except for strike-shortened 1981 season
  1980—Joe Charboneau is Rookie of the Year, never again plays regularly
  1982—Draw 62,443 to home opener on a 38° day
  1985—102 losses tie franchise record
  1986—Win 84 games for best year between 1968 and 1991; lead majors in runs and BA
  1987—Typify club's one step forward, two steps back kind of progress by finishing last in AL while finishing twelfth in the loop in runs and last in the majors in ERA with a 5.28 mark, the worst in the majors in thirty-one years; Tom Candiotti leads the team in wins with seven, the fewest in this century by a club leader
  1988—Finish 6th in AL East but only eleven games out of 1st place
  1989—3.65 staff ERA is club's best since 1976
  1990—Pitchers sag to 4.21 ERA, next to last in AL
  1991—Drop club-record 105 games as decent pitching is undermined by woeful attack that tallies the fewest runs in the majors

HITTING		PITCHING	
Batting Ave.	.341, Miguel Dilone, 1980	Wins	19, Bert Blyleven, 1984
Slugging Ave.	.527, Andre Thornton, 1977	Losses	19, Wayne Garland, 1977
			19, Rick Wise, 1978
Home Runs	35 Joe Carter, 1989	Innings	283, Wayne Garland, 1977
RBIs	121, Joe Carter, 1986	Games Started	38, Wayne Garland, 1977
Total Bases	341, Joe Carter, 1986	Complete Games	21, Wayne Garland, 1977
Hits	200, Joe Carter, 1986	Strikeouts	191, Dennis Eckersley, 1977
Runs	108, Brett Butler, 1984	Bases on Balls	106, Tom Candiotti, 1986
	108, Joe Carter, 1986		
Doubles	36, Joe Carter, 1988	Winning Pct.	.731, Bert Blyleven, 1984
Triples	14, Brett Butler, 1985, 1986	ERA	2.87, Bert Blyleven, 1984
Bases on Balls	111, Mike Hargrove, 1980	Saves	43, Doug Jones, 1990
Stolen Bases	61, Miguel Dilone, 1980	Shutouts	4, Bert Blyleven, 1985
			4, Greg Swindell, 1988

Start with the fact that only two names on the chart, Eckersley and Swindell, are products of the Indians' farm system, bear in mind that Hargrove is the club's all-time season record holder for walks, note carefully that Garland and Dilone did next to nothing for the Tribe after their record-setting seasons, and you begin—but only just begin—to understand why this franchise has tread water for so many years while continuing to drift farther and farther from the shore.

SEATTLE MARINERS

Pennants: None
Manager: Darrell Johnson, 1977–80
Park: Kingdome
Best Year: 1991 (83–79, .512)
Worst Year: 1978 (56–104, .350)
Top Rookie: Alvin Davis, 1984
Biggest Disappointment: Mike Parrott, 1980
Best Deal: Robbing Cleveland of Jack Perconte and Gorman Thomas, 1984
Worst Deal: Presenting Dave Henderson and Spike Owen to Boston, 1986
Other:

1977—Finish 6th in AL West in first year of existence, ahead of A's, the division winner just two years earlier

1981—George Argyros buys control of the club

1983—First ML team in the twentieth century to go through an entire season without playing a doubleheader

1986—Team's batters fan AL-record 1148 times

1987—4th-place finish in AL West is highest to date

1990—Set new club record with 3.68 staff ERA as young pitchers lead team to 77 wins, second most in franchise history

1991—Get off to worst start in club history by losing first six games of season, but rally to break .500 for the first time ever

HITTING		PITCHING	
Batting Ave.	.327, Ken Griffey, Jr., 1991	Wins	19, Mark Langston, 1987
Slugging Ave.	.527, Ken Griffey, Jr., 1991	Losses	19, Matt Young, 1985
			19, Mike Moore, 1987
Home Runs	32, Gorman Thomas, 1985	Innings	272, Mark Langston, 1987
RBIs	116, Alvin Davis, 1984	Games Started	37, Mike Moore, 1986
Total Bases	319, Phil Bradley, 1985	Complete Games	14, Mike Moore, 1985
			14, Mark Langston, 1987
Hits	192, Phil Bradley, 1985	Strikeouts	262, Mark Langston, 1987
Runs	109, Ruppert Jones, 1979	Bases on Balls	158, Randy Johnson, 1991
Doubles	42, Ken Griffey, Jr., 1991	Winning Pct.	.667, Erik Hanson, 1990
Triples	11, Harold Reynolds, 1988	ERA	3.24, Erik Hanson, 1990
Bases on Balls	101, Alvin Davis, 1989	Saves	33, Mike Schooler, 1989
Stolen Bases	60, Harold Reynolds, 1987	Shutouts	3, Floyd Bannister, 1982
			3, Mark Langston, 1987, 1988
			3, Mike Moore, 1988

It's taken an unconscionably long time for the Mariners to pull their act together. The chart says a lot. Playing in a park that's a hitter's paradise, Seattle has yet to unearth a top-notch slugger but, paradoxically, has developed many fine young pitchers, most of them now playing elsewhere. It's impossible right now to pick the club's best hurler since 1977. Whichever one has the best season in 1992 will probably be as good a candidate as any. Griffey, however, is everyone's choice for the Mariners' best all-around player.

THE BEST, THE WORST AND THE WEIRDEST TEAMS BETWEEN 1977 AND 1991

• •

NATIONAL LEAGUE

> ### THE BEST

1986 NEW YORK METS
W-108 L-54
Manager: Davey Johnson

Regular Lineup—1B, Keith Hernandez; 2B, Wally Backman/Tim Teufel; 3B, Ray Knight; SS, Rafael Santana; RF, Darryl Strawberry; CF, Lenny Dykstra/Mookie Wilson; LF, Kevin Mitchell/George Foster; C, Gary Carter; P, Dwight Gooden; P, Roger McDowell; P, Sid Fernandez; P, Doug Sisk; P, Rick Aguilera; P, Jesse Orosco; P, Ron Darling; P, Bob Ojeda

After sailing through the regular season without even the faintest suggestion of a challenge from any of the other five clubs in their division, the Mets were severely tested in the LCS by the Astros and then again by the Red Sox in the World Series. That they emerged triumphant in both is a greater testimony to their strength than their regular season record, which, alone, must rank them among the best teams since expansion. As had happened in 1969 and again in 1973, the Mets won primarily with pitching, although, for once, two of their everyday players, Carter and Hernandez, received considerable support in the MVP balloting. Indeed, the club, for virtually the first time in its twenty-five-year history, was able to field a reasonably solid regular lineup. Owing to Johnson's faith in platooning, however, it was seldom the same lineup two days in a row as only one player, Hernandez, collected more than 500 at bats. The mound staff was similarly utilized. Eight of its members appeared in 28 or more games, and six of them won in double figures.

THE WORST

1985 SAN FRANCISCO GIANTS
W-62 L-100
Managers: Jim Davenport/Roger Craig

Regular Lineup—1B, David Green/Dan Driessen; 2B, Manny Trillo; 3B, Chris Brown; SS, Jose Uribe; RF, Chili Davis; CF, Dan Gladden; LF, Jeffrey Leonard; C, Bob Brenly; P, Mike Krukow; P, Dave LaPoint; P, Atlee Hammaker; P, Scott Garrelts; P, Vida Blue; P, Bill Laskey; P, Jim Gott; P, Mark Davis; P, Greg Minton

The Giants thrilled their sellout Opening Day crowd when they edged the defending NL champion Padres in an extremely well-played and well-pitched game for so early in season, won in relief by Blue, a huge local favorite who was returning from a year in exile. But it was the lone high point in what would become the first 100-loss campaign in the franchise's history. The pitching continued to be unexpectedly strong in the early weeks of the season, but the team, one of the NL's more potent units in 1984, was unable to generate any offense. By the time a few of the hitters had begun to come around, the pitching had collapsed and the Giants were out of the race. Davenport, too nice a guy to manage successfully in the present major league climate, received most of the flaying for the club's failure to produce, but the fault really lay in the front office, which had fired Frank Robinson late in the 1984 season. For several years Robinson had concealed the organization's hilarious ineptness by fashioning respectable records with sparsely talented teams. Craig exhibited a similar skill in 1986, bringing the Giants home third in their division and eliminating, with considerable help from Al Rosen, the club's new general manager, the undercurrent of apathy that had made the franchise one of the most moribund in the majors.

THE WEIRDEST

1978 SAN DIEGO PADRES
W-84 L-78
Manager: Roger Craig

Regular Lineup—1B, Gene Tenace/Broderick Perkins; 2B, Fernando Gonzalez/Darrel Thomas; 3B, Bill Almon; SS, Ozzie Smith; RF, Oscar Gamble/Jerry Turner; CF, Gene Richards; LF, Dave Winfield; C, Rick Sweet/Gene Tenace; P, Gaylord Perry; P, Randy Jones; P, Bob Owchinko; P, Bob Shirley; P, Rollie Fingers; P, Eric Rasmussen; P, John D'Acquisto; P, Mark Lee

A decent hitting team with abominable pitching the previous season, the Padres underwent a complete reversal in 1978 and in so doing finished with a winning record for the first time in their ten-year history. Craig's charges scored the fewest runs in the league and got a combined total of one home run and 50 RBIs from Gonzalez and Almon, two of their regular infielders. But the club's two senior starters, Perry and Jones, made Craig seem like a wizard, and events have since demonstrated that perhaps he was that year. Although the Padres led the NL in double plays, the vast majority of them were instigated by Smith. The rest of the cast, Winfield excepted, brought the mound staff far more aggravation than comfort with their glovework. That Craig had worked some kind of magic in San Diego ought to have become apparent the following year when the team sagged to the bottom again and did not resurface until 1983. Yet it was not until he performed a similar miracle in San Francisco that his managerial skills were finally acknowledged and the Padres' astonishing achievement in 1978 was recalled.

AMERICAN LEAGUE

| THE BEST |

1984 DETROIT TIGERS
W-104 L-58
Manager: Sparky Anderson

Regular Lineup—1B, Dave Bergman; 2B, Lou Whitaker; 3B, Howard Johnson; SS, Alan Trammell; RF, Kirk Gibson; CF, Chet Lemon; LF, Larry Herndon; C, Lance Parrish; DH, Darrell Evans; P, Jack Morris; P, Dan Petry; P, Milt Wilcox; P, Aurelio Lopez; P, Willie Hernandez; P, Dave Rozema; P, Juan Berenguer

There's a strong temptation to dismiss this team's great season as an aberration since it was followed by two straight mediocre finishes. But Detroit's best performance in a decade had immediately preceded it, and only one other team in the past twenty years, the 1976 Cincinnati Reds, has so thoroughly dominated the game for an entire season. The issue is not whether the Tigers were a one-year wonder. It's why they—and every other team that has flashed onto the scene with similar brilliance in recent years—could not hold lightning in a bottle for longer than a single season. The most commonly heard explanation is that the incentive to repeat as World Champions just isn't there any longer. If not, will it ever again exist? What will it take to create it? How many franchises, given the fact that they can keep somewhat of a lid on salaries and make as much or more money with teams that challenge but fall short of winning, are even interested in creating it? Those are the questions that taunt every observer who knows baseball's rich past and speculates apprehensively on its future. In 1984, however, Tigers adherents found nothing to be in question. Their team led the AL race from wire to wire after shattering every existing record for the best start in this century by an ML team. Though no Tiger topped the AL in a major batting or pitching department, Anderson never lacked for on-the-field leadership. Gibson, Parrish and Trammell provided the bulk of the offensive punch, Morris bagged 19 wins and Hernandez walked off with both the MVP and the Cy Young awards.

THE WORST

1987 CLEVELAND INDIANS
W-61 L-101
Managers: Pat Corrales/Doc Edwards

Regular Lineup—1B, Joe Carter; 2B, Tony Bernazard; 3B, Brook Jacoby; SS, Julio Franco; RF, Cory Snyder; CF, Brett Butler; LF, Mel Hall; DH, Pat Tabler; C, Chris Bando/Andy Allanson; P, Tom Candiotti; P, Ken Schrom; P, Phil Niekro; P, Scott Bailes; P, Greg Swindell; P, Steve Carlton, P, Rich Yett; P, Doug Jones

Oh, sure, the 1988 Orioles and the 1991 Indians were even more rotten teams, but Cleveland was not just bad in 1987—it was *shamefully* bad. Expected to contend in earnest after leading the majors in runs and homers the previous year, the club elected to stand pat despite knowing that its mound staff was marginal at best. The Tribe's reward in 1987 was a 5.28 staff ERA, the worst in the majors, and the horror of watching the team's hitters fail nearly as badly. In a season when scoring totals went through the roof just about everywhere else, the Indians' numbers actually declined. Corrales was fired, Schrom and his ghastly 6.50 ERA were quietly eased into early retirement, and a long-overdue housecleaning occurred. It failed, however, to extend into the front office, where the real people responsible for this club's woeful performance of late remain in hiding. Among the Tribe's finer moments in 1987 was benching early on Andre Thornton, the incumbent DH and probably Cleveland's best player during the current era, and forcing him to sit for almost his entire last season in the majors and helplessly witness the Wake beside the Lake.

THE WEIRDEST

1978 NEW YORK YANKEES
W-100 L-63
Managers: Billy Martin/Dick Howser/Bob Lemon

Regular Lineup—1B, Chris Chambliss; 2B, Willie Randolph; 3B, Graig Nettles; SS, Bucky Dent; RF, Reggie Jackson; CF, Mickey Rivers; LF, Lou Piniella; C, Thurman Munson; DH, Roy White; P, Ron Guidry; P, Ed Figueroa; P, Catfish Hunter; P, Goose Gossage; P, Sparky Lyle; P, Dick Tidrow; P, Jim Beattie

Some may question labeling a team that won its second World Championship in a row weird. But how many pennant winners have had a pitcher who started twenty-two games (Beattie) and completed none of them? Or a bullpen that had only two men (Gossage and Lyle) who were credited with saves and yet led the league in saves by a wide margin? Or a career .161 hitter (sub second baseman Brian Doyle) who emerged as the leading batter in the World Series? And that's over and above the way the Yankees roared back into contention after being given up for dead in the middle of the season and the wild route they took, both on the field and off, to win their division in a single-game playoff with the Red Sox. Amid all the tumultuous memories the 1978 Yankees left us with, Guidry's spectacular 25–3 record and 1.74 ERA are, already, sometimes forgotten, as is the fact that this team, for all the furor that surrounded it, was the last to win back-to-back World Championships. Lemon has never received his full due for making it happen. When he took over the club 95 games into the season after Martin was fired and Howser served for one day as the interim skipper, the Yankees were just nine games above .500. Under Lemon, the team won 48 of its last 68 contests and finished 37 lengths over the .500 mark.

SPECIAL FEATURE
TEAM: HARVEY'S
WALLBANGERS

● ●

1982 MILWAUKEE BREWERS
W-95 L-67
Managers: Buck Rodgers/Harvey Kuenn

Regular Lineup—1B, Cecil Cooper; 2B, Jim Gantner; 3B, Paul Molitor; SS, Robin Yount; RF, Charlie Moore; CF, Gorman Thomas; LF, Ben Oglivie; C, Ted Simmons; DH, Roy Howell/Don Money; P, Mike Caldwell; P, Pete Vuckovich; P, Moose Haas; P, Bob McClure; P, Rollie Fingers; P, Randy Lerch; P, Jim Slaton; P, Dwight Bernard

If the 1982 Brewers had not been piloted by Kuenn, they might still have been named after a drink. Try a Molotov Cocktail. Had Molitor tagged just one more home run, Milwaukee would have joined the elite group of teams that have had six players who hit twenty or more homers, and Money, who clouted 16 taters in just 275 at bats, was not far from being a seventh. Altogether, the Brewers banged out 216 home runs, three more than the two division winners in the NL, the Cardinals and the Braves, totaled combined.

Spearheaded by Yount, who had the greatest offensive season by a shortstop since Lou Boudreau in 1948, and Thomas, the most dangerous .225 hitter in history, Harvey's Wallbangers made Milwaukee County Stadium the only major league park in the past forty-eight years to be home to both an AL and an NL pennant winner. In June, with Milwaukee stumbling along in fifth place after having been the pre-season favorite to capture its division, the fiery Rodgers was replaced by Kuenn, a long-time coach and a former batting titlist. After grappling with cancer, heart trouble and life-threatening circulatory problems, Kuenn managed in the same mellowed-out fashion that his many health adversities had dictated he live. Under his relaxed guidance, the Brewers sauntered into the last month of the season with a sizable lead but then began to flounder after an elbow injury sidelined Fingers for the rest of the campaign and Baltimore suddenly caught fire. Down three games with four to play, the Orioles hosted the Brewers on the final weekend of the season. A doubleheader sweep by the Birds on Friday followed by a single-game victory the following afternoon created a tie and made Sunday's finale a winner-take-all affair. But the Brewers, behind Don Sutton, a late-season acquisition from Houston, drubbed Baltimore ace Jim Palmer, 10–2, to clinch the division and then won the LCS the following weekend by taking three straight from the Angels after returning to Milwaukee from Los Angeles down 2 games to 0. The loss of Fingers finally caught up to the Brewers in the World Series. Up 3–2 after five games were played, Milwaukee came up short when its relievers were strafed by the Cardinals in the last two contests.

When Fingers's injury proved severe enough to shelve him for all of 1983, Milwaukee skidded through the season but still finished twelve games above .500. Declining health forced Kuenn to step down before the 1984 campaign began. His replacement, Rene Lachemann, envisioned that having Fingers back in the bullpen would return the club to contention. Instead the Brewers fell prey to the wild fluctuations that marked the peformances of nearly every team during the eighties. A mere two years after they had paced the majors in runs and homers and utilized their explosive attack to capture a pennant and nearly a World Series, the Brewers compiled the fewest home runs in the AL and finished with the worst record.

Precipitous as Milwaukee's fall from the top perch was, it should not have been completely unexpected. Thomas, Cooper, Simmons and Oglivie were all on the wrong side of thirty in 1982, Molitor was playing one of his rare injury-free seasons, and each of the club's five regular starting pitchers—Vuckovich, Haas, Caldwell, McClure and Lerch—by 1986 was either out of the majors, in the bullpen, or spending most of his time on the disabled list. Too, the club had no rookies or even any players in their second or third seasons who could step into the breach when its older stars began to slip. Just five years later, in 1987, when the Brewers opened the season with a record thirteen straight wins, only three members of Harvey's Wallbangers—Yount, Gantner and Molitor—were still with the team. Each of the trio has since become a fixture on the Milwaukee scene. By 1991 the three had played a combined total of thirty-eight seasons in the majors and none had ever appeared in any uniform but that of the Brewers.

THE FIRST MINOR LEAGUE TEAM TO DRAW 1,000,000

• •

1983 LOUISVILLE RED BIRDS
W-78 L-57
Manager: Jim Fregosi

Regular Lineup—1B, Greg Guin; 2B, Jeff Doyle; 3B, Bill Lyons; SS, Jose Gonzalez; RF, Jim Adduci; CF, Tito Landrum; LF, Gene Roof; C, Tom Nieto; DH, Orlando Sanchez; P, Jeff Keener; P, Ricky Horton; P, Kevin Hagen; P, Eric Rasmussen; P, Ralph Citarella; P, Rick Ownbey; P, Kurt Kepshire

The American Association, for sixty years one of the premier minor leagues, disbanded for economic reasons after the 1962 season and then regrouped seven years later. Louisville, a charter member of the original AA (which took its name from the major league circuit that operated from 1882 through 1891), had joined the International League during the hiatus and won the IL pennant in 1972 before returning to the AA. The old club had been called the Colonels, in honor of the Louisville National League franchise of the 1890s, but the reorganized team was christened the Red Birds when it became the Cardinals' top farm affiliate.

In 1983 a combination of a good team, civic pride, sharp promotional tactics by the club and the slender hope that a strong showing at the gate might one day bring major league ball back to the Falls City drove the Red Birds to shatter every existing minor league season attendance record as 1,052,438 fans poured through the club's turnstiles. Louisville's mark has since been eclipsed by Buffalo, now also in the American Association and likewise in the hunt for a future major league franchise. But in 1983 Buffalo was a member of the Eastern League and drew only 200,531. As further evidence of the magnitude of Louisville's achievement, Denver, a fellow AA member, was the only other minor league club in 1983 to exceed 400,000 in attendance. Between them, Louisville and Denver accounted for roughly three-fifths of the AA's total attendance, and the Red Birds by themselves were responsible for 41 percent of it.

The quality of the team was probably the least important factor in the franchise's stunning accomplishment. Although Louisville took the Eastern Division title and had the best overall record in the loop, Denver, the Western Division champ, made short work of the Red Birds in the AA playoff final, winning in four straight games. Fregosi, in his first season as a minor league manager after having been fired by the California Angels, assembled a club that triumphed via a group effort. No member of the Red Birds finished among the top ten batters or ERA qualifiers, and none was named to the league All-Star squad that was chosen at the finish of the season. Several Red Birds nonetheless had fine years. Doyle and Roof both topped .300 at the plate, Adduci led the AA in RBIs, and Landrum was hitting .292 with eighteen homers when he was ticketed for Baltimore in early August to complete a deal made earlier in the season between the Cardinals and the Orioles. Among the pitchers, Keener was both the leading winner and the leading reliever, posting eleven victories and twelve saves. Horton was the only other hurler to win in double figures, finishing with an even ten victories, but Rasmussen was the team's best moundsman. After being sent down by the Cardinals, he bagged eight wins in nine decisions and posted a 2.28 ERA before being sold in August to the Kansas City Royals.

All of the Red Birds' regulars in 1983 (excepting Guin, who hit .222 and played just 58 games) subsequently earned at least a trial with the parent Cardinals, but the only ones to achieve more than moderate success in the majors were two players who were with the team that season for just a brief time before heading in opposite directions, Todd Worrell and Andy Van Slyke. Worrell, who set an all-time rookie record for saves in 1986, was still mainly a starter in 1983. Battered to the tune of a 4.74 ERA, he was demoted in midseason to Arkansas of the Texas League. Van Slyke, on the other hand, was promoted midway through the summer to the Cardinals after he hammered AA pitchers for a .368 BA in 54 games. St. Louis wisely decided, however, that third base, where he was stationed for most of his stay in Louisville, was perhaps not his best position. In 38 games at the hot corner, Van Slyke fielded .893 and ranked last among third sackers who handled more than 100 chances.

The complete AA standings and attendance figures for the 1983 season:

EASTERN DIVISION*	W	L	Attendance	WESTERN DIVISION	W	L	Attendance
Louisville	78	57	1,052,438	Denver	73	61	442,870
Iowa	71	65	255,830	Oklahoma City	66	69	226,079
Indianapolis	64	72	227,595	Wichita	65	71	128,756
Evansville	61	75	120,703	Omaha	64	72	137,545

*The AA played a 136-game schedule in 1983, with division rivals meeting each other 24 times and teams in the other division 16 times. As you can see, it was a strange year in the AA. While the division races were very one-sided, Denver finishing 7½ games ahead of Oklahoma City and Louisville topping Iowa by an identical margin, the teams finished tightly packed in the overall standings. Last-place Evansville came in only 17½ games behind Louisville, the overall winner.

Postscript: The baseball fever in Louisville carried over into the 1984 season. Although the Red Birds toppled to fourth place after the IL dispensed with its two-division setup and became an eight-team circuit, the franchise again had far and away the top attendance figure in the minors, drawing 846,878. What made the Red Birds' achievement even more extraordinary was that Louisville had dropped out of organized baseball after attendance fell to just 116,000 in 1972 and not returned until 1982 when it replaced the Springfield, Illinois, franchise in the AA.

ERA ALL-STAR TEAMS

	AMERICAN LEAGUE		NATIONAL LEAGUE
1B	Don Mattingly	1B	Will Clark
2B	Willie Randolph	2B	Ryne Sandberg
3B	George Brett	3B	Mike Schmidt
SS	Cal Ripken, Jr.	SS	Ozzie Smith
OF	Jim Rice	OF	Dale Murphy
OF	Rickey Henderson	OF	Tony Gwynn
OF	Dave Winfield	OF	Tim Raines
C	Carlton Fisk	C	Gary Carter
P	Ron Guidry	P	Steve Carlton
P	Jack Morris	P	Dwight Gooden
RELIEF	Dave Righetti	RELIEF	Bruce Sutter
UTIL	Eddie Murray	UTIL	Andre Dawson
MGR	Tony La Russa	MGR	Tommy Lasorda
*	Wade Boggs	*	Dave Parker

*Best player who failed to make the team

ALL-TIME
FRANCHISE
ALL-STAR TEAMS

• •

No book about teams would be complete without indulging in one of every baseball fan's favorite recreations. The following are the guidelines the panel used in making its selections:

A player or a manager must be with a team for a minimum of three seasons to be eligible for selection.

A player or a manager may be selected for more than one team.

No one can be selected as both a player and a manager for the same team.

Consistency and longevity, while important to the panel, were on occasion overridden by peak value—that is, a player or a manager who was an immense boost to a club for a few years as opposed to one who gave steady but not unduly noteworthy service over a long period.

For each of the sixteen franchises that existed in 1901 a first and second team was chosen. Only one team was chosen for the twelve expansion franchises.

NATIONAL LEAGUE

BOSTON/MILWAUKEE/ATLANTA BRAVES

	1ST TEAM		2ND TEAM
1B	Fred Tenney	1B	Joe Adcock
2B	Bobby Lowe	2B	Felix Millan
3B	Eddie Mathews	3B	Bill Nash
SS	Herman Long	SS	Rabbit Maranville
OF	Hank Aaron	OF	Hugh Duffy
OF	Dale Murphy	OF	Chick Stahl
OF	Wally Berger	OF	Tommy Holmes
C	Joe Torre	C	Hank Gowdy
RHP	Kid Nichols	RHP	Phil Niekro
LHP	Warren Spahn	LHP	Ed Brandt
RELIEF	Don McMahon	RELIEF	Gene Garber
UTIL	Bob Elliott	UTIL	Bob Horner
MGR	Frank Selee	MGR	George Stallings
*	Lew Burdette	*	Del Crandall

*Best player who failed to make the team

BEST TEAM: Boston—1898, Milwaukee—1957, Atlanta—1991

BROOKLYN/LOS ANGELES DODGERS

	1ST TEAM		2ND TEAM
1B	Gil Hodges	1B	Dolph Camilli
2B	Jackie Robinson	2B	Davey Lopes
3B	Ron Cey	3B	Jimmy Johnston
SS	Pee Wee Reese	SS	Maury Wills
OF	Zach Wheat	OF	Jimmy Sheckard
OF	Duke Snider	OF	Carl Furillo
OF	Mike Griffin	OF	Willie Davis
C	Roy Campanella	C	Mike Scioscia
RHP	Dazzy Vance	RHP	Don Drysdale
LHP	Sandy Koufax	LHP	Nap Rucker
RELIEF	Ron Perranoski	RELIEF	Clem Labine
UTIL	Pedro Guerrero	UTIL	Jim Gilliam
MGR	Walter Alston	MGR	Tommy Lasorda
*	Jake Daubert	*	Tommy Davis

BEST TEAM: Brooklyn, 19th century—1899, 20th century—1953, Los Angeles—1978

CHICAGO CUBS

	1ST TEAM		2ND TEAM
1B	Cap Anson	1B	Phil Cavarretta
2B	Ryne Sandberg	2B	Billy Herman
3B	Ron Santo	3B	Harry Steinfeldt
SS	Bill Dahlen	SS	Joe Tinker
OF	George Gore	OF	Andre Dawson
OF	Hack Wilson	OF	Billy Williams
OF	Jimmy Ryan	OF	Kiki Cuyler
C	Gabby Hartnett	C	Johnny Kling
RHP	Three Finger Brown	RHP	Ferguson Jenkins
LHP	Hippo Vaughn	LHP	Dick Ellsworth
RELIEF	Bruce Sutter	RELIEF	Lee Smith
UTIL	Ernie Banks	UTIL	King Kelly
MGR	Frank Chance	MGR	Joe McCarthy
*	John Clarkson	*	Bill Madlock

BEST TEAM: 19th century—1880, 20th century—1906

CINCINNATI REDS

	1ST TEAM		2ND TEAM
1B	Tony Perez	1B	Ted Kluszewski
2B	Joe Morgan	2B	Bid McPhee
3B	Heinie Groh	3B	Harry Steinfeldt
SS	Dave Concepcion	SS	Roy McMillan
OF	Frank Robinson	OF	Eric Davis
OF	Edd Roush	OF	Vada Pinson
OF	George Foster	OF	Cy Seymour
C	Johnny Bench	C	Ernie Lombardi
RHP	Bucky Walters	RHP	Dolf Luque
LHP	Noodles Hahn	LHP	Eppa Rixey
RELIEF	John Franco	RELIEF	Clay Carroll
UTIL	Pete Rose	UTIL	Hughie Critz
MGR	Bill McKechnie	MGR	Sparky Anderson
*	Charley Jones	*	Ken Griffey, Sr.

BEST TEAM: 19th century—1882, 20th century—1976

NEW YORK/SAN FRANCISCO GIANTS

	1ST TEAM		2ND TEAM
1B	Bill Terry	1B	Willie McCovey
2B	Frankie Frisch	2B	Larry Doyle
3B	Art Devlin	3B	Freddy Lindstrom
SS	George Davis	SS	Travis Jackson
OF	Willie Mays	OF	Ross Youngs
OF	Mel Ott	OF	George Burns
OF	Bobby Bonds	OF	Mike Tiernan
C	Buck Ewing	C	Chief Meyers
RHP	Christy Mathewson	RHP	Juan Marichal
LHP	Carl Hubbell	LHP	Rube Marquard
RELIEF	Frank Linzy	RELIEF	Hoyt Wilhelm
UTIL	Roger Connor	UTIL	Will Clark
MGR	John McGraw	MGR	Roger Craig
*	Joe McGinnity	*	Tim Keefe

BEST TEAM: New York, 19th century—1888, 20th century—1905, San Francisco—1987

PHILADELPHIA PHILLIES

	1ST TEAM		2ND TEAM
1B	Dick Allen	1B	Fred Luderus
2B	Nap Lajoie	2B	Manny Trillo
3B	Mike Schmidt	3B	Pinky Whitney
SS	Dave Bancroft	SS	Dick Bartell
OF	Chuck Klein	OF	Billy Hamilton
OF	Sam Thompson	OF	Gavvy Cravath
OF	Richie Ashburn	OF	Greg Luzinski
C	Jack Clements	C	Andy Seminick
RHP	Pete Alexander	RHP	Robin Roberts
LHP	Steve Carlton	LHP	Chris Short
RELIEF	Tug McGraw	RELIEF	Ron Reed
UTIL	Ed Delahanty	UTIL	Larry Bowa
MGR	Pat Moran	MGR	Harry Wright
*	Sherry Magee	*	Del Ennis

BEST TEAM: 19th century—1899, 20th century—1976

PITTSBURGH PIRATES

	1ST TEAM		2ND TEAM
1B	Willie Stargell	1B	Al Oliver
2B	Bill Mazeroski	2B	Claude Ritchey
3B	Pie Traynor	3B	Bill Madlock
SS	Honus Wagner	SS	Dick Groat
OF	Roberto Clemente	OF	Max Carey
OF	Ralph Kiner	OF	Kiki Cuyler
OF	Paul Waner	OF	Jake Stenzel
C	Manny Sanguillen	C	George Gibson
RHP	Babe Adams	RHP	Deacon Phillippe
LHP	Wilbur Cooper	LHP	Ed Morris
RELIEF	Roy Face	RELIEF	Dave Giusti
UTIL	Arky Vaughan	UTIL	Dave Parker
MGR	Danny Murtaugh	MGR	Fred Clarke
*	Tommy Leach	*	Glenn Wright

BEST TEAM: 19th century—1893, 20th century—1902

ST. LOUIS CARDINALS

	1ST TEAM		2ND TEAM
1B	Johnny Mize	1B	Ed Konetchy
2B	Rogers Hornsby	2B	Frankie Frisch
3B	Ken Boyer	3B	Joe Torre
SS	Ozzie Smith	SS	Marty Marion
OF	Stan Musial	OF	Enos Slaughter
OF	Joe Medwick	OF	Chick Hafey
OF	Lou Brock	OF	Curt Flood
C	Walker Cooper	C	Ted Simmons
RHP	Bob Gibson	RHP	Dizzy Dean
LHP	Harry Brecheen	LHP	Bill Hallahan
RELIEF	Bruce Sutter	RELIEF	Al Brazle
UTIL	Red Schoendienst	UTIL	Pepper Martin
MGR	Billy Southworth	MGR	Whitey Herzog
*	Jesse Burkett	*	Jim Bottomley

BEST TEAM†: 19th century—1899, 20th century—1967

†The original St. Louis Browns, although technically an ancestor of the Cardinals, were not viewed as such in selecting the Cards' best players and teams because not a single regular from the last Browns team in 1891 was with the club the following year when it joined the National League, making it apparent that the franchise was the same in name only.

NEW YORK METS

1B	Keith Hernandez
2B	Ron Hunt
3B	Howard Johnson
SS	Bud Harrelson
OF	Cleon Jones
OF	Darryl Strawberry
OF	Kevin McReynolds
C	Gary Carter
RHP	Tom Seaver
LHP	Jerry Koosman
RELIEF	Tug McGraw
UTIL	Rusty Staub
MGR	Gil Hodges
*	Dwight Gooden

BEST TEAM: 1986

HOUSTON COLT .45s/ASTROS

1B	Glenn Davis
2B	Joe Morgan
3B	Doug Rader
SS	Craig Reynolds
OF	Jose Cruz
OF	Jim Wynn
OF	Cesar Cedeno
C	Alan Ashby
RHP	Mike Scott
LHP	Bob Knepper
RELIEF	Dave Smith
UTIL	Bob Watson
MGR	Bill Virdon
*	Rusty Staub

BEST TEAM: 1986

MONTREAL EXPOS

1B	Andres Galarraga
2B	Ron Hunt
3B	Tim Wallach
SS	Hubie Brooks
OF	Tim Raines
OF	Andre Dawson
OF	Rusty Staub
C	Gary Carter
RHP	Steve Rogers
LHP	Woody Fryman
RELIEF	Jeff Reardon
UTIL	Bob Bailey
MGR	Buck Rodgers
*	Mike Marshall

BEST TEAM: 1979

SAN DIEGO PADRES

1B	Nate Colbert
2B	Roberto Alomar
3B	Graig Nettles
SS	Ozzie Smith
OF	Tony Gwynn
OF	Dave Winfield
OF	Gene Richards
C	Benito Santiago
RHP	Clay Kirby
LHP	Randy Jones
RELIEF	Rollie Fingers
UTIL	Gene Tenace
MGR	Dick Williams
*	Terry Kennedy

BEST TEAM: 1984

AMERICAN LEAGUE

BALTIMORE ORIOLES/NEW YORK YANKEES

	1ST TEAM		2ND TEAM
1B	Lou Gehrig	1B	Hal Chase
2B	Joe Gordon	2B	Tony Lazzeri
3B	Graig Nettles	3B	Clete Boyer
SS	Phil Rizzuto	SS	Kid Elberfeld
OF	Babe Ruth	OF	Dave Winfield
OF	Joe DiMaggio	OF	Earle Combs
OF	Mickey Mantle	OF	Roger Maris
C	Yogi Berra	C	Bill Dickey
RHP	Red Ruffing	RHP	Mel Stottlemyre
LHP	Whitey Ford	LHP	Ron Guidry
RELIEF	Dave Righetti	RELIEF	Sparky Lyle
UTIL	Tommy Henrich	UTIL	Don Mattingly
MGR	Joe McCarthy	MGR	Miller Huggins
*	Thurman Munson	*	Willie Randolph/Elston Howard

BEST TEAM: Baltimore—1901, New York 1939

BOSTON RED SOX

	1ST TEAM		2ND TEAM
1B	Jimmie Foxx	1B	Buck Freeman
2B	Bobby Doerr	2B	Billy Goodman
3B	Wade Boggs	3B	Larry Gardner
SS	Joe Cronin	SS	Everett Scott
OF	Tris Speaker	OF	Dom DiMaggio
OF	Carl Yastrzemski	OF	Harry Hooper
OF	Ted Williams	OF	Dewey Evans
C	Carlton Fisk	C	Sammy White
RHP	Cy Young	RHP	Roger Clemens
LHP	Mel Parnell	LHP	Lefty Grove
RELIEF	Ellis Kinder	RELIEF	Bob Stanley
UTIL	Babe Ruth	UTIL	Rico Petrocelli
MGR	Bill Carrigan	MGR	Dick Williams
*	Jim Rice	*	Johnny Pesky/Rick Burleson

BEST TEAM: 1912

CHICAGO WHITE SOX

	1ST TEAM		2ND TEAM
1B	Eddie Robinson	1B	Jiggs Donahue
2B	Nellie Fox	2B	Eddie Collins
3B	Buck Weaver	3B	Willie Kamm
SS	Luke Appling	SS	Luis Aparicio
OF	Joe Jackson	OF	Chet Lemon
OF	Minnie Minoso	OF	Fielder Jones
OF	Harold Baines	OF	Johnny Mostil
C	Ray Schalk	C	Sherman Lollar
RHP	Ed Walsh	RHP	Eddie Cicotte
LHP	Billy Pierce	LHP	Wilbur Wood
RELIEF	Bobby Thigpen	RELIEF	Hoyt Wilhelm
UTIL	Dick Allen	UTIL	Carlton Fisk
MGR	Al Lopez	MGR	Jimmy Dykes
*	George Davis	*	Red Faber

BEST TEAM: 1917

CLEVELAND INDIANS

	1ST TEAM		2ND TEAM
1B	Hal Trosky	1B	Andre Thornton
2B	Nap Lajoie	2B	Joe Gordon
3B	Bill Bradley	3B	Al Rosen
SS	Lou Boudreau	SS	Ray Chapman
OF	Tris Speaker	OF	Larry Doby
OF	Joe Jackson	OF	Earl Averill
OF	Elmer Flick	OF	Rocky Colavito
C	Jim Hegan	C	John Romano
RHP	Bob Feller	RHP	Early Wynn
LHP	Vean Gregg	LHP	Herb Score
RELIEF	Doug Jones	RELIEF	Ray Narleski
UTIL	Joe Sewell	UTIL	Terry Turner
MGR	Al Lopez	MGR	Steve O'Neill
*	Bob Lemon	*	Addie Joss

BEST TEAM: 1948

DETROIT TIGERS

	1ST TEAM		2ND TEAM
1B	Hank Greenberg	1B	Norm Cash
2B	Charlie Gehringer	2B	Lou Whitaker
3B	George Kell	3B	Aurelio Rodriguez
SS	Alan Trammell	SS	Donie Bush
OF	Ty Cobb	OF	Barney McCosky
OF	Al Kaline	OF	Bobby Veach
OF	Harry Heilmann	OF	Willie Horton
C	Bill Freehan	C	Lance Parrish
RHP	George Mullin	RHP	Jack Morris
LHP	Hal Newhouser	LHP	Mickey Lolich
RELIEF	John Hiller	RELIEF	Willie Hernandez
UTIL	Harvey Kuenn	UTIL	Rudy York
MGR	Hugh Jennings	MGR	Sparky Anderson
*	Sam Crawford	*	Kurt Gibson

BEST TEAM: 1984

MILWAUKEE BREWERS/ST. LOUIS BROWNS/ BALTIMORE ORIOLES

	1ST TEAM		2ND TEAM
1B	George Sisler	1B	Eddie Murray
2B	Del Pratt	2B	Bobby Grich
3B	Brooks Robinson	3B	Harlond Clift
SS	Cal Ripken, Jr.	SS	Vern Stephens
OF	Frank Robinson	OF	Ken Singleton
OF	Ken Williams	OF	Paul Blair
OF	George Stone	OF	Jack Tobin
C	Rick Dempsey	C	Hank Severeid
RHP	Jim Palmer	RHP	Urban Shocker
LHP	Dave McNally	LHP	Mike Cuellar
RELIEF	Dick Hall	RELIEF	Stu Miller
UTIL	Luis Aparicio	UTIL	Bobby Wallace
MGR	Earl Weaver	MGR	Luke Sewell
*	Wally Gerber	*	Boog Powell

BEST TEAM: Milwaukee—1901 (by default), St. Louis—1922, Baltimore—1970

PHILADELPHIA/KANSAS CITY/OAKLAND A'S

	1ST TEAM		2ND TEAM
1B	Jimmie Foxx	1B	Harry Davis
2B	Eddie Collins	2B	Max Bishop
3B	Home Run Baker	3B	Sal Bando
SS	Bert Campaneris	SS	Eddie Joost
OF	Al Simmons	OF	Bob Johnson
OF	Rickey Henderson	OF	Topsy Hartsel
OF	Reggie Jackson	OF	Jose Canseco
C	Mickey Cochrane	C	Wally Schang
RHP	Catfish Hunter	RHP	Jack Coombs
LHP	Lefty Grove	LHP	Eddie Plank
RELIEF	Dennis Eckersley	RELIEF	Rollie Fingers
UTIL	Lave Cross	UTIL	Gus Zernial
MGR	Tony La Russa	MGR	Connie Mack
*	Rube Waddell	*	Carney Lansford

BEST TEAM: Philadelphia—1913, Kansas City—1966, Oakland—1989

WASHINGTON SENATORS/MINNESOTA TWINS

	1ST TEAM		2ND TEAM
1B	Harmon Killebrew	1B	Mickey Vernon
2B	Rod Carew	2B	Buddy Myer
3B	Eddie Yost	3B	Ossie Bluege
SS	Joe Cronin	SS	George McBride
OF	Goose Goslin	OF	Clyde Milan
OF	Kirby Puckett	OF	Sam Rice
OF	Tony Oliva	OF	Heinie Manush
C	Earl Battey	C	Muddy Ruel
RHP	Walter Johnson	RHP	Camilo Pascual
LHP	Jim Kaat	LHP	Frank Viola
RELIEF	Firpo Marberry	RELIEF	Jeff Reardon
UTIL	Cecil Travis	UTIL	Cesar Tovar
MGR	Bucky Harris	MGR	Tom Kelly
*	Buddy Lewis	*	Gary Gaetti

BEST TEAM: Washington—1924, Minnesota—1991

LOS ANGELES/ CALIFORNIA ANGELS

1B	Wally Joyner
2B	Bobby Grich
3B	Doug DeCinces
SS	Jim Fregosi
OF	Don Baylor
OF	Brian Downing
OF	Leon Wagner
C	Buck Rodgers
RHP	Nolan Ryan
LHP	Chuck Finley
RELIEF	Bob Lee
UTIL	Rod Carew
MGR	Bill Rigney
*	Bobby Knoop

BEST TEAM: 1982

KANSAS CITY ROYALS

1B	John Mayberry
2B	Frank White
3B	George Brett
SS	Freddie Patek
OF	Amos Otis
OF	Hal McRae
OF	Willie Wilson
C	Darrell Porter
RHP	Dennis Leonard
LHP	Charlie Leibrandt
RELIEF	Dan Quisenberry
UTIL	Kevin Seitzer
MGR	Dick Howser
*	Lou Piniella

BEST TEAM: 1977

WASHINGTON SENATORS/ TEXAS RANGERS

1B	Rafael Palmeiro
2B	Julio Franco
3B	Buddy Bell
SS	Toby Harrah
OF	Ruben Sierra
OF	Frank Howard
OF	Jeff Burroughs
C	Jim Sundberg
RHP	Charlie Hough
LHP	Claude Osteen
RELIEF	Darold Knowles
MGR	Bobby Valentine
UTIL	Al Oliver
*	Mike Hargrove

BEST TEAM: Washington—1969, Texas—1973

SEATTLE PILOTS/ MILWAUKEE BREWERS

1B	Cecil Cooper
2B	Jim Gantner
3B	Paul Molitor
SS	Robin Yount
OF	Gorman Thomas
OF	Ben Oglivie
OF	Tommy Harper
C	Charlie Moore
RHP	Jim Slaton
LHP	Ted Higuera
RELIEF	Rollie Fingers
MGR	George Bamberger
UTIL	George Scott
*	Don Money

BEST TEAM: Seattle—1969 (by default), Milwaukee— 1982

SEATTLE MARINERS

1B	Alvin Davis
2B	Harold Reynolds
3B	Jim Presley
SS	Spike Owen
OF	Tom Paciorek
OF	Phil Bradley
OF	Ken Griffey, Jr.
C	Scott Bradley
RHP	Mike Moore
LHP	Mark Langston
RELIEF	Mike Schooler
UTIL	Edgar Martinez
MGR	Rene Lachemann
*	Leon Roberts

BEST TEAM: 1991

TORONTO BLUE JAYS

1B	Fred McGriff
2B	Damaso Garcia
3B	Kelly Gruber
SS	Tony Fernandez
OF	George Bell
OF	Jesse Barfield
OF	Lloyd Moseby
C	Ernie Whitt
RHP	Dave Stieb
LHP	Jimmy Key
RELIEF	Tom Henke
UTIL	Willie Upshaw
MGR	Bobby Cox
*	Alfredo Griffin

BEST TEAM: 1985

A HOLE IN ONE . . .

There's an epidemic with 27 million victims. And no visible symptoms.

It's an epidemic of people who can't read.

Believe it *or* not, 27 million Americans are functionally illiterate, about one adult in five.

The solution to this problem is you… when you join the fight against illiteracy. So call the Coalition for Literacy at toll-free **1-800-228-8813** and volunteer.

Volunteer Against Illiteracy. The only degree you need is a degree of caring.